Real Estate Principles

THE PRINCETON REAL ESTATE EXAMINATION GUIDE

Real Estate Principles

The Princeton Real Estate Examination Guide

Ralph A. Palmer, LL.B.

Gorsuch Scarisbrick, Publishers
8233 Via Paseo del Norte, Suite E–400
Scottsdale, AZ 85258

10 9 8 7

Library of Congress Catalog Card Number: 82-82531

ISBN 0-89787-905-8

Copyright © 1982, by Gorsuch Scarisbrick, Publishers

All rights reserved. No part of this publication may be reproduced, stored in a retrieval system, or transmitted, in any form or by any means, electronic, mechanical, photocopy, recording or otherwise, without the prior written permission of Gorsuch Scarisbrick, Publishers.

Printed in the United States of America.

Contents

Preface   vii

Part I   Preparing to Use the Text

1 How to Use the Guide   1

2 Studying for the Educational Testing Service Examinations   3
Format of the Examinations — Scores — Salesperson Examination — Broker Examination — Question Format — Test Regulations — Taking the Test

Part II   Understanding Real Estate Principles

3 Introduction to Real Estate   7
Characteristics of Real Estate — Physical Characteristics of Real Property — Economic Characteristics of Real Property — General Concepts of Land Use — Land Use Controls — The Real Estate Business — The Real Estate Market — Real Estate Transactions — Summary — Important Points — Important Terminology — Review Questions

4 Licensing of Real Estate Brokers and Salespersons   19
Broker and Salesperson Defined — Licensing Boards or Commissions — Standards of Conduct Required of Licensees — Summary of License Law Provisions — Important Points — Important Terminology — Review Questions

5 Property Ownership and Interests   33
Real Estate Defined — Estates in Real Property — Types of Estates — Freehold Estates — Ways in Which Title May Be Held — Real Property Ownership by Business Organizations — Leasehold Estates — Encumbrances — Encroachments — Easements — Profits — License — Liens — Important Points — Important Terminology — Review Questions

6 Contracts and Agency   57
Fundamentals of Contract Law — Methods of Creating Contracts — Bilateral and Unilateral Contracts — Essential Elements of a Valid Contract — Assignment of Contracts — Termination of Contracts — Statute of Frauds — Real Estate Contracts — Listing Contracts — Broker's Obligations as Agent — Types of Commission Arrangements — Types of Listing Contracts — Offer and Contract of Sale — Contract for Deed — Option to Purchase — Lease Contracts — Types of Leases — Summary — Important Points — Important Terminology — Review Questions

7 Transfer of Title to Real Property   91
Alienation During Life — Alienation After Death — Essential Elements of a Valid Deed — Types of Deeds — Title Examination — Title Insurance — Property Descriptions — Important Points — Important Terminology — Review Questions

8 Real Estate Financing   111
Notes — Mortgage and Deed of Trust — Requirements for Validity of a Mortgage or Deed of Trust — Rights of Lender — Rights of Borrower — Mortgage Clauses and Covenants — Foreclosure — Types of Mortgages — Sources of Real Estate Financing — Methods of Financing — Conventional Loans — FHA Insured Loans — Veterans Administration Guaranteed Loan Program — Qualifying Requirements for Mortgage Loans — Discount Points — Truth-In-Lending Law — Real Estate Settlement Procedures Act (RESPA) — Equal Credit Opportunity Act (ECOA) — Secondary Mortgage Market — Important Points — Important Terminology — Review Questions

9 Closing Real Estate Transactions   141
Preparation of Closing Statements — Cash Sale Statements — Practice Problem No. 1 — Purchase Money Mortgage Closing Statements — Reconciliation — Practice Problem No. 2 — Mortgage Assumption Statements — Practice Problem No. 3 — New First Mortgage Statement — Practice Problem No. 4 — Review Questions

10 Valuation of Real Estate   **163**
Concepts of Value — Value, Price, and Cost Distinguished — Types of Value — Competitive Market Analysis — Basic Valuation Principles — Approaches to Value — Important Points — Important Terminology — Review Questions

11 Land Use Controls   **181**
Development of Land Use Controls — Private Land Use Controls — Public Land Use Controls — Interstate Land Sales Full Disclosure Act — Environmental Protection Legislation — Responsibility of Real Estate Agents — Important Points — Important Terminology — Review Questions

12 Fair Housing   **191**
Fair Housing Act of 1968 — Sale or Rental of Housing — Financing of Housing — Real Estate Brokerage Services — Exemptions — Discriminatory Advertising — Blockbusting — Steering — Enforcement — Civil Rights Act of 1866 — Important Points — Important Terminology — Review Questions

13 Property Management and Insurance   **199**
Property Management — The Functions of a Property Manager — The Management Agreement — Insurance — Fire Insurance/Policies — Insurable Interest — Coinsurance — Mortgagee Insurable Interest — Homeowners Warranty Policies (HOW) — Important Points — Important Terminology — Review Questions

14 Tax Implications of Real Estate Ownership and Transactions   **207**
Tax Implications of Home Ownership — Tax Implications in the Sale of a Principal Residence — Long and Short-Term Capital Loss in the Sale of a Home — Rollover Rule — Computing Taxable Gain — Inheritance Basis — The Age Fifty-Five-and-Over Exclusion — Installment Sales — 30 Percent Rule Repealed — Two-Payment Rule Eliminated — Related Party Sales — Tax Implications of the Ownership and Sale of Business and Investment Property — Depreciation — Depreciation Methods — Tax Shelter — Accelerated Cost Recovery System (ACRS) — ACRS-Excluded Property — Alternate ACRS Method — Tax Implications in the Sale of Property — Capital Gains and Losses — Tax-Free Exchanges — Multiple Exchange — Starker Exchange — Exchanges Under Accelerated Cost Recovery System (ACRS) — Important Points — Important Terminology — Review Questions

15 Real Estate Mathematics   **229**
Fundamentals — Area Problems — Proration Problems — Capitalization Problems — Depreciation and Appreciation Problems — Taxation Problems — Percentage Lease Problems — Miscellaneous Problems — Review Problems and Solutions

16 The Language of Real Estate: A Glossary of Real Estate Terminology   **281**

Part III   Testing Your Understanding of Real Estate Principles

17 Diagnostic Practice Test   **299**
Introduction — Licensing — Ownership and Interests in Property — Contracts and Agency — Transfer of Title — Real Estate Finance — Closing Real Estate Transactions — Valuation of Real Estate — Land-Use Controls — Fair Housing — Property Management and Insurance — Tax Implications — Real Estate Mathematics

18 Sample Salesperson's Test   **313**

19 Sample Broker's Test   **323**

Appendix   **333**
Real Estate Construction Illustrated — Answers to Questions at End of Chapters — Answers to Diagnostic Practice Test — Answers to Salesperson's Test — Answers to Broker's Test

Index   **343**

Preface

This text covers, for the beginning student, the principles and practices basic to a career in modern real estate. It presents the subject matter and study materials needed in preparing for a real estate salesperson's or a broker's licensing examination. While such subject matter is common to testing programs administered by various agencies throughout the United States, the book gives specific attention to content and methods of the testing program administered by the Educational Testing Service of Princeton, New Jersey.

This book has evolved from my teaching and writing of other real estate books over many years. In covering the various subjects, every effort has been made to provide straight-forward and understandable explanations without neglecting the necessary legal and real estate terminology. The review questions, problems, and sample tests are included to supply the student with sufficient opportunity for self testing and assurance of adequate preparation necessary for success on either the salesperson's or broker's licensing examination.

The author would like to express his appreciation to those who have assisted in making this book a reality. My thanks to my publisher, John Gorsuch, and the reviewers who helped develop and mold the final manuscript. They contributed immeasurably to the quality and scope of the material.

Ralph A. Palmer

How to Use the Guide

This text is written expressly as an aid to prepare you, the real estate student, to enter the field of real estate and to be successful in taking the Uniform Licensing Examinations for brokers and salespersons prepared by the Educational Testing Service of Princeton, New Jersey. The only way in which you can be successful in these two endeavors is to become thoroughly knowledgeable of the subject matter presented in the following pages.

Part II of the book, "Understanding Real Estate Principles," provides an in-depth, logical and orderly discussion of the important real estate principles that you must understand. To assist you in obtaining this understanding, each chapter contains a listing of vital vocabulary contained in the chapter, a listing of the important points in the chapter, and review questions presented in the same format as the questions that you will encounter on the ETS Licensing Examinations.

Chapter 4, "Licensing of Real Estate Brokers and Salespersons," contains the basic and most important provisions of real estate license law legislation. The purpose of this chapter is to provide you with an understanding of these laws in the various jurisdictions. Every license applicant must be thoroughly knowledgeable of the license law and its applications in his or her particular jurisdiction. Copies of these laws and accompanying rules and regulations can be obtained, usually at no cost, from the licensing agency.

The license law questions on the ETS License Examinations are not generalized, but are strictly based on the license law and regulations of the state or jurisdiction where the test is being taken and to which license application is being made. An outline, to be completed by filling in the specifics of the license law provisions of your state of application, is included in this chapter.

Chapter 15, "Real Estate Mathematics," covers all the various problem types that may be encountered on the licensing examinations. Development of your problem-solving skills is acquired by the practice you will obtain by working the one hundred review problems at the end of the chapter. Solutions are included so that you can verify your results and methods.

Mastery of real estate terminology is extremely important for your success. Therefore, in addition to the vital vocabulary list at the end of each chapter, "The Language of Real Estate: A Glossary of Real Estate Terminology" is included as chapter 16. The review questions with each chapter enable you to master the definitions and the application of the terms.

Part III of the text, "Testing Your Understanding of Real Estate Principles," enables you to conduct your own comprehensive review. In this way you may reveal subject areas where you are deficient and need additional preparation in order to be successful on the licensing examination. The Diagnostic Practice Tests, the subject area in chapter 17, are specifically included for this purpose. These questions are grouped by chapters in the book so that you may re-study subjects in which you need reinforcement. After the diagnostic tests have been successfully completed, a score of at least 90 percent correct, proceed to the sample salesperson's and/or broker's tests.

The sample test questions are not copies of questions appearing on actual Educational Testing Service Real Estate Licensing Examinations nor have they been approved or recommended by the Educational Testing Service. However, the questions are representative of the type of questions appearing on the ETS examinations. The ETS examinations require the application of knowledge to various situations presented in the questions rather than a mere demonstration of knowledge of specific facts. This is not necessarily true of every question on the examinations, but it is the case for many questions—especially those on the broker's examinations.

The sample tests give you experience in taking the ETS type of examination and provide you with an additional opportunity to test your knowledge and understanding of the subject matter. The sample tests also enable you to evaluate your ability to apply the newly acquired knowledge.

Finally, to use this Guide successfully, it is imperative that you carefully read all of the material. Be sure that you understand each subject before you move on to the next. The book is written so that you will acquire knowledge one step at a time. Each chapter builds on preceding chapters to provide an accumulation of knowledge necessary for a successful real estate career.

Studying for the Educational Testing Service Examinations

2

Nearly two-thirds of the states and other jurisdictions in the United States have adopted the Real Estate Licensing Examinations prepared and administered by the Educational Testing Service of Princeton, New Jersey. These examinations consist entirely of objective multiple-choice questions. Each question provides four answer choices, only one of which is correct.

FORMAT OF THE EXAMINATIONS

There are two examinations, one for broker license applicants and one for salesperson license applicants. Actually, there are several different tests in that the questions vary from test to test. Also, the tests are continually revised so that the questions reflect current real estate laws and practices. Both the broker and salesperson examinations are in two parts—the state test and the uniform test.

The state test is based specifically on the license law and rules and regulations of the particular jurisdiction where the student has applied for a real estate license. In some jurisdictions, the state test also contains questions on real estate laws and practices applicable to that particular jurisdiction and, therefore, not appropriate for inclusion on the uniform test. The state tests consist of thirty to forty questions. Tests limited to questions on the license law and regulations usually have only thirty questions.

The uniform test covers a variety of subjects that are standard, or uniform, in all jurisdictions. The questions and, to some extent, the subject areas are different on the salespersons and brokers examinations. To be successful in taking the examinations, the applicant must pass both the state test and the uniform test. In the case of failure, some jurisdictions require the applicant to retake only that test, state or uniform, that was not passed rather than retake the entire examination. The regulation in this regard is completely determined by the particular state licensing agency.

The examinations must be completed within the time allotted by each jurisdiction. The time period may be up to four and a half hours. The amount of time allowed is sufficient to complete the examination successfully, if the applicant is adequately prepared and does not waste time.

SCORES

The passing score required for the examinations is established by each jurisdiction. Required scores are typically 70 percent to 75 percent of the questions answered correctly. A jurisdiction may specify a different percentage for the state test and the uniform test. Grading of the examinations is done by the Educational Testing Service (usually referred to as ETS). The ETS uses a factor that compensates for minor differences in the degree of difficulty that might occur between different forms of the examinations. Therefore, applicants are not benefitted or penalized as a result of taking a certain form of the examination.

Score reports are sent to applicants by the ETS. If an applicant is successful, the score report will read *PASS* and no score will be given. If the applicant is not successful, the report will state *FAIL* and will also give the results by subject area. The breakdown is: state test score; uniform test score; and results on the subject areas of contracts, financing, ownership, brokerage, and valuation. The results on these subject areas are reported as *Good* (81 percent to 100 percent correct), *Fair* (60 percent to 80 percent correct), and *Needs Improvement* (less than 60 percent correct). This method of reporting the results enables the applicant to determine the subject area(s) on which to concentrate in preparing to retake the examination. Neither ETS nor licensing agencies provide for a review of test results with applicants.

SALESPERSON EXAMINATION

Both the salesperson and broker examinations consist of the state test and uniform test. Since the state test only contains questions regarding laws and regulations of a particular jurisdiction, the widely varying subjects are impossible to discuss here. The uniform test on the salespersons examination questions the applicant in the following subject areas:

1. Real Estate Contracts—13 percent
   Elements and terminology on real estate contracts, including leases, options, listings, and contracts of sale.
2. Financing—24 percent
   Sources; government agencies and regulations such as FHA, VA, and Truth-In-Lending Act; financing instruments; loan procedures, types of mortgage loans; mortgage default and foreclosure.
3. Real Estate Ownership—22 percent
   Deeds; various types of ownership in real property; interests in real property and condominiums; and the Fair Housing Act of 1968 as amended.
4. Real Estate Brokerage—24 percent
   Law of agency; property management; and settlement procedures.
5. Valuation—17 percent
   Appraising; planning and zoning; property descriptions; real property taxes, special assessments, liens, and other tax factors.
6. Approximately 20 percent of the eighty questions on the subjects discussed above require arithmetic calculations to some extent. Many jurisdictions permit the use of calculators and slide rules. Calculators must be silent, hand-held, battery-operated, and without paper tape printing capabilities. The calculations necessary may be done without a calculator within the time allotted for taking the examination. The arithmetic questions are not grouped together on the test.

BROKER EXAMINATION

The eighty questions (same as salesperson examination) cover the following subject areas:

1. **Real Estate Brokerage—35 percent**
   A. Broker's responsibilities in listing, advertising, and showing property, including responsibilities imposed by the Law of Agency, and the Federal Fair Housing Act.
   B. Broker's responsibilities in the final settlement of real estate transactions, including the Real Estate Settlement Procedures Act.
   C. Broker's responsibilities when representing client as property manager.

2. **Contracts and Other Legal Aspects— 27 percent**
   A. Contracts: General contract law; listing, sales, leases, options, installment land contracts, and escrow agreements; referring buyers and sellers to seek legal advice from attorneys.
   B. Land-Use Controls: Public and private including zoning laws regulating the development of subdivisions, deed restrictions, and restrictive covenants.
   C. Deeds: General characteristics of a variety of types of deeds and the appropriate situations for the use of certain types.
   D. Property Ownership: Ownership rights and interests in real property; characteristics of various types of ownership, including individual and co-ownership, such as tenancy in common, joint tenancy, and time-sharing.
   E. Condominiums and cooperatives: Requirements for establishing condominium or cooperative; individual and common ownerships; conversion of

a property to a condominium or cooperative.
F. Other Legal Aspects: Public powers over real property, such as eminent domain, police power, taxation, and escheat; special interests in real property, such as easements, profits, and liens.

3. **Pricing and Valuation —15 percent**
   Principles of value; approaches to estimating value, using the comparative market analysis in pricing real estate in the absence of an appraisal report.

4. **Financing and Investment—23 percent**
   A. Costs in loan placement; FHA and VA, and the Truth-in-Lending Act.
   B. Characteristics of financing instruments, including notes, mortgages, deeds of trust, installment land contracts, and others.
   C. Types of mortgage loans; essential mortgage elements and special mortgage clauses; sources of junior loans; default and foreclosure.
   D. Tax ramifications of the ownership and sale of a principal residence, business, or investment property.

5. Approximately 20 percent of the eighty questions on the subjects discussed above require arithmetic calculations.

QUESTION FORMAT

The questions on the state test and the uniform test for broker and salesperson are entirely objective multiple choice. There are eight basic formats as illustrated in the following examples.

1. *Direct Question*
   Real property is which of the following?

   (a) Automobiles
   X (b) Land
   (c) Contracts
   (d) Notes

2. *Sentence completion*
   Land has the physical characteristic of

   (a) Destructibility
   (b) Mobility
   (c) Limitless supply
   X (d) Immobility

3. *Exception*
   All of the following are physical characteristics of land EXCEPT

   X (a) Mobility
   (b) Immobility
   (c) Indestructibility
   (d) Nonhomogenity

4. *Least or most*
   Which of the following would most likely be a benefit resulting from ownership of a particular parcel of land?

   (a) Profit
   (b) Leasehold estate
   X (c) Appurtenant easement
   (d) License

5. *Double right or wrong*
   Which of the following statements is (are) correct?
   I. The listing broker is the agent of the seller
   II. The listing broker may not misrepresent the property to the buyer

   (a) I only
   (b) II only
   X (c) both I and II
   (d) neither I nor II

6. *Narrative*
   A situation is presented in narrative form consisting of several paragraphs. Using this information, the applicant is required to answer two or more multiple-choice questions by application of knowledge of real estate subjects and transactions.

7. *Plats, tables and charts*
   These questions provide plats, tables, or charts to be used in answering the questions. Typical subject matter involved includes: (1) using mortgage loan payment tables to arrive at the monthly payment necessary to amortize a certain mortgage loan, or (2) reading a subdivision plat to identify various features.

*X indicates correct answer

8. *Mathematics*
Mathematic problems related to real estate are scattered throughout the uniform test. These questions provide four answer choices as do all questions on the examinations. A note of caution in answer selection: there will be wrong answers that will result from failure to complete all steps required or from incorrect calculations, such as multiplying instead of dividing.

TEST REGULATIONS

To insure fair and equitable testing conditions, the Educational Testing Service requires observance of the following regulations at the test center.

1. No books or papers may be taken into the testing room.
2. The allotted time for taking the test cannot be extended.
3. All scratch work must be done only on the margins or blank pages of the test books, not on the answer sheets. Scratch paper may not be brought into the test room. ETS supplies sufficient scratch work space in the test book.
4. Applicants may not leave the test room without the permission of the test supervisor.
5. Anyone engaging in misconduct during the test will be dismissed and reported to their licensing agency.

TAKING THE TEST

The following are suggestions that should prove beneficial in taking the licensing examinations.

1. Continue to study after you have completed your pre-licensing course until you take the examination.
2. Take the following items to the test:
   (A.) Three number 2 pencils with erasers
   (B.) Calculator (if permitted) with extra set of fresh batteries
   (C.) ETS admission ticket and other forms of identification
   (D.) Watch
3. Read each question and all the answer choices carefully before selecting an answer. Be sure you know what the question is asking.
4. Skip, for the time being, questions that are long and involved as well as questions to which you are not sure of the answer. Make certain that you also skip these on the answer sheet. When marking the answer, be sure you are marking the right number. Keep checking this throughout the examination.
5. Be alert to certain words that may determine the correct answer choice. For example: must and may, always and never, can and cannot.
6. Do not change an answer you have selected unless you are absolutely positive your first selection was incorrect. If you do change an answer choice, make certain that you erase the first choice completely on the answer sheet.
7. After you have answered all questions you are sure of, go back over the examination and answer any questions that you omitted. If you do not know the answer, guess. Do not leave any answers blank. Questions not answered are automatically incorrect. If you guess, your guess may be correct.

BULLETIN OF INFORMATION

The Educational Testing Service publishes a *Bulletin of Information for Applicants* that provides detailed information about the examinations, including sample questions that illustrate the types of questions on each of the two examinations. The bulletin is available at no charge from licensing agencies using the ETS examinations, from prelicensing real estate schools, or directly from the Educational Testing Service. The bulletin also contains an order form for sample uniform examinations that may be purchased for a reasonable amount. Correspondence should be addressed:

Real Estate Licensing Examinations
Educational Testing Service
Box 2837
Princeton, NJ 08541

Introduction to Real Estate

3

This text provides a real estate student with a logical and understandable step-by-step approach to the subjects that must be mastered in preparation for the real estate licensing examinations and for an entry-level position in the real estate brokerage business. This approach permits the student to build a solid foundation of information upon which to build a firm understanding of real estate.

This chapter provides an introduction by defining real estate, discussing the characteristics of real property, explaining the basic concepts of land use and land use controls, and providing a basic understanding of the real estate business and the transactions involved in the business. Most of the subject matter covered here is discussed in greater detail in subsequent chapters of the text.

CHARACTERISTICS OF REAL ESTATE

Real property has certain characteristics that set it apart from other marketable commodities. These characteristics are both physical and economic. However, the physical and economic characteristics are so interrelated that they each have a definite affect on the other and are sometimes difficult to separate in a practical sense. We will discuss both of these characteristics and their affect on real property value.

Real Estate Defined

Real estate or *real property* or *realty* (these terms are for most purposes interchangeable) consists of land and everything that is permanently attached to land. Ownership in land includes not only the surface of the earth but also the area below the surface to the center of the earth and the area above the surface theoretically to the highest heavens. These three aspects of ownership in land are separable. The owner of the land may retain the ownership of the surface and the air space above but sell or lease the mineral rights below the surface. The owner may also sell or lease the air rights above the surface.

Real estate includes not only land but everything that is permanently attached to land. Therefore, all structures on the land, as well as any other improvements, such as fences, swimming pools, flag poles, and things growing in the soil that grow naturally without cultivation, are all included in the definition of real estate. Therefore, the property owner, when conveying the title to his property, conveys all aspects of real estate, unless there is a prior agreement to exempt some portion of the real estate from the conveyance.

The only category of property defined in law other than real property is *personal property*. Therefore, by the definition of real property, we are able to determine that personal property is everything that is not land or not permanently attached to land. Personal property is everything that is readily moveable. Personal property is an entirely different commodity than real property and does not possess the special characteristics of real property.

PHYSICAL CHARACTERISTICS OF REAL PROPERTY

Immobility

A physical characteristic of major importance is the immobility of land. This is the primary distinguishing feature between land and personal property, which is highly mobile. The land cannot be relocated from one place to another. This is a unique feature of land as a commodity.

The physical characteristic of immobility is a major reason why the economic characteristic of location is so important and is a major factor in affecting land value. The characteristic of immobility also makes the market for land a local market.

It is because of this local aspect of the real estate market that there are thousands of real estate brokerage firms located in communities across the nation. It is necessary for those who have a specific knowledge of the local market in real estate to be available as specialists to serve the buyers and sellers in each community.

Indestructibility

Another unique feature of land is its physical characteristic of indestructibility. Land is a permanent commodity. Land cannot be destroyed. It may be altered substantially in its topography or other aspects of its appearance, but it still remains. Land values can, of course, change as a result of changing conditions in the area of the location of the land and may suffer from economic obsolescence, which results from changes in surrounding areas that adversely affect its value. For example, the construction of an interstate highway can radically affect land values of property located several miles away on a minor highway that loses a tremendous volume of traffic to the newly constructed nearby interstate.

The permanence or indestructibility of land makes it very attractive as a long-term investment. However, the investor should always be alert to changing conditions that may affect the value of the investment.

Nonhomogeneity

Another important characteristic of land is the fact that it is nonhomogeneous. No two parcels of land are identical although there may be similarities.

The special legal right of specific performance granted to parties in a contract to buy and sell real estate is a direct result of the fact that each parcel is unique. In these contracts, the law does not consider a suit for damages to be a sufficient remedy for the injured party and therefore the law makes available a legal action wherein the injured party can require the defaulting party to either buy or sell the land that is the subject of the contract.

ECONOMIC CHARACTERISTICS OF REAL PROPERTY

Availability

An important economic characteristic of real property is its availability or scarcity. Land is a commodity that has a fixed supply base. As we know, no additional physical supply of land is being produced to keep pace with the ever-increasing population.

However, the problems created by an ever-increasing demand for the limited supply of land have been substantially eased by the increase in the economic supply of land. This increase has come about as a result of the greater utilization of the existing physical supply of land. Farmers are continuing to increase the utilization of land in the agricultural area. Greater and greater crop yields per acre are being achieved as a result of scientific and technological advances. Today, the agricultural industry is producing more cattle per acre and more bushels of crops per acre than it did just a few years ago. Additionally, in urban areas, land is being utilized to a greater and greater extent.

As a result of advances in science and technology, we are able to create high-rise office buildings, apartment complexes, and multilevel shopping centers. Consequently, one acre of land serves many times the number of people who could utilize the land in the absence of these improvements.

Introduction to Real Estate

Modification by Improvement

Another factor that has increased the economic supply of land has been the construction of highways, bridges, water reservoirs, purification plants, and public utilities. The improvement and expansion of our public air and land transportation system also makes a significant contribution in this regard. These accomplishments in the field of construction and transportation have converted land that was previously not accessible and useful in a practical sense into land that may now be utilized. A substantial increase in the economic supply of land has resulted from modification by improvements to the land (not on the land) that have made previously inaccessible and unusable land now usable in a practical sense.

Permanence of Investment

Because of the physical characteristics of immobility and indestructibility of land, the investment of capital and labor to create improvements to the land and improvements on the land is an investment that is long-term in nature. Many years are required to recoup these investments made to improve the value and quality of land.

Location (Situs)

Location, or situs, is an extremely important economic characteristic of land and has the greatest effect on property value of any other characteristic. The physical characteristic of immobility dictates that the location of a parcel of land is permanent. Therefore, if the land is located in an area where there is a high demand for the available land, the land will have a substantially increasing value. Conversely, if the land is inaccessible from a practical standpoint or is located in an area with very little or no demand, the economic value will be depressed.

Although the location of land cannot be changed, the value of the location and consequently the value of the land can be increased as the result of improvements in access and improvements by other modification to the land and on the land.

Additionally, the value of the location can change as the result of the preferences of people. In the 1950s there was a great flight from the urban centers to the suburbs. This resulted in many cases in substantial property value reductions in urban areas. Recently, as a result of sky-rocketing energy costs and the consequent increased cost of transportation, this trend has been reversing itself. People are rediscovering the inner cities and rehabilitating older properties and restoring lost values.

GENERAL CONCEPTS OF LAND USE

Physical Factors Affecting Land Use

Physical factors affecting land utilization are both natural and artificial. Natural factors include such things as location, topography, soil conditions, size and shape, subjection to flooding, action of the sun, and the presence or absence of minerals. Artificial factors include items such as streets and highways, surrounding land use patterns, availability of sewage systems, water, and other utility services, proximity to public transportation, and the existence of commercial and social centers in the area. The natural and artificial physical factors must always be taken into consideration in making an analysis as to the utility of land and the various uses to which the land may be adapted.

Economic Factors Affecting Land Use

Economic factors affecting land use include local property tax assessments and tax rates, wage and employment levels in the community, availability of financing and levels of interest rates, directional growth of a community, the quantity of highly competitive uses within the area, the trading area covered from the site location, governmental regulations such as zoning laws, fire regulations, adequacy of city planning, building codes, the effectiveness of crime control, and the concept of highest and best use. All of these economic factors have a definite effect on the uses to which the land can be or should be adapted.

The concept of highest and best use is of extreme importance. In employing this concept to determine the highest and best use of land, all of the physical and economic factors are taken into consideration. The highest and best use of land is the use of the land which will provide a residual income to the land that results in the highest present value of the land. Land must be improved by the employment of capital and labor to make it productive.

The task of coordinating and combining capital and labor to create an improvement is performed by an expert in real estate. The expert must determine the use of the land that will provide the necessary income to the land after labor has been paid and capital has been paid. The expert may very well be a general partner in a limited partnership with the investors providing the capital, as limited partners.

The expert will establish, for example, the optimum size of a building to be constructed on a particular site. The space should not be overadequate or underadequate. The building must not contain more space than can be rented in the market, nor should it fail to provide the space that the market demands. Either an overimprovement or an underimprovement will not provide sufficient income to the land. In either of these cases, the income will be absorbed by the cost of constructing, maintaining, and operating the building and providing a return to the investors to the extent that insufficient income is left, after all of these expenses are paid, to be allocated to the land. As a result, the land has not been put to its highest and best possible use.

There is only one highest and best use for a particular parcel of land at any particular time. The loss of residual income to the land resulting from failure to employ the land to its highest and best use will cause the value of the property to diminish. This form of depreciation is a loss in value resulting from economic obsolescence.

LAND USE CONTROLS

Historical Need for Land Use Controls

Even though most land in the United States is privately owned, there is a vested public interest in land because the type of use of a particular property affects other property owners and the general public. Because of this interest of the general public and other property owners, the use of land requires some regulation for the benefit of all. The need for land use control has existed since the founding of our country. This is especially true in areas of high population density where land uses more radically affect a great number of people.

Public land use controls exist in the form of city planning and zoning, state and regional planning, building codes, suitability for occupancy requirements, and environmental control laws. Additionally, there is substantial public control of land use as a result of direct public ownership. Direct public ownership exists in the ownership of public buildings, public parks, watersheds, streets, and highways.

Regulation of land use in the private sector exists in the form of restrictive covenants established by developers, restrictions in individual deeds requiring the continuation of a specified land use or prohibiting a specified land use, and use restrictions imposed on the lessee in lease contracts.

THE REAL ESTATE BUSINESS

Scope of the Real Estate Business

The real estate business is extremely extensive in scope and is a very complex industry. Usually when people think of the real estate business they only think of real estate brokerage. However, brokerage is just one of several specializations within the real estate business. In fact, within the field of brokerage, there are several specializations including farm and land brokerage, residential property brokerage, commercial and investment property brokerage. In addition to brokerage, other specializations in real estate include property management, appraising, financing, construction, property development, real estate education, and government service.

Real estate transactions can be traced to early written records from biblical times. However, those transactions were between seller and buyer directly without participation of a real estate broker. The business of real estate brokerage is a product of the twentieth century. In 1917, the State of California became the first state in the nation to enact licensing law legislation. Today, all states in the nation require real estate brokers and salespersons to be licensed.

The establishment of the national Association of Real Estate Boards in 1908 was a major factor in the field of real estate brokerage. During the 1970s, the name was changed to National Association of REALTORS. The term REALTOR is a registered mark of the National Association of REALTORS and identifies members of local and state associations and the national association. Only the active members of these associations may use the term REALTOR or REALTOR ASSOCIATE.

One of the most salutary and beneficial accomplishments of the National Association of REALTORS was the creation of a code of ethics in 1913. This code has contributed significantly to the professional stature of real estate brokerage. Other significant contributions of the National Association of REALTORS have been efforts that have resulted in licensing laws being enacted in all states, the legislative activity on the federal level to safeguard rights of private ownership in real property from erosion by unnecessary and harmful legislation, and the provision of excellent programs of continuing education for members and nonmembers through the REALTORS National Marketing Institute.

Relationship of the Real Estate Business to Other Professions and Businesses

The fact that real estate represents more than 65 percent of the wealth in this country illustrates the extremely broad scope and importance of the real estate business. The size and complexity of the real estate business dictates that participants in the business have continual dealings with people in a substantial variety of other professions and businesses. Included are attorneys, abstract and title companies, builders, developers, architects, surveyors, and accountants or other tax experts.

THE REAL ESTATE MARKET

The Free Market Concept

The free market concept illustrates a market in which there is ample time for buyer and seller to effect a mutually beneficial purchase and sale without undue pressure or urgency. The real estate market is an excellent example of this concept. Properties available for sale are given substantial market exposure, particularly on the local level. Properties are available for inspection by prospective buyers and prospective buyers have the opportunity to inspect several such properties prior to making a final selection.

Special Characteristics of the Real Estate Market

The physical characteristics of land create special characteristics of the real estate market that do not exist in other markets. The immobility of real estate causes the market to be local in character, requiring local specialists who are currently familiar with local market conditions, property values, and availability. The nonhomogeneity, or uniqueness, of each parcel of real estate also requires that the market be local in character. Each parcel of real estate is unique primarily because of its particular location.

The physical characteristic of immobility also results in a market that is slow to react to changes in supply and demand. When supply substantially exceeds demand, existing properties may not be withdrawn from a local market area and relocated to an area in which there is a higher demand because of the characteristic of immobility. Conversely, when the demand exceeds supply, new supplies of housing and business properties cannot be constructed quickly. Therefore, after a recession, it always takes many months for the supply to equal or exceed demand in the real estate market.

Factors Affecting Supply and Demand in the Real Estate Market

There are many factors affecting supply and demand in the real estate market, both on the local and national levels. Examples of these factors include interest rates, availability of financing for purchase and construction, population migrations, variations in population trends and family formations, government regulations, local and national economic conditions, and the availability and cost of building sites, construction materials, and labor.

Historical Trends in the Real Estate Market

Just as the economy as a whole is subject to peaks and valleys of activity that have recurred over the years with fairly reasonable regularity, the real estate industry as part of this economy has also been subjected to recurring periods of recession and prosperity. In recent years we have experienced recessions in the national economy and the real estate industry in 1966, 1975, and during the period of 1979-1981.

The real estate industry is typically the first industry to feel the adverse effects of depressed conditions in the national and local economies. It also takes the real estate industry a longer period of time to climb out of a recession than the economy as a whole because of the inability of the real estate industry to react quickly to radical changes in supply and demand.

Another characteristic of the real estate cycle is that the real estate industry usually attains a much higher level of activity in prosperous times than does the economy in general.

REAL ESTATE TRANSACTIONS

The Real Estate Agent

The successful real estate agent is not engaged in applying techniques of the "hard sell." Rather, he or she is a counselor working diligently to solve the problems of buyers, sellers, and renters of real estate. Everyone that contacts a real estate office has a problem. The problem involves real property—the need to either buy, sell, or rent. The real estate agent's ability to solve these problems for the benefit of others results in a successful career.

A career in real estate can provide the practitioner with satisfaction from serving the needs of people and with accompanying financial rewards. Success in the real estate business is built upon knowledge, service to others, and ethical conduct in all dealings.

Listings

A listing is a contract wherein a property owner employs a real estate firm to market the property described in the contract within a specified period of time. The real estate firm becomes the agent of the selling property owner under this contract. Listings are the inventory of a real estate office and are the life blood of the business. Without listings, a real estate firm is severely handicapped and is limited to marketing the listings of other real estate offices.

As agent of the seller, the real estate broker and the associates working for that broker are empowered to act as a negotiator to market the listed property. The listing contract does not authorize the agent to bind the seller in a contract to sell the property. The agent's purpose is to find qualified prospective buyers for the property and present offers from these buyers to the property owner for acceptance or rejection. The ability to match up qualified buyers with specific properties enables the real estate agent to create purchase and sale contracts, thereby solving buyers' and sellers' problems and providing commission income to the agent.

Offer and Contract of Sale

A binding contract to buy and sell real property results from the written acceptance of a valid written offer from the buyer by the seller or the acceptance by the buyer of a new offer or counteroffer made by the seller. In presenting the offer, the real estate agent must always give the seller for whom he or she is acting as agent the benefit of all information regarding the qualifications of the buyer and the quality of the offer.

Financing

One of the most important aspects of real estate transactions is financing. If the property cannot be financed, usually it cannot be sold. Occasionally, a broker will have the good fortune of obtaining a prospective buyer that is able to pay cash for the full purchase price and does not wish to finance the transaction. These are the exceptions in the real estate business.

A broker's knowledge of financing and the use of imagination in this area will increase sales volume significantly. In a tight money market, the use of a second mortgage coupled with the assumption of the existing mortgage by the purchaser is an excellent financing arrangement. This is true even though the second mortgage may be at an unusually high interest rate. This is often offset by an existing mortgage available for assumption that has an interest rate that is below the going interest rate being charged.

A thorough knowledge of the various forms of mortgage loans available from lending institutions as well as all methods that may be used by a seller to finance the sale of a property for the buyer is essential to the broker. A real estate broker must continually keep in touch with the financial institutions in the area and keep current on the activities in the money market. The individual broker should establish a cordial relationship with the people in these financial institutions. The broker brings them prospective borrowers and the financial institution, in turn, assists the broker in making sales by financing the transactions for qualified buyers.

Final Settlement

The consumation of the real estate transaction occurs at closing or final settlement. This is the time when the buyer receives a deed giving title to the property, the seller receives the compensation for the sale of the property, and the real estate agent receives a well-earned commission. The real estate agent—along with an attorney, a loan officer of a lending institution, the buyer, and the seller—is a party to the closing and often arranges for the performance of the various activities preliminary to closing.

Other Aspects

In addition to the activities involved in the real estate brokerage business discussed previously, the real estate agent must be knowledgable in a variety of other subjects necessary to the satisfactory performance of the agent's obligations in real estate transactions. These other subjects, which will be discussed in depth in the various chapters of the text, include property ownership and interests, transfer of title to real property, fundamentals of residential construction, valuation of real estate, land use controls, Fair Housing Law, property management, insurance, and federal income tax implications in real estate ownership and sale. It is also very important for the real estate agent to understand and know the meaning of the various real estate and legal terms involved with real estate transactions. Finally, a basic understanding of the various types of arithmetic problems with which the practitioner may be confronted in the activities of real estate brokerage is necessary.

SUMMARY

Real property has special characteristics that set it apart from other marketable commodities. These characteristics are both physical and economic and have an important affect on real estate values. Additionally, these special characteristics create a real estate market that is substantially different from other markets.

Land utilization is affected by both physical factors and economic factors. The principle of highest and best use of land is an all-important concept in land utilization. Failure to make the highest and best use of land results in depreciation in the form of economic obsolescence.

Controls of land use are necessary to protect the vested interests of the general public as well as the interests of surrounding landowners. The need for land use controls has existed since the early days of our country and the need grows ever greater with increasing populations and increased land use density. Land use controls exist in the form of public and private controls.

The real estate business is highly complex and has an enormous scope that affects the lives of all people. The real estate business consists of a substantial variety of specializations and subspecializations. The real estate business has a very responsible relationship to many other professions and businesses.

The real estate market utilizes the free market concept wherein buyers and sellers have adequate time and information to reach a purchase and sale agreement without undue pressure and with factual knowledge of all important aspects of the transaction. The physical and economic characteristics of land create a market that is local in character and slow to react to fluctuations in supply and demand.

Historically, the real estate business has experienced cycles of recession and prosperity along with the national economy. The effects of depressed economic conditions are usually felt by the real estate industry before other segments of the economy. The real estate industry is typically slower to pull out of depressed economic periods, but typically reaches higher peaks of activity and prosperity than many other segments of the economy.

The real estate agent is a counselor working to solve the problems of buyers, sellers, and renters of real estate. Success in the real estate business is built upon ethical conduct, service to others, and knowledge of the great variety of subjects covered in this text.

IMPORTANT POINTS

1. Real property consists of land and everything permanently attached to land.

2. Personal property is everything that is not real property.

3. Real property has certain physical and economic characteristics that set it apart from other commodities.

4. Land use controls are necessary to protect the interests of the public and the property owners.

5. The real estate market is local in character and is an example of the free-market concept.

6. For the benefit of others, a real estate agent acts as a counselor in solving real estate problems.

IMPORTANT TERMINOLOGY

Final Settlement
Free Market
Highest and Best Use
Immobility
Indestructibility
Land Use Controls
Listing
Nonhomogeneity

Offer and Contract of Sale
Real Estate
Real Property
REALTOR®
REALTOR® Associate
Realty
Situs
Supply and Demand

Introduction to Real Estate

REVIEW QUESTIONS FOR CHAPTER 3

1. All of the following are separable ownerships in land EXCEPT

   (a) Surface of the land
   (b) Area below the surface
   (c) Nonhomogeneity
   (d) Air rights

2. The characteristic of land that causes the real estate market to be essentially a local market is the physical characteristic of

   (a) Indestructibility
   (b) Immobility
   (c) Availability
   (d) Natural features

3. The nonhomogeneity of land
   I. Is the basis for the legal remedy of specific performance
   II. Results from the uniqueness of every parcel of real estate

   (a) I only
   (b) II only
   (c) both I and II
   (d) neither I nor II

4. The increase in the economic supply of land has resulted from
   I. Increased utilization of the physical supply of land
   II. Modification by improvements of the land

   (a) I only
   (b) II only
   (c) both I and II
   (d) neither I nor II

5. The quality of the location of land and consequently the value of the land can be changed by

   (a) The principal of nonhomogeneity
   (b) Relocation of the land
   (c) Changes in the national scope of the real estate business
   (d) Improvements to the land that result in accessibility not previously available

6. The employment of the concept of highest and best use
   I. Includes consideration of the physical and economic factors affecting land use
   II. Results in the greatest present value of the land

   (a) I only
   (b) II only
   (c) both I and II
   (d) neither I nor II

7. The type of depreciation resulting from an overimprovement or an underimprovement on land is described as:

   (a) Physical deterioration
   (b) Functional obsolescence
   (c) Modification by improvement
   (d) Economic obsolescence

8. Public land use controls exist in the form of:

   (a) Restrictive covenants
   (b) Zoning laws
   (c) Deed restrictions
   (d) Assessments

9. Specializations within the real estate business include which of the following?

   (a) Transportation
   (b) Farming
   (c) Accounting
   (d) Property management

10. The physical characteristics of land create a real estate market that has special characteristics that are not inherent in other markets, including:
    I. The characteristic that the real estate market is slow to react to changes in the supply of and demand for real estate.
    II. The characteristic of the necessity for local specialists to adequately serve the buying and selling public.

    (a) I only
    (b) II only
    (c) both I and II
    (d) neither I nor II

11. The real estate market may be described in all the following ways EXCEPT

    (a) Free market
    (b) Local market
    (c) Movable market
    (d) Market that is slow to react to changes in supply and demand

12. The function of a real estate agent in dealings with buyers and sellers in the real estate market may be best described as which of the following?

    (a) Financier
    (b) Counselor
    (c) Contractor
    (d) Salesperson

13. A real estate firm becomes an agent of a property owner as a result of which of the following?

    (a) Contract of sale
    (b) Final settlement
    (c) Specialized knowledge
    (d) Listing contract

14. The typical real estate agent must have specialized knowledge of a variety of subjects which include all of the following EXCEPT

    (a) Financing
    (b) Contracts
    (c) Excavation
    (d) Valuation

15. Which of the following is (are) an accurate statement regarding a successful career in real estate?
    I. A successful career in real estate is based on ethical conduct and service to others.
    II. A successful career in real estate is based on knowledge of a great variety of subjects.

    (a) I only
    (b) II only
    (c) both I and II
    (d) neither I nor II

16. All of the following are real property EXCEPT

    (a) Surface of the earth
    (b) Area below the surface
    (c) Readily movable items
    (d) Area above the surface

17. Economic characteristics of real property include which of the following?

    (a) Situs
    (b) Immobility
    (c) Indestructibility
    (d) Nonhomogeneity

18. Which of the following has the greatest affect on real property value?

    (a) Tax rates
    (b) Location
    (c) Availability
    (d) Indestructibility

19. Which of the following is an example of of the private control of land use?

    (a) Zoning
    (b) Restrictive covenants
    (c) Building codes
    (d) Environmental controls

20. The real estate market is
    I. An example of the free market concept.
    II. Local in character.

    (a) I only
    (b) II only
    (c) both I and II
    (d) neither I nor II

21. The term REALTOR® designates
    I. Any real estate licensee.
    II. A real estate licensee that is a member of the national association of REALTORS®

    (a) I only
    (b) II only
    (c) both I and II
    (d) neither I nor II

Introduction to Real Estate

22. Which of the following is a contract wherein a property owner employs a real estate broker to market the property?
    - (a) Assumption
    - (b) Contract of sale
    - (c) Consumation
    - (d) Listing

23. The real estate market is subject to
    I. The cyclic changes in the national economy.
    II. The law of supply and demand.
    - (a) I only
    - (b) II only
    - (c) both I and II
    - (d) neither I nor II

24. Which of the following statements regarding the real estate business is (are) correct?
    I. Real estate transactions can be traced to Biblical times.
    II. The business of real estate brokerage is a product of the Twentieth Century.
    - (a) I only
    - (b) II only
    - (c) both I and II
    - (d) neither I nor II

Licensing of Real Estate Brokers and Salespersons

4

Today, all states require that people engaged in the real estate business be licensed by the state. The authority of the state to require licenses falls under the police power of the state. This is a power that every state has to enable it to fulfill its obligation to protect the health, safety, welfare, and property of the citizens of the state.

The purpose of license law legislation is to protect the general public. License laws require a licensee to possess the necessary knowledge, skill, and reputation for honesty, fair dealing, and ethical conduct to enter the real estate business. License laws also govern the conduct of licensees in their real estate business activities.

Since only a generalized presentation is possible in a textbook designed for use in many states, it is imperative that a real estate student become thoroughly familiar with the license law and rules and regulations in his or her particular state or other jurisdiction. Assistance in this regard is provided by a checklist at the end of the chapter.

Variations

Although there are variations in license law legislation from state to state, the most important provisions are very similar, if not identical, and are based on the model recommended by the National Association of REALTORS. Substantial uniformity in the major provisions of license law statutes has also resulted from efforts of the National Association of Real Estate License Law Officials (NARELLO). Organized in 1930, NARELLO consists of license law officials representing every state. NARELLO and the National Association of REALTORS® have made substantial contributions to license law legislation that have resulted in elevating the standards of the real estate industry.

Variations in license law legislation from state to state usually involve administrative matters such as requirements for license eligibility. Variations in eligibility occur in such requirements as minimum age for licensing, amount of education required, residency, apprenticeship, license renewal requirements, and fees. All states require that license applicants pass a licensing examination for either a broker's license or salesperson's license. As of this writing, approximately thirty-five states and jurisdictions are using a license examination prepared by the Educational Testing Service (ETS) of Princeton, New Jersey.

Broker and Salesperson Defined

The definition of real estate broker and the definition of real estate salesperson are substantially uniform in the various state licensing laws. *Real estate broker* is any person, partnership, association, or corporation, who for a payment or other valuable consideration, or a promise of payment or other valuable consideration, lists or offers to list, sells, or offers to sell, buys or offers to buy, auctions or offers to auction, or negotiates the purchase, sale, or exchange of real estate, or who leases or rents or offers to rent any real estate for others. A *real estate salesperson* is any person who performs any of the acts set forth in the definition of real estate broker for compensation or valuable consideration or promise of compensation or valuable consideration but does so only while associated with and supervised by a licensed broker.

From these definitions it can be determined that a real estate broker can own and operate a business whereas a salesperson licensee can only engage in the real estate business when associated with and supervised by a broker. Therefore, a salesperson can not operate independently.

Exceptions

License law statues typically provide for exceptions to the requirement of being licensed in order to legally receive a compensation in a real estate transaction. The following is a list of usual exceptions:

1. Owners or lessors acting with reference to property owned or leased by them.
2. Any person acting as attorney-in-fact under a duly executed power of attorney authorizing the final consummation of any contract of sale, lease, or exchange of real estate. An attorney-in-fact is a person or organization appointed to perform certain legal acts on behalf of another under a duly executed power of attorney.
3. An attorney-at-law is exempt regarding acts or services rendered by an attorney-at-law if the services are performed in behalf of clients as part of an attorney's provision of legal services to those clients.
4. Receivers, trustees in bankruptcy, guardians, administrators, or executors acting under a court order.
5. A trustee acting under a trust agreement, deed of trust, or will or the trustee's salaried employees.

Licensing Boards or Commissions

The responsibility for the enforcement of real estate license law statutes is assigned by the statute to a licensing board or commission. These organizations are authorized to issue licenses to qualified applicants and to revoke or suspend licenses in the event of statutory violations by the licensee. These organizations are also empowered by statute to prosecute unlicensed persons committing acts in violation of the license law statute. Violations of license law statutes are misdemeanors (not felonies) and courts are empowered by the license law statutes to punish the violator by either fine or imprisonment or both fine and imprisonment, in the discretion of the court.

Standards of Conduct Required of Licensees

The sections of license law statutes requiring every licensee to maintain certain standards of conduct are the major portions of license law legislation and are substantially uniform among the various states. These standards of conduct reinforce the obligations of the licensee to his or her principal—typically the listing seller—and the obligations of the licensee to the general public. These standards of conduct are absolutely necessary for the protection of the general public. This is the major purpose of license law legislation. Violations of these statutory requirements by a licensee subjects the licensee to license revocation or suspension.

Typical Prohibitions

The following is a list of typical violations that subject a licensee to license revocation or suspension:

1. Obtaining a license under false or fraudulent representations.
2. Having been convicted or entered a plea of no contest upon which a finding of guilty and final judgment has been entered in a court of competent jurisdiction for the criminal offense of embezzlement, obtaining money under false pretenses, conspiracy to defraud, forgery, or any similar offense or offenses involving moral turpitude.
3. Making any substantial and willful misrepresentation. It is a violation for a broker or salesperson to make an intentional false statement regarding an important matter in a real estate transaction to induce someone to contract. It is also a violation for a broker or salesperson to indicate knowledge of an important matter in a real estate transaction when in fact the individual has no such knowledge. Example: If a broker or a salesperson tells a buyer that a house is well-insulated when either (a) the broker or salesperson does not know whether the house is insulated or not, or (b) knows that it is not properly insulated, he or she has made a substantial and

willful misrepresentation. A misrepresentation occurs in the case of a false statment if the agent should have known the facts because of his or her training and knowledge as a real estate expert.

4. Making any false promises of a character likely to influence, persuade, or induce someone to contract. A false promise is simply an untrue promise to a party that something will or will not occur in a real estate transaction. It is a false promise if a broker or salesperson tells a prospective buyer that something will or will not happen when in fact the licensee knows that just the opposite is true. It is also a false promise if a licensee promises something when he or she does not know whether or not the promise will be kept on the part of the party supposed to perform the promise or when in fact there is no basis for making such a promise

5. Pursuing a course of misrepresentation or making of false promises through agents or salespersons or advertising or otherwise. This is simply a continuing program of making misrepresentations or false promises by a broker.

6. Acting for more than one party in a transaction without the knowledge of all parties for whom the salesperson acts. It is a violation for a real estate broker to represent both a buyer and seller in a real estate transaction without informing both parties of the dual representation and obtaining their agreement.

7. Accepting compensation from someone other than the supervising broker. A salesperson licensee is required to accept compensation in a real estate transaction only from the broker under whom he or she is supervised. Also, the salesperson may not represent another broker without the knowledge and consent of the broker with whom he or she is principally associated.

8. Failing to account for and remit funds belonging to others that have come into the licensee's possession. All brokers must maintain trust or escrow accounts in insured banks or thrift institutions for the deposit of other peoples' monies, and are prohibited from comingling the funds of others with their business or personal funds. Brokers are required to maintain adequate records regarding the deposit and disbursement of funds from this account. Salesperson licensees are required to promptly remit to their supervising broker all funds belonging to others that come into their possession.

9. Paying an unlicensed person a commission or valuable consideration for services in a real estate transaction. It is just as much a violation of the license law statute for someone to pay an unlicensed person a compensation for services in a real estate transaction as it is for the unlicensed person to receive the compensation. Both payor and payee are in violation of the law. The real estate agent should be thoroughly knowledgeable of the policy of his or her particular state in this regard.

10. Performing or attempting to perform any legal service as prohibited by the state statutes concerned with the unauthorized practice of law. A licensee may not, in most states, prepare legal documents such as deeds or mortgages, may not give an opinion as to the legal validity of any document or the legal rights of others, and may not perform a title examination and render an opinion as to the quality of the title. These are some examples. In essence, a licensee may not perform any service that must be performed by an attorney-at-law. In all legal matters affecting buyers and sellers, the licensee should recommend that the parties retain the services of a competent attorney.

11. Failing to deliver all necessary documents handled by the licensee to buyers and sellers in a real estate transaction. Licensees are required to present every offer in writing to the seller. It is the seller's prerogative to accept or reject any offer. Licensees are also required to provide copies of all documents executed by buyer, seller, or both to the buyer and seller. The buyer must receive a copy of the offer and both buyer and seller must receive copies of the executed contract. The seller must always be provided with a copy of the listing contract. Additionally, copies of any other documents—such as options, contract for deed, or contracts of lease—must be provided to the parties.

12. Failing to deliver to buyers and sellers completed copies of closing statements

reflecting the receipt and disbursement of funds in a real estate transaction. License law statutes do not typically require brokers to prepare closing statements, but they often hold brokers responsible for delivery of these statements even though they are prepared by someone else.

13. Violating any rule or regulation promulgated by the licensing board or commission. The rules and regulations are usually incorporated into the statutes by statutory reference, which makes a violation of the rules and regulations a violation of law. The rules and regulations have the effect of administrative law.

Knowledge of the License Law Essential

It is absolutely essential that the real estate student be thoroughly knowledgeable of the license law statute and rules and regulations currently in effect for his or her particular state or jurisdiction. The student may obtain copies of the license law statute and rules and regulations from the licensing authority in the state to which the student is making application for a real estate license. This knowledge is absolutely necessary for the student to pass the state licensing examination.

The ETS real estate licensing examination is divided into two parts. One part consists of questions about the license law statute and rules and regulations in effect in the particular state to which license application is being made. The other part of the examination consists of eighty questions covering all other real estate subjects of which the applicant must be knowledgeable. The applicant for license must pass both parts of the examination.

It is also extremely important that the real estate student be knowledgeable of his or her state's license law and rules and regulations to be assured that conduct in their activities in the real estate business is in accord with the standards required by law after they are licensed. For these purposes the student should fill in the license law provisions of his or her state on the following outline.

SUMMARY OF LICENSE LAW PROVISIONS

I. General Provisions
   A. Define—real estate broker

   B. Define—real estate salesperson

   C. Cite exemptions from license requirements

   D. List broker office requirements

   E. Give experience requirements—broker

   F. Note experience requirements—salesperson

   G. Cite educational requirements—broker

Licensing of Real Estate Brokers and Salespersons

    H. List educational requirements—
       salesperson

    B. Qualifications for license:
       1. Salesperson

II. Real Estate Commission
    A. Give the number of members

       2. Broker

    B. List the qualifications and appointment

       3. Corporation

    C. Note the powers of enforcement

       4. Partnership

    D. List all penalties for violation

    C. Application procedures and fees for:

    E. Cite the consent agreements and fees

    D. Displaying of licenses

III. General Licensing Requirements
    A. Give reasons for the necessity for license

    E. Expiration and renewal of licenses

F. Effect of revocation of broker license on licenses of salespersons in his employ

G. Transfer of license

H. Branch offices

I. Discharge or termination of employment of salesperson

J. Change of location requirements

K. Death of broker

L. Effect of contracts negotiated by licensed persons, unlicensed persons

M. Provisions for trust accounts

N. Bonding

O. Convictions

P. Sponsorship

Q. Fee splitting with unlicensed persons

R. Comingling

S. Fingerprinting

T. Other rules or regulations for:
  1. Rental housing
  2. Appraisals
  3. Advance fees
  4. Guaranty fund
  5. Trust accounts
  6. Steering/blockbusting
  7. Reciprocity
  8. Interstate land sales
  9. Business opportunity sales

U. Grounds for suspension or revocation of license

SUMMARY

All states today require that people engaged in the real estate business be licensed by the state. In every state there are two types of licenses: a broker's license and a salesperson's license.

The distinction between these two types of licenses is that a broker licensee may operate a real estate business whereas a salesperson licensee may only function in the real estate business while supervised by and associated with a licensed broker. License law statutes provide certain exceptions to the requirement that a person or organization be licensed to legally receive a compensation in a real estate transaction.

While there are variations among the states in license law statutes, the important portions of the statutes are substantially uniform from state to state. These important parts of license law statutes set forth the standards of conduct required of licensees for the protection of the general public. These standards include the agent's obligations to the principal as required by the law of agency. Additionally, these standards include requirements for the protection of buyers and other members of the public.

It is absolutely essential that the real estate student be thoroughly knowledgeable of the license law statute and rules and regulations currently in effect in the student's state of license application. This is absolutely necessary in order to pass the license examination and to enable the student to meet the required standards of real estate practice after being licensed.

IMPORTANT POINTS

1. License laws are an exercise of the police power of a state.

2. The purpose of license laws is to protect the public.

3. All states require that people be licensed to engage in the real estate business. However, there are certain exemptions to the requirement to be licensed.

5. A broker is defined as a person or organization who, for a consideration or promise of a consideration, performs or offers to perform aspects of real estate transactions for others.

6. A salesperson is one who performs acts authorized to be performed by a broker but does so on behalf of a broker with whom he or she is associated.

7. Real estate commissions are responsible for the enforcement of license laws in their state or jurisdiction.

8. License laws establish standards of conduct for licensees.

9. Real estate commissions are empowered to issue and revoke or suspend licenses.

10. License applicants must be knowledgeable of all the provisions of the license law, commission rules, and other regulations in their particular state or jurisdiction.

IMPORTANT TERMINOLOGY

Attorney-at-law
Attorney-in-fact
Broker
Comingle
Commission
Escrow Account
False Promise
License

Licensee
Misrepresentation
NARELLO
National Association of REALTORS®
Police Power
Salesperson
Trust Account
Unauthorized Practice of Law

REVIEW QUESTIONS FOR CHAPTER 4

1. Specifically exempted from the licensing law requirements is (are)
   I. Trustees in bankruptcy
   II. Attorneys-at-law

   (a) I only
   (b) II only
   (c) both I and II
   (d) neither I nor II

2. A broker must
   I. Submit all written offers to the seller
   II. Furnish the seller with a copy of the executed sales contract

   (a) I only
   (b) II only
   (c) both I and II
   (d) neither I nor II

3. A licensee's license may be revoked or suspended for
   I. Making a substantial and willful misrepresentation
   II. Acting for more than one party in a transaction without the knowledge of all parties for whom he or she acts

   (a) I only
   (b) II only
   (c) both I and II
   (d) neither I nor II

4. A real estate salesperson
   I. Must accept commissions only from the employing broker
   II. Must not represent a broker other than the employing broker without the knowledge and consent of the employing broker

   (a) I only
   (b) II only
   (c) both I and II
   (d) neither I nor II

5. It is a violation of the license law
   I. To pay an unlicensed person a commission
   II. For an unlicensed person to receive a commission

   (a) I only
   (b) II only
   (c) both I and II
   (d) neither I nor II

6. A licensee's license may be revoked or suspended for
   I. The violation of any rule promulgated by the board or commission
   II. Preparing a deed for a client

   (a) I only
   (b) II only
   (c) both I and II
   (d) neither I nor II

7. Which of the following most correctly states the purpose of a license law legislation?

   (a) To provide protection for licensed brokers and salespersons from competition by unlicensed people.
   (b) To control the number of people entering the real estate business.
   (c) To give protection for the general public by requiring the people entering the real estate business to be adequately qualified.
   (d) To establish a board of arbitration to settle disputes between licensees.

8. The legal authority of a state to require that real estate brokers and salespersons be licensed is derived from which of the following?

   (a) Enabling power
   (b) Regulatory power
   (c) Commission power
   (d) Police power

9. The license law statutes authorize the licensing commission or board to enforce the statutory provisions against
   I. Licensed brokers and salespersons
   II. Unlicensed people who are engaged in activities prohibited by the license law statute

   (a) I only
   (b) II only
   (c) both I and II
   (d) neither I nor II

10. A person with a salesperson's license must
    I. Be associated with and supervised by a licensed broker to engage in the real estate business
    II. Present every offer to the seller

    (a) I only
    (b) II only
    (c) both I and II
    (d) neither I nor II

11. A broker may legally receive a commission from both buyer and seller in a real estate transaction
    I. Provided both buyer and seller are aware that both are paying a commission to the broker
    II. Provided the broker's business is organized as a corporation

    (a) I only
    (b) II only
    (c) both I and II
    (d) neither I nor II

12. If an unlicensed person initiated a legal action against a seller for a commission in a real estate transaction, which statement regarding the situation is incorrect?

    (a) The court would probably not hear the case.
    (b) The seller would be in violation of the license law if he or she paid the commission.
    (c) The unlicensed person would be in violation of the license law if he or she received the commission.
    (d) The commission payment would be legal if it were a flat fee rather than a percentage of the sales price.

13. In an effort to induce a prospective buyer to enter into a contract to purchase a home, a real estate broker told the buyer that the home was only four years old when it was actually eight years old. The broker knew the actual age of the home. Relying on the broker's statement, the prospect entered into a contract to purchase the property. Given this information, which of the following statements is (are) true?

    (a) The broker is in violation of the licensing law.
    (b) The broker has committed an act of willful misrepresentation.
    (c) The buyer can have the contract set aside.
    (d) All of the above.

14. A real estate broker employed a salesperson who had received notification that she had passed the state license examination but had not received her license. In light of these facts, which is (are) true?
    I. The broker is in violation of the license law.
    II. The salesperson is in violation of the license law.

    (a) I only
    (b) II only
    (c) both I and II
    (d) neither I nor II

15. A buyer was induced to enter into a contract to purchase a house by the broker's statement that the house was fully insulated. The broker knew that the house actually had no insulation at all. Given this information, which is (are) true?
    I. The buyer has the option to void the contract.
    II. The broker is guilty of having made a misrepresentation of a material fact and is subject to revocation or suspension of his or her license.

    (a) I only
    (b) II only
    (c) both I and II
    (d) neither I nor II

16. While showing a house to a prospective buyer, a salesperson told the buyer that the house was attractive, comfortable, and nicely landscaped. In light of these facts, which is (are) true?
    I. The salesperson has violated the license law prohibition against misrepresentation.
    II. The statements are "sales talk" to which the doctrine of *caveat emptor* applies.

    (a) I only
    (b) II only
    (c) both I and II
    (d) neither I nor II

17. A broker listed a property with a price of $50,000, which was the broker's estimate of the market value. The broker received an offer of $37,000, but he did not present it to the seller because he did not consider it to be a reasonable offer. Given this information, which is (are) true?
    I. The broker is in violation of the license law.
    II. The broker has violated his fiduciary position as agent of the seller.

    (a) I only
    (b) II only
    (c) both I and II
    (d) neither I nor II

18. A seller executed a listing contract that provided for payment of an 8 percent commission to the broker. In negotiating the sale of the property, the broker obtained a commitment from the buyer to pay a commission of 7 percent to the broker. The broker did not reveal the buyer's commission agreement to the seller or the seller's commission agreement to the buyer. In light of these facts, which is (are) true?
    I. The broker acted properly as a negotiating agent.
    II. The broker is subject to having her license suspended or revoked.

    (a) I only
    (b) II only
    (c) both I and II
    (d) neither I nor II

19. A seller was so pleased with the manner in which a salesperson handled the listing and sale of her property that she decided to pay an extra commission to go entirely to the salesperson. The salesperson may accept this special commission provided

    (a) The salesperson receives it directly from the seller.
    (b) The salesperson has the broker's approval.
    (c) The broker shares in the extra commission.
    (d) The seller pays the extra commission to the broker who in turn passes it on to the salesperson.

20. If a licensed broker wants to list property in an adjoining state, which of the following is correct?

    (a) The broker must file a request for permission to do so with the real estate commission in the adjoining state.
    (b) The broker must submit a request for authorization in his state of residency.
    (c) The broker must obtain a nonresident license from the real estate commission in the adjoining state.
    (d) There is no way in which a broker can lawfully negotiate a real estate transaction in a state where he is a nonresident.

21. A broker may do all of the following without being in violation of the license law EXCEPT

    (a) Market her own property through her real estate office
    (b) Witness a sales contract
    (c) Charge varying rates of commission on several different listings
    (d) Advise a seller as to the validity of a purchase money deed of trust taken by the seller from the buyer in a real estate transaction

22. Over a period of several months a broker advertised lots for sale with all utilities and services available all the while knowing the area in which the lots were located did not have water, sewage, or electricity available. Which of the following statements regarding this action by the broker is (are) correct?
    I. The broker's action constituted a course of misrepresentation for which he is subject to license revocation or suspension.
    II. Since the untrue information was only provided by advertising rather than verbal statements by the broker to prospective buyers, the broker is not in violation of the license law.

    (a) I only
    (b) II only
    (c) both I and II
    (d) neither I nor II

23. An owner listed her property for sale because the broker told her that the market value of the property was $75,000. However, the broker knew the property value was approximately $60,000. As a result, which of the following is (are) correct?
    I. The broker is guilty of an act of misrepresentation and is in violation of the license law.
    II. The broker has violated his responsibility as a fiduciary of his principal, the seller.

    (a) I only
    (b) II only
    (c) both I and II
    (d) neither I nor II

24. Brokers and salespersons are required to deliver to the parties copies of all of the following EXCEPT

    (a) Offers and contracts
    (b) Abstracts of title
    (c) Written leases
    (d) Options

25. Included in the responsibility of licensing commissions or boards is (are) which of the following?
    I. To issue licenses to qualified applicants
    II. To see that the qualifications and activities of brokers and salespeople are in accord with law and in the best interests of the public

    (a) I only
    (b) II only
    (c) both I and II
    (d) neither I nor II

26. Which of the following statements about license laws is (are) correct?
    I. License laws are an exercise of the police power of the state.
    II. The purpose of license laws is to protect the general public.

    (a) I only
    (b) II only
    (c) both I and II
    (d) neither I nor II

27. Typically exempt from the requirement to be licensed is which of the following individuals?

    (a) A person who only lists property for sale.
    (b) A person who only negotiates leases for others.
    (c) A person engaged in the real estate brokerage business only a few months each year.
    (d) A person acting for another as an attorney-in-fact in a real estate transaction.

28. The broker must deliver to the seller
    I. All written offers that the broker considers to be reasonable offers.
    II. All written offers.

    (a) I only
    (b) II only
    (c) both I and II
    (d) neither I nor II

29. A licensee's license may be revoked or suspended for
    I. The violation of any rule promulgated by the commission.
    II. Preparing a deed for a client.

    (a) I only
    (b) II only
    (c) both I and II
    (d) neither I nor II

30. All funds received by a real estate broker acting in a fiduciary capacity as an agent
    I. Must be deposited in a trust or escrow account.
    II. May not be comingled with the broker's personal or business funds.

    (a) I only
    (b) II only
    (c) both I and II
    (d) neither I nor II

Licensing of Real Estate Brokers and Salespersons

31. A real estate broker failed to pay the license renewal fee at the end of the license year. The effect of the broker's failure to pay the renewal fee is
    I. The broker's license is expired.
    II. The licenses of the salespersons under the broker's supervision are suspended.

    (a) I only
    (b) II only
    (c) both I and II
    (d) neither I nor II

32. To be in compliance with the license law statute, a trustee in bankruptcy selling the real property of another
    I. Must have a broker's license.
    II. Must have a salesperson's license.

    (a) I only
    (b) II only
    (c) both I and II
    (d) neither I nor II

Property Ownership and Interests

5

In this chapter we will expand the definition of real property, discuss the various types of ownership in real property as well as the interests that may exist, and point out the conditions that can adversely affect a title to real property.

REAL ESTATE DEFINED

In chapter 3, we learned that real property consists of land and everything permanently attached to the land. Ownership in land includes not only the surface of the earth, but also the area below the surface to the center of the earth and the area above the surface theoretically to the highest heavens. Real property also includes everything that is permanently attached to the land. Therefore, the owner of the land owns all structures on the land as well as any other improvements such as fences, swimming pools, flag poles, and retaining walls.

In addition things that grow in the soil may be included in the definition of real property. Growing things that do not require planting or cultivation but grow naturally and are perenials are called fruits of the soil and are designated in law as real property. These include forest trees, native shrubs, and wild berries. Growing things that require planting and cultivation are called fruits of industry and are designated in law as personal property. Examples include crops such as corn, wheat, melons, and soybeans. These fruits of industry are called emblements and are annual crops. The term emblements is also used to denote the right of a tenant to reenter the property and harvest the emblements after the termination of the tenancy.

Air Rights

Ownership of land includes ownership of and the rights to the area above the surface of the earth. The right of ownership of the air space enables the land owner to use that space to construct improvements on the land, to lease the air space to others, and to sell the air space to others.

However, the right of ownership and control in the air space is limited by zoning ordinances and federal laws providing for the use of the air space by aircraft. Zoning ordinances often restrict the height of improvements constructed on the land, and federal laws permit the use of the air space by air traffic flying at an altitude above a minimum height specified by the government.

Mineral Rights

A mineral right is the right of the property owner to take minerals from the earth. The owner may conduct mining operations or drilling operations personally or may sell or lease these rights to others on a royalty basis. A mineral lease is one that permits the use of land for mineral exploration and mining operations, if the exploration reveals the existence of minerals in sufficient quantity and quality to be economically profitable. The lease may be for a definite term or for a period as long as the land is productive. A mineral royalty is income received from leases of mineral land.

Fixtures
chattel

Personal property that has become real property by reason of its permanent attachment to real estate is called a fixture. In deciding whether or not personal property has become part of the real estate, a court takes three things into consideration. One, the intention of the person making the attachment. That is, did the person making the attachment intend for the property to be permanently attached to the real estate? Two, the method of attachment. Will removal damage the property remaining? Three, the position of the person making the attachment. An owner is usually presumed to be making a permanent attachment, whereas a tenant is presumed to be making a temporary attachment.

A permanent attachment converts the personal property into real property. Therefore, the attachment of personal property by the property owner converts the personal property to real property, whereas an attachment made by a tenant is typically considered to be temporary and therefore the attached item continues to be personal property. Included in this category are agricultural fixtures and trade fixtures. These are items installed by a tenant under an agricultural or commercial lease for use in a farming or business operation.

An exception to the general rule that a tenant is not presumed to be making a permanent attachment exists in cases where removal of the item would severely damage the remaining structure.

Effect of the Uniform Commercial Code (UCC)

A special situation occurs when the property owner has financed the purchase of an item. The Uniform Commercial Code (UCC), adopted by a majority of states, provides for the lender to retain a security interest in a chattel (personal property) until the lender is paid in full. The security interest is available to the lender even though the chattel is installed in real property. The security interest is created by an instrument called a *security agreement*.

The existence of such an agreement is evidenced on the public record by the filing of a notice called a financing statement. This notice is filed in the office of the Register of Deeds or other appropriate public office. The filing of the financing statement provides constructive notice to all the world that there exists a security interest in the item that is the subject of the security agreement. As a result, the attached item will not become a fixture and therefore a part of the real property until the security agreement has been satisfied by full payment. Consequently, the lender can remove the article even though it has been attached to real property in the event that the buyer/borrower defaults in payment. Subsequent purchasers of the real estate as well as any subsequent mortgagee are bound by the filing of the financing statement. Therefore, a purchaser of the home or a mortgagee accepting the property as security for a mortgage, would either have to complete the payments or permit the removal of the item by the lender in the event the property owner did not satisfy the debt.

ESTATES IN REAL PROPERTY

Systems of Property Ownership

The original system of land ownership was the feudal system that originated in English law almost a thousand years ago. Under the feudal system, only the king could hold title to real property. The king granted feuds to loyal subjects. These feuds did not provide ownership in land but simply a right of use and possession of land as long as the holder of the feud provided certain services to the king. The feuds were approximately equivalent to the modern concept of leasehold estates. Under the feuds outright ownership could never be obtained. Ownership of a feud could continue only as long as the owner provided services to the king.

One of the basic reasons for the American Revolution was the colonists' insistence on outright and absolute ownership of land in this country. As a result, the system of land ownership in the United States is the allodial system and not the feudal system. In this country, title to real property may be held absolutely by individuals. However, even the allodial system of property ownership is subject to four very important powers of federal and local governments. These powers are (1) the power of eminent domain, (2) police power, (3) power of taxation, and (4) the power of escheat.

Property Ownership and Interests

Power of Eminent Domain

The power of eminent domain is the power to take private property for public use. Governments exercise this power themselves and also delegate it to public utility companies. The taking of property under the power of eminent domain is called condemnation.

There are two limitations on the power of eminent domain. They are (1) the property condemned must be for the use and benefit of the general public and (2) the property owner must be paid the fair market value of the property lost through condemnation. The property owner has the right to appeal to the courts if he or she is not satisfied with the compensation offered by the condemning authority.

Police Power

The police power is the power that government has to enable it to fulfill its responsibility to provide for the health, safety and welfare of the public. Examples of the exercise of the police power affecting property use are zoning ordinances, subdivision ordinances, building codes, and environmental protection laws. Property owners affected by the exercise of the police power are not compensated for the restrictions on their use of property resulting from the exercise of this power.

Power of Taxation

The government's power of taxation is well known to everyone. Taxes are imposed upon real property on an *ad valorem* basis. This simply means that real property is taxed according to value. Every county has an official with the title Tax Assessor who is responsible for establishing the value of property within the county. This value is then taxed on the basis of an assessment or assessed value. The assessment resulting in tax value may be 100 percent of estimated market value or a substantially lower percentage.

A tax rate, either in dollars or mills, is applied to the assessed value to determine the amount of property tax. The rate must be sufficient to provide the amount of revenue required by property taxes to accomplish the budgetary requirements of the local government unit. Real property taxes are by far the largest source of income for local governments.

Power of Escheat

If a property owner dies and leaves a valid will, the individual's property is distributed to heirs as specified in the will. However, if an owner dies without having left a valid will, the deceased's property is distributed to heirs in accordance with state statutory provisions. These statutes are usually called "statutes of intestate succession" and specify how property will be distributed based on the relationship of heirs to the deceased.

In the event of there is no one qualified to receive title to property left by the deceased, the property then escheats to the state. In other words, if there is no one legally eligible as designated by statute to receive title to the property, the state takes title.

TYPES OF ESTATES

This subject deals with the various types of ownership and interests in land. The following discussion of these ownerships and interests is intended to provide a basic knowledge to the real estate student.

An estate in real property is an interest in the property sufficient to give the owner of the estate the right to possession of the property. Here, we must distinguish between the right of possession and the right of use. The owner of an estate in land has the right of possession as opposed to a mere right to use the land, as in the case of an easement.

The Latin translation for the word estate is *status*. This indicates the relationship in which the estate owner stands with reference to rights in the property and establishes the degree, quantity, nature, and extent of interest that a person has in real property.

Lands, Tenements, and Hereditaments

A concept of the law of real property is that real property consists of lands, tenements, and hereditaments. What then does each of these three things include?

Land is the surface of the earth and also the area below the surface (including minerals) theoretically to the center of the earth itself. The term lands also includes the air above the surface of the earth to the highest heavens.

Tenements includes all of those things that are included in the definition of land; in addition it includes both corporeal and incorporeal rights in land. Corporeal things are tangible things — things that can be touched and seen. Incorporeal rights are things that are intangible. Tenements includes buildings (corporeal). Tenements also includes rights in the property of another, such as an easement (incorporeal).

Hereditaments is a term that includes everything included in the term land and everything included in the term tenements. The term hereditaments includes every interest in real property that is capable of being inherited.

Groups of Estates in Land

Estates in land are divided into two groups. These are estates of freehold and estates of less than freehold (leasehold estates). Each of these two major divisions have various groupings or subheadings within them. The material following provides a description of each of these types of estates.

FREEHOLD ESTATES

The freehold estates are (1) the various fee simple estates and (2) life estates. Fee simple estates are inheritable; life estates are not.

Fee Simple Absolute

The estate of fee simple absolute provides the greatest form of ownership available in real property. This estate may be described as fee simple absolute, fee simple, or ownership in fee. Ownership in fee simple absolute provides certain legal rights usually described as a "bundle of legal rights." This bundle includes the right to possession of the property; the right of quiet enjoyment of the property; the right to dispose of the property by gift, sale by deed, or by will; and the right to control the use of the property within the limits of the law.

The owner in fee simple absolute may convey a life estate to another either in reversion or in remainder; pledge the property as security for a mortgage debt; convey a leasehold estate to another; grant an easement in the land to another; or give a license to conduct some activity on the property to another. Certain of these rights may be removed from the bundle leaving the other rights intact. For example, if the owner pledges the title as security for a mortgage debt, the balance remaining is a fee simple title subject to the mortgage debt. Also, if the owner conveyed an estate for years or conveyed an easement in the property to another, the remaining rights would be a fee simple subject to a lease or subject to the existance of an easement.

Fee Simple Subject to a Condition Subsequent

The fee simple subject to a condition subsequent can continue for an infinite period as is the case with the fee simple absolute. However, the fee simple subject to a condition subsequent can be defeated and is, therefore, a defeasible title.

The fee simple subject to a condition subsequent is created by the grantor (the one conveying title) specifying in the conveyance of title a use of the property that is prohibited. For example, a grantor conveys property with the condition that it can never be used as a landfill. As long as the property is never used for this purpose, the title will continue indefinitely in the initial grantee or any subsequent grantee. However, at any time in the future if the property is used for a landfill, the original grantor and/or his or her heirs may reenter the property and take possession or go to court and sue to regain possession. By doing so the title holder's estate is terminated.

Fee Simple Determinable

This is another inheritable freehold estate in the form of a fee simple estate. However, it is a defeasible fee and, therefore, the title can be terminated by the grantor. An example of the fee simple determinable is a situation in which a grantor conveyed title to a college and in the conveyance stipulated that the title is good as long as the property is used for scholastic purposes. Title received by the college can be for an infinite period of time. However, if the property is not used for the purpose specified in the conveyance, the title will automatically terminate and revert to the original grantor or the grantor's heirs.

Notice that in the case of a fee simple determinable the estate in the grantee automatically terminates in the event that the designated use of the property is not continued. This is contrasted with the fee simple subject to a condition subsequent in which the termina-

Property Ownership and Interests

tion is not automatic. In the latter case, the grantor and/or the heirs must either reenter the property or go to court to obtain possession of the property and to terminate the estate in the grantee.

Life Estates

A life estate is a freehold estate that is not inheritable. It may be created for the life of the named life tenant or for the life of some other named person. A life estate created for the duration of the life tenant's own life is called an estate for life. When the life estate is for the life of another person other than the life tenant, it is called an estate *per autre vie* (for the life of another).

There are actually two types of life estates. One is an estate in remainder and the other is an estate in reversion. If the conveyance is from grantor to A for life and then to a named person or persons upon the death of A, it is an estate in remainder. The person or persons receiving the title upon the death of A (the life tenant) are called remaindermen and the conveyance is a conveyance in remainder. The remaindermen receive a fee simple title. The life tenant has only an estate or ownership for his or her life. Immediately upon his or her death or upon the death of some other person named in the conveyance, the title automatically vests in the remainderman. If the conveyance does not specify a person or persons to receive the title upon the death of the life tenant or other specified person, a life estate in reversion is created and the title will revert to the grantor or the grantor's heirs upon the death of the life tenant. The grantor has a reversionary interest in the estate.

In addition to being created by an intentional conveyance, life estates can also be created by operation of law. Life estates created by act of the parties are called conventional life estates, whereas life estates created by operation of law are called legal life estates.

Many states provide dower or curtesy rights to a surviving spouse. This is a right that a surviving spouse has to a life estate in the property of the deceased spouse that was owned while they were married. If the surviving spouse had not joined in a conveyance of the property, he or she has a right to a life estate (usually limited to ⅓ the value) in the property that was owned while they were married. Dower is a wife's right and curtesy is the husband's right (except in Arkansas, Illinois, Kansas, Kentucky, Maryland, Ohio, and Pennsylvania, where the husband's right is also called dower instead of curtesy).

Estates and Rights In Real Property
(In Descending Order Of Importance)

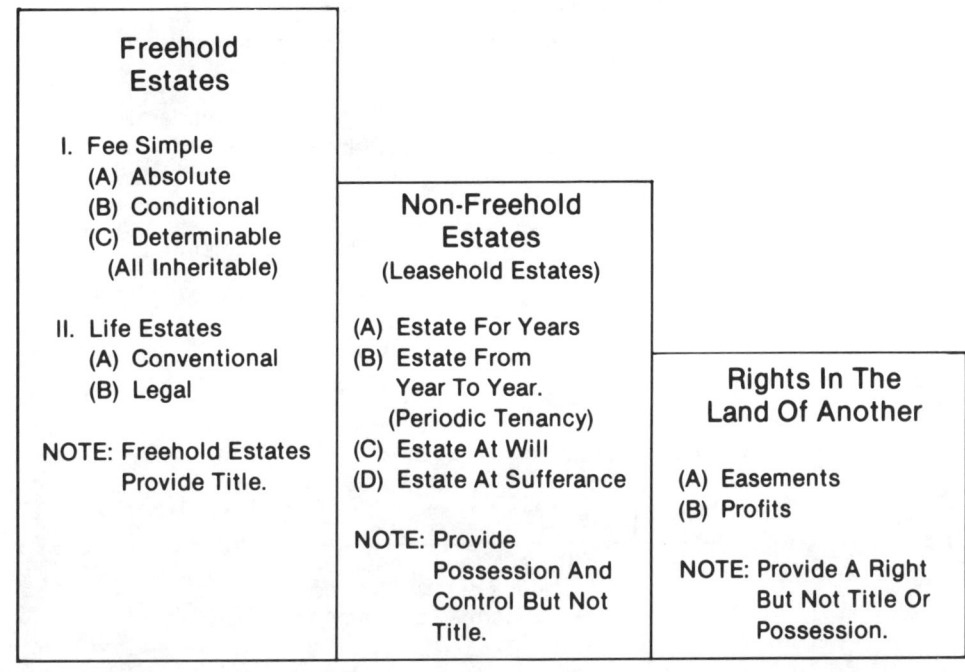

Figure 5.1

In those states where dower and curtesy have been abolished, there is usually a substitute provided by an intestate succession. Intestate succession statutes set forth the manner in which the property of an intestate (one who has died without leaving a valid will) is distributed to heirs. These statutes also normally provide for a life estate to the surviving spouse in those properties owned during marriage in severalty by the deceased spouse wherein the surviving spouse did not join in the conveyance by executing a deed.

From these requirements, it can be readily seen that it is extremely important for both husband and wife to join in the conveyance of any property owned by either of them while they are married. In many states, there can only be a valid deed if both husband and wife sign the deed. In dower and curtesy states, the right of dower or curtesy must be renounced on the deed. Married persons holding title as community property must both participate by conveying their undivided one-half ownership.

Rights and Responsibilities of Life Tenants

A life tenant has the right of alienation. That is, the life tenant may transfer his or her title to another person or pledge the title as security for a debt. Of course, the individual cannot give a title for a duration longer than his or her life or the life of the person named in the creation of a life estate to establish its duration. The life tenant also has the right to the net income produced by the property, if any. The life tenant may legally mortgage the life estate. However, it is unlikely that a lending institution would accept a life estate as security for a mortgage since the estate terminates on the death of the life tenant or some other named person.

Figure 5.2 *Life Estate in Remainder*

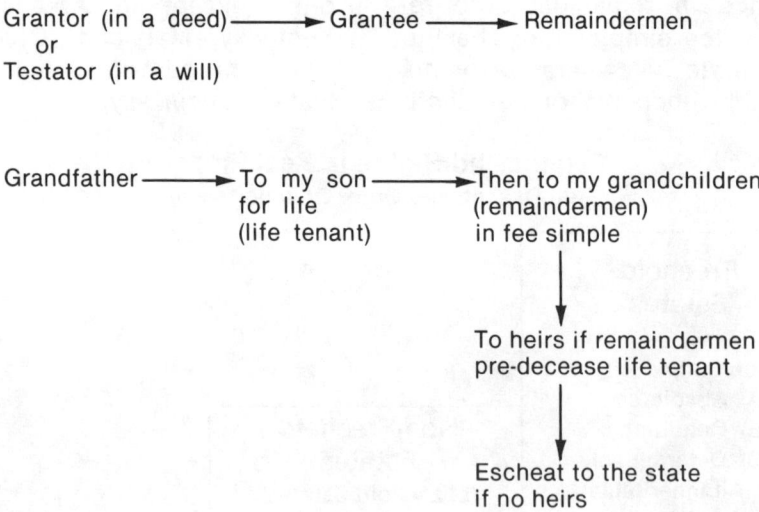

Figure 5.3 *Life Estate in Reversion*

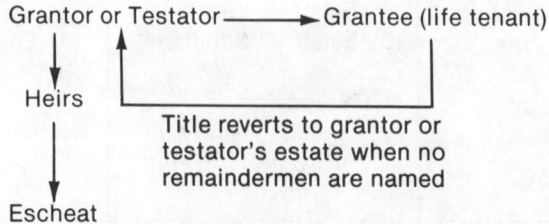

Property Ownership and Interests

A life tenant has certain responsibilities. Basically, the individual must preserve the estate for the benefit of the remainderman or reversionary interest. However, the life tenant has a legal right called the right to estovers. The right to estovers provides that a life tenant may cut and use a reasonable amount of timber from the land to repair buildings or to use for fuel. However, the individual may not cut and sell the timber for profit. A violation of the right of estovers is called an act of waste.

A life tenant has an obligation to pay the real property taxes on the property in which he or she has a life estate. The life tenant also has the duty to pay any assessments levied against the property by a county or municipality for improvements to the property. Assessments are levied against land for improvements made to the land, such as paving of streets and laying of water lines and sewer lines.

The life tenant has a duty to make repairs to the improvements on the land. He cannot permit the property to deteriorate because of lack of repairs and thus cause depreciation to existing improvements.

WAYS IN WHICH TITLE MAY BE HELD

Ownership in Severalty

When title to real property is held in the name of only one person, it is called ownership in severalty. The person holding title is the sole or only owner. If the title holder is married, the property is called separate property. The owning spouse holds title separately from the other spouse.

Co-Ownership

Simultaneous ownership of real property by two or more people is called co-ownership. There are various types of co-ownership. The rights of the owners are dependent upon the type of ownership that they have. The types of co-ownership are: tenancy in common, joint tenancy, tenancy by the entireties, and community property.

In studying the matter of co-ownership, you should realize that the co-owners may hold title in the same manner as owners in severalty — for example, fee simple absolute, fee simple subject to a condition subsequent, fee simple determinable, and life estate.

Tenancy in Common

Tenancy in common is characterized by there being two or more owners, each owning an undivided interest in the entire property, with no right of survivorship.

Anyone can hold title as a tenant in common. Each title holder owns an undivided interest in the property. Each owns a share of the entire property rather than one specific geographical section of the property. No right of survivorship means that upon the death of a tenant in common, the deceased's share will go to the person's heirs.

A tenant in common may sell his or her interest. The individual may sell to one of the other tenants in common or to a third party. A tenant in common may also pledge the interest as security for a mortgage; this creates an encumberance against the share of ownership. It is not necessary for each tenant in common to have the same degree of interest. One may own a one-half interest, another a one-third interest, another a one-sixteenth interest, and so forth.

A tenant in common has a right to have the lands partitioned so that each tenant in common may own a separate, specific section of the property in severalty. A partition is a proceeding by which the land is divided between two or more tenants in common. To have this done, tenants in common must bring legal action. If the land can feasibly be divided equitably between the tenants in common, the court will have this done. If the land is such that an actual physical partition is not feasible, the property may be sold and the proceeds of the sale divided among the tenants in common according to their degree of ownership.

Joint Tenancy

Unlike tenancy in common, joint tenancy includes the right of survivorship. In the event of the death of a joint tenant, the deceased's share goes not to heirs but to the surviving joint tenants. This is an automatic transfer of ownership upon death without the requirement of probate. A joint tenant, therefore, may not convey ownership by will to another.

This form of co-ownership requires unity of time, title, interest, and possession. Joint tenants must have the same interest in the property, receive their title at the same time from the same source and they must have the same degree of undivided ownership and right to possession in the property. For example, if there are three joint tenants, each must own an undivided one-third interest in the property, they must all receive their title from the same source at the same time, and must continue to hold possession concurrently.

If a joint tenant sells his or her share of ownership, the effect is to destroy the joint tenancy. The sale violates the requirement of unity of time, title, interest, and possession. A purchaser from a joint tenant has received title at a different time from the remaining joint tenants, and from a different grantor. Upon the sale of an interest by a joint tenant, the ownership is converted to a tenancy in common, thereby eliminating the survivorship. Joint tenancies are terminated by a sale of a joint tenant's share, by a court-ordered partition, or by the death of one of the joint tenants.

The right of survivorship is not favored in law today except in joint ownership by husband and wife as tenants by the entirety. Therefore, a court will not recognize a joint tenancy unless the deed of conveyance makes it absolutely clear that the right of survivorship is intended by the parties. The granting clause must contain wording such as: to A, D, and C as joint tenants, to their survivor, and to the survivor's heirs and assigns forever.

Tenancy by Entirety *Not La-*

Ownership as tenants by the entirety is limited to husband and wife. To receive title as tenants by the entirety, there must be a legal marriage at the time that the husband and wife receive title to the property. In many states, it is not necessary for the deed to read "to husband and wife as tenants by the entirety" to create a tenancy by the entirety. The deed only needs to convey the property to John A. Jones and his wife, Mary A. Jones, and a tenancy by the entirety is automatically created. Tenancy by the entirety contains the right of survivorship. The surviving spouse receives title to the property automatically by operation of law. Creation of tenancy by the entirety requires unity of time, title, interest, possession, and marriage.

A husband or wife owning land as tenants by the entirety may not legally convey property to a third party without the other spouse joining in the deed. A spouse who is a tenant by the entirety may convey the property only to the other spouse only if the signature of the conveying spouse is on the deed. There can be no partition of real property held by tenants by the entirety.

Tenancy by the entirety exists as long as the tenants hold title to the property and are legally married. Tenancy by the entirety is abolished by decree of divorce. A mere legal separation is not sufficient. However, when a final decree of absolute divorce is obtained, the ownership is automatically changed to tenancy in common by operation of law, eliminating the right of survivorship.

Married people may, if they elect to do so, own property as tenants in common. It is not necessary for them to take title as tenants by the entirety. A husband or wife may also own separate property in severalty. However, it should be noted that in most states it will still be necessary for the other spouse to join in the deed if the title is to be conveyed.

Community Property

Eight states (Arizona, California, Idaho, Louisiana, Nevada, New Mexico, Texas, and Washington) are community property states. In these states, husband and wife may acquire title to real estate as community property. A husband and wife may hold title to both real and personal property as community property. Title may also be held as husband or wife in severalty as separate property. These concepts of title originated in Spanish law, and all community property states were subject to the influence of Spanish law at the time of their early settlement.

The theory of community property is that husband and wife share equally in the ownership of property purchased by their joint efforts during the community of marriage. The title to such property will vest in husband and wife as community property whether the deed is made only to the husband, only to the wife, or to both husband and wife.

This general rule is in effect except in California and New Mexico where there is a rebuttable presumption that property deeded to a married woman in her name only is separate

Property Ownership and Interests

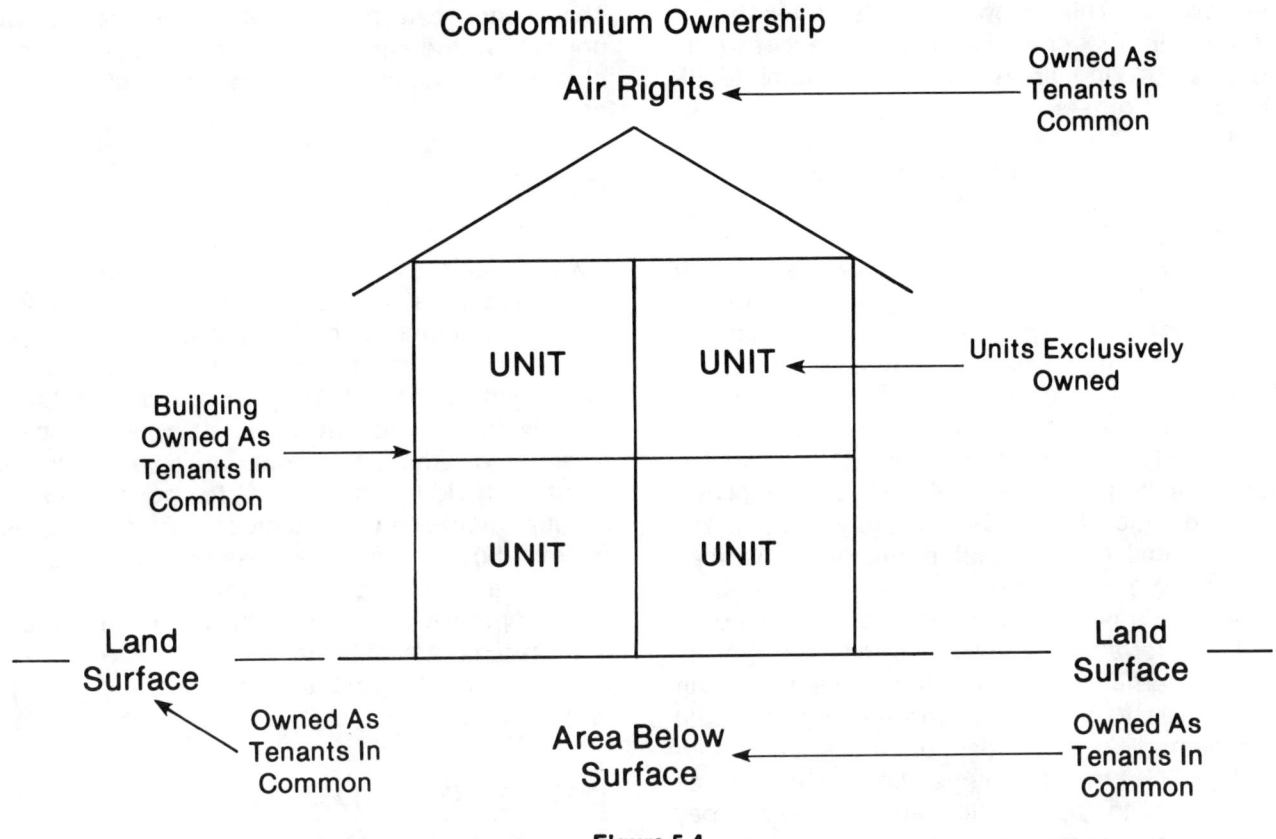

Figure 5.4

property. The presumption may be rebutted by proof that the property was purchased with community funds.

There is no right of survivorship in community property and therefore the one-half interest of a deceased spouse will descend to heirs and will not automatically go to the surviving spouse. To pledge or convey title to community property during life, both husband and wife must sign the deed.

In community property states, separate property is any property acquired by one spouse during marriage by gift or inheritance. Also, any property purchased with the separate funds of the husband or wife becomes the separate property of the purchasing spouse. Property acquired prior to marriage by either husband or wife is also separate property. Since community property states do not recognize dower or curtesy, a spouse may mortgage or convey title to separate property without the participation of the other spouse. In these states, separate property is completely under the ownership and control of the spouse holding title in severalty. However, in most of the community property states, both husband and wife must execute deeds and mortgages involving the separate property of either spouse where the property is being used as their home.

Condominiums

Condominium ownership is a form of ownership that is now recognized in all states. All states have statutes that define this type of ownership and set forth the requirements for the creation of a condominium. The first condominium statute enacted in the fifty States was the California Horizontal Property Act. Though the titles of the laws creating condominium ownership vary from state to state, the fundamental principles are reasonably uniform.

A condominium purchaser receives a fee simple title to an apartment the same as in any other real estate. The owner can convey title by deed or leave it to an heir by will. In addition to ownership in the apartment, the individual also has a co-ownership in the common areas of the condominium along with the other apartment owners. This co-ownership is as tenants in common in the common areas—the corridors, grounds, parking areas, and recreational facilities, among others.

Condominium statutes set forth the manner in which a condominium is to be created. These will include a declaration (master deed), articles of association, and by-laws.

The declaration includes a legal description of the property, a plat of the property with the location of buildings, plans and specifications for the buildings and the various units (apartments, etc.), a description of the common areas, and the degree of ownership in the common areas available to each unit owner. It may also include a "right of first refusal" clause giving the association the first opportunity to purchase an individual owner's unit if the owner wishes to sell. This same clause may be found in a lease for the benefit of the lessee and including the lease for a cooperative apartment.

The articles of association establish an association to provide for the maintenance and management of the common areas and other services for the owner-members. Owners, as members of the association, are assessed to pay for these necessary services.

The by-laws set forth the various offices in the association, how they are elected, and the requirements for amending the by-laws.

In order to be valid, the declaration, articles, and by-laws must be recorded on the public record in the county where the property is located.

The creation of a condominium is not limited to residential purposes. Other purposes may be office space, parking space, an industrial park, and so forth. The particular purpose of the condominium must be set forth in the declaration as required by state statute.

A condominium unit can be mortgaged just as any other property. FHA financing has been available for condominiums since 1961. Also, the Veterans Administration will guarantee mortgage loans for the purchase of condominiums.

Time sharing is a fairly recent innovation in condominium ownership. In the time-sharing ownership concept, the owner takes title to an apartment for a period of time. This time period may be one week, two weeks, a month, and so forth, in each calendar year during ownership. The purchaser receives a title to an apartment for the same period of time each calendar year.

The owner can sell all of the share or any portion of the time share. The sale is accomplished by a deed of conveyance as with all real property.

Cooperatives

Ownership in a cooperative results from ownership of shares of stock in a corporation that owns a building containing cooperative apartments. The right of stockholders to occupy an apartment is provided by a proprietary lease, usually for a long term. The only real property interest of the stockholders is a leasehold estate providing the right to possession of an apartment. The stockholders, as lessees, pay no rent but do pay an assessment to cover the cost of maintaining and operating the building, real property taxes, and debt service if there is a mortgage against the building. The owners' rights and obligations are specified in the lease and the stock certificate.

REAL PROPERTY OWNERSHIP BY BUSINESS ORGANIZATIONS

Business organizations can take several different forms. These forms include the sole proprietorship, partnership, corporation, syndicate, joint venture, and real estate investment trust. All of these business organizations can receive, hold, and convey title in the various ways previously discussed.

Sole Proprietorship

A sole proprietorship is simply a business owned by one individual. The individual may use his or her own name as the name of the business or may assume a name for this purpose. If the business name does not contain the owner's surname (in any form of business organization), the business must be registered with a Register of Deeds or some other comparable authority, depending upon the state of location.

The owner of the sole proprietorship is fully liable for the business debts. If business debts exceed the assets of the business, the personal assets of the owner may be attached by creditors for satisfaction of the business debts.

The sole proprietor can receive, hold, and convey title to real estate either in his or her own name or in the name of the business.

Partnerships

A partnership is a form of business organization in which the business is owned by two or more persons called partners. A partnership is created by contract between the partners as contrasted with a corporation, which is created by the state when it issues the corporate charter. The partners do not have to have the same degree of interest in the partnership. One may own a half interest and two others each a quarter interest, for example. Under the Uniform Partnership Act, which has been adopted by most states, a partnership may hold title to real property in the name of the partnership. Additionally, under the common law, partnerships may hold title to real property in the names of the individual partners.

A general partnership is one in which the parties conduct the business for the joint benefit of the partners. In the general partnership, the partners are personally liable for partnership debts exceeding partnership assets. Partners are jointly and severally liable. That is, any individual partner is personally liable for the partnership debts exceeding partnership assets as well as all the partners being jointly liable.

A limited partnership is one consisting of one or more general partners who are jointly and severally liable like partners in a general partnership. In addition to the general partner or partners, there are one or more special, or limited partners who contribute money to the extent of their ownership in the partnership. The limited partners are not liable for the debts of the partnership beyond the amount of money they have contributed to the partnership and may not participate in the management of the partnership.

The limited partnership organization is frequently used for participation in real estate investments. Typically, a general partner(s) will conceive of the investment opportunity and obtain the money to either construct an improvement or purchase an existing improved property for a number of limited partners. The general partner(s) will do all of the work necessary to create the investment and the limited partners provide the funds. The purpose of the investment may be to provide an income return as well as an eventual capital gain to the investors when the property is sold.

A limited partnership is an excellent way to participate in a real estate investment. The advantages of this form of ownership are limited liability on the part of the limited partners, income tax advantages to each individual limited partner resulting from depreciation, and other write-offs and the avoidance of double taxation in operating and resale profits as is the case in the corporate form of business organization.

Corporation

"A corporation is an artificial being, invisible, intangible, and existing only in contemplation of law." A corporation is created by a charter granted to it by its state of incorporation. The incorporators must comply with the statutory requirements for incorporating in any particular state. The corporation's activities are essentially limited to the state within which it is incorporated and may not "do business" in another state without the permission of the Secretary of State of such other state. A corporation is called a domestic corporation within the state in which it is incorporated. A corporation doing business in another state is called a foreign corporation in that state. The term "doing business" is defined in the Uniform Foreign Corporation Act as being the situation when "some part of the corporation's business substantial and continuous in character and not merely 'casual or occasional'" is transacted within a state.

Corporations are divided into two classes according to their objectives and purposes. Public corporations are the various governmental corporations such as cities, towns, counties, school districts, and special bodies for public improvements. Private corporations are those corporations not organized to perform governmental functions.

Ownership in a corporation is evidenced by shares of stock. These shares are transferrable without having to dissolve the corporation. The stockholders do not have personal liability for the debts of the corporation. Only the corporate assets are subject to the claims of creditors.

To create a corporation, the organizers (most states require at least three who are citizens of the United States, with at least one being a citizen of the state of incorporation) file an application for a corporate charter with the Secretary of State. The application must contain the names and addresses of the incorporators, the name of the corporation, the object for which it is formed, its duration, location of the principal office, total authorized stock, the names and addresses of the first board of directors, and the terms for which the directors are to serve.

If all is in order, the Secretary of State issues a charter to the corporation that contains all of the information on the application and sets forth the powers, privileges, and rights granted to the corporation. The charter must be recorded in the office of the Register of Deeds in the county where the corporate headquarters are located or in such other proper recording office as is prescribed by a particular state.

A corporation has the power to receive, hold, and convey title to real property for all purposes for which the corporation is created. The power to hold, receive, and convey title to real property is normally expressly given in the corporate charter. Corporations are empowered to hold a mortgage on real estate to secure a financial obligation due the corporation and are also empowered to pledge corporate property as security for a mortgage to obtain money to accomplish corporate objectives.

Syndications

A syndication is an organization of investors in real estate (or other types of investment). A syndicate normally includes some specialists in real estate such as a developer, a broker, and a property manager. A syndicate may exist in the form of a general or limited partnership or as a corporation. Syndications are typically used in cases of multiple continuing projects that require the investment of substantial sums of money.

Joint Venture

A joint venture is an organization consisting of two or more parties for the purpose of investing in real estate or any other type of investment. The joint venture may be in the form of a corporation or partnership, or the parties may hold title as joint tenants or as tenants in common. Joint ventures are usually used where the investment is in only one project and the amount of investment is not too substantial.

Trusts

Title to real property may be held in trust for the benefit of the property owner. A land trust is created by transferring the title to a trustee who holds the title for the benefit of others called beneficiaries. The power of the trustee is limited to the power granted by the beneficiary when the trust is created. The instrument creating a land trust may be a will or a deed in trust. The trustee may be an individual or a corporation in the form of a trust company. The trust beneficiary may retain control and possession of the property and instruct the trustee to deal with the property for the benefit of the beneficiary.

Real estate investment trusts (REIT) were created in 1967 as a result of changes in the Internal Revenue Code that became effective in September of that year. Qualified real estate investment trusts are given special tax treatment so that they do not pay any federal income tax on trust profits that are distributed to shareholders. However, to qualify, the REIT must distribute each year at least 90 percent of their ordinarily taxable income to the shareholders. Congress has provided this special tax treatment to qualified REITs to enable small investors to participate in large real estate investments that provide expert management and to help make funds available for financing large real estate developments.

REITs are unincorporated associations that operate in the form of business trusts. The purpose of the REIT is to provide, as an investment for the REIT, funds necessary to finance all phases of real estate development. REITs may invest in single-and multi-family residential mortgages, interim purchase mortgages, commercial mortgages, and construction and development loans. Also, REITs may invest in mortgages by purchasing them from the Federal National Mortgage Association. REITs are regulated by the federal government as to the form of or types of loans in which they can invest. Essentially, the loan must be secured by real property.

Property Ownership and Interests

LEASEHOLD ESTATES

These estates are less than freehold and are of limited duration. The four leasehold estates are (1) estate for years, (2) estate from year-to-year, (3) estate at will, and (4) estate at sufferance. The leasehold estates are created by contract and therefore provide contractual rights and obligations as well as real property rights and obligations. Leasehold estates provide a right of possession only and not a title to real property. They create a relationship of landlord and tenant between the parties.

Estate for Years

An estate for any fixed period of time, regardless of the duration, is an estate for years. The term of the estate may be for six months, six years, or sixty years; it is still called an estate for years. The major requirement for creating an estate for years is that the duration of the estate be for a specifically definite period of time. If there is any indefiniteness in this regard, the contract will not create an estate for years. The estate for years automatically terminates when the time period in the contract expires. It is not necessary that notice of termination be given by landlord to tenant or vice versa to terminate an estate for years.

In conveying an estate for years the usual words used by the lessor are "have granted, demised, and by these presents do grant, demise, and let." The term demise is synonomous with lease or let and implies a covenant for quiet enjoyment and a covenant of good title on the part of the lessor. The contract creating an estate for years may fall under the Statute of Frauds, depending upon the duration of the estate, and, therefore, it must be written to be valid.

Statutes in most states specify that a lease (estate for years) for a term exceeding one year must be in writing. In a minority of states, the requirement for a written lease contract exists when the duration exceeds three years. If the lease is required by statute to be in writing, it must be recorded on the public record to protect the lessee from purchasers of the property from the lessor.

If the lease term is less than the statutory minimum and therefore not required to be written, the fact that the lessee is in possession of the property at the time of a sale by the lessor will protect the lessee in the lease and therefore the lease must be honored by a purchaser from the lessor. Contracts creating an estate for years are discussed in depth in chapter 6 "Contracts and Agency."

Estate from Year-to-Year

The more popular name for this estate is periodic tenancy. This estate automatically continues for successive periods until it is terminated by the parties. The successive periods may be from year-to-year, quarter-to-quarter, month-to-month, or week-to-week. Termination is accomplished by formal notice of termination by either landlord to tenant or tenant to landlord. Notice of termination must be given for one full period prior to the termination date, unless the successive periods are three months or longer. Therefore, if the periods are for more than three months, at least three months prior notice of termination must be given. If the periods are less than three months, notice must be given one full period in advance of the termination date. For example, in the case of successive periods of month-to-month, notice of termination must be given one month in advance. If the periods are year-to-year, only three months advance notice is required.

Estate at Will

In the estate at will, the duration of the term is completely unknown at the time the estate is created. This is because the estate at will may be terminated by either party at will, by simply giving the other party notice. Statutes require that the notice of termination be given at least thirty days prior to the date upon which termination is to be effected.

Estate at Sufferance

This is not truly an estate. The term is simply used to describe someone who was originally in lawful possession of another's property after that person's right to possession has terminated. This could occur upon termination of any of the three previously discussed leasehold estates. The term is used to make a distinction between the tenant at sufferance who was originally in lawful possession of the property and someone who was on the property illegally from the beginning (trespasser). The estate at sufferance will continue until such time that the property owner brings a legal action to evict the person wrongfully holding over or until the one holding over vacates voluntarily. During this period the occupier is called a tenant at sufferance.

ENCUMBRANCES

An encumbrance is a claim, lien, charge, or liability attached to and binding upon real property. Some examples of encumbrances are liens of all types, restrictive covenants, easements, encroachments, inchoate dowers (a wife's interest in the real property of her husband during marriage and during his life, which will become a right of dower upon his death), government regulations controlling the use of property, and restrictions in individual deeds limiting the use of property.

The following is a discussion of encroachments, easements, and specific and general liens. Restrictive covenants, deed restrictions, and government regulation of land use are covered under the heading of "Land Use Controls."

ENCROACHMENTS

An encroachment is a trespass on the land of another as a result of an intrusion or invasion by some structure or other object such as a wall, fence, overhanging balcony, or driveway. The encroaching owner may obtain title to the area of the land upon which the encroachment exists by adverse possession (discussed in the chapter on transfer of title) or may obtain an easement by prescription in the case of the encroaching driveway if the owner of the land subject to the encroachment does not take appropriate legal action. The owner may sue for damages (a judgment by the court requiring the encroacher to compensate the owner for the encroachment) or may petition the court for a decree ordering the encroachment to be removed. Figure 5.4 illustrates an encroachment by owner B on the land of owner A.

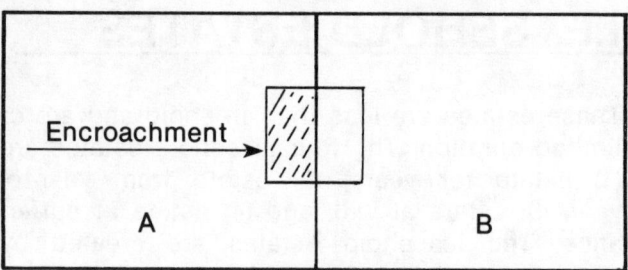

Figure 5.5 *An encroachment by owner B on the land of owner A.*

EASEMENTS

An easement is a nonpossessory interest in land owned by another. An easement provides a right of use in land and not a right of possession.

Typical Examples of Easements

Easements can exist for a great variety of legal uses such as a right-of-way for ingress and egress; a party wall; the right to take water from the land of another; the right to use a water course flowing through the land of another; the right of receiving air, light, or heat from over the land of another; the right to obtain water from a well or spring on the land of another; and a right-of-way for the purpose of putting utility lines under and above the surface of the land.

Party Walls

A party wall is a wall used by two structures as the sidewall of each structure. A party wall is usually constructed so that the property line runs longitudinally down the center of the wall. In this case half of the wall is on each property and the adjoining property owners on whose land the wall is located have an undivided ownership interest in the property as tenants in common. However, if the wall is built entirely within the property of one adjoining owner who will have complete ownership in the wall, the owner may convey a right to use the wall to the adjoining property owner in the form of an easement. The adjoining owner can then use the wall as the side wall for a structure built on his or her property. Since the lands are adjoining, an appurtenant easement is created.

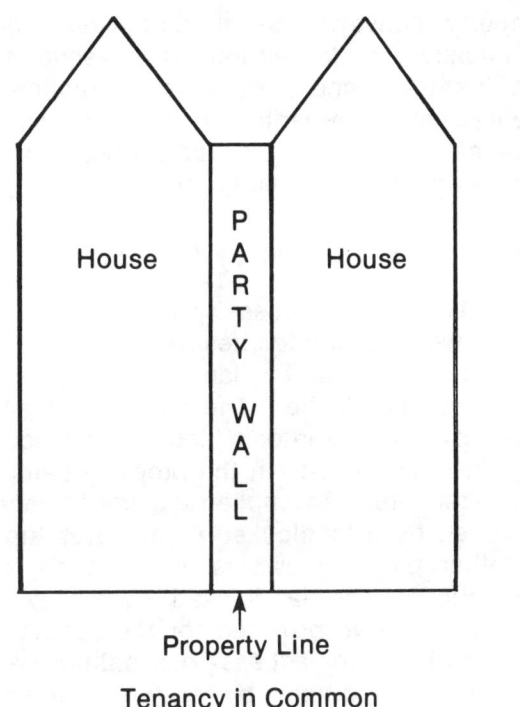
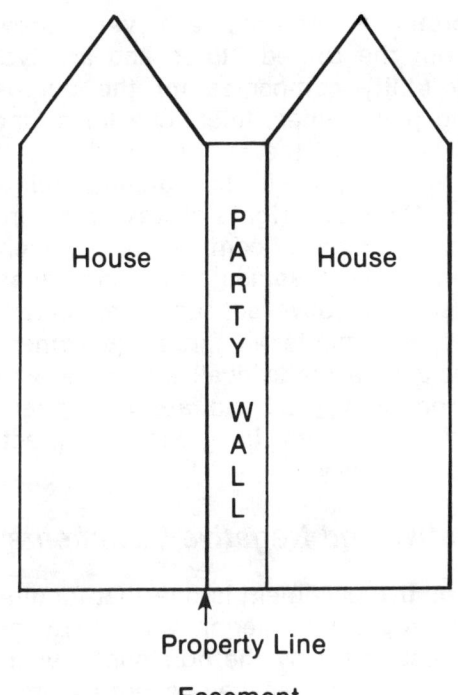

Figure 5.6 *Ownership and Interests*

Apurtenant Easement

An appurtenance is something that has been added to something else and as a result becomes an inherent part of that to which it has been added. In real property law, an appurtenance is the right that one property owner has in the property of another as a result of the property owner's ownership in a particular parcel of real estate. For example, if a purchaser receives a title to a tract of land and included in this title is an easement in the form of a right-of-way across the adjoining land of another, this easement is an appurtenance to that title. Whenever the titleholder conveys that title to another, the conveyance includes the easement since the easement is appurtenant to the title. Since an easement appurtenant moves with a title, it is said to "run with the land."

The land that is benefited by the easement is described as the dominant tenement. The land encumbered by the easement (the land in which the easement exists) is described as the servient tenement. The two property owners are called the dominant owner and the servient owner. An appurtenant easement can only be used for the benefit of the dominant tenement and may not be used for the benefit of any other land, including land acquired by the dominant owner after the creation of the easement.

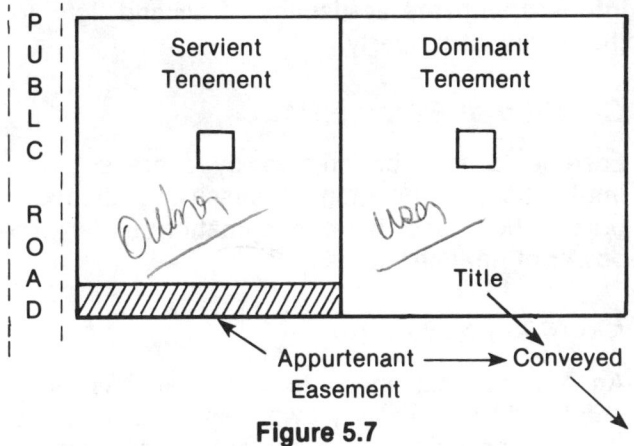

Figure 5.7

Easements in Gross

Unlike appurtenant easements, easements in gross are not dependent upon ownership of an adjoining property. Typically, the owner of an easement in gross does not own property in the area of the property in which the easement exists.

The most prevalent use of easements in gross is in the form of commercial easements.

Commercial easements are very prevalent throughout the United States and are typically held by utility companies for the purpose of installing power lines, telephone lines, and gas lines either above the surface of the earth, on the earth itself, or in the ground below the surface. Railroad rights-of-way are another prominent example of commercial easement.

Commercial easements in gross are assignable, can be conveyed, and are inheritable. Personal easements in gross (easements in gross held by an individual) are not assignable, cannot be conveyed, and are not inheritable. Personal easements in gross are practically non-existent today.

Affirmative and Negative Easements

An affirmative easement is one that requires the servient property to permit an activity on the servient easement by the dominant owner (e.g., the right to cross over the servient easement for access to a public way). A negative easement is one that prohibits the owner of the servient land from doing something, otherwise lawful, upon the owner's land because it will affect the dominant land. An example, would be an easement prohibiting the servient owner from erecting a structure on the land that would interfere with the availability of air and light to the dominant property.

Creation of Easements

Easements may be created by express grant, implication, reservation, necessity, dedication, prescription, and by condemnation under the power of eminent domain.

Express Easements

An express easement is one that has been created by the property owner specifically granting or conveying as easement to another by deed of easement. An express easement may also be created by reservation. An easement by reservation is created when a grantor reserves a right of use in land conveyed to another by the grantor. The reservation is made in the deed conveying the title to the property.

Implied Easements

Easements are implied by law in cases where the actions of a party demonstrate an intent to create an easement and in cases where the property conveyed to another would not be practically usable without an easement over the grantor's land. Examples of implied easements are easements created by necessity, easements created by dedication, and easements created by prescription.

Easements Created by Necessity

An easement by necessity is implied in those cases where a grantee desires to gain access to a public way over the land of a grantor but is otherwise landlocked. The absence of an easement over the grantor's land to gain access to a public way results in the property being of no practical value. An implied easement cannot be acquired by a landlocked owner over the lands of other property owners who did not convey the title to the landlocked owner except in states that have provided for the acquisition of a right-of-way for access to a public road over the land of others by statute. Under such statutes, the property owner (or owners) over which the right-of-way is created must be compensated for providing the right-of-way even though it is required by statutory law.

Easements Created by Dedication

A dedication is an appropriation of land for the use of the public. The dedication is made by the landowner and must be accepted for such use by or in behalf of the public by the appropriate public authority. Such a dedication creates an express easement on the part of the property owner to the general public.

An implied easement by dedication can be created as the result of an act or course of conduct by the property owner from which a reasonable implication of intent may be established. For example, when a developer of a residential subdivision conveys title to lots in that subdivision and describes the property by reference to a recorded plat demonstrating the existence of streets in the subdivision, an easement by dedication is implied by law for use of the streets by the general public as well as purchasers of property in the subdivision.

Easements Created by Prescription

An easement in another's land can be acquired by prescription or use without permission of the owner. The use must be open and well known to others, continuous and uninterrupted for the required statutory period, and against the interest of the property owner. To obtain an easement by prescription, the user must satisfy a court that he or she has fulfilled all of the statutory requirements for obtaining an easement by this means. If successful, the claimant will be awarded an easement for the specific use made by the claimant during the period of prescription.

The time period for continuous and uninterrupted use varies from state to state. Typical statutory requirements are periods of ten, fifteen, or twenty years.

Easements Created by Condemnation

Condemnation is the exercise of the power of eminent domain. Eminent domain is a statutory power held by governmental bodies and public utility corporations. This power enables the holders to take private property for public use. The taking is called condemnation or exercise of the power of eminent domain.

In all cases, the property owner must be compensated as to the difference in fair market value of the property before and after condemnation. The property taken must be for the use or benefit of the public. Condemnation may be for the purpose of creating an easement for the use of the general public, or the condemnation may be for the purpose of acquiring title to the property rather than a mere right of use in the general public. Usually condemnations for rights-of-way for various public uses are easements and not for acquisition of title.

Termination of Easements

Easements may be terminated as follows:

1. By the release of the easement by the dominant owner to the servient owner;
2. By combining the dominant and servient lands into one tract of land;
3. By abandonment of the easement by the dominant owner;
4. When the purpose for which an easement was created ceases to exist the easement is terminated;
5. By the expiration of a specified period of time for which the easement was created.

PROFITS

The complete legal term used to describe this real property right in the land of another is *profit à prendre*. A profit is a right of one person in the land of another by participation in the profits of the soil. The term *profit à prendre* includes the right to take soil, minerals, gravel, timber, or grass from the land of another. It does not include the right to take running water from another's land since the water is not a product of the soil. Profits are created in the same way that easements are created.

LICENSE

In real property law a license is defined as permission to do a particular act or series of acts on land of another without possessing any estate or interest in the land. A license is a personal privilege and may be revoked by the licensor at any time unless the licensee has compensated the licensor for giving the license in which case the licensor must permit the activity to continue for the agreed time period.

A license is not assignable and is not inheritable. A license is personal property and not real property. Therefore, the agreement may be oral, it does not have to be written. Examples of activities that may be permitted by licenses are the privilege to hunt or fish on the land of another; the rental of space for camping, parking, or selling merchandise; admission to a concert, movie, or sporting event. From these examples it can be seen that a license is not only a personal privilege but is also a temporary privilege.

LIENS

A lien is a claim that one person has against the property of another for some debt or charge. The lien entitles the lienholder to have the claim satisfied from the property of the debtor. Liens are of two types: (1) specific liens, which are liens that attach to one particular property only, and (2) general liens, which are liens that attach to all of the property, within the jurisdiction of the court, owned by the person whom the lien is against.

Specific Liens

Mortgage Liens

A mortgage creates a lien against the property that is pledged as security by a mortgage. In the event that the borrower under the mortgage defaults, the property is subject to a foreclosure sale to satisfy the mortgage lien. For a full discussion of this matter, please refer to chapter 8 "Real Estate Financing."

Mechanics and Materialmens Liens

State statutes provide specific liens to those who furnish labor and/or materials for the construction or repair of a house or other improvement on land. In the event they are not paid for their services or materials, these people may file a claim of lien against the property.

Some states provide a special priority for these liens by backdating and making them effective as of the first day of labor or when materials were first supplied to the construction.

Real Property Tax and Assessment Liens

The taxes levied by a local government constitute a specific lien against the real estate. State laws provide that real property tax liens have priority over all other liens.

Property is taxed on an ad valorem basis, that is, according to value. The assessment of property for tax purposes involves establishing the value of each parcel of land to be taxed within the taxing unit. An official with the title of tax assessor is responsible for the valuation of property for tax purposes. Property values must be reasonably uniform to provide for equal taxation of property owners. In most states real property is assessed at its full market value or a 100 percent assessment. Some states, however, assess property at a fixed percentage less than 100 percent of its full market value.

An assessment is a levy against a property for payment of a share of the cost of improvements made to areas adjoining the property. Examples of these are: paving of streets, installation of sewer or water lines, and construction of sidewalks. The assessment will constitute a specific lien against the property until paid.

Vendors and Vendees Liens

Vendors (sellers) liens come into existence upon the sale of real property and conveyance of title to the buyer when the seller does not receive the full purchase price at the time of conveyance. The seller is given a specific lien against the property for the amount of the balance of the purchase price due. If the lien is not satisfied by the purchaser, the seller can foreclose to obtain the money to satisfy the lien.

Vendees (buyers) liens are created in the case of default by the seller under a contract of sale for real property. In such case, a buyer has a lien against the property in the amount of money the individual had paid toward the purchase price. The vendees lien can be enforced by foreclosure.

Lis Pendens

This is a notice that a lawsuit is pending (awaiting trial) and that a resulting judgment may create a lien against the property of the defendant. The recording of the lis pendens provides constructive notice of the forthcoming legal action and the potential lien. As a result, a lien resulting from the lawsuit will attach to the property even though the title was transferred to someone else if the transfer occurred after the notice of lis pendens was placed on the public record in the county where the property is located.

Bail Bond Liens

A bail bond is a bond executed by a defendant under criminal charges to obtain temporary release from custody, conditional upon an appearance to court in answer to the charges. If real property is pledged as security for the bail bond, the bond will create a specific lien against the property pledged. If the defendant does not appear in court as scheduled, the bond will be forfeited and the lien will be executed. The result will be a lien foreclosure sale of the property and the proceeds will be applied to the satisfaction of the financial obligations created by the bond.

General Liens

Judgment Liens

A judgment is a court decree establishing that one person is indebted to another and the amount of that indebtedness. A judgment constitutes a general lien against all of the real and personal property that the judgment debtor owns in the county in which the judgment is recorded. The lien takes effect from the time the judgment is recorded. A judgment creditor may record a judgment in any other county in

Property Ownership and Interests

the state and it will constitute a general lien against all the property of the judgment debtor in that county. The judgment will also create a lien against any property that the judgment debtor acquires subsequent to the judgment during the existence of the judgment.

A general lien will not apply to real property owned by husband and wife by the entireties, as joint tenants, or as community property, if the judgment is against only one of them. For the lien to attach to property in such cases, the judgment must be obtained against both husband and wife on a debt they both incurred.

A judgment lien remains in effect for a period of time specified by state statute unless the judgment is paid. Judgment may be renewed and kept in force for an additional period if the creditor brings another action on the original judgment before the original period has elapsed.

Judgment liens have a priority relationship based on the time of recording. The creditor who records a lien before another creditor records a lien against the same judgment debtor will have a prior claim. The judgment debtor's obligation to the creditor having priority must be satisfied before creditors with a lower priority.

Judgment liens are enforced by an order called an execution. This is an order that is signed by the clerk of court that instructs the sheriff to sell the property of the judgment debtor and apply the proceeds of the sale to the satisfaction of the judgment.

Income Tax Liens

The Internal Revenue Service of the United States government and a State Department of Revenue may create a general lien against all the property of the taxpayer for taxes due and unpaid. This lien is created by filing a certificate of lien against the landowner in the county in which the taxpayer's land is located.

Estate and Inheritance Tax Liens

All states impose a tax upon the inheritance of real property (as well as personal property). This tax is called state inheritance tax. The tax is a lien on the property to be inherited until the tax is paid. To satisfy the tax bill, the estate can sell sufficient property.

The federal government imposes a tax on the estate of deceased persons. This tax is called the federal estate tax. This tax creates a lien that attaches to all of the property—both real and personal—in the estate and continues until the tax is paid. The inheritance tax is paid by the heirs inheriting the estate. The federal estate tax is levied against the estate and is paid from the assets of the estate.

Priority of Liens

For most liens, their priority in relationship to other liens is based on the time (day and hour) they were recorded with the proper court officer or, in the case of mortgages, with a Register of Deeds. However, certain liens have special priority by statute, as is the case with mechanics and material liens in some states. The highest priority of all liens is given to liens for real property taxes in most states.

IMPORTANT POINTS

1. Real property consists of land and everything attached to the land, including things that grow naturally without requiring planting and cultivation.

2. Annual crops that require planting and cultivation are personal property and are called emblements.

3. Ownership in land includes the surface of the earth and the area above and below the surface.

4. A fixture is personal property that has become attached to real property.

5. The allodial system of real property ownership is used in the United States.

6. The four powers of government are eminent domain, police power, taxation, and escheat.

7. Estates in land are divided into two groups: freehold and estates of less than freehold (leasehold).

8. The freehold estates are the fee simple estates, which are inheritable, and life estates, which are not inheritable.

9. The greatest form of ownership in real property is fee simple absolute.

10. Life estates may be in reversion or in remainder.

11. The duration of a life estate may be measured by the life tenant or by the life of another (*per autre vie*).

12. Conventional life estates are those created by someone's intentional act. Legal life estates are created by operation of law.

13. A life tenant has the right of alienation, the right of encumbrance, and the right of possession and enjoyment of the property.

14. A life tenant is obligated to preserve and maintain the property for the benefit of the future interest.

15. Title held in the name of one person only is called ownership in severalty, which is also called separate property if the owner is married.

16. When title is held simultaneously by two or more persons or organizations it is called co-ownership (also, concurrent ownership). The forms of co-ownership are tenancy in common, joint tenancy, tenancy by the entirety, community property, and certain aspects of condominiums and cooperatives.

17. Joint tenancy and tenancy by the entirety include the right of survivorship and require the unities of time, title, interest, and possession. Tenancy by the entirety is limited to husband and wife and requires a fifth unity—marriage (or unity of person).

18. The owner of a condominium unit holds title to the unit either in severalty or as co-owners with another as well as title to the common areas as tenant in common with the other unit owners.

19. The creation of a condominium requires the recording of a declaration (also called a master deed), articles of association, and by-laws.

20. Ownership in a cooperative results from stock ownership in a corporation that owns a building containing cooperative apartments. Stockholders occupy apartments under a lease.

21. Business organizations may receive, hold, and convey title to real property.

22. The less than freehold estates are also called leasehold estates and are estates of limited duration, providing possession and control but not title (as in the case of freehold estates).

23. The leasehold estates are estate for years, estate from year-to-year (periodic tenancy), estate at will, and estate at sufferance.

24. An encumbrance is a claim, lien, charge, or liability attached to and binding upon real property. Examples are encroachments, liens, restrictive covenants, easements, inchoate dower, deed restrictions, and government control of land use.

Property Ownership and Interests

IMPORTANT TERMINOLOGY

Affirmative Easement
Air Rights
Alienation
Appurtenant Easement
Bundle of Rights
Community Property
Condemnation
Condominium
Conventional Life Estate
Convey
Cooperative
Co-ownership
Curtesy
Declaration
Dedication
Deed in Trust
Demise
Dower
Easement in Gross
Emblements
Eminent Domain
Encroachment
Encumber
Encumbrance
Escheat
Estate at Sufferance
Estate at Will
Estate for Years
Estate from Year-to-Year
Estovers
Fee Simple Absolute
Fixture
Freehold Estate
Future Interest
General Lien
Intestate Succession
Joint Tenancy

Judgment Lien
Landlocked
Leasehold Estate
Legal Life Estate
Less than Freehold Estate
License
Lien
Life Estate
Life Tenant
Lis Pendens
Master Deed
Mineral Rights
Mineral Royalty
Negative Easement
Operation of Law
Party Wall
Per Autre Vie
Periodic Tenancy
Police Power
Prescription
Profit à Prendre
Remainder
Remainderman
Reversion
Right of Survivorship
Separate Property
Severalty
Specific Lien
Taxation
Tenancy by the Entirety
Tenancy in Common
Time-Sharing
Trust
Unities
Vendee
Vendor

REVIEW QUESTIONS FOR CHAPTER 5

1. Personal property attached to real property is prevented from becoming real property by which of the following?

   (a) Ownership
   (b) An appurtenance
   (c) Security Interest and Financing Statement
   (d) Mineral rights

2. Which of the following is a right that results from ownership in a particular parcel of real estate?

   (a) Easement in gross
   (b) Appurtenant easement
   (c) License
   (d) Condemnation

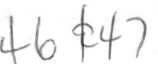

3. Which statement(s) below is (are) correct?
   I. An easement provides a nonpossessory interest in land.
   II. The land in which an easement exists is the servient tenement.

   (a) I only
   (b) II only
   (c) both I and II
   (d) neither I nor II

4. One property owner held an enforceable right to prevent a second property owner from erecting a structure that would interfere with the passage of light and air to the property of the owner holding the enforceable right. This right is in the form of which of the following?

   (a) Implied easement
   (b) Easement by necessity
   (c) Easement by prescription
   (d) Negative easement

5. Easements may be created in all of the following ways EXCEPT

   (a) Condemnation
   (b) Dedication
   (c) Prescription
   (d) Assessment

6. An easement is terminated
   I. When the purpose for which the easement was created ceases to exist.
   II. When the adjoining dominant and servient tenements are combined into one tract of land.

   (a) I only
   (b) II only
   (c) both I and II
   (d) neither I nor II

7. A property owner gives another person permission to fish in a lake on the property. The permission is a temporary privilege and exists in the form of which of the following?

   (a) License
   (b) Easement
   (c) Lease
   (d) Appurtenance

8. The creation of an easement by condemnation results from the exercise of which of the following?

   (a) Prescription
   (b) Eminent domain
   (c) Dedication
   (d) Implication

9. An estate in fee simple determinable is an example of a
   I. Freehold estate
   II. Defeasible fee

   (a) I only
   (b) II only
   (c) both I and II
   (d) neither I nor II

10. A widow inherits an estate by will granting her the right of use and possession of a parcel of land for the rest of her life with the provision that the estate will go to her children in fee simple upon her death; she has received
    I. a noninheritable freehold estate
    II. a life estate in remainder

    (a) I only
    (b) II only
    (c) both I and II
    (d) neither I nor II

11. The highest and best form of estate in real property is which of the following?

    (a) Easement appurtenant
    (b) Defeasible fee
    (c) Life estate in reversion
    (d) Fee simple absolute

12. A life estate created by the exercise of the right of dower is called

    (a) Conventional life estate
    (b) Estate *per autre vie*
    (c) Legal life estate
    (d) Community property

13. Which of the following is not a right or responsibility of a life tenant?

    (a) Estovers
    (b) Inchoate dower
    (c) Alienation
    (d) Preservation

Property Ownership and Interests

14. Estates for years, estates for year-to-year, estates at will, and estates by sufferance
    I. Are leasehold estates.
    II. Create a legal relationship between the parties of landlord and tenant.

    (a) I only
    (b) II only
    (c) both I and II
    (d) neither I nor II

15. When title to real property is held in the name of one person only,
    I. It is called ownership in severalty.
    II. If the owner is a married person, it is called separate property.

    (a) I only
    (b) II only
    (c) both I and II
    (d) neither I nor II

16. Which of the following types of ownership requires unity of interest, title, time, and possession?

    (a) Cooperative
    (b) Tenancy in common
    (c) Joint tenancy
    (d) Community property

17. None of the following include the right of survivorship EXCEPT

    (a) Tenancy in common
    (b) Joint tenancy
    (c) Life estate
    (d) Community property

18. The purchaser of a condominium unit receives title to the land whereon the condominium is situated as a

    (a) Tenant by the entirety
    (b) Tenant in common
    (c) Joint tenant
    (d) Tenant at sufferance

19. The purchaser of a condominium time share
    I. Receives a title for the same time period (or periods) each calendar year.
    II. May convey this title to anyone else.

    (a) I only
    (b) II only
    (c) both I and II
    (d) neither I nor II

20. In the cooperative form of ownership
    I. Ownership is evidenced by shares of stock in a corporation holding title to the building.
    II. Each owner owns an interest in the corporation.

    (a) I only
    (b) II only
    (c) both I and II
    (d) neither I nor II

21. A tenant in common
    I. May sell his or her interest in the property.
    II. May pledge his or her interest as security for a mortgage loan.

    (a) I only
    (b) II only
    (c) both I and II
    (d) neither I nor II

22. Ownership as tenants by the entirety includes which of the following?

    (a) The right of one owner to convey title to his or her share of ownership without the participation of the other owner.
    (b) The right of survivorship.
    (c) Ownership of an unequal interest in the property with another.
    (d) Is converted to ownership as joint tenants if the owners are divorced.

23. The levy against real property to provide the funds to defray all or part of the cost of an improvement to the property is which of the following?

    (a) Mechanics lien
    (b) Special assessment
    (c) General lien
    (d) Judgment lien

24. All of the following are examples of specific liens EXCEPT

    (a) Income tax liens
    (b) Mortgage liens
    (c) Vendors liens
    (d) Real property tax liens

25. Which of the following statements regarding judgment liens is (are) correct?
    I. Judgment liens will not attach to property to which title is held by a husband and wife as tenants by the entirety, joint tenants, or as community property unless both participated in the creation of the debt and are both named as defendants in the judgment.
    II. Judgment liens have a priority relationship based on the time of docketing and are enforced by an execution order.

    (a) I only
    (b) II only
    (c) both I and II
    (d) neither I nor II

26. Liens, easements, encroachments, and restrictive covenants are all examples of which of the following?

    (a) Emblements
    (b) Estovers
    (c) Estates
    (d) Encumbrances

27. Which of the following is (are) characteristics of leasehold estates?
    I. They are estates of unlimited duration.
    II. The holder of a leasehold estate has title to the property.

    (a) I only
    (b) II only
    (c) both I and II
    (d) neither I nor II

28. All of the following statements regarding an estate for years is correct EXCEPT
    (a) The duration of the estate must be definite.
    (b) The duration of the estate must be at least one year.
    (c) The estate automatically terminates without notice.
    (d) The contract creating an estate for years may be required to be in writing for validity.

29. Which of the following is an estate that automatically renews itself for consecutive periods?

    (a) Estate at will
    (b) Life estate
    (c) Estate from year-to-year
    (d) Estate for years

30. After the termination of a lease, the tenant continued in possession of the property without permission of the property owner. The tenant's status is

    (a) Tenant at will
    (b) Lessee
    (c) Trespasser
    (d) Tenant at sufferance

Contracts and Agency

6

Contracts play an extremely important part in the real estate business and are involved in the listing of property, the sale or exchange of property, the leasing of property, optioning of property and property management. Before learning the specifics of the various contracts normally encountered in the real estate business, the student must first develop a knowledge of the basic fundamentals of contract law. These basic fundamentals apply to real estate contracts as well as other contracts.

FUNDAMENTALS OF CONTRACT LAW

Definition

A contract is an agreement between competent parties upon legal consideration to do, or abstain from doing, some legal act. A contract may be valid, voidable, or void.

Valid Contracts

A valid contract is one that is binding and enforceable. The parties to a valid contract are legally obligated to abide by the terms and conditions of the contract. If a party to a valid contract defaults in the performance of obligations under the contract, the individual is subject to legal action by the other party or parties to the contract. In creating contracts, every effort should be made to insure that a valid contract is created.

Voidable Contracts

A voidable contract results from failure to meet the legal requirements for validity in the negotiation or creation of the contract. A voidable contract is neither enforceable nor binding upon the parties. A party to such a contract can avoid the effects of the contract without consequence. A contract can be voidable insofar as only one party is concerned or voidable for all parties.

The parties to a voidable contract are not required to elect a set aside or avoid the contract. The parties to a voidable contract may fulfill their obligations under the contract and receive their benefits. A voidable contract can be voluntarily performed by the parties. However, at any time prior to complete performance of the contract, any party or parties can elect to discontinue. Examples of conditions which result in the creation of voidable contracts appear in the subsequent discussion of requirements for contract validity.

Void Contracts

A void contract is one that is absolutely unenforceable and has no legal force or effect. If a contract is void, it is void as to all the parties to the contract. By comparison, a voidable contract is one that can be avoided by one or more parties to the contract. A void contract has no legal force or effect from its inception; whereas, a voidable contract is not avoided (or made void) until some party to the contract takes action to create this result.

Methods of Creating Contracts

Contracts may be either express or implied. An express contract is one in which the parties to the contract have definitely expressed all the terms and conditions as agreed upon between

57

them. For most purposes, an express contract can be either verbal or written. However, as we shall see subsequently, certain types of contracts must be in writing to be enforceable.

A real estate listing contract and a real estate sales contract are examples of express contracts. All the terms and conditions of the contractual agreement are set forth in each of these contracts. The contracts are entered into expressly by the parties.

Implied Contracts

An implied contract is a contract that is implied from the conduct and actions of the parties. Implied contracts are enforced when the conduct of the parties clearly illustrates their intention to contract. A court will imply a contract if a benefit has been received by one party at the expense of the other party. A court will require the recipient of the benefit to pay a reasonable compensation to the party rendering the benefit unless the benefit was actually a gift. An implied contract is created, for example, if one party orders merchandise from another party without stipulating the price to be paid for the merchandise. An implied contract to pay the reasonable value of the merchandise when delivered is created.

Bilateral and Unilateral Contracts

A contract may be either bilateral or unilateral. A bilateral contract is one based on mutual promises. The mutal promises provide the consideration for the contract. For example, a real estate sales contract is typically a bilateral contract based on the purchaser's promise to buy and the seller's promise to sell and convey a marketable title. A unilateral contract is one in which there is a promise on the part of one party to the contract in return for a specific action from the other party. For example, a unilateral contract is created when merchandise is ordered with a promise to pay upon delivery. A unilateral contract may be revoked by the promisor at any time prior to performance by the other party.

Executed and Executory Contracts

A contract that has been fully performed by the parties is called an executed contract. All contracts that have not been fully performed (there are still things to be done as required by the contract) are executory contracts.

Essential Elements of a Valid Contract

The objective in drawing a contract is to create an agreement that is binding and enforceable. The essential elements required to create a valid, enforceable contract follow:

Competent Parties

The parties to a contract must have contractual capacity. They must be legally competent to contract. Most people possess contractual capacity and therefore this subject is discussed by pointing out the few conditions resulting in incompetency; these are minors and mental incompetents. Minors are those who have not reached the age of majority as established by statutory law in each particular state. Most states specify this to be age eighteen.

If either party to the contract is incompetent, the contract is voidable by the incompetent party and unenforceable against the incompetent. In the case of minors, the contract is voidable at the option of the minor. The minor may hold an adult to a contract but the adult cannot legally hold the minor to the contract. The contract is not legally enforceable against the minor. A minor may fulfill the terms of the contract and if he or she does, and does not take steps to terminate the contract after reaching the age of majority, the individual is said to have ratified the contract as an adult and it will be binding. If a party to a contract is intoxicated or under the influence of drugs at the time of entering into the contract so that the person does not understand what is happening, the individual is considered temporarily mentally incompetent to contract and, therefore, the contract will be unenforceable against the person.

Mutual Assent

To create a valid contract, it must be entered into voluntarily by the parties. The parties must mutually assent (agree) to the terms and conditions in the contract. If a person has entered into a written contract as evidenced by his or her signature on the contract, the individual is presumed to have assented to the terms and conditions of the contract.

The consent of the parties to enter into a contractual agreement must be a real consent. This is a consent that is based on the parties having an accurate knowledge of the facts concerning the terms and conditions of the contract. The failure of contract validity because of the lack of real and mutual consent by the parties results from the presence of misrepresentation, fraud, undue influence, or duress.

MISREPRESENTATION. An unintentional misrepresentation occurs as a result of an innocent misconception as to the facts on the part of the person making the unintentional misrepresentation. A contracting party who has entered a contract in reliance upon an unintentional misrepresentation of a material fact (important fact) is legally entitled to rescind the contract. The contract is voidable by any party who relied upon the unintentional misrepresentation as a basis for entering the contract.

FRAUD. Fraud is an intentional misrepresentation of a material fact made for the purpose of inducing someone to enter into a contract. If a party enters into a contract because of fraud, the defrauded party can avoid the contract. A false representation is deemed to be fraudulent when (1) a party making the representation knows it to be false or (2) the person making the false representation does not know in fact whether the statement is true or untrue and should have known that the statement is untrue.

If a real estate broker, as agent of an owner of real property, commits an act of fraud, the injured party may rescind any contract entered into with the seller. Also, the agent is liable to the injured party and the seller for damages incurred.

UNDUE INFLUENCE. Undue influence is any improper or wrongful influence by one person over another whereby the will of a person is overpowered so that he or she is induced to act or prevented from acting on free will. Undue influence occurs when one person takes advantage of another person's lack of mental ability or takes advantage of a special relationship between the parties that enables one party to have an unusual influence over the other party, as in the relationship between legal advisor and client or employer and employee. If a person is induced to enter a contract because undue influence is exerted, the individual may avoid the contract.

DURESS. The essential element of duress is the inability of a party to exercise personal free will at the time of the creation of the contract because of fear of another party to the contract. The fear may result from a threat of bodily injury or a threat of criminal prosecution of the contracting party. Also, the unlawful retention of another's property, a threat to retain property of another unlawfully, or a threat to destroy the property of another all constitutes duress. The presence of duress in inducing someone to contract prevents the reality of consent as required for contract validity. Therefore, duress in the contract negotiation renders the contract voidable and the contract can therefore be avoided by the party or parties who were the subject of the duress.

Offer and Acceptance

Each contract must contain an offer and an unconditional acceptance of the offer. The party making an offer is the offeror and the party to whom the offer is made is the offeree. Since an offer may be withdrawn at any time prior to acceptance, it is very important that any offer be expeditiously presented. The contract is created at the time of the unconditional acceptance of the offer. The requirement of mutual assent, necessary for contract validity, is evidenced in the contract by the unconditional acceptance of an offer.

The offer must be definite and specific in its terms. If the offer is vague and indefinite and, therefore, subject to various interpretations, its acceptance will not result in the creation of a valid contract. For example, if an offer is made to a seller to purchase a house in the Executive Heights Subdivision without a specific property description and the seller actually owns three houses in that subdivision, the offer is indefinite and an acceptance will not result in the creation of a valid contract.

The offer must not be illusory and, therefore, not binding upon the offeror if accepted. For example, a person cannot offer to buy seller's home in Security Estates if the offeror decides to move to Security Estates. Here the offer is not binding upon the offeror and is therefore illusory, since the offeror has complete control over whether or not to move to Security Estates. The acceptance of an illusory offer will not result in the creation of a valid contract.

A unilateral offer may be accepted only by the performance of the action specified in the offer; for example, a promise to pay money upon the delivery of goods. The acceptance of this unilateral offer is made by the delivery of the goods. A bilateral offer is accepted by a promise to do the things requested in the offer.

The acceptance of a bilateral offer must be communicated to the offeror for a contract to be created. The acceptance must be absolutely unconditional in the case of either a bilateral offer or unilateral offer. If the acceptance varies in any way from the offer as presented, it will not qualify as an acceptance and instead is actually a rejection of the offer. Sometimes an offer will specify the manner in which the acceptance of the offer must be communicated to the offeror by the offeree. In the absence of any specific provision in this regard, the communication of acceptance may be made in any reasonable manner by the offeree. In the event that acceptance is by mail, the communication is effective and a contract is created at the time the acceptance is mailed by the offeree.

A contract for the sale of real property is a bilateral contract because it is based on the mutual promises of the seller to sell and the promise of the buyer to buy. Therefore, the acceptance of the offer must be communicated to the offeror to create the contract.

In presenting an offer to purchase real property, the broker should counsel the seller regarding all aspects of the offer. If the broker feels that acceptance of a particular offer is not in the best interests of the seller, the broker should so advise him. However, if the broker believes that the offer is probably the best that can be obtained, the broker should urge the seller to accept. In any case, it is the seller's prerogative to accept or reject any offer.

In the event that a seller rejects an offer, the broker should encourage the seller to make a counteroffer. A counteroffer is actually a new offer wherein the seller becomes the offeror and the prospective purchaser the offeree. The counteroffer then must be presented by the broker to the prospective buyer for acceptance or rejection. In some real estate transactions there are several offers and counteroffers before both the buyer and seller reach an acceptable agreement.

TERMINATION OF OFFERS. Offers may be terminated in the following ways: (1) by the expiration of a time limit specified by the offeror prior to acceptance; (2) by the death or insanity of either the offeror or the offeree prior to acceptance; (3) by the revocation of the offer by the offeror prior to acceptance; (4) by the expiration of a "reasonable" period of time after the offer is made and prior to acceptance; (5) by the failure of the offeree to comply with the terms of the offer as to the specific manner in which the acceptance must be communicated; (6) by the expiration of a power of attorney when either offeror or offeree are acting as attorney-in-fact under a power of attorney; or (7) by acceptance of the offer by the offeree. When the offer is accepted, a contract is created.

Consideration

Consideration must be present in every contact for the contract to be valid and enforceable. Consideration may consist of a promise in return for the performance of a specified act as is the case in unilateral contracts. Unless there are mutual promises in a bilateral contract, the contract will not be valid. For example, if one party promises to make a gift to another party, the contract will not be enforced because the one to receive the gift has furnished no consideration. There must be mutuality. Each party to the contract must do something or promise to do something. There are two exceptions to the general rule that mutual promises will constitute consideration: (1) a promise to fulfill a moral obligation and (2) a promise to fulfill a legal obligation.

Legality of Object

The contract must be for a legal purpose. A contract for an illegal purpose is void. Examples of illegal contracts include contracts to sell a public office, contracts in restraint of trade, contracts to promote litigation or stifle prosecution, and contracts that restrain freedom to marry.

Assignment of Contracts

A contract is assignable provided there is no prohibition against assignment spelled out within the contract itself. The assignment of the contract, however, does not relieve the assignor of the responsibility for performance in the event that the assignee fails to perform unless the assignor has been specifically released by the other contracting party who accepts the assignee in place of the assignor.

Termination of Contracts

Contracts may be terminated by (1) complete performance, (2) mutual agreement of the parties, (3) accord and satisfaction, (4) novation, (5) impossibility of performance, (6) operation of law, or (7) breach of the contract.

Complete Performance

The usual manner of terminating contracts is by complete performance. When all the terms of the contract have been fully performed by all parties, the contract is executed and terminated.

Mutual Agreement

Executory contracts may be terminated by the mutual agreement of all parties to the contract. The release of each party by the other supplies the consideration.

Accord and Satisfaction

An accord consists of a new agreement between contracting parties whereby one of them is to do something different from that required by the original contract and the other party is to receive something different from that specified in the original contract. The accord is satisfied and terminated when the terms of the accord are fully performed. When the accord is fully performed, the original contract is also terminated.

Novation

A novation is the substitution of a new contract for a prior contract. To create a novation the parties to the original contract are changed. A new party to the contract agrees to satisfy a former contracting party's obligation to another party in a previous contract. When the novation (new contract) is created, the old contract is discharged. The requirements for a novation are a previous valid contract, an agreement of the parties to a new contract, the termination of the old contract, and the validity of the new contract.

Impossibility of Performance

The general rule is that even though it is impossible for a party to a contract to perform obligations under the contract, the party is still not relieved of liability. The reasoning behind this is that the one who cannot perform should have provided against this possibility by a provision in the contract relieving him from liability.

However, there are exceptions to the general rule. One exception is in the case of a personal service contract. If a person contracts to render services to another person that cannot be rendered by someone else, the person obligated to render the service is relieved from liability in the event that the individual dies or becomes incapacitated so that he or she cannot render the service. This is the only case in which contractual obligations are terminated by death or incapacity. Another exception to the general rule occurs when the performance of an obligation under a contract becomes illegal as a result of a change in law after the contract was created. As a result, the obligated parties are relieved of liability.

Operation of Law

The term operation of law describes the manner in which the rights and/or liabilities of parties may be changed by the application of law without the act or cooperation of the parties affected. The following are examples of discharge of contracts by operation of law.

The time within which a legal action may be brought against a party to a contract by another party to that contract is limited by statute in every state. The statutes are called Statutes of Limitations. If a party to a contract fails to bring a law suit against a defaulting party to a contract within the statutory time period, the right of legal remedy is lost to the injured party by operation of law brought about by the expiration of the time period specified in a Statute of Limitations.

The bankruptcy of a party to a contract as established by the Federal Bankruptcy Act has the effect of terminating contracts because the bankruptcy law relieves the bankrupt from liability under contracts to which he or she is a party as of the date of filing the bankruptcy petition with the federal court.

The intentional cancellation or alteration of the written evidence of an agreement has the effect of discharging the agreement. There must have occurred an intentional and material alteration to create this effect. This most frequently involves negotiable instruments: notes, bonds, or checks. Examples of typical alterations are changes in the date of payment, changes in the amount of payment, or changes in the interest rate.

Breach of Contract

The term breach of contract may be defined as "failure, without legal excuse, to perform any promise which forms the whole or part of a contract." The effect of the breach of contractual obligations by a party to a contract is to terminate the contract. However, the breach does not terminate the right to legal remedies against the defaulting party by the injured party. The injured party is entitled to receive compensation for any financial loss caused by the breach as may be awarded by a court. This is called compensatory damages. Additionally the court will award punitive damages if the breach of contract was willful, malicious, and committed intentionally to do harm to the plaintiff. Often the amount of punitive damages will exceed the amount of compensatory damages.

Statute of Frauds

For most purposes, a verbal contract is just as valid and enforceable as a written contract. The difficulty with verbal contracts lies in the fact that they lead to misunderstanding of the rights and obligations of the parties, and they may be extremely difficult to prove in a court proceeding if that should become necessary.

Contracts involving the creation or conveyance of an interest in real property must be written to be enforceable. This requirement is created by the Statute of Frauds. This statute was derived from an English statute by the same name. To prevent fraud in real estate contracts, this statute requires that they be written and contain all the elements essential for contract validity. Verbal testimony will not suffice to create obligations under a contract involving transfer of title to real property.

The statute does not require any particular form of writing. To be sufficient to satisfy the requirements of the statute, the writing may be a short memorandum, a telegram, a receipt, and so forth. The contract need not necessarily be in one document. Several documents can be put together to create the contract. However, the best form is to have the entire contract in one writing and signed by the parties.

Examples of real estate contracts falling under the Statute of Frauds are contracts to buy and sell real estate, options, contracts for deed (also called installment contracts, land contracts, and conditional sale contracts) and contracts for the exchange of real estate. Also, lease contracts fall under the Statute of Frauds if the lease term exceeds the statutory time period in a particular state (more than one year in most states).

Other types of contracts falling under the Statute of Frauds are contracts wherein one party becomes responsible for the debt of another, contracts in which executors or administrators of estates agree to become liable from their own property for the debts of the estate, contracts that are not possible of completion within one year, contracts for the sale of goods exceeding a specified statutory dollar value, and contracts created in contemplation of marriage.

REAL ESTATE CONTRACTS

Listing Contracts

The first contract that we encounter in the real estate business is the listing contract. A listing contract is a contract whereby the owner of property employs a real estate broker to find a buyer for his or her property. This contract creates an agency relationship in which the seller is the principal and the broker is the seller's special agent for this particular purpose. If a buyer hires a broker to obtain property that he or she may purchase, the broker is the agent of the buyer who is his or her principal. However, the usual situation is that the broker is employed by the seller and is, therefore, the seller's agent.

No transfer of interest in real property is going to occur under this contract. No title will pass between the seller and the broker. Therefore, this contract does not fall under the Statute of Frauds in all states. Consequently, it need not be reduced to writing to be enforceable in those states. However, most states require the listing contract to be in writing because contracts for the conveyance of title must be written; and since listing contracts relate to the sale of real property, they must also be in writing.

Also, many states require the listing contract to be in writing for the broker to be eligible to receive a commission. The broker must prove the existence of an employment contract. A written contract clearly spells out the fact that the broker has actually been hired by the seller and sets forth all the terms and conditions of employment. The requirement for the listing contract to be in writing substantially reduces lawsuits between brokers and property owners concerning matters of the broker's employment. There are approximately sixteen states that require listing contracts to be in writing to enable the broker to be legally entitled to a commission. These states include Arizona, California, Idaho, Indiana, Iowa, Kentucky, Michigan, Montana, Nebraska, New Jersey, Ohio, Oklahoma, Oregon, Utah, Washington, and Wisconsin.

Listing contracts should always be created for a definite period of time. The contract should specify an origination date and a termination date. The definiteness of the time period for which the broker is employed is necessary for the protection of the broker and the seller. The definite termination date protects the seller by eliminating any doubt as to the end of the seller's employment of the broker. In the event that the seller sells the property to a prospect not generated by the broker after the termination date, there is clearly no obligation for the seller to pay any compensation to the broker. In the absence of a definite listing term, a court would rule that the agent was employed for a reasonable length of time. If the broker finds a prospect after the expiration of what a court would consider a reasonable time, the broker is not entitled to any commission. In some states, North Carolina for example, brokers are required to set forth a definite termination date in listing contracts. In these states, a broker is subject to license revocation or suspension if he or she writes an "open-ended" listing contract.

Broker's Obligations as Agent

The broker, as agent of the seller, is in a fiduciary relationship to his or her principal. It is a position of trust. The broker as agent of the seller has certain obligations to the principal as required of every agent by law. The agent's duties and responsibilities include (1) the requirement to be loyal to the principal, (2) to obey all reasonable instructions of the principal, (3) not to be negligent, (4) to account for all money or property received for the benefit of the principal and (5) to inform the principal of all facts that materially affect the subject matter of the agency.

Loyalty

The real estate broker as agent of the seller must be loyal to the seller and must work diligently to serve the best interests of the principal under the terms of the employment contract creating the agency. The agent may not work for personal interests or interests of others adversely to the interests of the principal. The real estate broker cannot legally represent any other person in the activities of his or her agency without disclosing this fact to the principal and obtaining the principal's consent. Therefore, a real estate broker cannot represent both buyer and seller in a transaction and cannot receive a commission from both without the knowledge and consent of both buyer and seller. It is also a violation of the requirement of loyalty for a broker to purchase the listed property without knowledge by the principal that the broker is in fact the purchaser.

Instructions

It is the duty of the broker to obey all reasonable instructions given by the principal as long as the instructions fall within the broker's duties as contemplated by the employment contract. For example, if the principal specifies certain times when the property may be shown to prospective buyers, the broker must abide by these instructions. Or, if a seller instructs the broker not to include the listed property in a multiple listing service, the broker must follow these instructions. Of course, if the broker is instructed to do something that is illegal or unethical, the instructions do not have to be and must not be followed. Also, the agent does not have to adhere to instructions that go beyond the performance of the employment contract.

Negligence

In offering services as a real estate broker to the public, the broker is asserting that he or she is possessed of the necessary skill and training to perform the employment requirements. In performing duties as an agent, the broker must exercise the degree of skill and diligence the public is entitled to expect of real estate brokers. If a broker's principal incurs a financial loss as a result of the broker's negligence and failure to meet the standards of skill, diligence, and reasonable care the public is entitled to expect from brokers, the broker is liable for any loss incurred by the principal. Additionally, the principal would not be required to pay any compensation to the broker as agreed in the employment contract.

Accounting

A real estate broker must account for and promptly remit as required all money or property entrusted to the broker for the benefit of others.

The broker is required to keep adequate and accurate records of all receipts and expenditures of other people's money so that a complete accounting can be provided. A real estate broker must maintain a special account for the deposit of other people's money. This account must be entitled either "trust account" or "escrow account" and must be maintained in an insured bank or insured savings and loan association. It is a violation of the law of agency and the real estate licensing laws in the various states for a broker to commingle funds or property that he or she is holding in trust for others with personal money or property.

Disclosure of Information

A real estate broker is required to keep the principal fully informed of all important matters involved with the purpose of the broker's employment. Any information that is material to the transaction for which the broker is employed must be communicated promptly and totally to the principal. The requirement to disclose information includes the requirement that the broker present every offer in writing to the seller. It is the seller's prerogative to decide whether to reject or accept any offer for the purchase of the property. In presenting the offer, the broker should provide the principal with any knowledge of all circumstances surrounding the offer. An offer must be presented even though the seller has several offers under consideration at the time an additional offer is made. The broker must continue to present offers during the term of the listing contract until there is an acceptance of an offer by the seller.

A broker also has an obligation to the principal not to disclose certain information to third parties. For example, if a broker knows that a seller will actually accept a price for the property lower than the listed price, the broker is obligated not to disclose this information to others. The broker may offer the property only at the listed price. It is a violation of the broker's fiduciary obligation to the seller to offer the property at any price other than the listed price.

Even though one of the broker's obligations to the seller includes the requirement not to disclose certain confidential information to third parties that would be injurious to the seller, the broker may not misrepresent the property in any way to the buyer. The law provides that liability may be imposed upon a broker for the misrepresentation of the existence of a defect in the real estate. Liability may be imposed upon the broker for concealing defects in the property or for failing to disclose the existence of defects. This liability may be imposed for both an intentional and an unintentional misrepresentation by the broker.

The basis for the imposition of liability in the case of a misrepresentation consists of (1) a false representation of a material fact; (2) the fact that the person making the false representation knew or should have known it to be false; (3) the fact that the misrepresentation was made with an intent to induce the party to act or refrain from acting in reliance upon the misrepresentation; (4) the fact that the party relied upon the misrepresentation in acting or failing to act; and (5) the fact that there was damage to the party who relied upon the misrepresentation in acting or not acting.

A positive misrepresentation by a broker occurs when he or she conceals a defect in the property from the buyer or makes a misrepresentation to the buyer regarding the existence of a defect. An unintentional misrepresentation occurs when the broker makes a false statement to the buyer about the property and the broker does not know in fact whether the statement is true or untrue. In either of these situations the broker is liable to a buyer who suffers a loss as a result of acting or failing to act in reliance upon the misrepresentation.

The broker is not excused from liability for making a misrepresentation of the property based upon statements made to the broker by the seller. The broker is required to make a personal diligent investigation of the property before accepting the listing. Liability is imposed upon the broker even though he or she is the agent of the seller who is the client and is not the agent of the buyer. The broker is obligated by law to represent the property honestly, fairly, and accurately to all prospective buyers.

Buyer as Principal

In the typical real estate transaction, the broker is the agent of a property owner who wishes to sell the property and employs a broker as agent in a listing contract. Sometimes, however, a buyer will become a principal and broker's client in a contract whereby the buyer employs a broker as an agent to locate a certain type of property for him or her to purchase under specified terms. In these situations, the buyer-principal may wish to remain anonymous to the property owner. Therefore, the buyer may enter into the agency relationship as an undisclosed principal.

An undisclosed principal often authorizes the agent to enter into contracts to purchase real estate on his or her behalf within terms and conditions set forth in the employment contract between the buyer and the broker. In these cases the undisclosed principal is responsible for all contracts entered into by the agent that are within the scope of the agent's authority as spelled out in the contract of employment.

Other Agency Relationships

As previously discussed, the real estate broker is appointed agent of the seller under the terms and conditions of a listing contract. Also, as we have seen, the broker may represent a buyer as agent in locating or acquiring property for the buyer. However, there are other agency relationships that exist in the activities of real estate brokerage. The other agency situations involve: (1) the sales associates affiliated with a real estate broker and (2) other brokers cooperating in the sale of real estate with the listing broker.

Sales Associates

The sales associates affiliated with a real estate firm are agents of the brokerage firm. This is true whether the associates are licensed as real estate salespersons or brokers. The relationship between the broker and his or her sales associates is that of principal and agent wherein the broker is the principal and the sales associates are the broker's agents for the purposes of the brokerage business.

As the principal, the broker is responsible for the acts of all agents while they are engaged in the activities of the agency. The sales associates in their capacity as agents of the broker are required to comply with all the requirements of the law of agency as previously discussed.

Cooperating Brokers

A cooperating broker who works through a listing broker to effect a sale of property is the agent of the listing broker. The cooperating broker as agent must comply with the requirements of the law of agency in all dealings with the listing broker. The cooperating broker has the responsibility to work for the best interests of the property owner who is paying the commission in which the cooperating broker will share. Cooperating brokers and all sales associates are subagents of the seller through the listing broker.

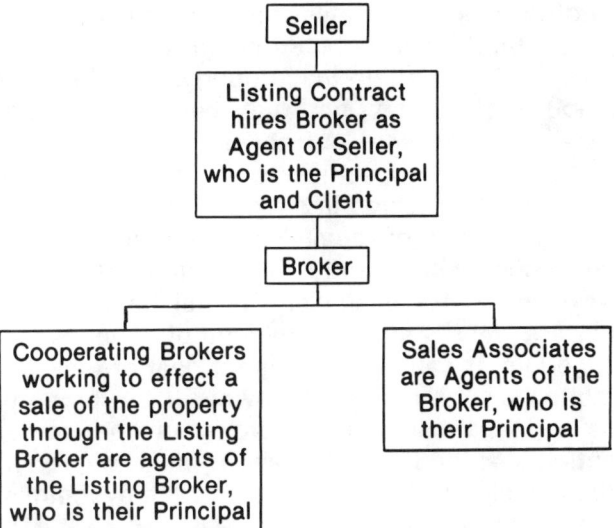

Figure 6.1 *Agency Relationships in Typical Real Estate Transactions*

TYPES OF COMMISSION ARRANGEMENTS

Negotiability

The amount or rate of commission to be charged by or paid to a real estate broker is strictly a negotiable matter between the broker and the listing seller. It is a violation of federal law for any person or organization—either governmental or private—to even recommend a commission schedule to a broker or group of brokers. It is also illegal for two or more brokers to agree to charge certain rates of commission to listing sellers. These activities are "price fixing" and are acts in the restraint of trade in violation of the Sherman Anti-Trust Act.

Percentage of Final Sold Price

The most usual type of commission arrangement found in listing contracts is for the commission to be a specified percentage of the final sales price of the property. Notice that this is not a percentage of the listed price (unless the listed price and sold price are identical) but is the price for which the property actually sells.

Net Listing

Another type of commission arrangement is the net listing. This is a situation in which the seller, when listing the property, specifies an amount of money net that he or she must receive in the sale. All above the net amount that the seller specifies is designated as the broker's commission in effecting the sale.

This type of commission arrangement is not recommended and is illegal in some states, New Jersey for example. The net listing is, at best, a very poor arrangement of commission schedule. It can lead to a great deal of dissatisfaction on the part of the owner if the property sells for substantially more than the owner anticipated and thereby results in a disproportionate share of the proceeds as the commission to the broker.

When you consider the broker's responsibility to his or her principal, the owner, and look at it in the light of the fact that one of the broker's responsibilities is to establish a fair market price for the property, it would seem that the broker is fulfilling the responsibility in a much better and more professional manner by recommending a fair market price, which would include a reasonable rate of commission established as a percentage of the sales price.

Flat Fee

Another form of commission arrangement is the flat fee. The broker takes the listing based on a specified payment of money by the seller to the broker at the time of listing the property. The broker is entitled to retain this fee for efforts in attempting to market the property. The broker's compensation, in this case, does not depend on the sale of the property. The amount of the flat fee is typically substantially less than the broker would normally receive had the compensation been based on a percentage of the price for which the property sold. Often in these arrangements, the broker will only advertise the property and put together a sales contract when buyer and seller agree on the terms. As far as showing the property and negotiating the sale, the broker does not participate. The seller has the sole responsibility for these aspects of the transaction.

Commissions of Sales Associates

Commissions to be paid to sales associates in a real estate office are established by an agreement between the real estate firm and the associates. This is true whether the associates are licensed as real estate salespersons or as brokers. Under the usual agreement, there are two commissions that may be earned by sales associates. One is a commission for listing the property; it is paid when the property is sold. The other is a commission for selling the property. If a sales associate sells a property that he or she has listed, the sales associate will receive both the listing and the selling commission. The combination of these two commissions usually amounts to approximately 50-60 percent of the commission that the real estate firm receives in the transaction.

Commissions Paid to Cooperating Brokers

When a property is sold as the result of cooperating efforts of two real estate firms, one of which is the listing firm and the other the selling firm, the commission agreed upon in the listing contract is paid to the listing broker by the property owner. This commission is shared by the listing broker with the selling broker on a predetermined basis. The division of the commission to be received by the listing broker should be determined by agreement between the two cooperating brokers prior to the participation of the selling broker in the transaction.

Referral Fees

Brokers typically pay a referral fee to other brokers who refer prospective buyers and sellers to them. The fee is usually about 10 percent of the commission earned by the broker to whom the prospect is referred and is paid on the closing of the transaction.

TYPES OF LISTING CONTRACTS

There are three types of listing contracts in general use. These are the open listing, the exclusive agency listing, and the exclusive right to sell listing. Each of these contracts give different rights to the broker and seller. A brief description of each type of listing contract follows.

Open Listing

Under an open listing, the seller lists a property with the assistance of one or more brokers. The broker effecting the sale is entitled to the commission. However, if the owner sells the property (not to a prospect generated by the broker), the owner owes no commission.

This type of listing is not beneficial to the owner or the broker. Usually, a broker cannot afford to spend advertising dollars and sales staff on an open listing. The broker is competing with the owner and with every other broker who has an open listing on the property or who may learn about the availability of the property and obtain an open listing. This type of listing also can lead to disputes over commissions between brokers and can present legal problems for the owner.

Exclusive Agency Listing

In this type of listing, the property is listed exclusively with one broker. This is the basis for the name "exclusive" listing. If the broker effects a sale of the property, he or she is legally entitled to the commission agreed upon. However, under this type of listing, if the owner sells the property then the broker earns no commission.

This type of listing is somewhat better than the open listing in that only one broker is involved. However, the broker is still competing with the owner. The broker's advertising programs, including the office's "for sale" sign on the property, may generate prospects for the owner.

Exclusive Right to Sell Listing

This is the best type of listing contract from both the standpoint of the broker and the seller. Under this listing contract, the property is listed with only one broker (exclusive). If the property is sold by anyone during the term of the listing contract, the broker is legally entitled to the commission. The seller is legally obligated to pay the broker's commission if the broker or the seller or some third party effects a sale of the property during the term of the listing contract.

The exclusive right to sell listing contract benefits the owner because the broker is secure enough in the opportunity to earn a commission that he or she can afford to spend time and advertising dollars to effect a quick and satisfactory sale of the listed property. Also, with the agreement of the seller, the broker may put the listing in a multiple listing service and thereby provide significantly increased market exposure for the property.

Multiple Listing

The term "multiple listing" refers to an organized method of placing listings in a pool of listings by member brokers. The listing broker is the agent of the property owner; and the other member brokers participating to effect a sale of another broker's listing are agents of the listing broker. Multiple listing provides a substantially increased market exposure for the listings placed in the pool. For this reason, a multiple listing service is of significant benefit to both brokers and sellers.

Unilateral and Bilateral Listing Contracts

A listing contract may be drawn so that it is a bilateral or unilateral contract. Care should be taken by the broker to draw the listing contract so that it is bilateral. A unilateral listing contract is one in which the property owner promises to pay a commission when the broker has performed the required act of producing a ready, willing, and financially able buyer or an offer that is accepted by the seller. A unilateral listing contract may be revoked by the seller at any time prior to performance by the broker. However, if the contract is bilateral, based on mutual promises of the seller and broker, the owner may not legally revoke the contract before the specified termination date provided the broker is fulfilling his or her legal obligations as promised.

Figure 6.2 shows an exclusive right to sell listing contract. Since it is based on the mutual promises of seller and broker, is a bilateral contract. As can be seen from this contract, the broker is promising to do certain things. These promises are (1) to use her best efforts to procure a buyer, (2) to take all actions considered appropriate to effect a satisfactory sale of the property, including advertising the property twice weekly during the listing term, and (3) to provide the owner the benefit of the office staff's knowledge of financing, surveying, and other real estate matters. Additionally, the broker promises to enter the listing in the multiple listing service. So we see that the broker as well as the seller has promised to do certain specific things, thereby creating a bilateral listing contract.

The exclusive right to sell listing contract illustrated in figure 6.2 is broken down into fourteen numbered sections for reference to the discussion of the contract following.

Section 1 contains a recital of consideration, "the mutual promises hereinafter set forth", and the names of the parties to the contract, namely Mr. and Mrs. Seller and Action Realty Company. We also see that the Sellers grant to Action Realty the "exclusive right to negotiate for the sale or exchange" of the property described in the contract.

Section 2 contains the property description. In the description the street address and subdivision are included primarily for the purpose of enabling agents of Action Realty Co. to locate the property and to provide the same information to cooperating brokers acting as agents of Action Realty Co. The additional descriptions are used to identify the property by reference to recorded documents. These references eliminate any doubt as to the specific property listed.

Section 3 again sets forth the fact that the listing is an exclusive right to sell and exchange and also specifies the definite term of the listing contract by providing an inception date and time and a date and time when the listing automatically terminates. 19CY stands for "current year."

Section 4 specifies the asking price of the property and establishes the terms of payment acceptable to the seller. In this contract Mr. and Mrs. Seller agree to accept a cash payment, an offer subject to the buyer obtaining a conventional loan, or an offer subject to the buyer obtaining a VA guaranteed loan. It also states that the seller is willing to finance a portion of the sale price for the purchaser. This section also instructs the listing broker to enter the listing in the multiple listing service.

Section 5 sets forth the agreement of the seller to execute and deliver a fee simple title with the usual covenants of warranty with certain exceptions including taxes, recorded easements, zoning regulations, and restrictive covenants, if any.

Section 6 specifies that Action Realty Company will receive and hold in trust for the benefit of the principals all earnest money deposits paid toward the purchase price of the property until final settlement or other termination of the contract. The earnest money deposits should always be held by the listing broker.

Section 7 provides for the division of the earnest money between the seller and the broker in the event that the buyer defaults on a contract of sale with the seller and forfeits the earnest money as specified in the contract. It should be noted that the broker's share of the forfeited deposit may not be in excess of the amount of commission the broker would have earned had the transaction been consummated.

Section 8 contains specific promises on the part of Action Realty Company in marketing the property. These specific promises reinforce the bilateral aspect of this particular listing contract form.

Section 9 establishes the rate of commission agreed upon by Action Realty Company and Mr. and Mrs. Seller as a result of their negotiations. This section also includes a "carry-over clause" to protect the broker for a reasonable period of time after the expiration of the listing contract. This clause provides for the broker's commission in the event of a sale to a prospect that was interested in the property by Action Realty Company or its agents (including cooperating brokers) that Action Realty Company has registered with the owner within five days after the expiration of this listing contract.

Contracts and Agency

1   In consideration of the mutual promises hereinafter set forth, <u>Samuel E. Seller and wife Sarah A. Seller</u>, owner, grants to <u>Action Realty Company</u> the exclusive right to negotiate for the sale or exchange of the real property described as: <u>House and lot located at Number 6 Amortization Drive, Mortgage Heights Subdivision, Sellerstown, Homestate, and being Lot. No. 20 in said</u>

2 <u>subdivision as recorded in Plat Book 5, Page 40, Deed Book 301, Page 64, in the office of the Register of Deeds in Home County, Homestate.</u>

3   The owner gives <u>Action Realty Company</u> the exclusive right to sell or exchange this property from noon, <u>July 1</u>, 19 <u>CY</u> until noon, <u>October 1</u>, 19 <u>CY</u>, at a price of $ <u>75,000.00</u> payable in cash, or for such other price or terms as the owner may subsequently approve. Terms of sale: Cash <u>X</u> Conventional <u>X</u> FHA ___,

4 VA <u>X</u>, Owner Financing <u>X</u>. This listing (shall be) (XXXXXXXXX) entered in the <u>Sellerstown Multiple Listing Service</u>.

5   It is understood and agreed that if the property is sold or exchanged during the period set forth herein, owner will execute and deliver a fee simple deed with the usual covenants of warranty, subject only to current ad valorem taxes (which are to be prorated on the calendar year basis to the date of closing the transaction), recorded easements, zoning regulations and restrictive covenants, if any.

6   All earnest money deposits paid upon the purchase price shall be held in escrow by <u>Action Realty Company</u> until the consummation or termination of the transaction.

7   In the event any deposit money is retained by reason of the buyer failing to make settlement, then the monies retained shall be divided equally between the seller and the broker, but in no event shall the sum paid to the broker be in excess of the rate of the professional brokerage fee due.

8   <u>Action Realty Company</u> promises to use their best efforts to procure a buyer for the property, to take all actions that they consider appropriate to effect a satisfactory sale of the property, including advertising the property at least twice weekly, and to provide the owner the benefit of their knowledge of financing, advertising, surveying, and other real estate matters.

9   The owner agrees to pay <u>Action Realty Company</u> an amount equal to <u>7</u> percent of the final sales price upon the sale or exchange of said property, whether made by owner or any other person during the term of this contract, or within <u>45 days</u> after the expiration of this contract to any person <u>Action Realty Company</u> or its agents have interested in the property and registered with the owner within <u>5</u> days after the expiration of this contract.

10   The owner agrees to refer to <u>Action Realty Company</u> all inquiries or offers received for the proposed purchase or exchange of said property.

11   The owner (does) (XXXXXXX) authorize <u>Action Realty Company</u> to place a "for sale" sign on the property.

12   The owner agrees that the property described above is offered for sale without respect to race, color, religion, sex, or national origin.

13 Other conditions: Seller agrees to: give possession not later than 10 days after final settlement; permit assumption of existing $61,000.00 assumable mortgage; accept a purchase money second mortgage not exceeding $5,000.00, payable in 60 monthly installments with interest at 11% per annum; pay discount points required for VA loan.

14   <u>Action Realty Company</u>   *Samuel E. Seller* (Owner)

By *Mary E. Beaver* (Agent)   *Sarah A. Seller* (Owner)

June 30, 19CY   Date

Figure 6.2 *Exclusive Right to Sell Listing Contract*

Section 10 sets forth the agreement of the seller to refer to the listing broker any inquiries or offers made directly to them.

Section 11 specifies whether or not Action Realty Company is authorized to place a for sale sign on the property.

Section 12 sets forth the owner's agreement that they will not discriminate in the sale of the property on the basis of race, color, religion, sex, or national origin. In doing so, the seller's promise that they will abide by the requirements of the Fair Housing Act in offering the property for sale and in contracting with a buyer for its purchase.

Section 13 contains other conditions specifically involved in this particular listing contract. Every listing contract form should provide a space to set forth any special conditions applicable to the particular agreement. One thing that should be established with the seller as precisely as possible at the time of listing is the time when the seller will give possession of the property to the purchaser. In this case, Mr. and Mrs. Seller have agreed to give possession not later than ten days after final settlement. The date of possession must be specifically established at the time the sales contract is created. (This matter is discussed further in the material related to the offer and contract of sale.)

In addition to the time of possession, the conditions agreed to by the sellers are: to permit the assumption of their existing $61,000 assumable mortgage by buyer; to accept a purchase money second mortgage not exceeding $5,000; to pay discount points as required to enable a veteran buyer to obtain a VA guaranteed loan. The subject of discount points is fully discussed in the chapter on real estate financing.

Section 14 provides for the execution of the listing contract by Mr. and Mrs. Seller as owners and Action Realty Company represented by its agent Mary E. Beaver. The listing contract must always be prepared in sufficient counterparts to provide each executing party with a copy.

Other Types of Listing Contracts

Figure 6.2 is an exclusive right to sell listing contract and contains wording regarding the broker's right to commission under that type of contract. Reference is made to section 9 of the exclusive right to sell contract wherein it is specified that the owner agrees to pay the specified commission to the listing broker "whether the sale is made by owner or any other person during the term of the contract." In the event that the purpose of the listing contract is to create an exclusive agency, the wording in this regard would be substantially different. Appropriate wording regarding the commission for an exclusive agency listing is "the owner agrees to pay Action Realty Company an amount equal to 7 percent of the final sales price upon the sale or exchange of this property if effected by Action Realty Company. However, it is understood that owner may sell the property himself without obligation for payment of any commission to Action Realty Company."

If the purpose of the contract is to create an open listing agreement, the following wording is appropriate: "owner agrees to pay Action Realty Company an amount equal to 7 percent of the final sales price upon the sale or exchange of this property if effected by Action Realty Company. However, it is understood that owner may sell the property himself or may accept an offer through another real estate broker without obligation for payment of any commission to Action Realty Company." In both the exclusive agency contract and the open listing contract, the words "exclusive right to sell" do not appear in the contract.

Commission Entitlement

The exclusive right to sell listing contract entitles the broker to a commission if the property is sold during the listing term even though the broker may not have been the procuring cause of the sale. What are the broker's rights to commission under other types of listing contracts, the open listing or exclusive agency listing.

Under other types of listing contracts the broker's entitlement to commission is determined by two tests. The first is the ready, willing, and able test. If the broker brings a buyer to the seller who is ready to buy, is willing to buy, and is able (financially) to buy under the terms and conditions of the listing contract, the broker is legally entitled to the commission. The broker has done the job that he or she was hired to do in the listing contract; that is, find a buyer who

Contracts and Agency

will pay the listed price in cash. When the broker does this, the commission has been earned under the ready, willing, and able test. It does not matter whether or not the owner actually agrees to sell the property to the prospective buyer. Remember, the seller may reject any offer.

The next test, and more usual way in which the broker becomes legally entitled to a commission, is on the basis of acceptance. If the broker brings a buyer who is accepted by the seller, the broker is legally entitled to the commission. This acceptance would be on some price or terms other than the listed price in cash. For example, the listing contract may have specified $80,000 to be payable in cash. A broker may bring an offer to the seller of $78,500 and the offer may not be for payment in cash but may be subject to the assumption of seller's existing mortgage by the buyer. If the seller accepts this offer, the broker is legally entitled to the commission on the basis of acceptance. The broker has brought the seller a buyer that is acceptable to the seller.

These tests are not both required. This is an "either/or" situation. The broker earns a commission either on the basis of having brought a ready, willing, and able buyer or on the basis of having brought a buyer that is accepted by the seller.

OFFER AND CONTRACT OF SALE

Once a real estate agent has obtained a listing, as evidenced by an executed listing contract, his or her efforts are directed toward obtaining a buyer for the listed property. The agent must find a buyer that the property satisfies and who either has the purchase price or is able to obtain the necessary financing. Once such a buyer is located by the agent, the agent presents an offer to purchase the property on behalf of the buyer to the listing seller.

Figure 6.3 is the offer and contract of sale. The offer is created when the document is executed by the purchaser and gives the real estate agent the deposit of earnest money in the amount specified. The acceptance of the offer by the seller is evidenced by the seller's execution of the contract created by the acceptance of the offer when such acceptance is communicated to the purchaser. The offer and contract of sale must always be in writing as required by the State of Frauds, since an obligation to purchase and convey a title to real property is created.

The following is a discussion of each of the numbered sections of the offer and contract of sale illustrated in figure 6.3.

Section 1 sets forth the names and marital status of the seller and the purchaser. This section also contains the mutual promises of seller and purchaser, wherein the seller agrees to sell and convey and purchaser agrees to purchase. The contract, therefore, is bilateral because it is based on the mutual promises of seller and purchaser.

Section 2 provides the property description. The first part of the description is the address of the property and is not a legal description. The remainder of the description is a legal description by reference. This portion starts with the words "being lot number 20."

Section 3 establishes that the contract is conditional upon the seller having the ability to convey a marketable title free from encumbrances with the exceptions as specified. In the event that a title examination reveals an incurable defect in seller's title, the contract will be unenforceable. This provision is included for the protection of the purchaser. In purchasing the property, the purchaser expects and is entitled to receive a good and marketable title from the seller.

Section 4 contains the financial provisions agreed upon between seller and purchaser. First, the purchase price in the amount of $74,000 is definitely established. Secondly, the purchasers made a deposit at the time they made their offer in the amount of $5,000, by personal check. The method of payment of deposit of earnest money should always be shown for the protection of the broker. In the event that the broker accepted the buyer's personal check for deposit and did not specify that the deposit was by personal check, the seller would be entitled to rely upon the fact that the broker is holding $5,000 in cash in the agency's escrow account for the benefit of the parties. In the event that the buyer's personal check failed to clear the bank, the seller could hold the broker responsible for the $5,000.

The next paragraph of the financial portion provides for the payment of $61,000 of the $74,000 purchase price by the assumption of the unpaid principal balance on the seller's existing

1   This agreement for the sale of real property between ___Samuel E. Seller and wife Sarah A. Seller___ hereinafter called Seller, and ___William B. Buyer and wife Mary A. Buyer___ hereinafter called Purchaser; Witnesseth, that Seller agrees to sell and convey and Purchaser agrees to purchase the real property described as follows:

2   House and lot located at No. 6 Amortization Drive, Mortgage Heights Subdivision, and being Lot No. 20 in said subdivision as recorded in Plat Book 5, Page 40, Deed Book 301, Page 64, in the office of the Register of Deeds _____ located in the City of ___Sellerstown___, County of ___Home___, State of ___Homestate___.

3   This Contract is conditional upon Seller having the ability to convey a marketable title free from encumbrances except restrictive covenants, recorded easements, zoning regulations, and ad valorem taxes which are to be prorated as of the closing date.

The purchase price for the above described property is $ ___74,000.00___ and is payable as follows:

$ ___5,000.00___ By Deposit of Earnest Money Herewith, paid by cash ( ), personal check (X), bank or certified check ( ), to be held in escrow by ___Action Realty Company___.

4   $ ___61,000.00___, by the assumption of the unpaid principal balance on the existing loan secured by a ___First Mortgage___ on the property at an interest rate of ___10___ % as of ___June 30, 19CY___, to be adjusted to the actual balance as of the date of final settlement.

$ ___5,000.00___, by a promissory note from Purchaser to Seller secured by a ___Second Purchase Money Mortgage___ on the property with interest at the rate of ___11___ % per annum payable as follows: ___$108.72 per month including principal and interest in 60 equal installments due the fifteenth (15th) day of each month. Purchaser may prepay without penalty.___

$ ___3,000.00___, the balance of the purchase price in cash at final settlement;

This contract is subject to purchaser obtaining a ___N/A___ loan in the principal amount of $ ___N/A___ for a term of ___N/A___ years, at an interest rate not exceeding ___N/A___ %. This contract will be void and deposit returned if purchaser, after making diligent efforts to obtain a firm commitment, is unable to do so no later than ___N/A___.

5   In the event that Purchaser fails to perform the covenants contained in this Contract and is in default, Purchaser waives claim to the deposit which becomes the property of the Seller. However, a forfeiture by the Purchaser shall not affect any other remedies available to Seller. If this offer is not accepted or if there is a default of this contract by the Seller, the deposit will be returned to the Purchaser; however, a return of the deposit shall not affect any other remedies available to Purchaser.

6   The risk of loss by fire or other casualty prior to final settlement shall be upon the Seller.

7   Seller warrants that the plumbing, electrical, heating, and air conditioning systems and appliances will be in good working condition on the day of final settlement.

Figure 6.3 *Offer and Contract of Sale*

Contracts and Agency

Additional Conditions

8 Seller is to pay Purchaser rent of $24.00 per day for each day after final settlement that Seller remains in possession of the property. In no event is Seller to remain in possession for more than ten days after closing. Seller to furnish Purchaser with a Certificate of Occupancy as required by the City of Sellerstown. Seller agrees to furnish Purchaser a satisfactory certificate from a licensed pest control operator that the property is free from damage or infestation by termites or other wood destroying insects.

Purchaser agrees to pay Seller for the fuel in the tank on the property as of the date of final settlement based on a measurement by an oil distributor at the price per gallon prevailing at the time of settlement.

Final settlement of this Contract to be made on or before __August 30, 19CY__

9 at a location designed by __Seller__. Deed is to be made to __William B. Buyer and wife Mary A. Buyer as tenants by the entirety__.

10 Seller to deliver possession of the property __10 days after final settlement__.

11 This offer and contract is executed in __six__ counterparts, with each executing party being provided with an executed counterpart.

__William B. Buyer__ Purchaser   __Sarah A. Seller__ Seller

__Mary A. Buyer__ Purchaser   __Samuel C. Seller__ Seller

Offer Date __August 10, 19CY__   Acceptance Date __August 11, 19CY__

__Elizabeth Ellens__   __Albert Action__
Agent/Firm As To Buyer   Agent/Firm As To Seller

__Albert Action__ acknowledges receipt of the earnest money deposit and the trust created thereby.

August 10, 19CY   Action Realty Company
Date of Deposit Receipt   Firm

                                      By: __Albert Action__
                                          Agent

Figure 6.3 *Continued*

mortgage. The amount of $61,000 was determined at the time that the listing was given to the broker. At the time of writing the offer this is the only known amount. At the time of the offer, the exact date of closing the contract is not known; and, therefore, the exact balance to be assumed by the buyer cannot be established at the time the offer is made. Therefore, the known amount of $61,000 is used with the provision that the balance will be adjusted to the actual balance on the date of the final settlement.

In the next paragraph of the financial agreement, the seller agrees to finance $5,000 of the sales price for the purchaser by accepting a second purchase money mortgage from the buyer in this amount. In this way, the seller is financing $5,000 of the difference between the $61,000 loan to be assumed and the $74,000 purchase price. Whenever a purchase money mortgage is used in a contract of sale, the annual interest rate and the method of payment should always be set forth in detail to avoid any misunderstanding between the parties in this regard.

To this point we have accounted for $71,000 of the $74,000 purchase price. Therefore, the purchaser will have a payment of $3,000 upon final settlement of the transaction.

The last paragraph of the financial portion of the contract is used when the contract is contingent upon the purchaser obtaining a new mortgage loan from a lending institution. This clause must always specify the type of loan the purchaser requires. For example, an FHA insured loan, a VA guaranteed loan, or an insured or uninsured conventional loan. The amount of the loan, the term of years, and the per annum interest rate must also be definitely specified. This clause also provides that the purchaser is to make diligent efforts to obtain a loan commitment; however, in the event that the individual is unable to obtain a commitment, the contract will be void, the purchaser completely released, and the earnest money deposit returned. It is to be noted that since this clause is not used in this particular transaction, all blank spaces contain a notation "n/a" indicating that this portion is *not applicable* for this particular contract. Spaces should never be left blank thereby leaving a possible doubt that the space should have been filled in but inadvertently was not.

Section 5 provides for the forfeiture of purchaser's deposit in the event that the purchaser fails to perform any promises as set forth in the contract. The clause also states that the fact that the purchaser has forfeited the earnest money deposit when in default and will not prevent the seller from seeking other legal remedies against the purchaser available to the seller. The clause protects the purchaser by guaranteeing the return of the earnest money deposit in the event that the offer is not accepted by the seller or if a contract is created in which the seller defaults. Other remedies in the case of default by the seller after a contract is created are not lost by the purchaser as a result of accepting the return of the deposit.

Section 6 imposes the risk of loss by fire or other casualty prior to transfer of title upon the seller. A contract should always definitely impose the risk of loss during this period on one of the parties. The seller is the logical party to bear the risk because he or she is typically the one in possession of the property and usually has insurance protection in effect in the case of loss.

Section 7 provides protection to the buyer as a result of the seller's guarantee that the various operating systems and appliances in the property will be in good working order on the day of final settlement.

Section 8 provides for additional conditions that are specifically appropriate to this particular transaction. Every offer and contract of sale form should provide sufficient space for this purpose. The inclusion of conditions, in addition to the standard conditions previously and subsequently set forth, is necessary to insure against misunderstandings by the parties regarding special circumstances surrounding a particular contract.

Section 9 provides for final settlement of the purchase and sale and specifies that the final settlement is to be made on or before August 30, 19CY. The final settlement date must always be included in the contract. By specifying that final settlement may be "on or before" a specified date, a degree of flexibility is provided for closing the transaction. In this example, if all parties are ready to close on August 20, the closing could be held at that time. It would not be necessary to wait until August 30. In the event that the final settlement date specified is not adhered to, the contract would still be enforceable by the parties for a "reasonable length of time" beyond the specified date. However, it is good practice to have the parties execute an agreement based on mutual considerations to extend the final date of settlement to "on or before" a subsequent date when it apears that the date specified cannot be adhered to. Additionally, this section names the party to designate the location of the final settlement. This section also sets forth the name of the party or parties to be named in the deed as grantee or grantees and the manner in which they will hold title. For example, the purchasers may wish to take title as tenants by the entirety, as joint tenants, or as tenants in common. Additionally, either could take title only in his or her name in severalty as separate property.

Section 10 specifies the time when the seller is to deliver possession of the property to the purchaser. In figure 6.3, the sellers are agreeing to delivery possession ten days after final settlement. If the sellers are retaining possession after final settlement, it must be determined whether or not seller is to pay purchaser rent during the time of possession after final settlement. Purchaser is entitled to rent money during this time because the title is vested in him as of the date of final settlement. The date of possession and the amount of rent, if appropriate, should never be left in doubt. These items must be clearly and specifically established at the time the contract is created and be precisely and specifically set forth in the contract.

Section 11 provides for the execution of the contract by all parties and also specifies that each executing party is to receive a copy of the contract. It should be noted that when only the purchasers have executed the document, an offer is created. When the seller's signatures also appear indicating their acceptance of the offer, a contract is created.

Other Provisions

In addition to the standard provisions and additional conditions set forth in the contract as discussed above, there are often other matters that must be taken into consideration in a particular real estate transaction and provided for in the contract. Some typical matters of this nature are as follows:

1. The contract should specify who is to pay for certain settlement expenses incurred by buyer and seller. In the case of FHA insured loans and VA guaranteed loans, the contract must set forth who is to pay the various settlement expenses and prepaid items. These matters are discussed in detail in the chapter 8, "Financing Real Estate Transactions."

2. In the event that seller wishes to prevent assignment of the contract by purchaser, he or she must specifically spell out a prohibition against assignment in the contract. In the absence of such a prohibition, the contract is assignable as discussed earlier in this chapter. If the purchaser desires the contract to be assignable and to be relieved of liability in the event of an assignment, the purchaser must provide for this release of liability in the contract.

3. In the event that a mortgage is being assumed wherein the borrower is required to maintain an escrow account with the lender for the payment of real property taxes and insurance, disposition of this escrow account must be provided for in the contract. The best method is for the assumptor of the mortgage to agree, in the contract, to purchase this escrow account on a dollar-for-dollar basis from the seller. In this way, the seller receives payment for the amount on deposit in escrow with the lender at the time of settlement and the lender transfers credit for the amount of the escrow account to the purchaser assuming the loan.

Doctrine of Specific Performance

At this point we need to have an understanding of the legal doctrine of specific performance. In the event that a party to a contract breaches the contract and thereby damages the other party, the damaged party can sue for breach of contract and obtain a judgment from the court for money damages to the extent he or she can prove financial losses.

However, the law considers each parcel of real property to be unique. Therefore, the violation of a contract involving transfer of title to real property can result in an action for specific performance by the injured party. If the seller refuses to fulfill the terms of the contract by transferring title to the buyer, the buyer can bring an action for a decree of specific performance in which the court will require the seller to specifically perform the contract and transfer title to the property to the buyer upon the payment of the agreed sales price. This is because of the uniqueness of real estate. The law considers that money damages may not satisfy the injured party. The only real satisfaction may be for the title to be transferred. This is the reason for specific performance in a contract involving transfer of title to real property as an alternative to an action for breach of contract.

CONTRACT FOR DEED

This type of agreement for the purchase and sale of real property is also known as a conditional sale contract, installment sale contract, and installment and land contract. However, the essence of this contract is that the purchaser is contracting to obtain title to the property by paying the purchase price in installments and the seller is agreeing to transfer the title to the purchaser by the delivery of a deed upon payment of the purchase price by the purchaser. Therefore, it appears to this writer that a most appropriate name for this contract is "Contract for Deed." It is both a form of sales contract and a financing instrument.

In a contract for deed, the purchaser typically makes a down payment, agrees to pay the dollar balance of the purchase price in specified installments of principal and interest. The seller's obligation under the contract is to deliver a deed and thereby convey a marketable title to the purchaser when the purchaser has paid the purchase price. The contract for deed must be in writing to be enforceable, as required by the Statute of Frauds.

The following is a discussion of each of the numbered sections of contract for deed as illustrated in figure 6.4:

Section 1 sets forth the date on which the contract was executed and the names of the purchaser and seller. Seller agrees to surrender possession and occupancy of the property to the purchaser on the date that the contract is executed. Additionally, seller agrees to sell and convey the title in fee simple by general warranty deed upon the completion by the purchaser of the terms and conditions in the contract.

Section 2 provides a description of the property.

Section 3 covers the financial terms of the contract, including the amount of down payment, the total purchase price, and the provision for the installment payments of the balance of the purchase price including principal and interest until paid in full.

Also, this section contains the forfeiture clause providing for forfeiture by the purchaser to the seller in the event that a payment becomes overdue and unpaid for sixty days. As a result of the forfeiture, the purchaser forfeits to the seller all payments already made toward the purchase price. These forfeited payments are retained by the seller as due or accumulated rent. Upon forfeiture, the agreement becomes a rental contract providing for a monthly rental payment payable by the seller on the first day of each month. Additionally, the seller is granted the right of reentry and possession of the property in the event that the purchaser fails to make the monthly rental payments.

Section 4 requires the purchaser to pay all real property taxes and assessments starting with the tax year following the year in which the contract is executed. The contract could also provide for the prorating of taxes and any assessments for the year in which the contract was created. This section requires the purchaser to keep the property insured against fire and storm in a specified amount (typically at least 80 percent of value) and also requires the purchaser to maintain the buildings in a proper state of repair and preservation.

Section 5 contains a provision against assignment without the written agreement of all parties to the contract. However, in the event that written agreement is obtained, the contract provides that the assignment will be binding upon the assignee and his or her heirs, thereby relieving the assignor (original party to the contract) of further liability.

Section 6 provides for the execution of the contract by purchaser and seller under seal.

Section 7 contains an acknowledgement of execution of the contract by all parties thereto. The acknowledgement is necessary to make the contract eligible for recording in the county where the property is located. The recording provides constructive notice to all the world of the existence of the obligation between the parties.

Contracts and Agency

This Contract for Deed, executed this __11__ day of __August__, 19 __CY__, by and between __William B. Buyer and wife Mary A. Buyer__, hereinafter called Purchaser and __Samuel E. Seller and wife Sarah A. Seller__, hereinafter called Seller; Witnesseth that Seller agrees to surrender possession and
1 occupancy of the real property described below to Purchaser at the time of execution of this contract by all parties hereto. Seller additionally agrees to sell and convey title in fee simple to the real property described below to Purchaser free from encumbrances except restrictive covenants, recorded easements and zoning regulations, by good and sufficient __General Warranty__ deed upon the completion by Purchaser of the terms and conditions hereinafter set forth.

House and lot located at Number 6 Amortization Drive, Mortgage Heights Subdivision, Sellerstown, Homestate, and being Lot No. 20 in said subdivision as recorded
2 in Plat Book 5, Page 40, Deed Book 301, Page 64, in the office of the Register of Deeds in Home County, Homestate.

Purchaser has deposited with Seller the sum of $ __10,000.00__, the receipt of which is acknowledged by Seller, to be applied to the payment of the purchase price of $ __74,000.00__. The balance of the purchase price to be paid by Purchaser in equal monthly installments of $ __881.61__ including principal and interest at the rate of __11__ % per annum on the unpaid balance until paid in full. If any one
3 of said payments or any part thereof be overdue and unpaid for __60__ days, this Contract for Deed shall be forfeited and terminated within __15__ days after receipt by the Purchaser of the declaration of intent to forfeit and terminate by the Seller by registered mail, and the Purchaser shall forfeit all payments made on this Contract, and such payments shall be retained by the Seller as due or accumulated rent on the property, and the Purchaser shall become liable to the Seller for monthly rental of $ __882.00__ due and payable on the first day of each month. In the event of nonpayment of such rent, the Seller shall have the right to re-enter and take possession of the premises.

The Purchaser agrees to pay all real property taxes and assessments when due starting
4 with the tax year of 19 __NY*__; to keep the property insured against loss by fire and storm in the amount of $ __67,000.00__, and to keep the buildings in a proper state of repair and preservation.

This Contract may not be assigned without the written agreement of all parties hereto.
5 In the event that this contract is assigned by agreement as provided, this Contract will be binding on the Assignee and his heirs.

IN WITNESS WHEREOF, the parties have hereunto set their hands and seals the day and year first above written.

Figure 6.4 *Contract for Deed*

William B. Buyer (SEAL) _Sarah A. Seller_ (SEAL)
Purchaser   Seller

Mary A. Buyer (SEAL) _Samuel E. Seller_ (SEAL)
6 Purchaser   Seller

STATE OF ____Homestate____ , ____Home____ COUNTY.

I, ____Elizabeth Hedger____ , a notary public of said county, do certify that ____William B. Buyer and wife Mary A. Buyer____ , Purchaser and ____Samuel E. Seller and wife Sarah A. Seller____ , Seller, personally

7 appeared before me this day and acknowledged the execution of the foregoing Contract.

Witness my hand and notarial seal this __11__ day of __August__, 19 __CY__ . My Commission expires: __October 9__ , 19 __CY__

Elizabeth Hedger N.P. (SEAL)

(Notary Seal)

STATE OF ____Homestate____ , ____Home____ COUNTY.

The foregoing Certificate of ____Elizabeth Hedger____ is certified to be
8 correct. This instrument was presented for registration this __11__ day of __August__ , 19 __CY__ at __2:12__ XXX., p.m. and duly recorded in the office of the Register of Deeds of ____Home____ County, in Book __306__ Page __88__ .

Richard T. Recorder   by _Druella Dotson_
Register of Deeds   Assistant, Deputy Register of Deeds

*NY means next year.

Figure 6.4 *Continued*

Section 8 contains the certificate that the acknowledgement is correct; the date and exact time when the contract was filed for recordation; and the book and page number wherein the contract is recorded.

Even though this type of contract originally came into existence to provide for the purchase and sale of small and relatively inexpensive parcels of vacant land, there is no reason that it cannot be used as an agreement to purchase and sell improved property. It can be an especially useful tool in times of extremely high interest rates and/or unavailability of mortgage loans. If the property to be purchased under the contract is encumbered by a mortgage, the purchaser could agree in the contract to take title "subject to" such existing mortgage.

Caution should be observed in instances where the mortgage contains a "due on sale" clause. These clauses specify that the entire principal balance due on the mortgage must be paid if a sale of the property is effected. In some situations, the lending institution holding the mortgage may declare the contract for deed to be a sale of property and thereby require the mortgage to be paid off by the seller.

Consultation with legal counsel prior to the creation of the contract for deed is necessary for the protection of all parties. This is especially important if the property is encumbered by a mortgage containing a due on sale clause. In all cases where the property being purchased under a contract for deed is encumbered by a mortgage, the contract must specify that either the seller is to pay off the remaining principal balance due at the time of conveyance of title or provide for the assumption of the mortgage balance at that time by the purchaser.

Option to Purchase

An option is a contract wherein a property owner (optionor) sells a right to purchase his or her property to a prospective buyer (optionee). The price paid for the option is not escrow money or earnest money or binder, but is money paid for the right to purchase the property at the price specified in the option contract provided the optionee exercises his or her right within the time period set forth in the option. Therefore, the option money is paid directly to the property owner and is retained by that individual as agreed in the option contract. Usually a broker does not receive a commission for negotiating an option, but will be paid a commission as agreed in the listing contract if the option is exercised and the property sold.

So we see in figure 6.5 that our optionees are purchasing a right to buy the property under the terms and conditions set forth in the option contract. Once the optionees have paid for the option they have no further obligation under the contract. They have the right to exercise their option and purchase the property, but they are not required to do so.

However, the option is binding upon the optionor. The optionor is obligated to convey the title to the property if the option is exercised and the purchase price paid as agreed in the contract. Once the option is exercised, it becomes a contract of sale and is therefore binding on both buyer and seller as is the case in any sales contract.

The following is a discussion of each of the numbered sections of the option to purchase illustrated in figure 6.5.

Section 1 sets forth the date the option is granted, the names of optionor and optionee described as seller and purchaser, and a recital of the consideration paid for the option.

Section 2 provides a legal description of the optioned property by the government rectangular survey system for property description (discussed elsewhere in the text under the heading "Property Descriptions").

Section 3 contains the time period that the option is binding upon the seller. This section also sets forth the purchase price for the property and the manner in which it is to be paid in the event that the option is exercised.

Section 4 specifies the manner in which the option is to be exercised by the purchaser (optionee). This section also reinforces the optionor's right to retain the option money in the event that the option is not exercised within the time limit.

Section 5 establishes the date of final settlement in the event that the option is exercised and requires the seller to convey a marketable title free from the usual encumbrances. Also, in this section, the purchaser is given possession of the property on the date of final settlement.

Section 6 sets forth an additional or special condition for this particular transaction guaranteeing that the seller will convey an easement

This option to purchase is granted this __14__ day of __February__,
1 19 __CY__, by __Samuel E. Seller et ux Sarah A. Seller__, hereinafter
called Seller, __William B. Buyer et ux Mary A. Buyer__, hereinafter called
Purchaser. Seller for consideration of $__1,200.00__ paid by Purchaser, grants
to Purchaser the exclusive right to purchase the real property described as follows:
__Northwest 1/4, of Northwest 1/4, Section 10, Township 2 North, Range 3 East of__
2 __the Michigan Meridian, Home County, State of Homestate.__

This option shall be binding upon the Seller from this date until noon,
__April 14__, 19 __CY__. The purchase price for the above described property shall be $ __40,000.00__ and is paid as follows:
3 $ __1,200.00__ consideration as stated above and paid Seller for this option.
$ __8,800.00__ cash at closing and delivery of deed. $ __N/A__
by the assumption of a present mortgage on the property as of __N/A__,
to be adjusted to the balance as of the date of closing. $ __30,000.00__ by a
promissory note from Purchaser to Seller secured by a __First Deed of Trust__
on said property payable as follows:
In equal monthly installments of $396.46 including interest at 10% per
annum beginning on the first day of June 19CY

This option shall be exercised by written notice to the Seller and signed by the
Purchaser within the time limit set forth above. Should the Purchaser not exercise this
4 option within the time limit, the consideration for this option in the amount of
$ __1,200.00__ will be retained by the Seller.

Should the Purchaser exercise this option as provided, final settlement is to be
made on or before __May 14, 19CY__. Seller to convey a marketable title free
from encumbrances except restrictive covenants, recorded easements, zoning regula-
5 tions, and ad valorem taxes which are to be prorated as of the closing date. Possession
of the property to be given Purchaser on __date of final settlement__.

Additional Conditions

Seller warrants the conveyance of title to Purchaser will include
the conveyance of an easement 15 feet in width over Seller's adjoining
6 land for access by the Purchaser to and from the public road identified
as Highway 222.

This Contract contains the entire agreement between the parties.

Purchaser __Mary A Buyer__   Seller __Sarah A Seller__

7

Purchaser __William B. Buyer__   Seller __Samuel E. Seller__

Figure 6.5 Option to Purchase

Contracts and Agency

for access to and from the specified public road.

Section 7 contains the execution of the option to purchase by buyer and seller.

Following the option to purchase contract figure 6.6 illustrates the exercise of option document for this particular transaction. The option contract and the exercise of option must be in writing as required by the Statute of Frauds.

Lease Contracts

As discussed in chapter 5, "Property Ownership and Interests," the non-freehold estates are leasehold estates, namely estates for years, estates from year-to-year or periodic tenancies, estates at will, and estates at sufferance.

The most important of these is the estate for years. This estate is created by a lease contract that specifies a definite period of time for the existence of the estate. The lease automatically terminates upon the date specified in the contract without notice by either party. The following is a discussion of lease contracts including the requirements for validity, rights of the parties, various terms and conditions, types of leases, and the manner in which leases may be terminated.

Requirements for Validity

The lease, creating an estate for years, must be for a definite period of time. If there is any indefiniteness or vagueness regarding this matter, the contract will not create a lease in the form of an estate for years but will create a periodic tenancy or estate from year to year. A definite time period creates a lease in the form of an estate for years even though the period may be for only three months, six months, or even less.

In most states the lease creating an estate for years must be in writing if the lease term is more than one year. Statutes in some states specify this requirement for writing to be in effect if the lease is for more than three years. If a written lease is required by statute, the lease must be recorded in the county where the property is located to protect the lessee against purchasers of the property from the lessor. If a lease required by statute to be in writing is not recorded, a purchaser of the property is not required to honor the lease. However, if the lease is of short duration and therefore does not have to be in writing, the fact that the lessee is in possession of the property at the time of a sale by the lessor will protect the

_____ April 10_____, 19 CY

To Samuel E. Seller et ux Sarah A. Seller :

This is to notify you that pursuant to the option executed by us on the __14__ day of __February__, 19 __CY__, we hereby give notice that we elect to exercise said option to purchase the real property described therein in accordance with the terms and conditions agreed upon.

William B. Buyer
Optionee

Mary A. Buyer
Optionee

Figure 6.6 *Exercise of Option*

lessee and thereby require the purchaser to honor the lease for the remainder of the term.

The parties to the lease contract must be legally competent to contract as is required for the creation of a valid contract. For validity the lease must contain a recital of consideration as is required for validity of any type of contract. The consideration is the conveying of the leasehold estate to the lessee by the lessor and the agreement on the part of the lessee to pay the specified rent to the lessor. As with other contracts, the lease must be for a legal purpose. If the lease is created for the purpose of permitting the lessee to use the property in a manner that is illegal, the lease will not be valid.

In essence, the lease contract must meet all requirements for validity for contracts in general and in addition must meet certain special requirements as discussed above.

Rights of the Parties

A lease is both a contract and an estate in land. Under the contract, the lessor and lessee have specific rights as agreed to in the contract. The real property right in the lessee is the estate for years, which provides the lessee with the exclusive right of possession and control of the property during the lease term. Since the lessor retains the title to the property during the lease term, the lessor has the right of possession of the property upon the termination of the lease.

Under the lease contract, the lessor is entitled to receive the rent agreed upon and the lessee is obligated to make timely payments. The lessor must keep the property suitable for occupancy by the lessee. The lessee is obligated to return the property at the end of the lease in good condition, reasonable wear and tear excepted. The lessee is entitled to remove trade fixtures upon termination of the lease. The lessee is not entitled to make alterations in the property without the consent of the lessor or specific authorization in the contract. The lessee may only use the property for the purposes agreed to by the lessor in the lease contract.

In the absence of a specific prohibition against an assignment of the lease or subleasing the premises, the lessee is entitled to assign the lease to another or sublet to another. An assignment transfers the lessee's entire interest in the lease without providing for any reversion of interest to the lessee. For example, if the lessee has a remaining term of ten years in a lease and transfers the right to possession of the entire remaining ten-year term to another, an assignment is created. However, if the lessee transfers only six years of the remaining ten-year term to another, this is a sublease or subletting of the premises.

Subletting has the effect of creating a new lease wherein the original lessee becomes a lessor and the subtenant the lessee. This new lease is called a "sandwich lease." The new leasehold interest is sandwiched in between the original lessor and the sublessee.

The lease may contain a "right of first refusal" clause. This provides the lessee with the right to be offered the opportunity to purchase the property before it is offered to anyone else during the term of the lease contract.

The lease contract may include an option to renew for the lessee at the end of the lease term, or even a series of renewal options that may be exercised by the lessee at the end of each of several lease terms created by the exercise of options to renew.

Lease Contents

Lease contracts must contain the following:

1. The names of lessor and lessee.
2. A description of the leased premises.
3. The specific term of the lease, including a beginning and ending date.
4. A recital of consideration, the payment of rent by the lessee and the giving of the use of the property by the lessor.
5. The purposes for which the leased premises may be used by the lessee.
6. Any particular provisions agreed upon between lessee and lessor, such as right of entry by lessor for inspection purposes; right of lessee to make alterations; option to purchase; option to renew; or agreement by lessee to participate in the payment of real property taxes, property insurance, utilities, maintenance, and similar expenses.
7. The execution of the lease by lessor and lessee. Execution by lessor is essential. It is preferable that lessee also execute. The date of execution must also be specified.

8. As a practical matter the lease should always be in writing regardless of its duration. It is essential for validity that the lease be in writing if it exceeds the statutory period for verbal leases in a given state.
9. The contract must be acknowledged and recorded if the lease is required to be in writing for protection of lessee.
10. The lease must be delivered to and accepted by the lessee.

Types of Leases

Fixed

Types of leases are named according to the basis for establishing the amount of rent to be paid by the lessee. The basic type of lease is one in which the rental amount remains the same for each rental period over the entire lease term. This type of lease is called a fixed, flat, straight, or gross lease. Lessor pays all the expenses for the operation and maintenance of the property in addition to taxes and mortgage interest and principal.

Graduated

A graduated lease is one in which the rental amount changes from period to period over the lease term. The change in rental amount is specified in the lease contract. For example, a lease may be at $300 per month for the first year, $350 per month the second year, and $400 per month the third year.

Escalated

An escalated lease provides for rental changes in proportion to the changes in the lessor's costs of ownership and operation of the property. As changes occur in the lessor's obligations for real property taxes and operating expenses, the lease will change in specified proportions.

Index

An index lease is one in which the rental amount is changed in proportion to changes in the Consumer Price Index (CPI) published by the United States Department of Labor. The lease will specify a percentage change in relation to the number of points the CPI changes annually.

Reappraisal

A reappraisal lease is one in which changes in rental amount are based on changes in property value as demonstrated by periodic reappraisals of the property. Such appraisals may occur at three-or five-year intervals in the case of a long-term lease. The rent changes a specified percentage of the previous year's rent as spelled out in the contract.

Percentage

Many commercial leases are percentage leases. The rent in a percentage lease includes a fairly low fixed amount of rent per month plus an additional monthly rent which is a percentage of the lessee's gross sales. The majority of commercial leases are percentage leases in cases where the lessee is using the property to conduct a retail business. This is especially true of shopping malls. The percentage lease provides the lessor with a guaranteed monthly rental plus the opportunity to participate in the sales volume of the lessee on a percentage basis.

Net Lease

In a net lease, the lessee agrees to pay, in addition to the fixed rental, all costs and expenses associated with the property. These costs and expenses include such things as real estate taxes and assessments, maintenance, insurance, and utilities. As a result of these payments by the lessee, the rental income is a net income to the lessor.

Ground Lease

This is a lease of unimproved land. The ground lease normally contains a provision that a building will be constructed on the land by the lessee. The lease should always contain a provision as to the disposition of the improvements on the land constructed by the lessee at the end of the lease term. In the absence of a provision as to the disposition of the improvements at the end of the lease term, the improvements will automatically belong to the lessor as owner of the land. The ground lease is a long-term lease because the lessee must have sufficient time to recoup any costs and earn a profit during the term of the lease.

Sale and Leaseback

A sale and leaseback is a transaction wherein a property owner sells a property to an investor and in the sales contract the investor agrees to immediately lease the property back to the seller. This type of transaction is usually used by an owner of business property wishing to free up capital invested in the real estate and still retain possession of the property under a lease.

Termination of Leases

Leases may be terminated in the following ways: expiration of the lease term, agreement of lessor and lessee, breach of condition, condemnation, actual eviction, and constructive eviction.

Expiration of Lease Term

As previously noted, a lease creating an estate for years automatically terminates upon the expiration of the lease term. No notice is required by the lessor to the lessee or vice versa.

Agreement of the Parties

A lease, as other executory contracts, may be terminated by the mutual agreement of the parties. The release by each party of the other provides the consideration for the agreement to terminate.

Breach of Condition

If either the lessor or lessee fails to conform to the conditions set forth in the lease contract, the lease may be terminated. Examples of conditions usually imposed upon a lessee are: requirement to pay rent on a timely basis, adherence to the permitted use specified, and requirement to keep the property in good condition. Conditions commonly imposed on the lessor include the following examples: make repairs or furnish specified services, make the property available and suitable for occupancy within a reasonable period of time after the start of the lease term, and provide appropriate utility services.

Condemnation

A lease may be terminated by condemnation under the power of eminent domain. If the entire property is condemned, the lessee is entitled to compensation from the lessor for the remaining value of his or her leasehold interest. If only a part of the leased property is condemned, the lease may provide a lessee with the option to terminate the lease or to remain in possession of the remainder of the premises at a reduced rent.

Actual Eviction

If the lessee fails to adhere to the conditions of the lease, the lessor has the right to reenter and take possession of the property. In the event that the lessee fails to surrender possession upon demand, the lessor may resort to legal action to evict the tenant after giving the tenant sufficient notice before filing the suit. If the lessee does not surrender possession voluntarily after the lessor has been awarded a judgment for possession by the court, the lessee may be forcibly removed by an officer of the court.

Constructive Eviction

Constructive eviction results from some action or inaction by the lessor that renders the premises unsuitable for the use agreed to in the lease contract. For example, if the lease obligates the lessor to provide heat, water, and electricity, and the lessor fails to do so through personal fault or negligence, the lessee is entitled to abandon the premises, terminate the lease, and sue for damages.

SUMMARY

Contracts play an extremely important and essential role in the real estate business. One or more contracts are involved in every real estate transaction. Therefore, it is essential that real estate agents have a knowledge of the law of contracts.

To be adequately prepared for license examinations and entry into the real estate business, students must have a good knowledge of the fundamentals of contract law as discussed and a good and thorough understanding of the typical contracts involved in real estate transactions. Also of special importance is the agency relationship created by the listing contract and the responsibilities placed on real estate agents to their principals, and to the buying public with whom they are dealing.

Even though real estate agents are not authorized by law to "draw" contracts, most states permit the use of contract forms drawn by attorneys. In using these prepared forms, the real estate agent is filling in blank spaces provided and inserting appropriate additional conditions. The real estate agent must understand the meaning of all the contract clauses in the form being used as well as the effect of additional conditions.

IMPORTANT POINTS

1. A contract is an agreement between competent parties, upon legal consideration, to do or abstain from doing some legal act.

2. Bilateral contracts are based on mutual promises. Unilateral contracts are based on a promise by one party and an act by another party.

3. The requirements for contract validity are: (1) competent parties, (2) mutual assent, (3) offer and acceptance, (4) consideration, (5) and legality of object.

4. An offer must not be indefinite or illusory.

5. An offer may be revoked by the offeror at any time prior to acceptance.

6. A contract is created by the unconditional acceptance of a valid offer. Acceptance of bilateral offers must be communicated. Communication of the acceptance of unilateral offers results from the performance of an act by the promisee.

7. Mutual assent is defeated and a contract made voidable by (1) misrepresentation, (2) fraud, (3) undue influence, or (4) duress.

8. Contracts are assignable in the absence of a specific prohibition against assignment in the contract.

9. The statute of frauds requires that certain contracts be in writing to be enforceable. Included are contracts for the sale of interests in real property.

10. A listing contract is one in which a property owner employs a broker to find a buyer for his or her property. The contract creates an agency relationship wherein the seller is the principal and the broker is the special or limited agent of the seller.

11. An agent is a fiduciary and, therefore, has the following obligations to the principal: (1) loyalty, (2) obedience of all instructions, (3) professionalism and lack of negligence, (4) accounting for all money or property, and (5) information.

12. Even though a real estate agent does not represent the buyer in the typical real estate transaction, the real estate agent must represent the property honestly, fairly, and accurately to all prospective buyers.

13. The types of listing contracts are: (1) open, (2) exclusive agency, and (3) exclusive right to sell.

14. If a contracting party defaults in the performance of contractual obligations, then the injured party may sue for damages in a suit for breach of contract. If the contract is one for the purchase and sale of real property then an alternate remedy in the form of a suit for specific performance is available to the injured party.

15. A contract for deed is also called an installment land contract, conditional sale contract, or land contract. It is a contract of sale and a method of financing by the seller for the buyer. Title does not pass until all or some specified part of the purchase price is paid by the buyer.

16. An option provides a right to purchase property under specified terms and conditions. During the option term, the contract is binding on the optionor but not the optionee. When an option is exercised it becomes a contract of sale and is, therefore, binding on both parties.

17. A lease is created by contract and, therefore, the parties each have contractual rights and obligations as well as real property rights and obligations.

18. The transfer of the entire remaining term of a lease by the lessee is an assignment. A transfer of part of the lease term with a reversion to the lessee is a subletting.

19. A lease contract must be executed by the lessor and delivered to and accepted by the lessee.

20. The various types of leases are indentified according to the basis for establishing the amount of rent.

21. Leases are terminated by (1) expiration of lease term, (2) mutual agreement, (3) breach of condition, (4) condemnation, (5) actual eviction, or (6) constructive eviction.

IMPORTANT TERMINOLOGY

Acceptance
Accord and Satisfaction
Accounting for Funds
Actual Eviction
Agent
Assignee
Assignment
Assignor
Avoid
Bilateral Contract
Breach of Contract
Carry Over Clause
Commission Entitlement
Competent
Complete Performance
Conditional
Consideration
Constructive Eviction
Consumate
Contract
Contract for Deed
Cul-De-Sac
Damages
Date of Possession
Disclosure of Information

Duress
Earnest Money Deposit
Escalated Lease
Exclusive Agency
Exclusive Right to Sell
Executed Contract
Executory Contract
Exercise of Option
Express Contract
Final Settlement
Fixed Lease
Flat Lease
Forfeiture Clause
Fraud
Graduated Lease
Gross Lease
Ground Lease
Implied Contract
Impossibility of Performance
Index Lease
Instructions
Installment Land Contract
Land Contract
Lease
Legality of Object

Contracts and Agency

Lessee
Lessor
Listing Contract
Loyalty
Misrepresentation
Multiple Listing
Mutual Agreement
Mutual Assent
Net Lease
Net Listing
Novation
Offer
Offer and Contract of Sale
Open Listing
Option
Option to Renew
Percentage Lease
Principal

Ready, Willing, and Able
Real Consent
Re-appraisal Lease
Revoke
Right of First Refusal Clause
Sale and Leaseback
Specific Performance
Statute of Frauds
Straight Lease
Sublease
Subletting
Undisclosed Principal
Undue Influence
Unilateral Contract
Valid
Void
Voidable

REVIEW QUESTIONS FOR CHAPTER 6

1. A contract in which each party promises something to the other party or parties is which of the following?

    (a) Multilateral
    (b) Unilateral
    (c) Bilateral
    (d) Promissory

2. Of the following statements regarding voidable contracts, which is (are) correct?
    I. A voidable contract may be avoided by one or more parties.
    II. A voidable contract may be legally consumated by the parties.

    (a) I only
    (b) II only
    (c) both I and II
    (d) neither I nor II

3. All of the elements listed are essential for contract validity EXCEPT

    (a) Competent parties
    (b) Offer and acceptance
    (c) Legality of object
    (d) Undue influence

4. A false representation is deemed to be fraudulent when
    I. The party making a false representation knows it to be false.
    II. The party making a false representation does not know if the statement is true or false, but should have known.

    (a) I only
    (b) II only
    (c) both I and II
    (d) neither I nor II

5. The basis of duress is which of the following?

    (a) Fear
    (b) Mistake
    (c) Indefiniteness
    (d) Illusion

6. Which of the following is (are) examples of mutual promises providing consideration for a bilateral contract?
    I. A promise to pay a legal debt.
    II. A promise to make a contribution to a charity.

    (a) I only
    (b) II only
    (c) both I and II
    (d) neither I nor II

7. A contract to sell real property may be terminated by all of the following EXCEPT

    (a) Complete performance
    (b) Death
    (c) Mutual agreement
    (d) Breach of contract

8. Which of the following has the effect of terminating contracts?

    (a) Consideration
    (b) Bankruptcy
    (c) Exercise
    (d) Assignment

9. A contract in which a property owner employs a broker to market the property creates an agency relationship between which of the following?

    (a) Buyer and seller
    (b) Buyer and broker
    (c) Broker and seller
    (d) Broker, seller, and buyer

10. An agent's duties to the principal include all of the following EXCEPT

    (a) Loyalty
    (b) Accountability
    (c) Obedience
    (d) Misrepresentation

11. Which of the following is (are) agency relationships?
    I. The relationship between a sales associate and the broker with whom the associate is associated.
    II. The relationship between a listing broker and a cooperating broker participating in marketing the listed property.

    (a) I only
    (b) II only
    (c) both I and II
    (d) neither I nor II

12. An agreement between a broker and a property owner wherein the owner employs the broker to market the owner's property and agrees to pay the broker a percentage of the sales price if the property is sold by anyone during the specified time period of the broker's employment is which of the following?

    (a) Exclusive right to sell listing
    (b) Net listing
    (c) Exclusive agency listing
    (d) Open listing

13. A real estate salesperson presented an offer to the property owner during the listing term for the listed price payable in cash with no contingencies and a 10 percent earnest money deposit. In this situation, which of the following statements is (are) correct?
    I. The property owner is not required to accept the offer.
    II. The listing brokerage company is legally entitled to the commission agreed upon in listing contract.

    (a) I only
    (b) II only
    (c) both I and II
    (d) neither I nor II

14. The clause in a listing contract that protects the broker's commission entitlement beyond the listing term in the event of a sale of the property by the owner to a prospect that was interested in the property by the listing firm or its agents is called which of the following?

    (a) Forfeiture clause
    (b) Carry-over clause
    (c) Settlement clause
    (d) Exclusive right clause

Contracts and Agency

15. When an offer is contingent upon the buyer obtaining a new first mortgage loan, which of the following provisions is (are) necessary for the protection of the parties?
    I. A requirement that the buyer make diligent efforts to obtain a loan commitment.
    II. Detailed specifications regarding the loan upon which the contract is contingent.

    (a) I only
    (b) II only
    (c) both I and II
    (d) neither I nor II

16. All of the following should always be present in offers and contracts of sale EXCEPT

    (a) Date of final settlement
    (b) Date possession will be given purchaser
    (c) Date of commission payment
    (d) Date of contract inception

17. In the event that a seller defaults in his or her obligation to convey title to the purchase as agreed in a contract of sale, which of the following remedies is (are) available to the purchaser?
    I. Suit for breach of contract
    II. Suit for specific performance

    (a) I only
    (b) II only
    (c) both I and II
    (d) neither I nor II

18. Which of the following most accurately describes an agreement wherein a property owner agrees to convey title to the property when another party satisfies all obligations agreed to in the contract?

    (a) Lease contract
    (b) Listing contract
    (c) Legal contract
    (d) Land contract

19. During the term of an option, which of the following is (are) correct?
    I. The option is binding upon the optionee.
    II. The option is not binding upon the optionor.

    (a) I only
    (b) II only
    (c) both I and II
    (d) neither I nor II

20. When a party purchases an option the optionee is purchasing which of the following?

    (a) Right
    (b) Title
    (c) Land
    (d) Exercise

21. Which of the following describe(s) the situation existing after an option is exercised?
    I. The option is converted into a contract of sale.
    II. The contract is now binding upon all parites to the contract.

    (a) I only
    (b) II only
    (c) both I and II
    (d) neither I nor II

22. All of the following are requirements of options EXCEPT

    (a) Options must be in writing to be enforceable.
    (b) Options must contain a description of the property.
    (c) Options must be exercised.
    (d) Options must contain a recital of consideration.

23. Which of the following is (are) correct statements regarding the real property and contractural rights of the lessor and lessee as created by a lease contract?
    I. The lessee has the exclusive right to possession and control of the leased premises during the term of the lease.
    II. The lessor retains the title to the leased premises during the term of the lease and has the right to regain possession upon the termination of the lease.

    (a) I only
    (b) II only
    (c) both I and II
    (d) neither I nor II

24. All of the following are typical provisions that may be found in lease contracts creating an estate for years EXCEPT
    (a) Provision for a term of indefinite duration
    (b) Right of first refusal
    (c) Right to make alterations
    (d) Option to renew

25. A transaction in which a lessee transfers the remainder of a lease term without reversion is which of the following?
    (a) Assignment
    (b) Option to renew
    (c) Sandwich lease
    (d) Sublease

26. A lease in which the rental amount is changed a specified percentage of the changes in consumer prices is which of the following?
    (a) Percentage
    (b) Index
    (c) Escalated
    (d) Graduated

27. A transaction in which a property owner sells the property and leases it from the purchaser is described as which of the following?
    (a) Option to renew
    (b) Sales and leaseback
    (c) Ground lease
    (d) Sublease

28. A lease may be terminated by all of the following EXCEPT
    (a) Constructive eviction
    (b) Condemnation
    (c) Breach of condition
    (d) Right of first refusal

29. Upon the receipt of a buyer's offer, the seller accepted all of the terms of the offer except the amount of earnest money, which the seller agreed to accept an amount 50 percent higher than the buyer had offered. This fact was promptly communicated to the offeree by the real estate agent. Which of the following most accurately describes these events?
    (a) The communication created a bilateral contract.
    (b) The seller accepted the buyer's offer.
    (c) The seller conditionally rejected the buyer's offer.
    (d) The seller rejected the buyer's offer and made a new offer or counter offer to the buyer.

30. A real estate agent advised a buyer that a property was zoned for commercial use of the type the buyer intended to make of the property. In reliance upon the agent's advice, the buyer contracted to purchase the property. In making the statement regarding the zoning, the agent did not know what zoning applied to the property. The buyer subsequently learned that the zoning was such that he could not use the property as he intended. Which of the following is (are) correct?
    I. The agent committed an act of misrepresentation and is liable to the buyer for any loss the buyer suffered as a consequence.
    II. Since the agent did not know the true facts regarding the zoning, no misrepresentation of the property to the buyer took place and therefore the agent is not liable.

    (a) I only
    (b) II only
    (c) both I and II
    (d) neither I nor II

Transfer of Title to Real Property

7

The transfer of a title to real property is described in law as alienation. The property owner is alienated or separated from the title by transfer of the title to another. The alienation may be voluntary or involuntary and may occur during life or after death.

INVOLUNTARY ALIENATION DURING LIFE

During life, title to real property may be transferred by involuntary alienation as a result of a lien foreclosure sale, adverse possession, or condemnation under the power of eminent domain.

Lien Foreclosure Sale

In chapter 5 we discussed the fact that real property may be sold at public auction to satisfy a specific or general lien against the property. These foreclosure sales are without the consent of the property owner who incurred the debt resulting in a lien. Foreclosure sales are ordered by a court and title is conveyed to a purchaser at the sale by judicial deed. A judicial deed is executed by the official authorized by the court to conduct the sale and transfer the title. In these cases, titles are typically conveyed by a sheriff's deed, trustee's deed, commissioner's deed, etc., generally without the participation of the property owner who lost the title as the result of the foreclosure.

Adverse Possession

Title to real property may be obtained without the consent of the owner by adverse possession. Title to the occupied property may be obtained by the occupant if the following conditions are met.

1. The possession or occupation must be open and well known to others (notorious).
2. The possession of the property must be under color of title or claim of title. That is, the occupant of the property must have some reasonable basis to believe that he or she is entitled to possession of the property. This basis is typically in the form of a defective deed or a quit claim deed.
3. The possession must be without the permission of the true owner and must be exclusive (not shared with the true owner).
4. The possession must be continuous and uninterrupted for a period specified by statute in the state where the property is located. The states provide by statute a shorter period of time if possession is under "color of title" than when possession is under a "claim of title". A claim of title occurs when possession is based on some type of claim against the land rather than based on some written document as in the case of color of title. Statutory requirements vary from state to state. However, the period may be as short as five to seven years under color of title and as long as twenty-one years without color of title.

The adverse possessor does not automatically acquire title to the property by merely meeting the four requirements just listed. To perfect the claim and obtain a title to the property, the claimant must satisfy the court that he or she has fulfilled the requirements of the adverse possession statute in the particular state by suit to "quiet title." If the court is satisfied that the statutory requirements have been met, then the court will award the title to the claimant under adverse possession.

Condemnation Under Eminent Domain

The federal government, states and their agencies, counties, cities, towns, and boroughs have the power of eminent domain. This power provides the right to take private property for public use. The taking of the property under the power of eminent domain is called condemnation. The property is condemned under eminent domain. The property that is condemned must be for the use and benefit of the general public. The property owner must be compensated for the fair market value of the property lost through condemnation. The condemning authority must use due process of law (that is, adequately notify the property owner of the condemnation) and the property owner must have the right to appeal the value of the property as established by the condemning authority through the court system. However, the property owner cannot prevent the condemnation and, therefore, the loss of title is involuntary.

INVOLUNTARY ALIENATION AFTER DEATH

If a person dies and leaves a valid will, the individual's property will be distributed to heirs according to the terms of the will. In the absence of a will, property is distributed to heirs by descent according to the state statute enacted for this purpose. These statutes are called intestate succession statutes because a person who has died without leaving a valid will has died intestate. Escheat occurs when there is no one eligible to receive the property of the intestate as provided by statute. If a diligent search fails to reveal qualified heirs as specified by the statute, the property escheats to the state. This means that in the absence of heirs the state takes title to the property of the deceased. Since the deceased has no control over the transfer of title to the state this results in an involuntary alienation after death. This is the only form of involuntary alienation after death.

VOLUNTARY ALIENATION AFTER DEATH

Voluntary alienation after death occurs as a result of a valid will or in the absence of a valid will with qualified heirs existing to receive title to the property.

If a person dies and leaves a valid will, he or she is said to have died testate. The deceased is called a testator if a man and testatrix if a woman. A person appointed in a will to carry out the provisions of the will is called an executor or executrix. Probate is the judicial determination of the validity of a will by a court of competent jurisdiction. A gift of real property by will is a devise and the recipient is a devisee. A gift of personal property by will is a bequest and the recipient is the beneficiary.

In the absence of a valid will, the property of the deceased is distributed by descent according to the provisions of the interstate succession statute. The person appointed by a court to distribute the property of an intestate according to the provisions of the statute is called an administrator or administratrix.

VOLUNTARY ALIENATION DURING LIFE

This is the type of alienation that is of primary importance to the real estate business. Voluntary alienation, or transfer of title during life, is accomplished by the delivery of a valid deed by the grantor to the grantee during the life of both of them. The contract of sale for real property is consumated by the delivery of a valid deed by the grantor to the grantee as required in the contract.

Essential Elements of a Valid Deed

The following is a discussion of the various requirements necessary for the creation of a valid deed and the conveyance of title.

Writing

The deed must be in writing. As required by the statute of frauds, every deed must be written. A verbal conveyance is ineffective. The written form of the deed must meet the legal requirements of the state in which the property is located.

Grantor  Owner

The grantor (one conveying the title) must be legally competent, that is, the individual must have the capacity to contract. This is the same requirement that exists for all parties to a valid contract. The grantor must have reached the age of majority and must be mentally competent at the time of deed execution. Also, the grantor must be named with a certainty. It must be possible to positively identify the grantor.

A corporation may receive, hold, and convey title to real property in the corporate name. Therefore, a corporation may be a grantor. If the conveyance of title by the corporation is in the ordinary course of business of the corporation, the deed may be executed on behalf of the corporation by the corporate president or vice president and countersigned by the secretary or assistant secretary. If the transfer of title is not in the ordinary course of business of the corporation, there must be an authorization for the conveyance by resolution by the board of directors of the corporation authorizing the transfer of title. When the resolution has been made, the signatures, of the individuals discussed above are sufficient.

Under the Uniform Partnership Act adopted by practically every state, a partnership may receive, hold, and convey title to real property in the partnership name, in the name of an individual general partner, or in the name of a trustee acting for the partnership for this purpose.

From the foregoing it can be seen that title to real property may be held in an assumed name; and if title is in an assumed name, it can be transferred under that name. Examples are titles in the name of a corporation or partnership. The names of these organizations have been created or adopted by the people who formed the organization to identify the organization. Just as organizations may assume a name for the purpose of receiving, holding, and conveying title to real property, so can an individual. Although title may be held and transferred in an assumed name, title may not be held or transferred in the name of a fictitious person or organization. The person or organization must actually exist.

Grantees  Buyer

It is not necessary that grantees have legal capacity. Therefore, a minor or mental incompetent can receive and hold title to real property. However, these people cannot convey title on their own since they are not qualified to be grantors. Therefore, to effect a conveyance of title held in the name of an incompetent there must be a guardian's deed executed by the incompetent's guardian as grantor. The conveyance by the guardian may only be accomplished with the approval of the court.

Grantees must be named with a certainty. It must be possible to identify the grantee. The grantee must actually exist and be either a natural person or an artificial person, such as a corporation or partnership. The grantee must be alive at the time of the delivery of the deed. A dead person cannot be a grantee.

Property Description

The deed must contain an adequate legal description of the property. The various methods of describing property are metes and bounds, government survey system, and description by reference. These various descriptions, and the jurisdictions wherein they are used, are discussed in detail later in this chapter.

Consideration

A technical requirement for deed validity is that it contain a recital of consideration paid by the grantee to the grantor. It is not necessary that the recital of consideration contain the actual price paid for the property. Typically, the recital of consideration will be a statement that the consideration is "$10.00 and other good and valuable consideration the receipt of which is hereby acknowledged by the grantor." Such a recital of consideration will satisfy the technical requirement for deed validity. In the event that the conveyance is by deed of gift, such as a gift of real property by a parent to a child, the recital of consideration will typically be "for love and affection."

Words of Conveyance

The deed must contain words demonstrating that it is the grantor's intention to transfer the title to the named grantee. These words of conveyance are contained in the granting clause. Typical wording is "as given, granted, bargained, sold, and conveyed" in the case of warranty deeds.

In addition to the granting clause the deed must also contain an habendum clause. This clause describes the estate granted and must always be in agreement with the granting clause. The habendum clause begins with the words, "to have and to hold." A typical habendum clause appearing in a deed conveying a fee simple title will read, "to have and to hold the above described premises, with all the appurtances thereunto belonging, or in anywise appertaining, unto the grantee, his heirs, and or successors and assigns forever." By contrast, the habendum clause in a deed conveying a life estate will read "to have and to hold the premises herein granted unto the grantee for and during the term of the remainder of the natural life of the herein named grantee."

Also if the property is being sold subject to specific encumbrances, these encumbrances may be set forth in the habendum clause. Examples of typical encumbrances accepted by the grantee are the lien of an existing mortgage being assumed by the grantee, recorded easements existing in the property, and restrictive covenants.

Execution

The deed must be signed by each grantor conveying an interest in the property. Notice, only the grantors execute the deed. The grantee does not sign. In a minority of states, proper execution includes execution under seal. In these states the word seal in parenthesis must appear at the end of the signature line provided for each grantor. Sometimes the letters LS (*locus sigilli*) follow the grantor's signature rather than the word seal. *Locus sigilli* means "the place of the seal." The deed will not convey the title unless properly executed by the grantors.

Witnessing

A few states require that the grantor's signature be witnessed on the deed by one or more witnesses for the deed to be valid. Among the states requiring witnesses are Alaska, Connecticut, Florida, Georgia, Maryland, Ohio, South Carolina, and Texas.

Acknowledgement

For a deed to be eligible for recording it must be acknowledged. The grantor must appear before a public officer who is eligible to take an acknowledgement, such as a notary public, and state that the signing of the deed was done by him or her and was a voluntary act. A deed will be perfectly valid between the grantor and grantee without an acknowledgement. However, without the acknowledgement the deed cannot be recorded by the grantee and thereby provide the grantee protection of title against subsequent creditors or purchasers of the same property from the same grantor who record their deed. Therefore, the grantee should always insist upon receiving a deed that has been acknowledged.

Delivery and Acceptance

To effect a transfer of title by deed there must be a delivery of a valid deed by the grantor to the grantee, and the deed must be accepted by the grantee. Delivery may be made directly to the grantee or to an agent of the grantee. The agent for this purpose will typically be the grantee's attorney, his or her real estate broker, or the lending institution providing the mortgage loan to finance the purchase of the property. In almost every case there is a presumption of acceptance by the grantee. This presumption is especially strong if the deed has been recorded and the conveyance is beneficial to the grantee.

Transfer of Title to Real Property

In some states all of the activities necessary to prepare for a closing or final settlement of a real estate transaction are performed by title companies or escrow companies. These companies also are in charge of the final settlement. In these situations the grantor deposits the deed with the escrow company to be delivered to the grantee when the grantee has fulfilled the obligations in the sales contract. The title passes from the grantor to the grantee when the deed is delivered to the grantee by the escrow company.

Recording

As previously discussed, a deed is eligible for recording on the public record when the grantor has acknowledged the execution of the deed and this acknowledgement appears in the deed. The purpose and benefit of recording the deed is to protect the grantee's title. This protection is provided by constructive notice. All the world is bound by knowledge of the existence of the conveyance of title and the fact that the title is now vested in the grantee.

Constructive notice is contrasted with actual notice. Constructive notice is binding on everyone though they have not actually read the deed as recorded. The result of the constructive notice provided by recording is to protect the title in the grantee. This protection is against everyone including other purchasers of the same property from the same grantor.

Figure 7.1 illustrates the possible effect of the failure of the grantee to record a deed and the protection provided to a grantee who does record a deed.

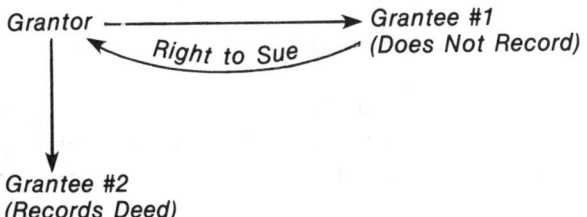

Figure 7.1 *The Possible Effects of Failure to Record a Deed*

As you can see in Figure 7.1, there was an effective transfer of title from Grantor to Grantee #1. However, the title in Grantee #1 has been defeated by the person's failure to record the deed and the subsequent conveyance of the same title by the Grantor to Grantee #2 who recorded the deed. Grantee #2 now holds the title and Grantee #1 has a right to sue Grantor to get his or her money back. This right may be worthwhile provided Grantor can be found and has money or property. To create the result described, Grantee #2 must be a bonafide purchaser for value. The individual must be completely unaware of the prior conveyance to Grantee #1 and he or she must have paid fair market value for the property.

In summary, figure 7.1 illustrates that a valid conveyance of title can exist between grantor and grantee without the deed being recorded. However, the deed must be recorded to protect grantee's title from third parties, such as purchasers from the grantor, subsequent creditors, or other lien holders of the grantor.

TORRENS SYSTEM There exists in some states a special form of recording called the Torrens System of title recordation. This system is available in California, Hawaii, Illinois, Massachusetts, Minnesota, New York, North Carolina, Ohio, Oregon, Georgia, Utah, South Dakota, and Virginia. Of these states Massachusetts, Hawaii, and Illinois are actively using the Torrens System. Also, in these states the regular method of recording titles is still used.

Under the Torrens System the title holder applies to the court to have the property registered. The court has the title examined by official title examiners who report the examination results to the court. If the results of the examination are satisfactory, the court issues instructions to the Register of Titles to record the title and issues Certificates of Registration of title after giving adequate public notice to provide an opportunity to anyone contesting the title to appear.

The Certificate of Registration of title contains the type of title that the applicant has and sets forth any encumbrances against the title. One certificate is issued to the Register of Titles and the other to the title holder who applied for registration of the title. The Certificate of Registration provides conclusive evidence of the validity of the title and it cannot be contested except for fraud. Title to properties recorded under the Torrens System cannot be obtained by adverse possession.

TYPES OF DEEDS

There are variations in types of deeds resulting from the different forms of warranty of title contained in the deed and variations based on a special purpose for which the deed is drawn. The following is a discussion of the various types of deeds both by type of warranty and special purpose.

General Warranty Deed

The general warranty deed contains the strongest and broadest form of guarantee of title of any type of deed and therefore provides the greatest protection to the grantee. The general warranty deed usually contains six covenants as discussed following.

1. Covenant of Seisin
   Typical wording of this covenant is, "grantor covenants that he is seised of said premises in fee." This covenant like the others in the general warranty deed is a specific covenant and provides an assurance to the grantee that the grantor holds the title which he or she specifies in the deed that he or she is conveying to the grantee. In the example cited, the grantor promises the grantee that he or she has fee simple title to the property.
2. Covenant of Right to Convey
   This covenant usually follows the covenant of seisin in the general warranty deed and typically reads, "and has the right to convey the same in fee simple." By this covenant the grantor provides an assurance to the grantee that the grantor has legal capacity to convey the title and also has the title to convey.
3. Covenant against Encumbrances
   This covenant will typically state, "that said premises are free from encumbrances (with the exceptions above stated, if any)." The grantor is assuring the grantee that there are no encumbrances against the title except those set forth in the deed itself. Typical encumbrances that are acceptable to grantees are the encumbrances of a lien of a mortgage when grantee is assuming grantor's existing mortgage, recorded easements, and restrictive covenants.
4. Covenant of Quiet Enjoyment
   This covenant may typically read, "the grantee, his or her heirs and assigns, shall quietly and peaceably have, hold, use, possess, and enjoy the premises." This covenant is an assurance by the grantor to the grantee that the grantee shall have a quiet possession and enjoyment of the property being conveyed and that the grantee will not be disturbed in the use and enjoyment of the property because of a defect in the title being conveyed by the grantor. In warranty deeds not containing a specific covenant of quiet enjoyment, the covenant of warranty itself assures the grantee of quiet enjoyment of the property.
5. Covenant for Further Assurances
   This covenant may typically read, "that he or she (grantor) will execute such further assurances as may be reasonable or necessary to perfect the title in the grantee." This covenant requires the grantor to perform any acts necessary to correct a defect that may exist in the title that is being conveyed and to correct any errors or any deficiencies that may exist in the deed itself.
6. Covenant of Warranty
   The warranty of title in the general warranty deed will provide that the grantor "will warrant and defend the title to the grantee against the lawful claims of all persons whomsoever." This is the best form of warranty for protection of the grantee and contains no limitations as to possible claimants protected against, since the grantor specifies that he or she will defend the title against "the lawful claims of all persons whomsoever." The covenant of warranty is the most important of all the covenants.

Grantee's Rights to Recovery

If the Covenant of Seisin or the Covenant of Warranty is broken, a grantee may recover from the seller any financial loss up to the price paid for the property. If the covenant against encumbrances is broken, the grantee may recover from the grantor any expense incurred to pay off the encumbrance. The amount that the grantee may recover in this case is also limited to the price paid for the property.

The Covenant of Quiet Enjoyment is not considered to be broken unless the grantee is actually dispossessed of the property. The mere threat or assertion of a claim by another party

State of _____
County of _____

This Indenture, made this _____ day of _____
by and between _____
hereinafter called Grantors, and _____
_____ hereinafter called Grantees whose address is
_____

(said designations shall include the respective parties, whether one or more, individual or corporate, and their respective successors in interest or assigns).

Witnesseth; That the Grantors, for and in consideration of the sum of Ten Dollars, and other good and valuable considerations to them in hand paid by the Grantees, the receipt whereof is hereby acknowledged, have given, granted, bargained, sold and conveyed, and by these presents do give, grant, bargain, sell, convey and confirm unto the Grantees their heirs and/or successors and assigns (subject, however, to any conditions, restrictions, limitations, reservations or exceptions appearing after the description below), the following particularly described real estate located in _____ County, _____ , to-wit:

To Have and to Hold the above described land and premises, with all the appurtenances thereunto belonging, or in any wise appertaining, unto the Grantees, their heirs and/or successors and assigns forever.

And the Grantors covenant to and with the Grantees, their heirs and/or successors and assigns, that the Grantors are lawfully seized in fee simple of said land and premises, and have full right and power to convey the same to the Grantees in fee simple, and that said land and premises are free from any and all encumbrances (with the exceptions above stated, if any), and that they will and their heirs, executors, administrators and/or successors shall forever warrant and defend the title to the said land and premises, with the appurtenances, unto the Grantees, their heirs and/or successors and assigns, against the lawful claims of all persons whomsoever.

In Witness Whereof, the Grantors have hereunto set their hands and seals, or, if corporate, has caused this Deed to be executed by its duly authorized officers and its seal to be hereunto affixed, the day and year first above written.

_____ (SEAL)   _____ (SEAL)

_____ (SEAL)   _____ (SEAL)

Figure 7.2 *General Warranty Deed*

State of _____, County of _____

I, _____, a Notary Public of said State and County, do hereby certify that
_____ personally appeared before me this day and acknowledged the due execution of the foregoing instrument.

Witness my hand and Notarial Seal, this _____ day of _____, 19_____.

My commission expires: _____, Notary Public.

State of _____ County of _____

I, _____, a Notary Public of said State and County, do hereby certify that
_____ personally appeared before me this day and acknowledged the due execution of the foregoing instrument.

Witness my hand and Notarial Seal, this _____ day of _____, 19_____

My commission expires: _____, Notary Public.

State of _____, County of _____

I, a Notary Public of said State and County, certify that _____

personally came before me this day and acknowledged that _____ he is _____

Secretary of _____ a corporation, and that, by authority duly given and as the act of the corporation, the foregoing instrument was signed in its name by its _____ President, sealed with its corporate seal, and attested by _____ self as its _____ Secretary.

Witness my hand and Notarial Seal, this _____ day of _____, 19_____

My commission expires: _____, Notary Public.

State of _____, County of _____

Each of the foregoing certificates, namely of _____
_____
_____
a notary or Notaries public of the State and County designated is certified to be correct.

This _____ day of _____, 19_____.

WILLIAM E. DIGGES
Register of Deeds, _____ County

By: _____, Deputy

Filed for registration on the _____ day of _____, 19_____ at _____ M.

WILLIAM E. DIGGES
Register of Deeds, _____ County

By: _____ Deputy

Figure 7.3 *General Warranty Deed (cont.)*

to some right in the property does not constitute a breach of the Covenant of Quiet Enjoyment. In the case of a dispossession, the grantee may recover from the grantee an amount up to the price paid for the property.

The Covenant for Further Assurances is not broken until it becomes necessary for the grantee to execute some instrument to perfect the grantee's title. Also the Covenant of Quiet Enjoyment and the Covenant of Warranty are not broken until the grantee is actually evicted from the property by someone holding a superior title.

Special Warranty Deed

In this type of deed, the warranty is limited to claims against the title arising out of the period of ownership of the grantor. Therefore, the warranty only goes back in time to the date when the grantor acquired the title as contrasted with the general warranty deed wherein the warranty is against defects in the title going back for an unlimited period of time.

Quit Claim Deed

Sale without Warranties

The quit claim deed contains no warranties whatsoever. It is simply a deed of release. It will release or convey to the grantee any interest, including title, that the grantor may have. However, the grantor does not state in the deed that he or she has any title or interest in the property. Execution of the quit claim deed by the grantor prevents the grantor from asserting any claim against the title at any time in the future.

Quit claim deeds may be used to clear a "cloud on a title." This terminology is used to describe the situation that exists when someone has a possible claim against a title. As long as this possibility exists the title is cloudy and therefore not a good and marketable title. To remove this cloud and create a good and marketable title, the possible claimant executes a quit claim deed as grantor to the true title holder as grantee. The granting clause in a quit claim deed will contain the words "remise, release, and quit claim" instead of "grant, bargain, sell, and convey," as used in warranty deeds.

Grant Deed

This is a special form of statutory deed used in western states where warranty deeds are rarely used. The warranties, rather than being expressly set forth in the deed, are implied from the state statute. These implied warranties include a warranty against encumbrances created by the grantor or anyone claiming title under him or her and a warranty that the grantor has not previously conveyed the same title to anyone else. The form of an individual grant deed is the simplest form of all the various types of deeds as can be seen by the example of an individual grant deed shown in figure 7.4.

Deed of Confirmation

This deed is also called a deed of correction and is used when a deed contains an error that requires correction. Examples of the types of errors that are corrected by this type of deed are errors in the names of the parties, errors in the property description, and mistakes made in execution of the deed.

Deed of Release

The primary use of this type of deed is to release a title from the lien of a mortgage when the debt secured by the mortgage has been paid in full, or in the case of a blanket mortgage, to release individual parcels of land from the lien of the blanket mortgage. A deed of release is also used to release a dower right in property.

Deed of Surrender

This type of deed is used by a life tenant to convey his or her estate to the reversionary interest or to the remainder interest, depending on the form of the life estate. This same result may be accomplished by the use of a quit claim deed.

Bargain and Sale Deed

This form of deed may be with or without covenants of warranty. However, in either case, there is an implied covenant on the part of the grantor that he or she has a substantial

FOR A VALUABLE CONSIDERATION, receipt of which is hereby acknowledged,

hereby GRANT(S) to

the following described real property in the

County of _____, State of _____

Dated _____

STATE OF _____ } SS.
COUNTY OF _____
On _____ before me, the undersigned, a Notary Public in and for said State, personally appeared _____
_____
_____
, _____ know to me to be the person _____ whose name _____ subscribed to the within instrument and acknowleded that _____ executed the same, WITNESS my hand and official seal.

NOTARIAL SEAL

Signature _____

Figure 7.4 *Individual Grant Deed*

title and possession of the property. Grantees in these deeds, for their protection, should require that the deed contain certain specific warranties, such as the warranty against encumbrances.

Deed of Gift

A gift of real property may be made by either general warranty deed or by quit claim deed. However, if the warranty deed is used, the warranties cannot be enforced against the grantor by the grantee because the grantor has received no compensation for conveying the title to the grantee since the conveyance is a gift. Either a warranty deed or a quit claim deed will convey the property provided the grantor has title to convey.

Judicial Deeds

The execution of these deeds results from a court order to the official executing the deed. The various types of judicial deeds receive their name from the title of the official executing the deed. The various names of these deeds include sheriff's deed, (referee's deed in foreclosure in some states), tax deed, guardian's deed, commissioner's deed (referee's deed in partition in some states), executor's deed, and administrator's deed.

Title Transfer Taxes

Approximately thirty-seven states impose a tax on the conveyance of title to real property. The name of the tax varies from state to state. Examples are real estate excise tax, documentary stamps, real estate transfer tax, and deed tax stamps. State statutes usually require the tax to be paid by the seller. The amount of tax is based on the consideration received by the seller in the sale of the property.

Some states exclude from tax the amount of a mortgage being assumed by the buyer in the transaction and impose a tax on the difference between the amount of the mortgage assumed and the purchase price. Students of real estate should determine if their state imposes such a tax, the tax rate, and the basis for applying the tax.

TITLE EXAMINATION

Regardless of the warranties set forth in a deed, the grantee should always retain the services of an attorney to conduct an examination of the public record to ascertain if in fact the grantee is receiving a good and marketable title free from encumbrances except those he or she has agreed to accept. The purpose of a title examination is to determine the quality of a title. It must always be performed by an attorney because only an attorney can give a legal opinion as to the quality of a title.

The title search consists of an examination of all the public records possibly affecting a title to real estate. The examiner establishes a chain of title, which must be unbroken for the title to be good, by tracing the successive conveyances of title on a consecutive basis starting with the current deed and going back an appropriate period of time, typically forty to sixty years. Additionally, the examiner searches all other public records, such as records of liens, restrictive covenants, easements, and any other recordings or documents possibly affecting the title.

Upon the completion of the title examination the examiner, in some states, provides an abstract of title, which is a condensed history of the title setting forth a summary of all links in the chain of title and any other matters of public record affecting the title. The abstract contains a legal description of the property and summarizes every instrument in chronological order that relates to the title being examined. An abstract continuation is an update of an abstract of title by memorandum of a new transfer of title. When the abstract is completed by the seller's attorney, it must be examined by the attorney for the purchaser for the preparation of his or her opinion of the title.

In states not requiring abstracts, the examining attorney provides a Certificate of Title Opinion, which sets forth the legal description of the property, a statement that the records have been carefully examined, the period of time covered by the examination, specific information about any liens or other encumbrances against the title, and the examiner's opinion of the quality of the title.

In cases of titles registered under the Torrens System, the Certificate of Title Opinion is not necessary because the Certificate of Title issued by the Register of Titles contains all of the current information regarding the property. Under this system, liens are not valid until they have been entered on the title certificate by the registrar. However, certain types of liens, such as tax and special assessment liens and liens of federal courts, are not required to be registered and therefore an examination of these records must be made. This examination and the results can be obtained from the register of titles under the Torrens System.

TITLE INSURANCE

It should be borne in mind that a title examination is only concerned with recorded documents appearing on the public record. Circumstances affecting the property that are not a part of the public record are not covered. Therefore, even though a title examination indicates that a title is good and marketable, this may not actually be the case.

To protect against a financial loss, the grantee may wish to take advantage of the protection afforded by a title insurance policy. The policy requires the title insurance company to compensate the insured for financial loss, up to the face amount of the policy, resulting from a title defect. The policy also requires the insurance company to defend against claims, including taking any action necessary to protect the title. The policy protects the insured against any title defect existing at the time that the insured received the title.

The policy will only be issued as the result of an acceptable abstract or title opinion. A title that is acceptable to the title insurance company is called an insurable title. The premium paid for a title insurance policy is a one-time premium paid at the time that the policy is placed in effect. There are three forms of title insurance policies as discussed following.

Owner's Policy

The owner's policy is for the protection of the owner and is written for the amount that the owner paid for the property. The amount of coverage remains the same for the life of the policy. The policy remains in effect for the duration of the insured's ownership of the property and continues in effect after the death of the owner to benefit heirs receiving an interest in the property.

Mortgagee's Policy

This policy only protects the mortgagee. Under the terms of the policy, the mortgagee is insured against defects in the title pledged as security in the mortgage. The mortgagee's insurable interest is only to the extent of the outstanding loan balance at any given time. Therefore, the mortgagee's policy decreases in face amount as the loan principal decreases but always provides coverage equivalent to the amount of the loan balance.

Leasehold Policy

This policy is written to protect a lessee (leaseholder) and/or a mortgagee against defects in the lessor's title. This policy is issued to a mortgagee in cases where the mortgagor has pledged a leasehold interest instead of a fee simple title as security for the mortgage debt.

PROPERTY DESCRIPTIONS

There are three types of property descriptions. These are metes and bounds, description by reference, and the government rectangular survey system.

Metes and Bounds

The property description used in the thirteen states that were the original thirteen colonies is the metes and bounds description. The metes and bounds description is also used in those states in which the primary description is the government rectangular survey system. In those states, the metes and bounds type of description is used to describe small, irregular land areas.

In the metes and bounds description, the *metes* are the distances from point to point in the description and the *bounds* are the directions from one point to another in the description.

A metes and bounds description is made from a survey performed by a licensed, registered land surveyor. One of the most important aspects of the metes and bounds description is the selection of the point of beginning. This point should be one that is reasonably easy to

Transfer of Title to Real Property

locate and that is well established. The surveyor, after starting at the point of beginning, sights the direction to the next point or monument. A "monument" may be a tree, or a rock, or an artificial boundary such as a road or a concrete marker. The directions in the metes and bounds description might read "north 45° east." There may be a further refinement of the direction. Degrees are divided into minutes, with 1 degree containing 60 minutes, and each minute divided into 60 seconds. A description, then, might read: "north 45°, 30', 10 sec. east." These bearings are illustrated in figure 7.5.

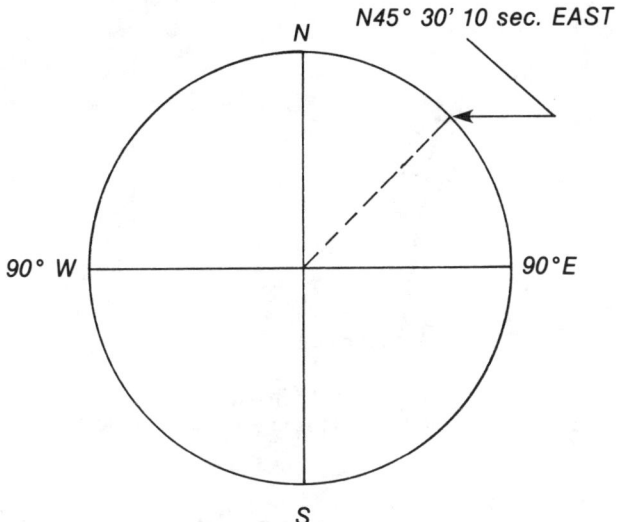

Figure 7.5

An example of a typical metes and bounds description and the plat resulting from that description follow.

*Being all of Lot No. 20 of the subdivision of a portion of the property of Mortgage Heights Land Company, Inc., as shown by plat thereof prepared by Worley and Gray, Consulting Engineers, dated October 1, 1965, and recorded in Book 5, page 40, Records of Plats for Buncombe County, and more particularly bounded and described as follows:

**BEGINNING on a stake in the northeast margin of Amortization Drive, south corner of Lot No. 20 of the subdivision or a portion of the property of Mortgage Heights Land Company, Inc., and runs thence North 6° 18' East 215.2 feet to a stake; thence North 8° 49' West 241.0 feet to a stake, common corner of Lot Nos. 20 and 19 of said subdivision; thence with the dividing line between said Lot Nos. 19 and 20, South 87° 50' West 138.5 feet to a stake in the east margin of a cul-de-sac; thence with the east margin of said cul-de-sac in a southwesterly direction along a curve with the radius of 50.0 feet, 61.2 feet to a stake in said margin; thence with the east margin of a drive leading to Amortization Drive, South 5° 19' West 132.8 feet to a stake in the point of intersection of said margin of said drive with Amortization Drive; thence with the northeast margin of said Amortization Drive, South 51° 17' East 84.7 feet to a stake in said margin; thence still with said margin of said drive, South 42° 27' East 47.2 feet to a stake in said margin; thence still said margin of said drive, South 29° 36' East 199.9 feet to the BEGINNING.*

---

*Description by Reference
**Description by Metes and Bounds

Description by Reference

A description by reference is a valid legal description. Sometimes an attorney will incorporate into the deed a description by reference in addition to a metes and bounds description. Sometimes the description by reference will be the only description in the deed.

A description by reference may be one in which a reference is made to a plat and lot number that has been recorded. The description would state the plat book number and page number in which the plat, or map, is recorded. The reader can refer to the plat and determine the exact location and dimensions of the property. Two examples of subdivision plats are shown in figures 7.6 and 7.7.

Sometimes a property will be described by reference to a previous deed that conveyed the same property. This reference incorporates the description in the previous deed by reference into the deed being prepared. If the description in the previous deed is accurate, all is well and good. However, if the description in the previous deed was faulty, the subsequent deed is still bound by that description.

Often a description will also contain a statement as to the number of acres or quantity of land being conveyed. In the event that this

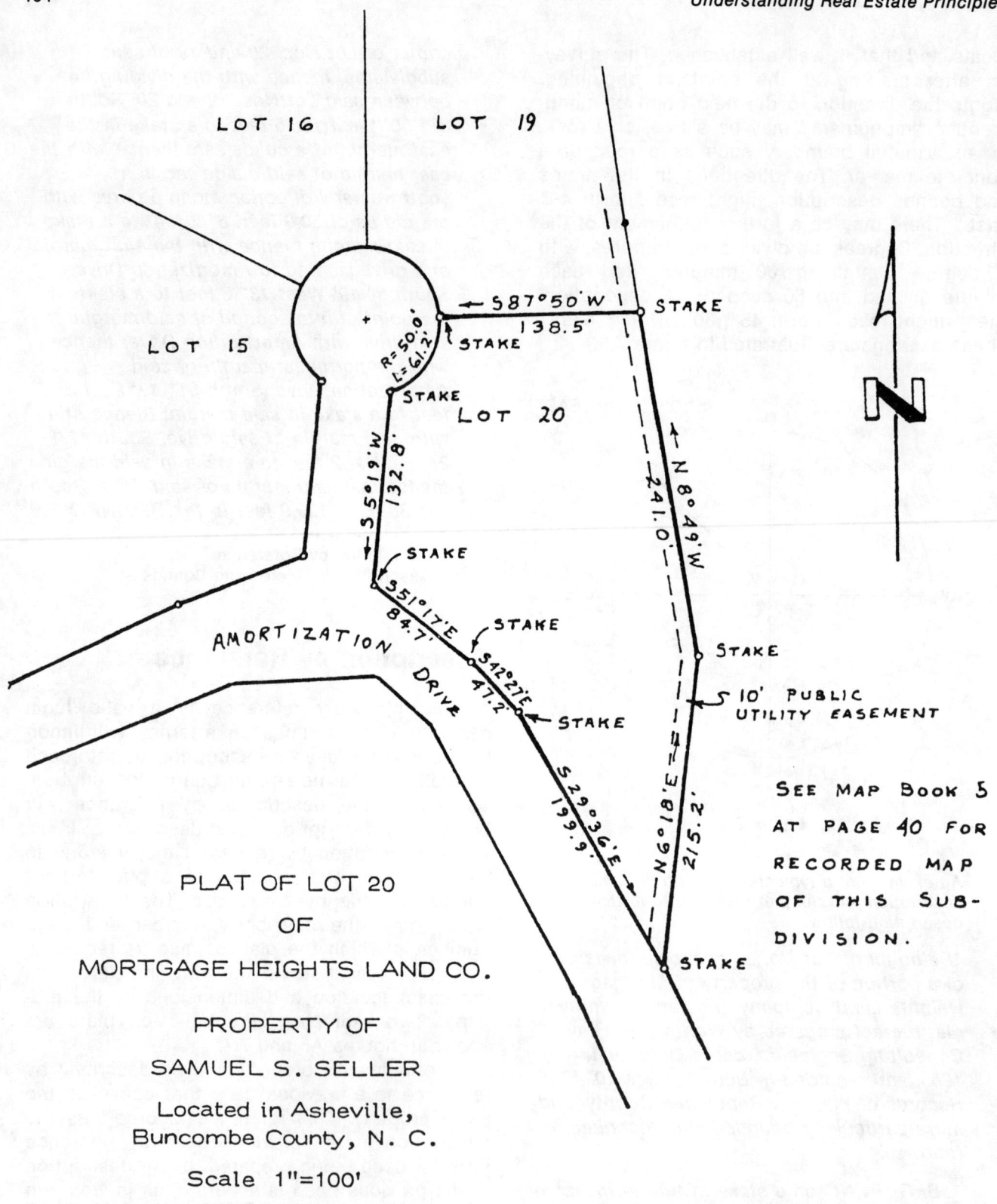

Figure 7.6

Transfer of Title to Real Property

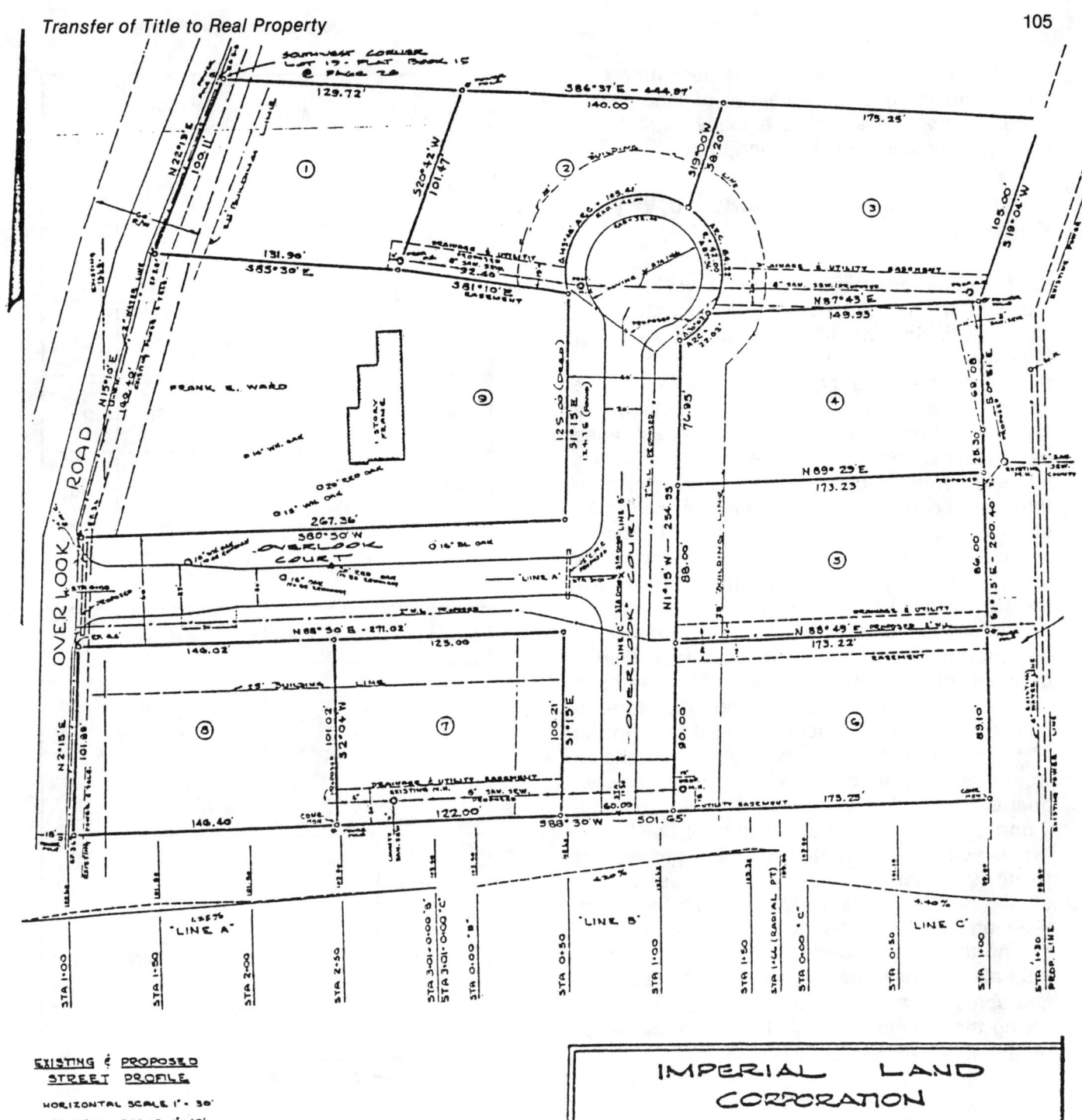

Figure 7.7

quantity is inconsistent with the description by metes and bounds, the quantity of land yields to the number of acres as actually established by the metes and bounds description.

Government Rectangular Survey System

In the government rectangular survey system, the country is divided by north-south lines called "principal meridians," and by east-west lines called "base" lines. The areas between the base lines and north-south meridians are called "ranges." Within the ranges, there are townships. Each township is a square, six miles by six miles, and is, therefore, thirty-six square miles in area. Each township is divided into thirty-six sections. Each section is one mile square, or one square mile. Figure 7.8 illustrates a township. As can be seen, the township is divided into thirty-six sections. Notice the manner in which the sections are numbered.

A section is divided into quarter-sections and may be subdivided into areas less than a quarter-section. Notice in figure 7.9 that each section contains 640 acres and, therefore, a quarter-section is 160 acres. A legal description of the southwest quarter of the section shown would read as follows: "All of the southwest quarter of section 25, range 1 east, township 1 north, Huntsville meridian and base line."

If you are confronted with the problem of trying to determine how many acres are included in a legal description such as the northwest one-fourth of the northwest one-fourth of the northwest one-fourth of section 25, simply multiply the fractions and multiply the result by 640 acres. In this example, the result of multiplying the fractions is 1/64. 1/64 times 640 acres results in an answer of 10 acres.

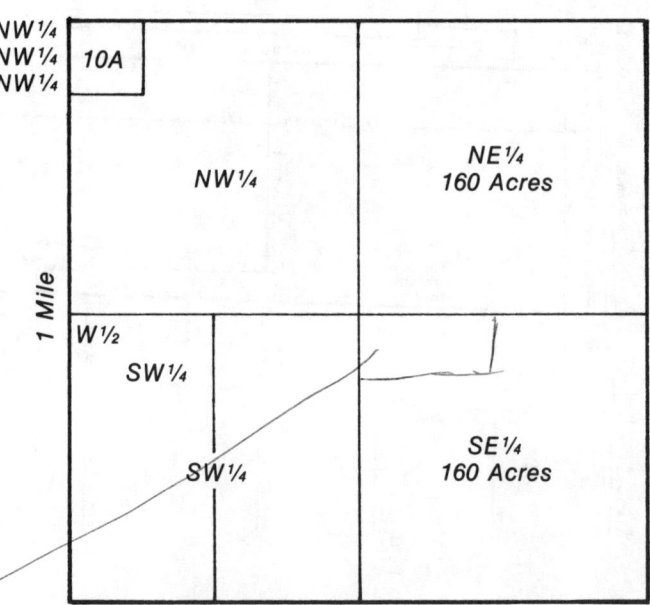

Figure 7.8 Township

Figure 7.9 Section 25 (640 Acres)

Transfer of Title to Real Property

IMPORTANT POINTS

1. Transfer of title is alienation. Involuntary alienation occurs during life as a result of adverse possession, lien foreclosure sale, and condemnation under the power of eminent domain. Involuntary alienation after death is escheat. Voluntary alienation after death is by will or descent. Voluntary alienation during life can occur only by delivery of a valid deed.

2. The requirements for deed validity are: (1) the deed must be written, (2) the grantor must be competent, (3) the competency of the grantees is not required, (4) the grantor and grantee must be named with a certainty, (5) adequate property description, (6) recital of consideration, (7) words of conveyance, (8) habendum clause, (9) proper execution by grantor, (10) witnessing (in some states), and (11) delivery and acceptance must occur to convey title.

3. To be eligible for recording on the public record a deed must be acknowledged. Recording protects the grantee's title against creditors of the grantor and subsequent conveyances by the grantor.

4. A general warranty is the strongest and broadest form of title guarantee. The general warranty deed typically contains six covenants; these are: seisin, right to convey, against encumbrances, quiet enjoyment, for further assurances, and warranty.

5. A quit claim deed is a deed of release and contains no warranties. It will convey any interest the grantor may have. The primary use of the quit claim deed is to remove a cloud from a title.

6. Other types of deeds are: (1) special warranty, (2) grant, (3) confirmation, (4) release, (5) surrender, (6) bargain and sale, (7) gift, and (8) judicial.

7. The purpose of a title examination is to determine the quality of a title. The examination must be made by an attorney. Only an attorney can legally give an opinion as to the quality of a title.

8. A title insurance policy protects the insured against a financial loss caused by a title defect. The three types of policies are: owner's, mortgagee's, and leasehold.

9. The three methods of property description in use in the United States are metes and bounds, reference, and rectangular survey.

IMPORTANT TERMINOLOGY

Abstract
Abstract Continuation
Acknowledgement
Administrator
Adverse Possession
Alienation
Base Line
Bargain and Sale Deed
Beneficiary
Bequest
Bona Fide Purchaser
Certificate of Title Opinion
Chain of Title
Constructive Notice
Covenant Against Encumbrances
Covenant for Further Assurances
Covenant of Quiet Enjoyment
Covenant of Right to Convey
Covenant of Seisin
Covenant of Warranty
Deed
Deed of Confirmation
Deed of Gift
Deed of Release
Deed of Surrender
Descent
Delivery and Acceptance
Description by Reference
Devise
Devisee
Execution
Executor

General Warranty Deed
Grant Deed
Grantee
Granting Clause
Grantor
Habendum Clause
Indenture
Intestate
Involuntary Alienation
Judicial Deed
Leasehold Policy
Lien Foreclosure Sale
Links in Chain of Title
Metes and Bounds
Mortgagee's Policy
Owner's Policy
Plat
Principal Meridian
Probate
Property Description

Quarter Section
Quit Claim Deed
Range
Recording
Rectangular Survey System
Section
Special Warranty Deed
Suit to Quiet Title
Testate
Testator
Title Examination
Title Insurance
Title Transfer Taxes
Torrens System
Township
Voluntary Alienation
Will
Witnessing
Words of Conveyance

REVIEW QUESTIONS FOR CHAPTER 7

1. Voluntary alienation may occur by which of the following?

    (a) Condemnation
    (b) Descent
    (c) Escheat
    (d) Adverse possession

2. Voluntary alienation during life may only occur in which of the following ways?

    (a) Will
    (b) Foreclosure sale
    (c) Deed delivery
    (d) Devise

3. Essential elements of a valid deed include all of the following EXCEPT

    (a) Acknowledgement
    (b) Writing
    (c) Competent Grantor
    (d) Execution by grantor

4. The purpose of a deed being acknowledged is to

    (a) Make the deed valid.
    (b) Make the deed eligible for delivery.
    (c) Make the deed eligible for recording.
    (d) Identify the grantee to a certainty.

5. The type of notice provided by recording is which of the following?

    (a) Actual
    (b) Reasonable
    (c) Protective
    (d) Constructive

6. Of the following types of deeds, which provides the grantee with the greatest assurance of title?

    (a) Special warranty
    (b) Deed of confirmation
    (c) Grant deed
    (d) General warranty

7. Which of the following covenants assures the grantee that the grantor has the legal capacity to transfer the title?

    (a) Covenant of quiet enjoyment
    (b) Covenant of right to convey
    (c) Covenant of seisin
    (d) Covenant for further assurances

8. A deed in which the wording in the granting clause is "remise and release" is which of the following?

    (a) Quit claim deed
    (b) Special warranty
    (c) Grant deed
    (d) Bargain and sale deed

9. Either a general warranty deed or a quit claim deed is equally suitable for which of the following?

    (a) Judicial deed
    (b) Deed of confirmation
    (c) Official deed
    (d) Deed of gift

10. A grantor left a deed for the grantee to find after the grantor's death. The result was to
    I. Convey the title during the grantor's life.
    II. Convey the title after the grantor's death.

    (a) I only
    (b) II only
    (c) both I and II
    (d) neither I nor II

11. The type of deed used to remove a mortgage lien when the debt is satisfied

    (a) Deed of surrender
    (b) Grant deed
    (c) Deed of release
    (d) Special warranty deed

12. If the covenants in a general warranty deed are broken, then the grantee's remedy is to
    I. Sue the grantor for damages in the amount of the loss up to the amount of the purchase price.
    II. Require the grantor to execute a deed of confirmation.

    (a) I only
    (b) II only
    (c) both I and II
    (d) neither I nor II

13. A claim of title by adverse possession may be defeated by the property owner by which of the following?

    (a) Permission
    (b) Confirmation
    (c) Will
    (d) Condemnation

14. The type of deed that guarantees the title against only defects that were created during the grantor's ownership is which of the following?

    (a) Bargain and sale
    (b) Special warranty
    (c) Surrender
    (d) Release

15. Which of the following statements regarding a title examination is (are) correct?
    I. The purpose of a title examination is to determine the quality of a title.
    II. A title examination must always be done by an attorney.

    (a) I only
    (b) II only
    (c) both I and II
    (d) neither I nor II

16. The successive conveyances of a title are called?

    (a) Releases
    (b) Remises
    (c) Links in the chain of title
    (d) Abstracts of title

17. Which of the following is a system of title recording?

    (a) Abstract continuation
    (b) Records of liens
    (c) Record of acknowledgement
    (d) Torrens

18. A title insurance policy may be written to protect all of the following EXCEPT

    (a) Owner
    (b) Licensee
    (c) Lessee
    (d) Mortgagee

19. A title insurance policy protects the insured against loss caused by
    I. Defects in the title existing at the time the insured acquired the title.
    II. Defects in the title created during the insured's ownership.

    (a) I only
    (b) II only
    (c) both I and II
    (d) neither I nor II

20. With reference to the metes and bounds property description, which of the following is (are) correct?
    I. It is a description by distances and directions.
    II. It is the primary method of description used in the original thirteen states.

    (a) I only
    (b) II only
    (c) both I and II
    (d) neither I nor II

21. A description by reference may refer to
    I. A prior deed.
    II. A recorded plat

    (a) I only
    (b) II only
    (c) both I and II
    (d) neither I nor II

22. Which of the following statements about the rectangular survey system is (are) correct?
    I. A township consists of thirty-six sections and is, therefore, thirty-six square miles.
    II. A section is one-mile square and contains 640 acres.

    (a) I only
    (b) II only
    (c) both I and II
    (d) neither I nor II

23. On the plat of Overlook Forest, which lot has the longest frontage on the cul-de-sac?

    (a) 4
    (b) 3
    (c) 1
    (d) 2

24. The following metes and bounds description identifies which lot in Overlook Forest: Beginning at a point in the eastern margin of Overlook Road, thence north 22°13' east 100.11'; thence south 86°37' east 129.72'; thence south 20°42' west 101.47'; thence 131.90' back to the point of beginning.

    (a) 8
    (b) 9
    (c) 1
    (d) 6

25. With reference to the plat of lot 20 in Mortgage Heights, which of the following observations is incorrect?

    (a) Lot 20 has a radius of 50 feet on the cul-de-sac.
    (b) Lot 16 is an adjoining lot.
    (c) There is a ten-foot public utility easement along the eastern boundary of lot 20.
    (d) The plat of the Mortgage Heights subdivision is recorded in Map Book 5 at page 40.

Real Estate Financing

8

In this chapter we will discuss financing instruments, such as mortgages and deeds of trust, and the various ways in which a real estate purchase may be financed. The knowledge of these financing methods is of great importance to real estate agents. Except in the unusual case of a cash sale, the knowledge or lack of knowledge of the ways in which a sale may be financed will make the difference between a successful or unsuccessful career in real estate. Lastly, the federal government regulation of lending institutions making mortgage loans and the secondary mortgage market will be covered.

NOTES

In making a mortgage loan, the lender requires the borrower to sign a promissory note (bond in some states). The note, which must be in writing, provides evidence that a valid debt exists. The note contains a promise that the borrower will be personally liable for paying the amount of money set forth in the note and specifies the manner in which the debt is to be paid. Payment is typically in monthly installments of a stated amount commencing on a certain date with a part of each payment applied first to payment of interest and the remainder applied to the reduction of principal. The note will also state the annual rate of interest to be charged on the outstanding principal balance.

MORTGAGE AND DEED OF TRUST

The personal liability of the borrower to pay the debt evidenced by the note does not provide sufficient security to the lender in making the loan. Therefore, the lender requires additional security. The borrower must provide the lender something of value from which the lender can recover the debt in case the borrower fails to pay. This security is provided in a real estate mortgage loan by the pledging (hypothecating) of real property by the borrower in a mortgage or deed of trust. Therefore, in every mortgage loan there are always two documents, the note and the mortgage or deed of trust.

There are three legal theories regarding the effect of a mortgage or deed of trust. These are the lien theory, the title theory, and the intermediate theory.

In all states a mortgage or deed of trust creates a lien against the property pledged to secure the payment of the note. In some states there is, in addition to the lien, an actual conveyance of title in the mortgage or deed of trust for the purpose of securing the debt.

In a mortgage, which is a two-party document between the mortgagor (borrower) and the mortgagee (lender), the title is conveyed to the mortgagee by the mortgagor. In a deed of trust, which contains a third party called a trustee appointed by and acting on behalf of the lender, the title is conveyed by the borrower to the trustee who holds it in trust for the benefit of the lender.

The intermediate theory provides for a conveyance of title to the trustee or mortgagee if the borrower defaults. There is no practical difference in these theories as far as the borrower is concerned. In any case, if the borrower fails to make loan payments on a timely basis, then the individual is subject to lose the property as a result of a foreclosure sale.

REQUIREMENTS FOR VALIDITY OF A MORTGAGE OR DEED OF TRUST

1. The mortgage or deed of trust must be in writing as required by the statute of frauds because the mortgage or deed of trust pledges or conveys title to real property to secure the payment of the note.
2. The mortgagor in a mortgage or the trustor (borrower) in the deed of trust must have contractual capacity. This is the same requirement of competency necessary for the creation of a valid contract as discussed in the chapter on contracts.
3. The mortgagee or trust beneficiary in a deed of trust and the trustee must have contractual capacity.
4. There must be a valid debt to be secured by the mortgage or deed of trust. The existence of the valid debt is evidenced by the note.
5. The mortgagor or trustor must have a valid interest in the property pledged or conveyed to secure the debt in the mortgage or deed of trust.
6. There must be a legally acceptable description of the property.
7. The mortgage or deed of trust must contain a mortgaging clause. In lien theory states using the mortgage form, this will be a statement that demonstrates the mortgagor's intention to mortgage the property to the mortgagee. In title theory states, the mortgaging clause takes the form of a deed of conveyance. The mortgaging clause in this case will read like the granting clause in a deed. There is a difference, however, in that this is not an absolute conveyance of title by the borrower but is a conditional conveyance made only to secure the payment of the note.
8. The mortgage or deed of trust will contain a defeasance clause that defeats the lien and conveyance of title when the mortgage debt is fully satisfied.
9. The mortgage or deed of trust must be properly executed by the borrower. Only the mortgagor or trustor signs the deed of trust. The lender does not sign.
10. The mortgage or deed of trust must be delivered to and accepted by the mortgagee or trust beneficiary (lender).

RIGHTS OF LENDER

1. The lender has the right to take possession of the property if and when the borrower defaults in mortgage payments.
2. The lender has the right to foreclose on the property in the event that the borrower defaults in the payments. The property may be sold at a foreclosure sale and the proceeds of the sale, after certain other items are paid, applied to the satisfaction of the mortgage debt.
3. The lender has the right to assign the mortgage or deed of trust. This right enables the lender to sell the mortgage, if he or she so desires, and thereby free up the money invested. The right of assignment provides liquidity to mortgages since the lender can sell the mortgage at any time and obtain the money invested rather than waiting for payment of the loan over an extended period of time.

RIGHTS OF BORROWER

1. The borrower has the right to possession of the property during the mortgage term as long as the borrower is not in default.
2. The defeasance clause gives the borrower the right to redeem the title and have the mortgage lien released at any time prior to default by paying the debt in full.
3. The borrower has the right of equity of redemption. This is the borrower's right, after default, to redeem the title pledge or conveyed to secure a mortgage debt up to the time of a foreclosure sale by paying the debt, interest, and costs.

MORTGAGE CLAUSES AND COVENANTS

The following are examples of the various clauses and covenants that may be included in a mortgage or deed of trust.

Real Estate Financing

1. The mortgage, which will be dated, contains the names of mortgagor and mortgagee. If the deed of trust form is used, the names of the borrowers will appear and they will be identified either as trustor, grantor, or mortgagor. Next, the name of the trustee will appear (perhaps called trustee or grantee) and, thirdly, the name of the lender who is the trust beneficiary and in some cases identified as noteholder.
2. The note executed by the borrower will be reproduced in the mortgage or deed of trust. The note will include an acceleration clause that enables the lender to declare the entire balance remaining immediately due and payable if the borrower is in default.
3. The note may provide that the borrower is permitted to pay off the loan at any time prior to the expiration of the full mortgage term without incurring a financial penalty for the early payoff or it may provide for a penalty to be imposed on the borrower (prepayment penalty) if the debt is satisfied prior to the expiration of the full term.
4. The mortgage will require the borrower to pay all real property taxes and assessments on a timely basis, keep the buildings in a proper state of repair and preservation, and protect the buildings against loss by fire or other casualty by an insurance policy written in an amount that is at least 80 percent of the value of the structures.
5. The mortgage will contain a defeasance clause and thereby provide for the borrower's right to defeat and remove the lien by paying the indebtedness in full.
6. The mortgage will provide the right of foreclosure to the lender in the event that the borrower fails to make payments as scheduled or fails to fulfill other obligations as set forth in the mortgage.
7. In the case of the deed of trust form, there will be a clause giving the lender the irrevocable power to appoint a substitute trustee or trustees without notice and without specifying any reason, by recording an instrument of appointment on the public record where the deed of trust is recorded.
8. Whether the mortgage form or deed of trust form is used, there will always be a covenant specifying that the mortgagor has a good and marketable title to the property pledged to secure the payment of the note.
9. The Mortgage or deed of trust may contain an alienation or "due on sale" clause. This clause entitles the lender to declare the principal balance immediately due and payable if the borrower sells the property during the mortgage term. This clause makes the mortgage unassumable without the lender's permission. Permission to assume the mortgage at an interest rate prevailing at the time of assumption will usually be given. The alienation clause in the FNMA/FHLMC uniform mortgage or deed of trust (discussed later in this chapter) reads as follows:

17. TRANSFER OF THE PROPERTY: ASSUMPTION. If all or any part of the Property or an interest therein is sold or transferred by Borrower without Lender's prior written consent, excluding (a) the creation of a lien or encumbrance subordinate to this Deed of Trust, (b) the creation of a purchase money security interest for household appliances, (c) a transfer by devise, descent or by operation of law upon the death of a joint tenant or (d) the grant of any leasehold interest of three years or less not containing an option to purchase, Lender may, at Lender's option, declare all the sums secured by this Deed of Trust to be immediately due and payable. Lender shall have waived such option to accelerate if, prior to the sale or transfer, Lender and the person to whom the Property is to be sold or transferred reach agreement in writing that the credit of such person is satisfactory to Lender and that the interest payable on the sums secured by this Deed of Trust shall be at such rate as Lender shall request. If Lender has waived the option to accelerate provided in this paragraph 17, and if Borrower's successor in interest has executed a written assumption agreement accepted in writing by Lender, Lender shall release Borrower from all obligations under this Deed of Trust and the Note.

Notice that this alienation clause provides for the release of the original borrower from liability if an assumption is permitted.

10. The mortgage or deed of trust will always provide for execution by the borrower. In some states witnesses may also be required.
11. The mortgage or deed of trust will provide for acknowledgement by the borrower to make the document eligible for recording on the public record for the protection of the lender.

FORECLOSURE

There are two types of foreclosure, namely, judicial and nonjudicial. Judicial foreclosure is also referred to as foreclosure by action. In this type of foreclosure, the lender must go through a court action to have the property sold to satisfy the debt when the borrower is in default. Nonjudicial foreclosure is also called foreclosure under power of sale and does not require the lender to bring a lawsuit against the defaulting borrower and obtain a judgment to foreclose.

Judicial Foreclosure

Judicial foreclosure requires that the lender bring a lawsuit against the borrower and obtain a judgment for the amount of the debt owed by the borrower. When the judgment is obtained, an execution is issued by the court, at the request of the lender, that instructs the sheriff to take possession of the mortgaged property and sell it at public auction to the highest bidder for cash. Title is conveyed to the purchaser by a sheriff's deed or trustee's deed.

Nonjudicial Foreclosure

Nonjudicial foreclosure, or foreclosure under the power of sale, requires the mortgagee or trustee to advertise the sale of the property by posting notice at the courthouse in the county where the property is located for a period of at least thirty days. Also, the mortgagee or trustee must advertise the sale in a newspaper, published in the county in which the property is located, at least once a week for a minimum of four consecutive weeks. In both cases the advertisement must describe the property and appoint a day and hour for the sale to be held. The sale is conducted by the trustee or sheriff, who conveys the title to the purchaser by a trustee's deed or sheriff's deed.

Equity of Redemption

After default and up to the time that a foreclosure sale is held, the borrower has an equitable right to redeem his or her property by paying the principal amount of the debt, accrued interest, and lender's costs incurred in initiating the foreclosure. The borrower's equity of redemption cannot be defeated by a mortgage clause. This right is terminated by the foreclosure sale. However, in states in which statutory foreclosure is permitted, the borrower may recover the property even after the foreclosure sale as discussed following.

Statutory Foreclosure

Some states provide a benefit to the borrower by statute. The borrower is granted the right to pay the debt plus accrued interest and costs in full after the foreclosure sale and thereby recover the property. The period of time during which the borrower may recover the property in this way varies from state to state, but it is usually six months to two years after the date of the foreclosure sale. Some statutes provide for possession of the property by the borrower during this period and the appointment of a receiver to collect rent from the borrower and to see that the property is adequately maintained.

Strict Foreclosure

Under this type of foreclosure, the lender may file a foreclosure petition with a court after the mortgagor is in default. The court in turn issues a decree requiring the mortgagor to satisfy the mortgage debt within a stated period of time. If the debt is not satisfied within this time period, the mortgagor's equitable right to redeem the title is lost and the mortgagor is prevented from asserting any rights in the title, which passes to the mortgagee. This type of foreclosure is not in favor in the United States.

Friendly Foreclosure

A borrower in default may simply convey the title to the property to the lender to avoid a record of foreclosure. This is also referred to as a deed in lieu of foreclosure.

Distribution of Sale Proceeds

The proceeds of the mortgage foreclosure sale are distributed in the following order of priority:

1. All expenses of the sale are paid. These will include court costs, trustees fee, advertising fees, legal fees, accounting fees, etc.
2. Next any real property tax liens and assessment liens against the property are paid.
3. If there are no other lienholders with liens having priority over the lien of the mortgage or deed of trust, the lender is paid.
4. Any other creditors holding liens against the property are paid.
5. Any remaining monies after items 1 through 4 have been satisfied are paid to the borrower.

Deficiency Judgments

The borrower in a mortgage loan is personally liable for the payment of the note. Therefore, in the event that the proceeds of a foreclosure sale are not sufficient to satisfy the balance due the lender, the lender can sue for a deficiency judgment on the note.

This is a suit for a judgment in the amount of money that the foreclosure sale was deficient in satisfying the mortgage. The judgment will create a lien against other property of the borrower both real and personal, so that this property can be sold to satisfy the lien created by the deficiency judgment.

Nonrecourse Note

Another situation in which deficiency judgments are not available to the lender is in the case of a nonrecourse note. This type of note is typically used in mortgage loans secured by commercial property. Nonrecourse means that the borrower assumes no personal liability for the payment of the note; and therefore, the lender may only look to the property pledged in the mortgage to obtain the money owed in the case of default by the borrower.

Mortgage Assumption

When a purchaser assumes the seller's existing mortgage, the purchaser assumes liability for the mortgage and personal liability for the payment of the note. Therefore, if the purchaser defaults in the mortgage payments, the purchaser is subject to lose property as a result of a foreclosure sale and is also subject to a deficiency judgment obtained by the lender.

In the case of a mortgage assumption, the seller whose mortgage was assumed remains liable on the mortgage and the payment of the note unless specifically released from liability by the lender. Therefore, if the purchaser defaults and the proceeds of a foreclosure sale are insufficient to pay off the mortgage, the seller whose mortgage was assumed is subject to a deficiency judgment by the lender. In the case of a mortgage assumption, if there is a default, the lender can foreclose against the current titleholder and sue the original borrower or anyone who has assumed the mortgage for a deficiency judgment if the proceeds of the foreclosure sale do not satisfy the mortgage debt.

Taking Subject to a Mortgage

If property is sold and title conveyed subject to the lien of an existing mortgage, the lender can foreclose against the property in the event of a default in mortgage payments. However, in taking title subject to a mortgage, the purchaser does not become liable for the payment of the note. Therefore, the lender cannot sue the purchaser for a deficiency judgment but may only obtain a deficiency judgment against the seller who remained personally liable for the payment of the debt as evidenced by the note.

TYPES OF MORTGAGES

There have been more innovations in the types of mortgages in the last few years than in the preceding fifty years. This is due to inflation and the accompanying increases in interest rates. Often these increases have been radical and on very short notice. As a result, lending institutions, for their protection, have shifted the burden resulting from rapid increases in interest rates from themselves to the borrowing public by making substantial innovations in mortgage loans. We will discuss the various types of mortgages including those of long-standing and those that have come into existence very recently.

Term Mortgage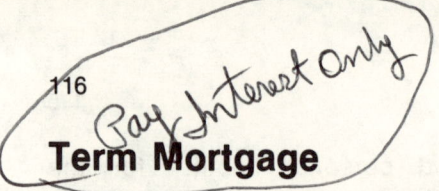

This type of mortgage requires the borrower to pay interest only for a specified term. At the end of the term, the borrower is required to pay the principal. This is the type of mortgage that was generally in use at the time of the depression of the 1930s. Many borrowers were unable to pay the principal when it came due and lenders had become unable to refinance the principal for the borrower as had usually been the case in more prosperous times. As a result, many homeowners lost their property through foreclosure.

Amortizing Mortgage 95%

The Federal Housing Administration (FHA) was created by the National Housing Act of 1934 for the purpose of insuring mortgage loans to protect lending institutions in the event of borrower default. FHA will only insure amortizing mortgages. As a result of this and as a result of the hardship that may be created for borrowers under the term mortgage, the typical home mortgage loan in use today is the amortizing mortgage.

Amortization provides for the paying of a debt by installment payments. A portion of each installment payment is applied first to the payment of interest and the remainder to the reduction of principal. The interest is always applied against the outstanding principal balance due at the time of an installment payment.

The rate of interest is an annual percentage rate as specified by the note and mortgage. The interest rate is calculated by multiplying the annual percentage rate by the unpaid principal balance and dividing the result by twelve (months) to determine the amount of interest due and payable for any monthly installment.

After deducting the interest, the remainder of the payment is used to reduce the principal balance. Therefore, the amount of interest paid with each installment reduces because the interest rate is applied against a smaller and smaller amount of principal. In this way, the loan is amortized so that the final payment in a fully amortizing mortgage will pay any remaining interest and principal.

The payment may be a fixed or constant payment and remain the same over the life of the loan. However, it may be a graduated payment or the payment may change as a result of a varying interest rate specified in the note and mortgage.

Balloon Mortgage

The balloon mortgage provides for installment payments that are not sufficient in amount to pay off the principal and interest over the term of the mortgage loan. Therefore, there must be a final payment that is substantially larger than any previous payment in order to satisfy the remaining principal and interest. If this so-called balloon payment is to be a substantial amount, the note will usually provide for refinancing by the lender to provide the funds to the borrower in the event that he cannot otherwise make the payment.

Open-End Mortgage

An open-end mortgage is one that may be refinanced without rewriting the mortgage and thereby incurring closing costs. The original mortgage provides the security for additional funds advanced to the borrower after the loan balance has been reduced to a specified amount. A closed-end mortgage is one that cannot be refinanced.

Open and Closed Mortgages

An open mortgage is a mortgage that can be paid off at a rate faster than that specified in the note without the mortgagor incurring a penalty for such prepayment. A closed mortgage is one that includes a penalty for payment at a rate faster than that permitted by the terms of the mortgage.

Graduated Payment Mortgage

In this type of mortgage the monthly payments are lower in the early years of the mortgage term and gradually increase at specified intervals until the payment amount is sufficient to amortize the loan over the remaining term. The monthly payments are kept down in the early years by not requiring the borrower to pay all of the interest. The unpaid interest is added back to the principal.

The purpose of this type of mortgage is to enable young adults to achieve home ownership as a result of the lower initial monthly payments. An outstanding example of this type

Table 8.1 *Amortization Schedule*

Monthly Payments of Principal and Interest per $1,000 of Loan Amount Necessary to Amortize a Mortgage Loan over a Definite Term of Years

Number of Years	9%	9¼%	9½%	9¾%	10%	10¼%	10½%	10¾%	11%	11¼%	11½%
5	$20.76	20.88	21.00	21.12	21.25	21.38	21.50	21.62	21.75	21.87	22.00
10	12.67	12.80	12.94	13.08	13.22	13.36	13.50	13.64	13.78	13.92	14.06
12	11.39	11.52	11.66	11.81	11.95	12.10	12.25	12.39	12.54	12.69	12.84
15	10.15	10.29	10.44	10.59	10.75	10.90	11.06	11.21	11.37	11.53	11.69
16	9.85	10.00	10.15	10.30	10.46	10.62	10.78	10.94	11.10	11.26	11.42
17	9.59	9.74	9.90	10.05	10.21	10.38	10.54	10.71	10.86	11.02	11.19
18	9.37	9.52	9.68	9.84	10.00	10.16	10.33	10.49	10.66	10.82	10.99
19	9.17	9.33	9.49	9.65	9.81	9.98	10.15	10.31	10.48	10.65	10.82
20	9.00	9.16	9.32	9.49	9.65	9.82	9.99	10.16	10.33	10.50	10.67
21	8.85	9.01	9.17	9.34	9.51	9.68	9.85	10.02	10.19	10.37	10.54
22	8.72	8.88	9.05	9.21	9.38	9.56	9.73	9.90	10.08	10.25	10.43
25	8.40	8.56	8.74	8.91	9.09	9.27	9.45	9.63	9.81	9.99	10.17
30	8.05	8.23	8.41	8.59	8.78	8.97	9.15	9.34	9.53	9.72	9.91
35	7.84	8.03	8.32	8.41	8.60	8.79	8.99	9.18	9.37	9.57	9.77
40	7.71	7.91	8.10	8.30	8.49	8.69	8.89	9.09	9.29	9.49	9.69

Number of Years	11¾%	12%	12¼%	12½%	12¾%	13%	13¼%	13½%	13¾%	14%
5	22.12	22.25	22.38	22.50	22.63	22.76	22.89	23.01	23.14	23.27
10	14.21	14.35	14.50	14.64	14.79	14.94	15.08	15.23	15.38	15.53
12	12.99	13.14	13.29	13.44	13.60	13.75	13.91	14.06	14.22	14.38
15	11.85	12.01	12.17	12.33	12.49	12.66	12.82	12.99	13.15	13.32
16	11.58	11.74	11.91	12.07	12.24	12.40	12.57	12.74	12.91	13.08
17	11.35	11.52	11.68	11.85	12.02	12.19	12.36	12.53	12.71	12.88
18	11.16	11.32	11.49	11.67	11.84	12.01	12.18	12.36	12.53	12.71
19	10.99	11.16	11.33	11.50	11.68	11.85	12.03	12.21	12.39	12.56
20	10.84	11.02	11.19	11.37	11.54	11.72	11.90	12.08	12.26	12.44
21	10.72	10.89	11.07	11.25	11.43	11.61	11.79	11.97	12.15	12.33
22	10.61	10.78	10.96	11.14	11.33	11.51	11.69	11.87	12.06	12.24
25	10.35	10.54	10.72	10.91	11.10	11.28	11.47	11.66	11.85	12.04
30	10.10	10.29	10.48	10.68	10.87	11.07	11.26	11.46	11.66	11.85
35	9.96	10.16	10.36	10.56	10.76	10.96	11.16	11.36	11.56	11.76
40	9.89	10.09	10.29	10.49	10.70	10.90	11.10	11.31	11.51	11.72

Number of Years	14.25%	14.5%	14.75%	15%	15.25%	15.5%	15.75%	16%	16.25%	16.5%
5	23.39	23.52	23.65	23.78	23.92	24.05	24.18	24.31	24.45	24.58
10	15.67	15.82	15.98	16.13	16.28	16.44	16.59	16.75	16.90	17.06
12	14.52	14.68	14.84	15.00	15.17	15.33	15.49	15.65	15.82	15.98
15	13.49	13.65	13.82	13.99	14.16	14.33	14.51	14.68	14.86	15.03
16	13.24	13.42	13.59	13.76	13.94	14.11	14.29	14.47	14.64	14.82
17	13.04	13.22	13.40	13.57	13.75	13.93	14.11	14.29	14.47	14.65
18	12.88	13.05	13.23	13.41	13.59	13.77	13.95	14.14	14.32	14.50
19	12.73	12.91	13.09	13.28	13.46	13.64	13.83	14.01	14.20	14.38
20	12.61	12.79	12.98	13.16	13.35	13.53	13.72	13.91	14.10	14.28
21	12.51	12.69	12.88	13.07	13.25	13.44	13.63	13.82	14.01	14.20
22	12.42	12.61	12.80	12.98	13.17	13.36	13.55	13.74	13.94	14.13
25	12.23	12.42	12.61	12.80	13.00	13.19	13.39	13.58	13.78	13.98
30	12.05	12.24	12.44	12.64	12.84	13.04	13.24	13.44	13.64	13.85
35	11.95	12.16	12.36	12.56	12.77	12.97	13.18	13.38	13.58	13.79
40	11.91	12.12	12.32	12.53	12.73	12.94	13.15	13.35	13.50	13.76

Number of Years	16.75%	17%	17.25%	17.5%	17.75%	18%	18.25%	18.5%	18.75%	19%
5	24.71	24.85	24.98	25.12	25.25	25.39	25.52	25.66	25.80	25.94
10	17.22	17.37	17.53	17.69	17.85	18.01	18.17	18.34	18.50	18.66
12	16.15	16.31	16.48	16.65	16.82	16.99	17.16	17.33	17.50	17.67
15	15.21	15.39	15.56	15.74	15.92	16.10	16.28	16.46	16.64	16.82
16	15.00	15.18	15.36	15.54	15.73	15.91	16.09	16.27	16.46	16.64
17	14.83	15.01	15.20	15.38	15.57	15.75	15.94	16.12	16.31	16.50
18	14.69	14.87	15.06	15.25	15.43	15.62	15.81	16.00	16.19	16.38
19	14.57	14.76	14.95	15.14	15.33	15.52	15.71	15.90	16.09	16.28
20	14.47	14.66	14.85	15.04	15.24	15.43	15.62	15.81	16.01	16.20
21	14.39	14.58	14.78	14.97	15.16	15.36	15.55	15.75	15.94	16.14
22	14.32	14.52	14.71	14.90	15.10	15.30	15.49	15.69	15.89	16.08
25	14.17	14.37	14.57	14.77	14.97	15.17	15.37	15.57	15.77	15.97
30	14.05	14.25	14.45	14.66	14.86	15.07	15.27	15.47	15.68	15.88
35	13.99	14.20	14.41	14.61	14.82	15.02	15.23	15.44	15.64	15.85
40	13.97	14.18	14.39	14.59	14.80	15.01	15.21	15.42	15.63	15.84

of mortgage loan is the FHA 245 graduated payment mortgage, which will be discussed later in this chapter.

Flexible Loan Insurance Program

This is a form of graduated payment mortgage that is called a FLIP mortgage. Under this program the borrower deposits a sum of money with the lender to be used to subsidize the borrower's monthly payments during the early years (usually five years). In this way the payments made by the borrower from current income are reduced without foregoing the payment of interest, which would be added to the principal if not paid.

As a result of this program, the borrower can obtain a loan in an amount requiring monthly payments exceeding the qualifying requirements of his or her current income and still be on a fully amortizing basis from the start.

Adjustable Rate Mortgage

In this type of mortgage the interest rate is adjusted up or down according to changes in interest rates established by an index used as a basis for making the rate changes.

The first type of adjustable rate mortgage to be authorized by the Federal Home Loan Bank Board was the renegotiable rate mortgage. This type of adjustable mortgage provides some specific safeguards for borrowers. The interest rate is revised every three years or every five years. The interest rate cannot increase more than a maximum of ½ percentage point per year and a maximum of five percentage points over the life of the loan. A typical index upon which interest rates are based is the National Average Mortgage Interest Rate as compiled and published by the Federal Home Loan Bank. Upward revisions in the interest rate are optional to the lender, but downward revisions are mandatory.

Variable rate mortgages have evolved to their present state as a result of a series of substantial liberalizations of restraints on lending institutions by the Federal Home Loan Bank Board and corresponding reductions in borrower safeguards. The present form of the variable rate mortgage was approved by the Federal Home Bank Board in April, 1981.

Under the current form the lending institution can change the interest rate according to an interest rate index selected by the lender. Changes in rates can be made as frequently as monthly. If the interest rate continues to increase so that the monthly payment will not amortize the loan over the remaining term, the lender may require the monthly payment to be increased or may extend the loan term to a maximum of forty years. Changes in monthly payment amount must be made at least once in every five years to provide for full amortization of the loan balance over the remaining term.

As far as the index is concerned, no specific interest rate index is required. However, the index must be free from the lenders control, the lender may not change the index during the loan term, and the index must be readily available to borrowers. A typical index being used is the interest rate for treasury bills. The interest rate on the mortgage does not have to be the same as the interest rate index. The mortgage rate may be a specified number of percentage points higher than the interest rate provided by the index at any given time.

Adjustable rate mortgages do contain some safeguards and benefits for the borrower. (1) The borrower may arrange new financing at any time that a lower interest rate fixed-rate mortgage becomes available; (2) the mortgages do not contain prepayment penalties; (3) and they are assumable. Additionally, the lender will usually make a variable rate mortgage at a beginning interest rate one to three percentage points lower than the going interest rate at that time for fixed-rate conventional mortgages.

Graduated Payment Adjustable Mortgage

Another innovation in mortgage loans was approved in July, 1981, by the Federal Home Loan Bank Board in the form of a graduated payment adjustable mortgage. This is a combination of the graduated payment mortgage and the variable rate mortgage. The purpose here is to make more borrowers eligible for mortgage loans by keeping the payments down in the early years as a result of the graduated payment and the variable rate features.

The liberalization of federal regulation of lending institutions has occurred in an effort to protect financial institutions making long-term

Real Estate Financing

loan commitments from the extreme fluxuations in short-term interest rates. These institutions borrow funds at the short-term rate but lend money on a long-term basis. As a result, they are caught in a squeeze between the price they must pay for the use of money in the form of interest and the interest they are earning on a long-term basis in making mortgage loans. In effect, the changes in types of mortgage loans have shifted the burden of fluxuating interest rates from lending institutions to mortgage loan borrowers.

Shared Appreciation Mortgage

This is another recent innovation in the types of mortgage loans. In this type of mortgage the lender shares in the appreciation of property value and in turn provides a lower rate of interest to the borrower. Typically, for a one-third share in value increase the lender will make the loan at a rate one-third less then the going rate for a fixed-term conventional loan at the time the loan is created.

The increase in value in which the lender shares is demonstrated by the price for which the lender shares is demonstrated by the price for which the property is sold by the borrower as compared to the price paid for the property. However, federal regulations require that if the property is not sold within ten years, there must be an appraisal of the property and the lending institution must receive its one-third share of the value increase as shown by the appraisal. This could result in a substantial hardship for the borrower who does not sell within the ten-year term. This borrower may often have to refinance in order to obtain the money to pay the lender the one-third share of value increase.

Price Level Adjusted Mortgage

In this mortgage plan, called PLAM, the interest rate is fixed and does not vary. However, the principal is variable on an annual basis. The changes in the principal are based on changes in the rate of inflation as measured by the Consumer Price Index. For example, if inflation increases 10 percent in a year, the principal will be increased 10 percent. The monthly mortgage payment is the amount of principal and interest necessary to amortize the loan over the remaining term and is changed annually.

The PLAM provides the lowest initial monthly payment of all the various alternative mortgage instruments because the rate of interest is very low in comparison to prevailing rates for other loan programs. In the early years of a mortgage loan, the interest portion of the payment is substantially greater than the part of the payment allocated to the reduction of principal. Therefore, a significant reduction in the rate of interest will result in a very large reduction in the monthly payment.

Participation Mortgage

Ther term *participation mortgage* is used to describe two different types of mortgages. One type is a mortgage in which two or more lenders participate in making the loan. The participation agreement between the lenders may provide that each participating lender owns a pro rata share of the mortgage and each will receive his or her share of mortgage payment of principal and interest as it is made. A different agrement occurs when one lender is making the substantial portion of the loan and another lender is lending a small amount of the loan. In this case the larger lender is provided with the first priority in the security pledged in the mortgage.

The other use of the term *participation mortgage* is to describe a mortgage in which the lender participates in the profits generated by a commercial property used to secure the payment of the debt in the mortgage loan. The borrower agrees to the lender's participation in the net income as an inducement for the lender to make the loans. In this case, the lender is receiving interest as well as a share of the profits.

Wrap Around Mortgage

The use of the wrap around, or all-inclusive, mortgage in financing the purchase of commercial properties dates back to the 1930s. It has achieved popularity as a financing method for residential properties only very recently. The wrap around mortgage is a second mortgage that is in an amount larger than the existing balance owed on a first mortgage against the same property. In this way it wraps around the existing first mortgage, which stays in place. The seller of the property makes a wrap around loan to the buyer, who takes title to the property subject to the existing first mortgage. The seller continues to make the payments on the first mortgage and the buyer makes the payments to the seller on the wrap around.

The wrap around mortgage can be very beneficial to both seller and buyer. The seller makes payments on the existing first mortgage at an old and lower interest rate and on a smaller initial loan amount. The seller receives the buyer's payments on a substantially larger loan amount at a higher rate of interest than the seller is paying on the existing first mortgage. In this way the seller is receiving principal payments on the second mortgage and earning interest income on the amount that the interest received on the wrap around exceeds the interest being paid on the existing first mortgage. Additionally, the use of the wrap around may enable the seller to effect a sale that may not be otherwise accomplished in times of high interest rates and tight money. The buyer's benefits in this situation are purchasing the property with a small downpayment and obtaining seller financing at a rate usually several percentage points below the prevailing rate for new financing at that time.

Lending institutions in some parts of the country have started making wrap around mortgage loans. In this case the borrower (buyer) assumes the existing first mortgage and the lending institution makes the wrap around loan to the borrower.

Wrap arounds will only work where the existing first mortgage is assumable. If the existing first mortgage contains a due on sale or alienation clause, the wrap around mortgage cannot be used. The alienation clause provides that the existing first mortgage must be paid in full if the title to the property is transferred by the first mortgage borrower without the lender's authorization. Lenders will usually give their approval provided the interest rate on the existing mortgage is increased to the current rate being charged by the lender.

Figure 8.1 illustrates the use and benefits of the wrap around mortgage.

Package Mortgage

This is a mortgage in which personal property in addition to real property is pledged to secure payment of the mortgage loan. Typical examples of these items are washer and dryer, range and oven, dishwasher, and refrigerator. The package mortgage is used frequently in the case of the sale of furnished condominium apartments and will include all furnishings in the apartment.

Blanket Mortgage

In this form of mortgage, two or more parcels of real estate are pledged as security for the payment of the mortgage debt. The blanket mortgage usually contains release clauses that provide for the release of certain parcels of property from the mortgage lien as the loan balance is reduced a specified amount. The mortgage should always provide that sufficient property value is subject to the mortgage lien to secure the remaining principal balance at any given time.

The blanket mortgage with release clauses is typically used by real estate developers. In this way the mortgagor can obtain the release

Figure 8.1 illustrates the use and benefits of the wrap around mortgage.

$100,000	Sale price
10,000	Buyer's down payment
$ 90,000	Wrap around mortgage given by buyer to seller
$ 40,000	Seller's existing first mortgage at 9 percent with monthly payments of $386.22 based on original loan amount of $48,000, term of 30 years, with a remaining term of 20 years.
$ 90,000	Wrap around mortgage to seller at 13½ percent with monthly payments of $1,086.64, term of 20 years (same as remaining term of seller's first mortgage). Seller will receive interest in the amount of $170,793 over the 20-year term in addition to the $90,000 of principal. On a monthly basis the seller retains the difference of $700.42 between the $386.22 he or she is paying on the first mortgage and the $1,086.64 being received from the buyer.

Figure 8.1 *Wrap Around Mortgage Given by Buyer to Seller*

Real Estate Financing

of certain parcels from the lien of the mortgage and convey a clear title to purchasers so as to generate a profit and provide the funds to make future mortgage payments.

Construction Mortgage

This is a form of interim, or temporary, short-term financing used to obtain the funds to create improvements on land. The applicant for a construction loan submits, for the lender's appraisal, the plans and specifications for the structure to be built and the property on which the construction is to take place. The lender will make the construction loan based on the value resulting from an appraisal of the property and the construction plans and specifications. The loan contract will specify that disbursements will be made at specified stages of the construction are completed. Interest is not charged until the money has actually been disbursed. Upon completion, the lender makes a final inspection and closes out the construction loan, which is then converted to permanent, long-term financing.

Often the lender will require the builder to be bonded for completion of the property. The bond is made payable to the lender in the event that the builder goes bankrupt and is unable to complete the structure. In this way, the lender has the funds to complete the construction to have a valuable asset to sell and recover the monies extended under the construction loan.

Purchase Money Mortgage

This is a mortgage given by a buyer to the seller to cover part of the purchase price. Here the seller becomes the mortgagee and the buyer the mortgagor. The seller has conveyed title to the buyer who immediately reconveys or pledges it as security for the balance of the purchase price. The seller is financing the sale of his property for the buyer in the amount of the purchase money mortgage. The purchase money mortgage may be a first mortgage or a junior mortgage, including a wrap around.

Leasehold Mortgage

The leasehold mortgage pledges a leasehold estate rather than a freehold estate to secure payment of a note. The leasehold acceptable to the lender is a long-term estate for years. The leasehold mortgage usually occurs in the case of a lease for vacant land whereon the lessee is to construct an improvement such as a shopping mall, hotel, or office building as an investment.

Junior Mortgage

This term describes any mortgage that is subordinate (lower in priority) to another mortgage. A junior mortgage may be a second mortgage, third mortgage, fourth mortgage, and so on. Each of these is subordinate to the prior mortgage on the same property. The second mortgage is subordinate to a first mortgage, the third mortgage is subordinate to the second, etc.

In the event of a foreclosure sale, the holder of the first mortgage has the first claim against the sale proceeds and the first mortgage debt must be fully satisfied before the holder of the second mortgage is entitled to any money from the sale. The holder of a third mortgage is not entitled to any of the sale proceeds until the second mortgage is fully satisfied, and so on down the line of priorities. The priority is established by the time (date and hour) that the mortgage is recorded on the public record in the county where the property is located.

Second mortgages are frequently used to finance part of the difference between the purchase price of a property and the loan balance being assumed in a purchase involving the assumption of the seller's existing mortgage. The seller will often take a short-term (five, seven, or ten years) purchase money second mortgage from the buyer for part of this difference when the buyer does not have the funds to pay the full amount.

Contract for Deed

As discussed in the chapter on contracts and agency, the contract for deed, or installment land contract, is both a contract of sale and a financing instrument. The seller is providing a method of purchasing the property for the buyer making installment payments.

The distinction between the contract for deed and the purchase money mortgage method of financing between buyer and seller is that in the purchase money mortgage the seller has conveyed title to the buyer who pledges it as security for the payment of the mortgage debt. In the contract for deed no title passes until the buyer completes the required installment payments totalling the purchase price.

SOURCES OF REAL ESTATE FINANCING

Savings and Loan Associations

Savings and loan associations supply more money for financing the purchase and construction of single-family dwellings than any other type of lending institution. These organizations may be state chartered or federally chartered. Approximately 2,000 of the total 4,600 savings and loans are federally chartered and regulated by the Federal Home Loan Bank Board.

The primary purposes for which savings and loans exist are to encourage thrift and to provide financing for residential properties. These organizations make loans for the construction of housing, for the purchase of existing housing, and to effect improvements in existing housing.

Mutual Savings Banks

Mutual savings banks are very similar to savings and loan associations as their main objectives are to encourage thrift and to provide financing for housing. These organizations exist in eighteen states, primarily in the northeast in Pennsylvania and northward along the coast. These banks are chartered by the state in which they exist and are regulated by those states. Mutual savings banks play a prominent role in the financing of housing in the states where they are located.

Commercial Banks

There are both federally and state chartered commercial banks. In either case, these banks are sources of mortgage money for construction, purchase of existing housing, and making home improvements. The loan policies of commercial banks are usually more conservative than other types of lending institutions.

Mortgage Bankers

Mortgage bankers, also called mortgage companies, make mortgage loans for the construction of housing and purchase of existing housing. They often specialize in making FHA insured loans and VA guaranteed loans.

There is a definite difference between a mortgage banker and a mortgage broker. A mortgage banker makes and services mortgage loans. A mortgage broker brings a lender and borrower together for a fee paid by the lending institution just as a real estate broker brings a buyer and seller of real property together for a fee.

Life Insurance Companies

At one time a number of life insurance companies were active in making loans directly to individual mortgage borrowers. Today, however, their activity is to provide funds to lending institutions to loan to individual borrowers and to provide funds for the purchase or construction of large real estate projects, such as apartment complexes, office buildings, and shopping malls.

Credit Unions

Credit unions may be an excellent source of mortgage money for their members. Usually, credit unions offer mortgage loans to their membership at an interest rate below the commercial rate at any given time. To be financially able to make long-term mortgage loans, the credit union must be of substantial size. The Federal Employees Credit Union, a state employees credit union, or the credit union of a major industry are examples of large credit unions.

Real Estate Investment Trusts

These organizations make loans secured by real property. They are owned by stockholders and enjoy a definite federal income tax advantage in that they do not pay federal income tax if they distribute at least 90 percent of their profits each year to the stockholders. They provide financing for large commercial projects, such as second home developments, apartment complexes, shopping malls, and office buildings.

Individual Investors

There are individuals in every area that invest in mortgages. These investors are usually an excellent source for second mortgage loans.

The seller of real property is definitely not to be overlooked as an individual investor. The seller may finance the sale of his or her property by taking a regular second mortgage, taking a second mortgage in the form of a wrap around, taking a purchase money first mortgage, or financing through means of a contract for deed. In times of extremely high interest rates a sale often cannot be made without the seller providing a substantial part of the financing for the buyer.

METHODS OF FINANCING

In this part of the chapter, we will discuss the various ways in which the purchase of real property may be financed by the buyer in obtaining a mortgage loan from a lending institution.

The various types of mortgage loans that may be obtained from lending institutions can be divided into two groups. (1) Conventional mortgage loans are Mortgage loans in which there is no participation by an agency of the federal government. (2) FHA or VA mortgage loans are those in which the federal government participates either by insuring the loan to protect the lender (FHA insured loans) or by guaranteeing that the loan will be repaid (VA guaranteed mortgage loans).

CONVENTIONAL LOANS

A conventional loan may be either a regular conventional loan or an insured conventional loan. In the regular conventional loan, the borrower's equity in the property is such that it provides sufficient security to the lender in making the loan and therefore insurance to protect the lender in case of the borrower's default is not required. In these cases, the borrower is obtaining a loan that does not exceed 75 to 80 percent of the property value and, therefore, has an equity of 20 or 25 percent. The regular conventional loan is less difficult to obtain than insured conventional loans or FHA and VA loans.

Insured conventional loans are typically conventional loans in which the borrower has a downpayment of only 5 percent or 10 percent and is therefore borrowing 90 to 95 percent of the property value. In these cases, the repayment of the top portion of the loan to the lender must be insured in the event that the borrower defaults. The insurance is called private mortgage insurance and the policies are issued by private insurance companies.

Today, more mortgage loans are insured by private mortgage insurance companies than are insured by the FHA. In the case of the 90 percent insured loan, the repayment of the top 20 percent of the loan is insured. In the 95 percent insured loan, the top 25 percent of the loan is insured. The premium for the insurance is paid by the borrower. The premium in the 90 percent loan is typically 2 percent the amount of the loan and 2½ percent in the case of the 95 percent loan. The borrower is usually permitted to pay a portion of the premium at the time the loan is obtained and the remainder in installments over a period of years. When the borrower's equity in the property reaches 25 percent as a result of appreciation and loan pay down, the individual may request a reappraisal of the property by the lender and discontinuation of the insurance requirement if the equity has, in fact, reached 25 percent or more.

FHA INSURED LOANS

The Federal Housing Administration (FHA) does not make mortgage loans but insures mortgage loans to protect lenders. This insurance protection enables lenders to provide financing when there is a very high loan-to-value ratio. This means that the loan amount is very high in comparison to the property value, thereby requiring only a small downpayment to be made by the borrower. The amount of insurance protection to the lender is always sufficient to protect the lender from a financial loss in the event of a foreclosure sale.

The insurance is called FHA mutual mortgage insurance and the premium is ½ percent of the average annual outstanding principal balance of the loan. The premium is paid by the borrower on a monthly basis along with his payments of principal and interest to amortize the loan.

The Federal Housing Administration has a number of different types of loans that it will insure. The following is a discussion of those programs of greatest importance to real estate brokers and salespeople.

(203B) FHA Regular Loan Program

This is the original and still the basic FHA program. This program provides for insuring loans for the purchase or construction of one-to four-family dwellings. As of this writing, maximum loan amounts range from $67,500 for the purchase or construction of a single-family dwelling up to $107,000 for the purchase or construction of a four-family dwelling. These loan amounts are based on the FHA appraised value of the property plus the FHA estimate of the borrower's closing costs, if the borrower is paying these costs. If the seller is to pay all or part of the closing costs for the buyer, the amount paid by the seller will not be included in the total.

The combination of the FHA appraised value and the buyer's closing costs is called the acquisition cost. The loan amounts are based on the acquisition cost. These loan amounts are 97 percent of the first $25,000 of acquisition cost and 95 percent of the acquisition cost exceeding $25,000 up to the maximum loan amount.

These loan percentages are available for dwellings that are more than one-year old or if less than one-year old were built to FHA specifications and under FHA supervision. If the dwelling is less than one-year old and not built to specifications or under supervision, the loan amount is 90 percent of the total acquisition cost. If the property is not to be occupied by the borrower, the loan amount is reduced to 85 percent of the acquisition cost.

The following calculations demonstrate the loan amounts available for the purchase or construction of a dwelling that is to be occupied by the borrower and meets all the FHA requirements. The calculation is based on a $55,000 FHA appraisal and estimated closing costs of $1,500 to be paid by the buyer.

$55,000	FHA appraisal
+ 1,500	FHA estimate of borrower's closing costs
$56,500	Acquisition cost

97% of first $25,000 =	$24,250
95% of balance of $31,500 =	29,925
Total Loan Amount	$54,175*
Rounded to	$54,150

*Loans must be in multiples of $50.

(FHA 245) Graduated Payment Mortgage

The purpose of this program is to assist young adults in becoming homeowners. Under the graduated payment plan, the payments are lower in the early years and increase at specified intervals until the payment reaches an amortizing basis. The monthly payment is kept lower in the early years of the mortgage term by not requiring the borrower to pay all of the interest due in those years. However, the unpaid interest is added back to the principal. As a result, the principal increases during those years but it may not increase to an amount that is in excess of 97 percent of the appraised value or acquisition cost.

The borrower may select any one of five plans that follow for annual increases in the monthly payment.

1. Annual increases of 2½ percent in monthly payment each year for five years.
2. Annual increases of 5 percent in monthly payment for five years.
3. Annual increases of 7½ percent in monthly payment for five years.
4. Annual increases of 2 percent in monthly payment for ten years.
5. Annual increases of 3 percent for ten years.

Under the five-year plans, the payments are at an amortizing level beginning with the sixth year and therefore remain the same for the remainder of the thirty-year term. Under the ten-year plans this occurs beginning with the eleventh year.

The FHA graduated payment mortgage is available for the purchase or construction of a single-family dwelling that is to be occupied by the borrower. The borrower must sign a certification that he or she is aware of the annual increases in monthly mortgage payment. Anyone assuming an FHA graduated payment mortgage must also sign a certificate that he or she is aware of the annual increases in monthly payment.

The graduated payment borrower may refinance the loan at any time to a level mortgage payment plan insured by the FHA. The maximum loan amount will be slightly lower under this program than for a regular FHA 203B loan to prevent the maximum principal balance exceeding 97 percent of the appraised value or acquisition cost during the years of graduated payments.

FHA 203B-2 (FHA-VA)

This is an FHA program available to veterans of military service. This program is not related in any way to the regular Veterans Administration loan program. The use of this program by a veteran does not affect his or her eligibility for a loan under the Veterans Administration program.

The definition of veteran under this program is much more lenient than the requirement of the Veterans Administration. Under the FHA-VA program a veteran is anyone who served at least ninety days of active duty at any time and was discharged or released under conditions other than dishonorable. The program is limited to the purchase or construction of a single-family dwelling to be occupied by the borrower.

The advantage of this program is that there is no downpayment on the first $25,000 of acquisition cost if the prepaid items are $200 or more. As in the case of the 203B regular loan, the loan amount is 95 percent of the amount exceeding $25,000 up to the maximum loan for a single-family dwelling. However, just as in the case of the regular loan program, if the property is less than one-year old and was not built under FHA or VA specifications and supervision, the loan is 90 percent of the appraised value.

FHA 222 (Inservice Loan Program)

The purpose of this program is to provide financing for the purchase or construction of a single-family, borrower-occupied dwelling for members of the armed forces. The borrower must be currently on active duty and must have completed more than two years of active service. The loan amount is the same as under the FHA 203B regular program.

The advantage under the FHA 222 program is that the borrower does not pay the FHA mortgage insurance premium while he or she is in the service. During this time the premium is paid by the Department of Defense. However, if the borrower leaves the service and is still obligated on the mortgage, the individual must start making the insurance premium payments.

FHA 221 (D) 2 (Low-Cost Housing for Families)

This program exists to provide for the financing of low-cost housing for families with lower downpayment requirements. The borrower must be a family as defined by FHA as follows: two or more people related by blood, marriage, or operation of law. Single persons who are age sixty two or over or are handicapped also qualify.

The maximum loan amounts are fixed by the FHA and are lower than those available under the FHA regular loan program. These amounts range from a low of $31,000 per family unit in normal housing cost areas and up to a maximum of $42,000 per unit in high housing cost areas. This program is available for the purchase or construction of one- to four-family structures.

The downpayment for properties that are more than one-year old, or if new construction or less than one-year old are built under FHA or VA supervision and to specifications, is a minimum of 3 percent of the acquisition cost. The downpayment will always be less than required under the FHA 203B program, unless the property is less than one-year old and was not built under FHA supervision. In that case, the loan amount is 90 percent of the total appraised value.

Contract Requirement

In the event that a sales contract contingent upon the buyer obtaining any FHA insured loan is created prior to an FHA appraisal and commitment to insure is made, the contract must contain the following wording as required by the FHA

It is expressly agreed, that notwithstanding any other provisions of this contract, the purchaser shall not be obligated to complete the purchase of the property described herein or to incur any penalty by forfeiture of earnest money deposit or otherwise unless the seller has delivered to the purchaser a written statement issued *by the Federal Housing Commissioner setting forth the appraised value of the property (exclusive of closing costs) of not less than $_____, which statement seller hereby agrees to deliver to the purchaser promptly after such appraised value statement is made available to the seller. The purchaser shall, however, have the privilege and option of proceeding with the consumation of this contract without regard to the amount of the appraised valuation made by the Federal Housing Commissioner. The appraised valuation is arrived at to determine the maximum mortgage the Department will insure. Hud does not warrant the value or the condition of the property. The purchaser sould satisfy himself/herself that the price and the condition of the property are acceptable.*

Certification Required on Existing Property in those states where FHA uses the modified cost approach for some appraisals. "We the seller, the purchaser, and the broker involved in the transaction each certify that the terms of the contract for purchase dated_____, and true to my best knowledge and belief and that any other agreement entered into by any of these parties in connection with this transaction is attached to the sales agreement."

VETERANS ADMINISTRATION GUARANTEED LOAN PROGRAM

Whereas the FHA programs are insured loans, the Veterans Administration program is a guaranteed loan. The Veterans Administration guarantees the repayment of the top portion of the loan to the lender in the event that the borrower defaults. The current guarantee made by the Veterans Administration to the lender is the lesser of 60 percent of the loan amount or $27,500. Also, unlike the FHA, the VA does not set maximum loan amounts. However, since $27,500 is the maximum guarantee and this equals 25 percent of $110,000, the maximum VA loan that a lender will typically make is $110,000 because the lender requires the security of having the repayment of the top 25 percent of the loan guaranteed.

The VA guaranteed loan is a 100 percent loan. The loan amount is 100 percent of the VA appraisal of the property set forth in the Veterans Administration "Certificate of Reasonable Value." This certificate is provided by the VA to the lending institution as a basis for making the loan. VA guaranteed loans are available for the purchase or construction of one-to four-family dwellings. However, unlike the FHA, the VA does not have a program for loans where the property being purchased or constructed is not to be occupied by the veteran borrower. The veteran must certify in writing at the time he or she obtains the loan that the property being purchased with the loan proceeds will be occupied by the owner. If the property is a multifamily dwelling (maximum of four units), the veteran must occupy one of the apartments.

Eligibility

For the borrower to be eligible for a VA guaranteed loan, he or she must qualify as a veteran under the requirements of the Veterans Administration. There are two groups of qualifying periods as follows.

Group I

Qualification in this group consists of at least ninety days of active duty during any one of the three wartime periods. Additionally, the veteran must have been discharged or released from duty under conditions other than dishonorable or may still be on active duty.

The periods of wartime are:

World War II - September 16, 1940, to July 25, 1947.

Korean Conflict — June 27, 1950, to January 21, 1955

Vietnam — August 4, 1964, to May 7, 1975

Group II

The three periods in this group are the periods between the wars and since Vietnam concluded up until the present time. To qualify in any of these groups, the veteran must have served at least 181 days of active duty and must have been discharged or released under conditions other than dishonorable or still be on active duty.

Real Estate Financing

The periods between wars are:

Post-World War II — July 26, 1947, to June 26, 1950

Post-Korean — February 1, 1955, to August 4, 1964.

Post-Vietnam — May 8, 1975, to present

Additionally, the not remarried spouse of a deceased veteran who had qualified under either group and died as a result of a service-connected disability or in the line of duty is qualified as the veteran would have been.

Restoration of Eligibility

The loan guarantee made by the Veterans Administration to lenders making VA loans has steadily increased over the years from the lesser of $2,000, or 50 percent of the loan amount, when the program was first initiated in 1944 to the present $27,500, or 60 percent that became effective October 7, 1980. In all there have been a total of six increases since the initial program.

When a veteran is discharged from the service, he or she receives a "certificate of eligibility." This certificate will state the maximum guarantee in effect at the time the veteran is discharged. Today, the certificate will provide an eligibility of $27,500. In the event that a veteran has used the full eligibility in obtaining a VA loan (a loan amount of $110,000 today) he or she may have that eligibility fully restored in one of two following ways:

1. The loan is paid in full and the veteran has disposed of the property; or
2. The veteran purchaser from the original veteran borrower assumes the VA loan and has as much remaining eligibility as the original veteran used to obtain the loan and also satisfies the VA requirements for income, credit, and occupancy. The assuming veteran must meet the same requirements as an original VA loan applicant.

These are only two ways in which the veteran borrower's eligibility can be restored. A mere release of liability by the lender and the VA does not in itself restore eligibility. Anyone can assume a VA loan. However, only an assumption by a qualified veteran will restore the selling veteran's eligibility.

Unused Eligibility

In the event that a veteran has used part of his or her eligibility and sold the property to a nonqualifying veteran or nonveteran who assumed the loan, the veteran may still have eligibility remaining. For example, if the veteran obtained the loan between May of 1968 and December of 1974, the maximum guarantee in effect was the lesser of $12,500, or 60 percent. Even if the veteran used all eligibility at that time by obtaining a loan in the amount of $50,000, the present eligibility is $15,000 providing a maximum loan of $60,000. This $15,000 is arrived at by subtracting the maximum eligibility of $12,500 existing at the time the loan was from the current maximum of $27,500.

In the event that a contract of sale subject to the buyer obtaining a VA guaranteed loan is created prior to an appraisal and commitment by the VA, the contract must contain the following statement as required by the Veterans Administration

It is expressly agreed that, notwithstanding any other provisions of this contract, the purchaser shall not incur any penalty by forfeiture of earnest money or otherwise or be obligated to complete the purchase of the property described herein, if the contract purchase price or cost exceeds the reasonable value of the property established by the Veterans Administration. The purchaser shall, however, have the privilege and option of proceeding with the consummation of this contract without regard to the amount of the reasonable value established by the Veterans Administration.

OTHER ASPECTS OF FHA AND VA LOANS

Escrow Account

These loans require that the borrower maintain an escrow account with the lending institution. The borrower must pay into this account an amount each month to accumulate money to pay the annual real property tax bill and the annual homeowners' insurance policy premium. Additionally, if the loan is used to purchase a condominium apartment, the escrow deposits must include an amount to pay the property owner's assessment.

At closing, the borrower must put money into the account to get it started and provide a headstart for accumulating the necessary funds. This will include two months' payments toward the next hazard insurance premium, several months toward the payment of the real property tax bill, and the equivalent of one months' FHA mortgage insurance premium if the loan is insured by the FHA. These monies deposited at the time of closing are called prepaid items and are included as a part of the borrower's actual closing costs; rather they are in excess of the closing cost.

The FHA requires that the borrower pay these prepaid items. Under the VA program, the seller is permitted, if he or she agrees, to pay the prepaid items for the buyer. Under either program, the seller may pay the buyer's closing costs or part of the closing costs.

Downpayment

In the event that the VA Certificate of Reasonable Value is less than the price the veteran is willing to pay for a home, the veteran may still obtain the VA loan and make a downpayment for the difference between the loan amount and the purchase price. In this case as well as in the case of the downpayment required under an FHA insured loan program, the borrower may not finance the downpayment. The borrower must have these funds on hand and must certify in writing that the money has not been borrowed and that there is no obligation to repay the money, in the event that the money was a gift.

Miscellaneous

The term of either an FHA or VA loan is thirty years. Both of these loans must be assumable and at the interest rate at which the loan was originally created. Therefore, mortgages securing these loans may not contain a due on sale or alienation clause.

Anyone can assume a VA loan. The assumptor does not have to be a veteran. Also, anyone can assume an FHA loan. In either assumption, the difference between the loan amount assumed and the purchase price can be financed. FHA and VA mortgages may not require a prepayment penalty.

Closing or Settlement Costs

At the time of closing or final settlement of a real estate transaction, both buyer and seller must satisfy the various expenses and obligations they have incurred in the transaction. The buyer's cost, where a new first mortgage from a lending institution is used, will typically be approximately 3 percent of the loan amount.

The seller's closing cost can vary widely depending on the obligations that must be satisfied at the closing. One such obligation of a very substantial nature that the seller may have is the requirement to satisfy an existing first mortgage against the property.

Examples of typical costs in the closing of a new loan and real estate transaction as incurred by the buyer may include the following:

1. Discount points paid to obtain a conventional loan or buy down the interest rate on a conventional loan.
2. The financing charge, which is called the loan origination fee or loan service charge, required by the lender. This fee may run anywhere from one-three percent of the loan amount.
3. Appraisal fee charged by the lender to estimate the market value of the property to be pledged as security in the mortgage or deed of trust.
4. Attorney's fee for title examination and document preparation.
5. Survey fee.
6. Credit report charge.
7. Assumption fee charged by the lender in the case of buyer assuming seller's existing mortgage.
8. Mortgage guarantee insurance premium required in 90 and 95 percent conventional insured loans.
9. Title insurance premium.
10. Cost of termite certification.

The various closing, or settlement, costs incurred by buyers and sellers in real estate transactions are discussed in detail in the text in the chapter on Closing Real Estate Transactions.

QUALIFYING REQUIREMENTS FOR MORTGAGE LOANS

In deciding whether or not to make any type of mortgage loan, a lending institution must take two things into consideration. These are: (1) the value of the property proposed to be pledged as security for the payment of the note and (2) the income, assets, and credit history of the loan applicant.

Property Appraisal

To estimate the value of the property, the lender retains the services of a qualified appraiser who performs an appraisal based on certain criteria specified by the lender. The appraisal is performed to estimate the value of the property. The lender's concern regarding the value is the amount of money that may be obtained in a foreclosure sale.

Income, Assets, and Credit History of the Loan Applicant

In evaluating the loan applicant, the lending institution requires the applicant to have an effective income sufficient to enable the borrower to make the loan payments and continue to meet other recurring financial obligations. The effective income may be a combination of an applicant's and co-applicant's income (husband and wife, for example). The applicant must also have a satisfactory credit history.

The applicant is required to furnish credit information covering the two-year period immediately preceeding the date of the application. If the applicant's credit history is unsatisfactory, then the application will be denied regardless of the amount and quality of the applicant's income in relation to the loan payments.

The applicant's assets are also taken into consideration by the lending institution. If the applicant's income is borderline in relation to the mortgage payment required but the individual has sufficient good-quality assets, the existence of these assets may make the difference between approval and disapproval of the loan application.

DISCOUNT POINTS

In making mortgage loans, lending institutions may charge discount points. The lender's purpose in charging these discount points is to increase the yield to the lender by increasing the effective interest rate in an amount exceeding a maximum rate that may be charged under certain conditions.

There are two aspects of discount points that must be understood for the student to be knowledgeable on this subject. These two aspects are:

1. The effect of the lender charging a discount point. Each point charged by the lender will increase the yield (effective interest rate) to the lender by 1/8th percentage point. Therefore, a lender wishing to increase the yield from 15 percent to 16 percent would charge eight discount points to make the loan.
2. The cost of discount points is the aspect that produces the effect described above. Each point charged by the lender costs somebody 1 percent of the loan amount. This cost must be paid at the time of loan closing.

The following example illustrates both the effect and cost of discount points. This example is based on an FHA insured or VA guaranteed mortgage loan. Both the FHA and the VA fix the maximum interest rate that a lender may charge in making these loans. The rate will be changed periodically by the FHA and VA as changes occur in the general market rate for conventional loans. However, the FHA and VA always establish a maximum allowable rate that is below the going rate for conventional loans at any given time. As a result, in making these loans the lender will invariably charge discount points to increase the yield from the maximum allowable rate to the going rate for conventional loans.

$50,000	FHA or VA loan at 14 percent
4,000	8 points charged by lender to increase yield to 15 percent
$46,000	Lender's *net* outlay

At the time the lender is making a $50,000 loan to the borrower, the lender is receiving

$4,000 in discount points charged as a requirement for making the loan. FHA and VA regulations prohibit the borrower from paying these points. Anyone other than the borrower is eligible to pay the points. The one paying is usually the seller. However, the seller is not obligated to pay unless the obligation is a condition of the sales contract.

Discount points may be charged by lenders in making conventional loans. In these situations, there is no prohibition against the borrower paying the points, and the borrower is the one who pays. In times of high interest rates and short supply of money for making mortgage loans, lenders will often charge one or two points in making 90 percent and 95 percent conventional loans. Also, in states having usury laws that fix a maximum allowable interest rate lower than the average national rate prevailing at any given time, lenders will require the payment of sufficient points to increase their yield above the statutory maximum to the equivalent of the national average rate.

Discount points may also be paid by conventional borrowers on a voluntary basis to "buy down" a mortgage interest rate at the time the loan is made. In this case, the lender reduces the interest rate ¼ percentage point for each point paid by the borrower. Therefore, the payment of six points by the borrower will result in a rate reduction of 1½ percentage points. For example, six points will reduce a prevailing rate of 16 percent to 14½ percent. This reduction in rate could result in a monthly payment for which the borrower could qualify if the individual did not qualify for a payment at 16 percent.

TRUTH-IN-LENDING LAW

The Truth-in-Lending Law is a part of the Federal Consumer Credit Protection Act, which became effective July 1, 1969. The Truth-in-Lending Act empowered the Federal Reserve Board to implement the regulations in the act. The Federal Reserve Board implemented these regulations by establishing Regulation Z.

Regulation Z does not regulate interest rates but instead provides specific consumer protections in mortgage loans for residential real estate. All real estate loans for personal, family, household, or agricultural purposes are covered by Regulation Z. The regulation does not apply to commercial loans. Regulation Z also standardizes the procedures involved in residential loan transactions. It requires that the borrower be made fully informed of all aspects of the loan transaction. In addition, the regulation applies to the advertisement of credit terms available for residential real estate. The specific requirements of Regulation Z are discussed in the following paragraphs.

Disclosure

At or before closing the lender must provide the borrower with a disclosure statement. The disclosure must set forth the true, or effective, annual interest rate on a loan. This rate is called the annual percentage rate (APR). This rate may be higher than the interest as expressed in the mortgage. For example, where certain fees and discount points charged by the lender are subtracted from the loan amount, the result will be to increase the true rate of interest. This is because the borrower, as a result of the subtraction, has received a smaller loan amount and is paying interest on a larger amount; therefore, the effect is to increase the interest rate being paid.

In addition to stating the true or effective annual interest rate on the loan, the disclosure statement must specify the finance charges, which include loan fees, interest, and discount points. It is not required that the finance charge include such things as title examination, title insurance, escrow payments, document preparation fees, notary fees, or appraisal fees.

If the borrower is refinancing an existing mortgage loan or obtaining a new mortgage loan and is pledging a principal residence already owned as security for such loan, the disclosure statement must provide for a right of rescission for the loan transaction. The right to rescind, or cancel, the loan must be exercised by the borrower prior to midnight of the third business day following the date that the transaction was closed. The three-day right of rescission does not apply where the loan is to finance the purchase of a new home or the construction of a dwelling to be used as a principal residence.

Advertising

Regulation Z also applies to advertising the credit terms available in the purchase of a home.

The only specific thing that may be stated in the advertisement without making a full disclosure in the advertisement is the annual percentage rate. If any other credit terms are included in the advertisement, a full disclosure must be provided. This full disclosure includes the cash price of the property, the annual percentage rate, the amount of downpayment, the amount of each payment, the date when each payment is due, and the total number of payments over the mortgage term. If the annual percentage rate is not a fixed rate but is instead a variable rate, then the ad must specify the rate to be a variable or adjustable rate.

Statements of a general nature regarding the financing may be made without a full disclosure being required. Such statements as "good financing available," "FHA financing available," or "loan assumption available" are satisfactory for this purpose. Real estate agents must take special care not to violate the advertising requirements of Regulation Z.

Penalties

The violator of Regulation Z is subject to criminal liability and punishment by fine up to $5,000, imprisonment for up to one year, or both. In the event the borrower has suffered a financial loss as the result of the violation, the borrower may sue the violator under civil law in federal court for damages.

REAL ESTATE SETTLEMENT PROCEDURES ACT (RESPA)

The Real Estate Settlement Procedures Act (RESPA) was enacted by Congress in 1974. It regulates lending activities of lending institutions in making mortgage loans for housing.

Purpose of the Act

RESPA was enacted by Congress for the following purposes:

1. To ensure that borrowers are provided with greater and more timely information on the nature and cost of the settlement process.
2. To protect borrowers from unnecessarily expensive settlement charges resulting from abusive practices.
3. To effect specific changes in the settlement process resulting in more effective advance disclosure of settlement costs to home buyers and sellers.
4. To eliminate referral fees or kickbacks that increase the cost of settlement services. In this regard, lenders are only permitted to charge for services that are actually provided to home buyers and sellers and in an amount that the service actually costs the lender.

RESPA Requirements

The following are required by the act:

1.) HUD Form no. 1

In making residential mortgage loans, lenders are required to use a standard settlement form that is designed to clearly itemize all charges to be paid by both borrower and seller as part of the final settlement. The form has become known as HUD Form No. 1. This form must be made available for inspection by the borrower at or before final settlement.

2.) Home Buyers Guide to Settlement Costs

At the time of loan application, the lender must provide the borrower with a booklet entitled *A Homebuyer's Guide to Settlement Costs.* The guide includes the following information:

a.) Clear and concise language describing and explaining the nature and purpose of each settlement cost.

b.) An explanation and sample of the standard real estate settlement forms required by the act.

c.) A description and explanation of the nature and purpose of escrow accounts.

d.) An explanation of choices available to borrowers in selecting persons or organizations to provide necessary settlement services.

e.) Examples and explanations of unfair practices and unreasonable or unnecessary settlement charges to be avoided.

3.) A Good Faith Estimate

At the time of loan application, the lender is required to provide the borrower with a good faith estimate of the costs likely to be incurred at settlement.

EQUAL CREDIT OPPORTUNITY ACT (ECOA)

This law was enacted by Congress in 1975. The purpose of ECOA is to prevent discrimination in the loan process on the part of lending institutions. The act requires financial institutions engaged in making loans to do so on an equal basis to all credit worthy customers without regard to discriminatory factors. The Equal Credit Opportunity Act is implemented by Regulation B of the Federal Reserve Board.

Requirements of ECOA

This act makes it unlawful for any creditor to discriminate against any loan applicant in any aspect of a credit transaction as follows:

1. On the basis of race, color, religion, sex, national origin, marital status, or age (unless the applicant is a minor and, therefore, does not have the capacity to contract).
2. Because part of the applicant's income is derived from a public assistance program.
3. Because the applicant has in good faith exercised any right under the Federal Consumer Credit Protection Act of which the Truth-in-Lending Law (Regulation Z) is a part.

SECONDARY MORTGAGE MARKET

Up to this point in the chapter we have been discussing the primary mortgage market. The primary mortgage market is the activity of lending institutions in making loans directly to borrowers. By contrast, the secondary mortgage market is the purchase and sale of mortgages that have been created in the primary mortgage market. One of the requirements for mortgage validity is that it be assignable. As a result, the lender holding the mortgage may assign or sell the rights in the mortgage to another. In this way, the lender may free up the money invested in the mortgage without waiting for the debt to be repaid by the borrower over the long mortgage term.

The sale of the mortgage by the lender does not in any way affect the borrower's rights or obligations. The original mortgagor will not usually even be aware that the mortgage has been sold because the lending institution typically continues to service the loan for the purchaser of the mortgage. Therefore, the mortgagor continues to make the necessary mortgage payments to the same lending institution that made the mortgage loan. Occasionally, the purchaser of the mortgage will prefer to service the mortgage itself. In these cases the original lender simply notifies the mortgagor to make payments to a different lender at a different address.

The benefit of the secondary mortgage market to lending institutions and in turn to the borrowing public is to provide liquidity to mortgages. The mortgage can be converted to cash (a liquid asset) by the lending institution selling the mortgage in the secondary market. The sale of the mortgage by the lender is especially beneficial in cases of low-yield mortgages. The lender may get the money out of these mortgages to reinvest in new mortgage loans at current higher yields. This provides stability in the supply of money for making mortgage loans. Therefore, the secondary mortgage market benefits the borrowing public by enabling lending institutions to make money available for loans to qualified applicants.

Mortgage liquidity available in the secondary market reduces the impact of disintermediation on lending institutions. Disintermediation is the loss of funds available to lending institutions for making mortgage loans and is caused by the withdrawal of funds from these institutions by depositors for investment in higher-yield securities in the times of unusually high interest rates. Without the secondary mortgage market, disintermediation would result in the "drying up" of funds available to lenders to the extent that these loans would be practically unavailable.

Secondary Market Activities

Not all lending institutions participate in the secondary mortgage market but instead limit their mortgage loans to their own assets. For those lenders that do participate in this market,

Real Estate Financing

there are two types of markets available. These are (1) the purchase and sale of mortgages between lending institutions and (2) the sale of mortgages by lending institutions to four organizations that provide a market for this purpose.

Activities Between Lending Institutions

A major activity of the secondary mortgage market is the purchase and sale of mortgages by and between lending institutions. In this way the market facilitates the movement of capital from those institutions having available funds to invest to lenders in short supply of money for this purpose. For example, at any given time, the demand for mortgage loans may be very low in a particular locality. As a result, institutions with funds available for making loans in those areas are unable to invest these funds in the local market by making primary mortgage loans. Consequently, the funds of these institutions that should be invested in mortgages and earning interest are lying idle. At this same time, in another part of the country, there may be a very high demand for mortgage loans. A lender in such an area may be in short supply of available funds to lend to qualified loan applicants. The problems of both of these lending institutions can be solved by the sale of existing mortgages on hand by the institution whose funds are in short supply to a lender in another area having a surplus of available funds and faced with a very low demand for mortgage loans. As a result, the lender with otherwise idle funds has them invested in mortgages earning interest as they should be and the lender in short supply of money has freed up capital invested in mortgages to meet the high demand for new mortgage loans in that area.

Sale to Organizations

There are four organizations that actively participate in the purchase of mortgages from financial institutions. These are the Federal National Mortgage Association (FNMA), the Government National Mortgage Association (GNMA), the Federal Home Loan Mortgage Corporation (FHLMC), and the Mortgage Guarantee Insurance Corporation (MGIC).

FEDERAL NATIONAL MORTGAGE ASSOCIATION (FNMA) The organization is usually referred to by its nickname "Fannie Mae." It is the oldest secondary mortgage institution and is the single largest holder of home mortgages. Fannie Mae was created in 1938 as a corporation completely owned by the federal government to provide a secondary market for residential mortgages. By 1968 it had evolved into a privately owned corporation. It is a profit-making organization with its stock listed on the New York Stock Exchange.

As a government-owned corporation, Fannie Mae was limited to purchasing FHA insured mortgages and VA guaranteed mortgages. As a privately owned corporation, it may now also purchase conventional mortgages. However, the overwhelming majority of its purchases are of FHA and VA mortgages, though it does purchase some conventional mortgages.

Fannie Mae buys mortgages in a bi-weekly free-market auction. Mortgage bankers are major sellers of mortgages to Fannie Mae. Additionally, savings and loan associations, mutual savings banks, commercial banks, and life insurance companies also sell mortgages to Fannie Mae. Fannie Mae sells interest-bearing securities (bonds, notes, and debentures) to investors. These securities are backed by specific pools of mortgages purchased and held by Fannie Mae.

GOVERNMENT NATIONAL MORTGAGE ASSOCIATION (GNMA) The popular name for this organization is "Ginnie Mae." It was established in 1968 when Fannie Mae was fully converted to a private corporation. Ginnie Mae is an agency of the Department of Housing and Urban Development (HUD).

Included in the various activities of Ginnie Mae is the purchase of mortgages to make capital available to lending institutions. As a government agency, Ginnie Mae is limited to the purchase of VA or FHA mortgages.

Ginnie Mae guarantees the "Ginnie Mae Pass Through," which is a mortgage-backed security providing participation in a pool of FHA insured or VA guaranteed mortgages. The pass throughs are originated by lending institutions, primarily mortgage bankers. Ginnie Mae guarantees these securities and thereby makes them very secure investments for purchasers. The yield on each pass through issue is guaranteed by the full faith and credit of the United States government, the pass throughs are secured by the FHA and VA guaranteed loans, and there is also a guarantee by the lending institution originating the pass through.

THE FEDERAL HOME LOAN MORTGAGE CORPORATION (FHLMC) Like the other organizations, this one also has a nickname—"Freddie Mac." Like the other two, Freddie Mac exists to increase the availability of mortgage credit and provide greater liquidity for savings associations. These objectives are achieved by the purchase of mortgages by Freddie Mac.

Freddie Mac was created by Act of Congress in 1970. A major reason for the creation of Freddie Mac was to establish a reliable market for the sale of conventional mortgages. Fannie Mae purchases a very small amount of conventional mortgages, and Ginnie Mae may not purchase conventional mortgages. Therefore, prior to the creation of Freddie Mac, lending institutions holding conventional mortgages were fairly well limited to the purchase and sale of these mortgages between each other.

Freddie Mac sells mortgage-participation certificates and guaranteed-mortgage certificates. These are securities that represent an undivided interest in specific pools of mortgages. The payment of principal and interest is guaranteed to the purchaser of PCs or GMCs by Freddie Mac.

Freddie Mac is part of and is wholly owned by the Federal Home Loan Bank System. Any member of the system and any other financial institution whose deposits or accounts are insured by an agency of the federal government is eligible to sell mortgages to Freddie Mac. Freddie Mac's purchase of residential conventional mortgages is primarily from savings and loan associations. However, it also purchases residential conventional mortgages from mutual savings banks and commercial banks.

THE MORTGAGE GUARANTEE INSURANCE CORPORATION (MGIC) This organization also has another name, "Maggie Mae," and is the first and largest private insurer of conventional mortgage loans. Maggie Mae also provides a market where primary lenders can sell conventional mortgages that are insured by Maggie Mae. The mortgages are consigned to Maggie Mae by lending institutions for sale to investors.

Maggie Mae sells interest-bearing securities backed by pools of these consigned mortgages. In this way lenders may free up capital they have invested in conventional mortgages.

Other Aspects of the Market

Primary lenders wishing to sell mortgages to Fannie Mae or Freddie Mac must use uniform loan documents meeting criteria established by FNMA and FHLMC. For example, these organizations will not purchase mortgages containing a prepayment penalty. This requirement is particulary advantageous to individual borrowers when they are required to pay off their mortgage as a condition of a contract of sale. In some cases prepayment penalties can be extremely high and, therefore, pose a real hardship to sellers.

In late 1980, Fannie Mae announced a new program that is very beneficial to home sellers willing to finance the sale for a buyer by taking a purchase money first mortgage. Under the Fannie Mae program, the seller can have the mortgage prepared by a lending institution qualified to sell mortgages to Fannie Mae using uniform FNMA and FHLMC documents. The lending institution will close the transaction between the seller and buyer and continue to service the loan for the seller for a fee. The institution collects the payments of principal and interest from the buyer and forwards them to the seller. In this way the seller has an on-site expert protecting his or her interests and rights in the mortgage.

A very important aspect of this Fannie Mae program is the guarantee of Fannie Mae to purchase the mortgage if the seller (mortgagee) desires to sell and get his or her money out without waiting for the completion of a series of payments over the mortgage terms. Prior to this, sellers holding purchase money first mortgages had no reliable market for these mortgages in the event they wished to sell. This Fannie Mae program should provide additional incentive to home sellers to take purchase money first mortgages.

Real Estate Financing

IMPORTANT POINTS

1. The purpose of a mortgage or deed of trust (trust deed) is to secure the payment of a promissory note.

2. The three legal theories regarding a mortgage or deed of trust are the lien theory, the title theory, and the intermediate theory.

3. The requirements for mortgage or deed of trust validity are: (1) writing, (2) competent parties, (3) valid debt, (4) valid interest, (5) description, (6) mortgaging clause, (7) defeasance clause, (8) execution by borrower, (9) delivery to and acceptance by lender.

4. The lender's rights are: (1) possession upon default, (2) foreclosure, and (3) assignment.

5. The borrower's rights are: (1) possession prior to default, (2) defeat lien by paying debt in full prior to default, and (3) equity of redemption.

6. The two types of foreclosure are judicial and nonjudicial. Foreclosure sale proceeds are distributed in a special order of priority. If the sale proceeds available to the lender are insufficient to satisfy the debt, then the lender may sue for a deficiency judgment.

7. A buyer assuming a seller's mortgage assumes liability on both the mortgage and the note. The seller remains liable on the note unless specifically released by a mortgage clause or by the lender. A buyer taking title subject to an existing mortgage has no liability on the note.

8. A fully amortizing mortgage requires payments of principal and interest that will satisfy the debt completely over the mortgage term.

9. Various types of mortgages include balloon, open end, closed end, graduated payment, FLIP, adjustable or variable rate, shared appreciation (SAM), PLAM, participation, wrap around, package, blanket, construction, purchase money, leasehold, and junior.

10. The major sources of residential financing are savings and loan associations, mutual savings banks, commercial banks, and mortgage bankers. Of these, savings and loan associations provide more funds than any other single source.

11. The methods of financing are insured and uninsured conventional mortgage loans, FHA-insured loans, VA-guaranteed loans, and the various types of seller financing.

12. Conventional loans are not required to be insured if the loan amount does not exceed 80 percent of the property value. Most conventional insured loans are 90 percent and 95 percent loans. The insurance is called private mortgage insurance (PMI). The premium is paid by the borrower.

13. FHA and VA loans are made by qualified lending institutions.

14. The FHA programs include 203B, 245, 203B-2, 222, and 221D2. The FHA insurance is called mutual mortgage insurance and protects the lender from a financial loss in the event of a foreclosure. The premium is paid by the borrower. The loan amount is a percentage of the acquisition cost as established by the FHA.

15. VA loans are guaranteed loans. The current guarantee is the lesser of $27,500 or 60 percent of the loan amount. VA loans are 100 percent of the property value established by a VA appraisal and stated in the certificate of reasonable value (CRV), which is issued by the VA.

16. FHA and VA loans require escrow accounts, are for thirty-year terms, are assumable, and do not impose a prepayment penalty. The downpayment cannot be borrowed.

17. The FHA and VA fix the maximum interest rate a lending institution may charge in making these loans. The allowable rate is always below the market rate for conventional loans at any given time. Therefore, lenders charge discount points to increase the yield to an approximate equivalent of the conventional loan rate. Borrowers may not pay these points in FHA and VA loans; however, the seller may pay and usually agrees to do so in the sales contract. Borrowers may pay points in conventional loans when required or to buy down the rate.

18. Federal laws that regulate lending institutions in making consumer loans include Regulation Z, RESPA, and ECOA.

19. The primary mortgage market is the activity of lending institutions making loans directly to individual borrowers. The secondary market is the activity of lending institutions selling and buying existing mortgages. The secondary market consists of the purchase and sale of mortgages between lenders and the sale of mortgages by lenders to Fannie Mae (FNMA), Ginnie Mae (GNMA), Freddie Mac (FHLMC), and Maggie Mae (MGIC). The market provides liquidity to mortgages, thereby reducing the affect of disintermediation for the benefit of lending institutions and borrowers as well.

IMPORTANT TERMINOLOGY

Acceleration Clause
Acquisition Cost
Adjustable Rate Mortgage
Alienation Clause
Amortizing Mortgage
Annual Percentage Rate (APR)
Balloon Mortgage
Blanket Mortgage
Beneficiary
Buy Down Rate
Certificate of Reasonable Value
Closed Mortgage
Closed End Mortgage
Commercial Bank
Construction Mortgage
Conventional Loan
Deed in Lieu of Foreclosure
Deed of Trust
Defeasance Clause
Deficiency Judgment
Disclosure Statement
Discount Points
Disintermediation
Due on Sale Clause
ECOA
Equity of Redemption
Escrow Account
Fannie Mae (FNMA)
FHA-Insured Loan
Finance Charge
Flexible Loan Insurance Program (FLIP)

Foreclosure
Foreclosure by Action
Foreclosure Under Power of Sale
Freddie Mac (FHLMC)
Friendly Foreclosure
Ginnie Mae (GNMA)
Good Faith Estimate
Graduated Payment Adjustable Mortgage
Graduated Payment Mortgage
Home Buyers Guide
HUD Form No. 1
Insured Conventional Loan
Intermediate Theory
Judicial Foreclosure
Junior Mortgage
Leasehold Mortgage
Lien Theory
Liquidity
Maggie Mae (MGIC)
Mortgage
Mortgage Assumption
Mortgage Banker
Mortgage Broker
Mortgagee
Mortgagor
Mutual Savings Bank
Nonjudicial Foreclosure
Nonrecourse Note
Note Holder
Open Mortgage
Open End Mortgage

Real Estate Financing

Package Mortgage
Participation Mortgage
Prepaid Items
Prepayment Penalty
Price Level Adjusted Mortgage (PLAM)
Promissory Note
Purchase Money Mortgage
Real Estate Investment Trust (REIT)
Regulation Z
Renegotiable Rate Mortgage
RESPA
Savings and Loan Association

Secondary Mortgage Market
Shared Appreciation Mortgage (SAM)
Statutory Foreclosure
Strict Foreclosure
Subject to a Mortgage
Term Mortgage
Title Theory
Trustee
Trustor
VA-Guaranteed Loan
Variable Rate Mortgage
Wrap Around Mortgage

REVIEW QUESTIONS FOR CHAPTER 8

1. All of the following statements are applicable to promissory notes EXCEPT
   (a) Must be written.
   (b) The borrower is personally liable for payment.
   (c) Provide evidence of a valid debt.
   (d) Executed by the lender.

2. Which of the following statements concerning a mortgage is (are) correct?
   I. The purpose of a mortgage is to secure the payment of a promissory note.
   II. The delivery of a mortgage may effect a conditional conveyance of title.
   (a) I only
   (b) II only
   (c) both I and II
   (d) neither I nor II

3. Which of the following is not a right given to lenders by a deed of trust?
   (a) Assignment
   (b) Possession after default
   (c) Foreclosure
   (d) Equity of redemption

4. The clause that makes a mortgage unassumable is which of the following?
   (a) Defeasance
   (b) Alienation
   (c) Mortgaging
   (d) Prepayment

5. Which of the following gives the borrower the right to pay the debt in full and remove the mortgage lien at anytime prior to default?
   (a) Defeasance
   (b) Prepayment
   (c) Equity of redemption
   (d) Foreclosure

6. The type of foreclosure that gives the borrower the right to recover the title after the foreclosure sale is which of the following?
   (a) Strict
   (b) Statutory
   (c) Friendly
   (d) Judicial

7. A deed in lieu of foreclosure conveys a title to which of the following?
   (a) Lender
   (b) Borrower
   (c) Trustee
   (d) Mortgagor

8. Which of the following is paid first from the proceeds of a foreclosure sale?
   (a) Mortgage debt
   (b) Real property taxes
   (c) Mortgagee's equity
   (d) Sale expenses

9. A deficiency judgment may be available to

   (a) Mortgagee
   (b) Mortgagor
   (c) Trustee
   (d) Trustor

10. A buyer assumed the seller's mortgage and subsequently defaulted. Which of the following is (are) correct?
    I. The buyer is personally liable for payment of the note.
    II. The seller is personally liable for payment of the note.

    (a) I only
    (b) II only
    (c) both I and II
    (d) neither I nor II

11. The type of mortgage requiring the borrower to pay only interest during the mortgage term is?

    (a) Balloon
    (b) Open
    (c) Term
    (d) Closed

12. The amount of interest paid in an amortizing mortgage for a month in which the principal balance is $73,000 and the rate is 12 percent is which of the following?

    (a) $876
    (b) $730
    (c) $600
    (d) $1,369

13. A mortgage that is not on a fully amortizing basis and, therefore, requires a larger final payment is called

    (a) Graduated mortgage
    (b) Balloon mortgage
    (c) Open mortgage
    (d) Flexible mortgage

14. Which of the following statements regarding variable rate mortgages is (are) correct?
    I. The interest rate changes according to changes in a selected index.
    II. Variable rate mortgages do not contain a due on sale clause or prepayment penalty.

    (a) I only
    (b) II only
    (c) both I and II
    (d) neither I nor II

15. The type of mortgage in which the lender reduces the interest rate for a part of the profit realized when the property is sold is a

    (a) Participation mortgage
    (b) Price level adjusted mortgage
    (c) Wrap around mortgage
    (d) Shared Appreciation mortgage

16. Which of the following statements about wrap around mortgages is (are) correct?
    I. The wrap around is a junior mortgage in an amount larger than the existing first mortgage.
    II. It is not necessary that the existing first mortgage is assumable.

    (a) I only
    (b) II only
    (c) both I and II
    (d) neither I nor II

17. A mortgage in which two or more parcels of land are pledged is called?

    (a) Blanket
    (b) Package
    (c) All-inclusive
    (d) Wrap around

18. A mortgage that is subordinate to another is called?

    (a) Leasehold
    (b) Blanket
    (c) Junior
    (d) Participation

Real Estate Financing

19. The priority of mortgages in relation to each other is based on which of the following?

    (a) Time of execution
    (b) Time of recording
    (c) Time of delivery
    (d) Time of acknowledgement

20. A mortgage given by buyer to seller to secure payment of part of the purchase price is which of the following?

    (a) Purchase money mortgage
    (b) Earnest money mortgage
    (c) Participation mortgage
    (d) Graduated payment mortgage

21. Which of the following provides more financing for the purchase or construction of single-family owner occupied dwellings than any other type of lending institution?

    (a) Mortgage bankers
    (b) Commercial banks
    (c) Mutual savings banks
    (d) Savings and Loan Associations

22. Insurance for the protection of lending institutions making conventional loans is called?

    (a) Mutual mortgage insurance
    (b) Conventional mortgage insurance
    (c) Institutional insurance
    (d) Private mortgage insurance

23. The FHA programs are for which of the following purposes?

    (a) Making housing loans
    (b) Guaranteeing housing loans
    (c) Purchasing housing loans
    (d) Insuring housing loans

24. The FHA bases its commitment on a percentage of which of the following?

    (a) Certificate of reasonable value
    (b) Purchase price
    (c) Selling price
    (d) Acquisition cost

25. Which of the following FHA programs provides for lower monthly payments in the early years of the mortgage term by not requiring the borrower to pay all of the interest at that time?

    (a) 203B
    (b) 203B2
    (c) 222
    (d) 245

26. Which of the following FHA programs is designed especially for people in the Armed Services?

    (a) 203B
    (b) 221D2
    (c) 245
    (d) 222

27. Which of the following statements about VA loans is (are) correct?
    I. The repayment of VA loans in the event of borrower default is guaranteed to the lender.
    II. VA loans are for 100 percent of the property value established by the VA.

    (a) I only
    (b) II only
    (c) both I and II
    (d) neither I nor II

28. All of the following statements about FHA and VA loans are correct EXCEPT

    (a) They are assumable.
    (b) They require a prepayment penalty.
    (c) The term is thirty years.
    (d) They require an escrow account.

29. Which of the following statements about discount points is (are) correct?
    I. Each point charged increases the lender's yield on the loan by 1/8 percentage point.
    II. Each point charged by the lender costs 1 percent of the loan amount.

    (a) I only
    (b) II only
    (c) both I and II
    (d) neither I nor II

30. All of the following statements about Regulation Z are correct EXCEPT

    (a) It applies to commercial mortgage loans.
    (b) It requires lenders to furnish a disclosure statement to the borrower.
    (c) It provides for a three-day right of recission if a residence already owned is pledged.
    (d) It regulates the advertising of credit terms of property offered for sale.

31. RESPA requires the lender to furnish the borrower all of the following EXCEPT

    (a) Homebuyers guide
    (b) Good faith estimate
    (c) Standard settlement form
    (d) Three-day right of recission

32. ECOA requires lenders to make consumer loans without regard to all of the following EXCEPT

    (a) Age
    (b) Occupation
    (c) Sex
    (d) Marital status

33. The activity of lending institutions making mortgage loans directly to individual borrowers is

    (a) Secondary mortgage market
    (b) Money market
    (c) Institutional market
    (d) Primary Mortgage market

34. Which of the following is a government owned corporation that purchases mortgages?

    (a) Fannie Mae
    (b) Ginnie Mae
    (c) Freddie Mac
    (d) Maggie Mae

35. The major benefit of the secondary mortgage market is to reduce the effect of which of the following?

    (a) Amortization
    (b) Liquidity
    (c) Disintermediation
    (d) Expensive settlement charges

Closing Real Estate Transactions

9

Closing is the final consumation of the sales effort that began when the broker or salesperson obtained a listing. This event is given different names in various parts of the country. In addition to closing, other names are: settlement, passing of papers, and coming out of escrow. At the closing the buyer receives a deed and the seller receives payment for the property. In some states, there are escrow companies that do all the preparatory work necessary to close the transaction and actually do the final closing. However, the states with escrow companies for this purpose are very few. Therefore, in the vast majority of states, necessary functions for closing a real estate transaction are performed by an attorney, a real estate broker, and (when a new loan is involved) a lending institution.

A listing of the documents that may be involved in closing a real estate transaction follows. Certainly not all of these will be involved in any particular transaction, but all are possibilities.

> Bill of Sale for personal property
> Certificate of Occupancy
> Closing or Settlement Statement
> Contract for Deed or Land Contract
> Deed
> Deed of Trust or Mortgage and Note
> Disclosure Statement
> Estopple Certificate
> Hazard Insurance Policy
> Homeowner's Warranty Insurance Policy
> HUD Form #1 as required by the Real Estate Settlement Procedures Act
> Lease
> Lien Waivers
> Mortgage Guarantee Insurance Policy
> Option and Exercise of Option
> Sales Contract
> Survey
> Termite Certification
> Title Insurance Policy
> Title Opinion or Abstract of Title

Prior to closing there are a number of things that must be accomplished for the closing to take place. These preliminaries to closing include: a title search or examination by an attorney, including a final check of the public record by the attorney at the last minute just before the closing procedure starts; the preparation of all the necessary documents as just listed; and the notification of all parties as to the date, hour, and location of the closing.

PREPARATION OF CLOSING STATEMENTS

There are four types of closing statements. These are cash sale, purchase money mortgage, mortgage assumption, and new first mortgage given to a lending institution. All four of these are based on the same fundamental principles. The variation occurs because of the different manner in which the purchase price is paid by the buyer.

In essence, a closing statement is simply an accounting of the funds involved in a particular real estate transaction. There are actually two statements, one for the buyer and one for the seller. Each closing statement must contain the date of closing, the name of seller and buyer, the location of the property, and the signature of the person who prepared the statement. Each party to the transaction should receive copies. These parties include the broker, the buyer and seller, the lending institution, and the attorney. The broker must retain a copy of each statement in his or her file.

A closing statement is an historical document prepared in advance. That is, the statement is prepared in advance of the closing, but it records what must happen at closing. The statement sets forth the distribution of monies involved in the transaction; that is, who is to pay a specific amount for each expense and who is to receive that amount.

In this chapter, you will learn to prepare debit-and credit-type closing statements. There are other formats for closing statements, but most are set up in this form. Additionally, a great majority of real estate examinations require you to have the ability to prepare debit and credit statements.

The first step in preparing statements is to list all items in the transaction. Some of these items involve both the buyer and the seller, other items are only of concern to the buyer, while a third category includes items only of concern to the seller. Entries that involve both parties appear in both statements, entries involving only the buyer appear only in the buyer's statement, and entries that involve only the seller appear only in the seller's statement. The following are examples of these three categories.

Both Statements

1. The purchase price.
2. Prorated insurance premiums.
3. Prorated real property taxes and assessments.
4. Prorated rent.
5. Seller's personal property taxes if unpaid. (In some states).
6. Purchase money mortgage given by buyer to seller.
7. Assumption of seller's mortgage by buyer.

Buyer's Statement Only

1. Cost of preparing note and mortgage.
2. Title search or abstract.
3. Recording fees.
4. Credit for deposit of earnest money or binder.
5. New first mortgage given by buyer to a lending institution.
6. Discount points when paid by buyer to obtain a conventional loan.
7. Other charges imposed by a lending institution when making a mortgage loan.

Seller's Statement Only

1. Current mortgage(s) to be paid off.
2. Cost of deed preparation.
3. Transfer taxes.
4. Broker's fee.
5. Prepayment penalties.
6. Discount points when paid by seller.

The allocation of these items between the statements as well as the determination of whether an entry is a debit or credit and to whom is mainly a matter of logic. Debit means that the item is to be paid for by the person in whose statement that item appears as a debit. In other words, it is an expense for that party. A debit can also mean a reduction in credits because of monies received to be applied toward the payment of a credit. Credit means that the money is received by the person in whose statement it appears as a credit. A credit is also given for monies paid against an expense obligation in the transaction. We will discuss these in the explanation of the illustrations that follow.

In the closing statement illustrations, each entry is based on the facts given for the particular statement. These are based, in most cases, on the typical allocations of the expense in a real estate transaction. You must realize, of course, that any of these typical or traditional allocations of expense items can be changed by the sales contract. In any given real estate transaction, either buyer or seller could agree in the sales contract to pay for various items normally paid by the other party.

Let's illustrate and analyze each of the four types of closing statements. After the analysis of each type of statement, you will find a practice problem. Solutions to these problems are found at the end of the chapter.

Many years of preparing students for real estate licensing examinations has taught that practice is of extreme importance in the learning process. You've heard the old cliche, "practice makes perfect." It's really true. To get the most benefit from all the chapters in this book, including this one, you should do all the practice problems. If you have difficulty with a practice problem, go back and restudy the illustration for that type of problem.

CASH SALE STATEMENTS

Starting the illustrations and analysis is the cash statement. This statement is usually the least complex of the four types because there are fewer items. Following is a list of items involved in the transaction. The statement prepared from this list is a typical example of a cash sale statement. After the statement, you will find an analysis of each entry. This analysis should be read and related to each entry in the illustration of the completed closing statement.

Closing Date: February 15, 19XX
Sales Price: $45,000
Earnest Money Deposit: $3,000
Annual Insurance Premium Paid by Buyer: $235
Real Property Taxes Unpaid: $720
Personal Property Taxes Unpaid: $198
Cost of Preparing Deed: $25
Cost of Recording Deed: $3.50
Title Search Paid by Buyer: $315
Transfer Taxes: $45
Broker's Fee at 7%: $3,150

Settlement Date: February 15, 19XX	Buyer's Statement		Seller's Statement	
	Debit	Credit	Debit	Credit
Purchase Price	$45,000	$	$	$45,000
Earnest Money		3,000		
Insurance Premium	235			
Prorated Real Property Taxes		90	90	
Personal Property Taxes		198	198	
Deed Preparation			25	
Deed Recording	3.50			
Title Search	315			
Transfer Taxes			45	
Broker's Fee			3,150	
Balance Due from Buyer		42,265.50		
Balance Due Seller			41,492	
Totals	$45,553.50	$45,553.50	$45,000.00	$45,000.00

Figure 9.1 *A Cash Sale Closing Statement*

ANALYSIS OF THE PRECEDING CASH SALE STATEMENTS

Settlement Date

The settlement date as shown for this transaction is February 15, 19XX. This is the date on which the closing took place. It is the calendar basis for all prorations that are involved in the closing statement. In making prorations, the day of closing or settlement date is always charged to the seller. The expenses for this date in a prorated item are to be paid by the seller. For the purposes of this text and the ETS licensing examinations, all prorations are performed on the basis of each month consisting of 30 days and therefore there are 360 days in a year.

Purchase Price

Both buyer and seller are involved with the purchase price. The buyer is paying and the seller is receiving. Since the buyer is paying, this is an expense and, therefore, appears as a debit in his or her statement. The seller is receiving, in gross, the corresponding amount; therefore, we have a credit to the seller in the amount of $45,000.

Earnest Money

When the buyer entered into the contract of sale with the seller, he made a deposit of $3,000 in the form of earnest money, escrow money, or binder, as it is called. The buyer receives credit in his statement for having paid this $3,000. This money is usually held in the broker's trust or escrow account until closing. The broker brings a check for the $3,000 to the closing for the benefit of the buyer. This money is available at the closing to be applied to the buyer's obligations in the purchase.

Insurance Premium

Every buyer wants to be protected against a financial loss resulting from a total or partial destruction of his property. Therefore, he will have in force at closing a hazard insurance policy. This policy is for his benefit; therefore, it is an expense to him—in this case, $235 appearing as a debit to the buyer.

Prorated Real Property Taxes

The real property taxes in figure 9.1 are $720 for the calendar year starting January 1 and ending December 31. As the facts set forth, these taxes are not paid. At the end of the year, when the tax bill is due, the property will of course belong to the buyer. If the real property taxes are unpaid, they will constitute a tax lien against the property. To make an equitable distribution of these taxes as of the date of closing, we collect the seller's share at closing by debiting the seller the prorated amount of the tax bill and give a corresponding credit to the buyer in his statement. The seller's share is for forty five days of taxes at $2 per day, providing an entry of $90.

Personal Property Taxes

These are the taxes for the seller's personal property associated with his residence that he is selling to the buyer. The seller's personal property taxes are his responsibility in full. In many states, unpaid personal property taxes constitute a lien against the real estate. Therefore, we are collecting these from the seller at closing by giving a credit to the buyer of $198 and a corresponding debit to the seller.

Deed Preparation

In the sales contract, the seller has agreed to convey a marketable title to the buyer. To accomplish this conveyance, the seller must deliver a valid deed to the buyer. Therefore, the seller retains an attorney to prepare this deed. Consequently, the cost of the deed preparation is an expense to the seller. In this illustration, we have an attorney's fee in the amount of $25 for this service. We enter this $25 as a debit (expense) to the seller in his statement only.

Deed Recording

The purpose of recording the deed is to protect the title in the buyer. Therefore, he usually pays this recording fee. We have an expense to the buyer entered as a debit in the amount of $3.50 in his debit column.

Title Search

Our facts set forth that the buyer is to pay a fee to an attorney in the amount of $315 for a title search. The buyer has retained an attorney to perform this search to assure himself that he is, in fact, receiving a marketable title from the seller. The attorney's fee for this service is an expense to the buyer; therefore, it is entered as a debit in his statement.

Transfer Taxes

Most states impose a small tax on the conveyance of real estate. This tax is based on the consideration that the seller receives in the transaction. The usual statutory requirement is that the seller pay these taxes; therefore, the amount of tax appears as a debit in the seller's statement only. The name given these taxes varies from state to state. Some examples of these are: deed stamps, real estate excise taxes, real estate conveyance taxes, and real estate transfer taxes.

Broker's Fee

In the listing contract, the seller has hired the broker to market his property. In this agreement, the seller has agreed to pay the broker a fee or commission of 7 percent of the final sales price of the property. Therefore, there is an entry of $3,150 as a debit to the seller.

Balance Due from Buyer

This is the amount of money that the buyer must pay at closing to satisfy his obligations in the transaction. The combination of the $3,000 earnest money and the $42,265.50 balance due from buyer will fulfill the financial responsibility. The balance due from the buyer is arrived at by totalling the buyer's debit column. This total shown on the statement is $45,553.50. From this total, we subtract the buyer's credits. His credits are $3,000 earnest money; $90 for the seller's share of the real property taxes; and $198 for the seller's personal property taxes. The total of these three credits is subtracted from the total of the buyer's debit column. The result is the difference between the buyer's debits and credits. He has $42,265.50 less in credits than in debits. Therefore, he must pay this amount at closing to satisfy his obligations. This amount is entered in the buyer's credit column because he paid it at closing.

Remember, this is an historical document prepared in advance. This is the amount that the buyer must pay at closing or there will be no closing. Now, of course, his debit and credit columns are identical in total.

Balance Due Seller

In this illustration, the seller has only one credit. This credit is the $45,000 purchase price. We subtract the seller's debits from this credit. These debits are prorated real property taxes, personal property taxes, deed preparation, transfer taxes, and broker's fee. By subtracting the total of those debits from the $45,000 credit, we establish a difference of $41,492. The seller has $41,492 more in credits than in debits. Therefore, to satisfy the obligations due him at closing, he must receive a check in this amount.

Since he received this check at closing, it is entered as a debit. Again, if he does not receive this amount, there will be no closing. With the entry of the amount due seller, his debit and credit columns are equal.

Other Comments

Notice that the totals of the buyer's statement and seller's statement are different. The reason for this is that the two statements are not completely related. The buyer has certain expenses and credits that the seller does not have. Also, the seller has certain expenses and credit for the purchase price that the buyer does not have. For this reason, the two statement totals are not the same.

Another entry in the seller's statement that is not atypical of a cash sale transaction is the satisfaction of the seller's existing mortgage. In the preceding illustration, if the seller had a mortgage on the property, he would have to pay this off to convey a clear title to the buyer. The cost of paying off such a mortgage by the seller would be an expense to the seller. Therefore, the cost of a seller's mortgage satisfaction would be a debit in the seller's statement. There would be no corresponding credit in the buyer's statement because the buyer is not involved in this cost.

PRACTICE PROBLEM NO. 1

Cash Sale

Use the following information to prepare statements on this worksheet. The solution to the problem is at the end of the chapter.

Closing Date: May 4, 19XX
Sales Price: $48,500

Earnest Money: $8,000

Hazard Insurance Premium to be Paid by Buyer: $294

*Real Property Taxes Unpaid: $1,620

Satisfaction of Seller's Existing Mortgage: $9,400

Cost of Preparing Deed: $35

Cost of Title Abstract to be Paid by Buyer: $485

Recording Fee: $5.50

Transfer Taxes: $97

Broker's Fee: 7¼%

*Note: No personal property taxes allocated to the property.

PURCHASE MONEY MORTGAGE CLOSING STATEMENTS

This type of closing statement involves the use of a mortgage given by the buyer to the seller for part of the purchase price. The seller is financing the sale of her property to the extent of the amount of the mortgage she takes from the buyer. In the discussion of this type of statement as well as the next two, we will use various terms to identify a mortgage. These

Practice Problem No. 1—*Worksheet*

Settlement Date:	Buyer's Statement		Seller's Statement	
	Debit	Credit	Debit	Credit
Totals				

Closing Real Estate Transactions

terms are mortgage, deed of trust, and trust deed. For the purpose of closing statements, all of these terms are interchangeable.

Now let us look at a typical list of items to be accounted for by statements for buyer and seller.

Closing Date: September 30, 19XX
Sales Price: $40,000
Earnest Money Deposit: $2,000
Insurance Premium Paid by Seller for one year on January 31: $240 (To be purchased by buyer)
Real Property Taxes Unpaid: $360
Personal Property Taxes Unpaid: $180
Seller's Existing First Mortgage to be Paid Off: $5,000
Purchase Money First Mortgage Given by Buyer to Seller: $25,000
Cost of Preparing Deed: $20
Cost of Preparing Mortgage and Note: $25
Cost of Recording Deed: $3.50
Cost of Recording Mortgage: $4.50
Title Search: $300 (To be paid by buyer)
Broker's Fee at 6%: $2,400

Figure 9.2 shows closing statements for the buyer and seller that would result from this information.

Settlement Date: September 30, 19XX	Buyer's Statement		Seller's Statement	
	Debit	Credit	Debit	Credit
Purchase Price	$40,000	$	$	$40,000
Earnest Money Deposit		$2,000		
Prorated Insurance Premium	80			80
Prorated Real Property Taxes		270	270	
Personal Property Taxes		180	180	
Purchase Money Mortgage		25,000	25,000	
Seller's Existing Mortgage			5,000	
Cost of Preparing Deed			20	
Cost of Preparing Note and Mortgage	25			
Cost of Recording Deed	3.50			
Cost of Recording Mortgage	4.50			
Title Search	300			
Broker's Fee			2,400	
Balance Due from Buyer		12,963		
Balance Due Seller			7,210	
Totals	$40,413	$40,413	$40,080	$40,080

Figure 9.2 *Purchase Money Mortgage Statement*

ANALYSIS OF THE PRECEDING PURCHASE MONEY MORTGAGE STATEMENTS

In making this analysis, we will only discuss entries that were not discussed in the analysis of the cash sale statement.

Prorated Insurance Premium

This is the first new item that we encounter. In the illustration of the cash sale statement, the buyer purchased a new insurance policy from his own insurance agent and therefore paid the premium in full at closing. In this illustration, the buyer is purchasing the unused value of the seller's existing hazard insurance policy. The seller had paid an annual premium on January 31 in the amount of $240. Using the skills we learned in chapter 15, we can prorate this premium. The premium amount, on a monthly basis, is determined by dividing $240 by twelve months. We find that the monthly average is $20. Eight months have elapsed since the inception of the policy therefore, the policy has a remaining life of four months. Multiplying four months by $20 per month, we establish an unused value for this policy in the amount of $80. This $80 payment is an expense to the buyer and appears in his debit column. There is a corresponding credit to the seller in the amount of the $80 she is to receive for selling the value of the policy to the buyer.

Purchase Money Mortgage

This is the next new entry that we find. The buyer is given credit for having given the seller a purchase money mortgage at closing. This is treated just as though the buyer had given the seller $25,000 in cash toward his purchase price obligation of $40,000. A mortgage is an obligation to pay money, typically with interest, over a period of time. The fact that the seller has received this mortgage from the buyer at closing results in an offsetting entry in the seller's statement debit column. So we have, for a purchase money mortgage, a credit to the buyer and corresponding debit to the seller.

Seller's Existing Mortgage

Here we have an example of the seller having to pay off an existing mortgage as discussed under "Other Comments" following the analysis of the cash sale closing statement illustration. To create a new first mortgage to be given by buyer to seller, we must pay off the seller's existing first mortgage. Since this is a seller's expense, the payoff amount appears as a debit to the seller.

Cost of Preparing Mortgage

The buyer must have a mortgage to deliver to the seller; therefore he pays an attorney to prepare these documents. This appears as a debit in the amount of $25 in this illustration in the buyer's statement.

Other Comments

All other entries appearing in this illustration are similar to those in figure 9.1 for the cash sale statement and a discussion would be repetitive. If you are not sure about the posting of these other entries, refer to figure 9.1 and the analysis of it.

RECONCILIATION

A good check to perform on statements for both buyer and seller is to determine the money available for disbursement to third parties for expenses involved in the transaction plus the balance due seller. For example, the following is a recap of this type of check for the buyer's and seller's closing statements immediately preceding:

Available

Earnest Money in Escrow	$ 2,000.00
Balance Due From Buyer	+ 12,963.00
Total	$14,963.00

Disbursements

Cost of Preparing Note and Mortgage	$ 25.00
Cost of Recording Deed	3.50
Cost of Recording Mortgage	4.50
Cost of Title Search	300.00
Seller's Existing First Mortgage	5,000.00
Cost of Preparing Deed	20.00
Broker's Fee	2,400.00
Balance Due Seller	+ 7,210.00
Total	$14,963.00

As can be seen from the preceding information, the money available for paying third-party expenses and balance due seller equals

Closing Real Estate Transactions

the amount of money to be disbursed to seller and third parties. In this way we have determined that between the amount of money we have in our escrow account and the amount of money we are collecting from the buyer at closing, we have sufficient funds.

PRACTICE PROBLEM NO. 2

Purchase Money Mortgage

Use the following information to prepare statements on the worksheet. The solution to the problem is at the end of the chapter.

Closing Date: March 15, 19XX
Purchase Price: $78,000
Earnest Money Deposit: $3,500
Insurance Premium: $540 (Paid by seller for three years on November 30 in the year immediately preceding the closing. Remaining policy value to be purchased by buyer)
Real Property Taxes, Unpaid: $1,440
Seller's Personal Property Taxes, Unpaid: $286
Transfer Taxes: $1.50 per $1,000 of consideration received by seller
Purchase Money Mortgage Given by Buyer to Seller: $50,000
Title Abstract: $415 (To be paid by buyer)
Seller's Existing Mortgage to be Satisfied: $4,400
Prepayment Penalty: $300 (To be charged by seller's mortgagee)
Cost of Preparing Deed: $30
Cost of Preparing Mortgage: $35
Recording Fees: $8
Broker's Fee: 7%

Practice Problem No. 2—*Worksheet*

Settlement Date:	Buyer's Statement		Seller's Statement	
	Debit	Credit	Debit	Credit
Totals				

MORTGAGE ASSUMPTION STATEMENTS

Now let us take a look at a statement in which the buyer is assuming the seller's existing mortgage. The buyer is paying part of the purchase price by the assumption of this mortgage. In assuming the seller's existing mortgage, the buyer is agreeing to make the payments of principal and interest as well as assuming responsibility for the other conditions set forth in the mortgage contract. In this illustration, $29,000 of the $35,000 sale price is being paid by the buyer in this fashion.

Closing Date: November 15, 19XX
Sale Price: $35,000
Earnest Money Deposit: $1,500
Annual Premium for New Insurance: $180 (To be purchased by buyer)
Real Property Taxes Prepaid: $300
Seller's Personal Property Taxes Prepaid: $108
Seller's Existing First Mortgage: $29,000 (To be assumed by buyer)
Interest from November 1 to November 15 @ 8%: $96.67 (Paid in arrears)
Mortgagee's Mortgage Assumption Fee: $35
Cost of Preparing Deed: $20
Cost of Recording Deed: $3.50
Broker's Fee 6.5%: $2,275

ANALYSIS OF MORTGAGE ASSUMPTION STATEMENT

Prorated Real Property Taxes

Notice that our closing date in this transaction is November 15, 19XX. With the closing so late in the year, we find that the seller had already paid his real and personal property taxes. The seller is only responsible for the real property taxes for the portion of the year during which he held title. Therefore, he is not responsible for the period after November 15 through the end of December. Since he has paid the taxes for this period, he must be reimbursed by the buyer. This reimbursement for one and one half months of taxes is $37.50. The reimbursement is reflected in the closing statement by a credit to the seller and a corresponding debit to the buyer.

Personal Property Taxes

Since the personal property taxes are the sole responsibility of the seller in a transaction and he has already paid these taxes, it is not necessary to reflect this by using debit and credit entries. However, the payment of the personal property taxes should be shown either as a footnote to the closing statement to the effect that the seller's personal property taxes in the amount of $108 were paid by seller prior to closing, or this may be reflected by debit and credit entries in the seller's statement only. In using the latter method, the seller would be debited to show that he owed the personal property taxes in the amount of $108 and there would be a corresponding credit to the seller to reflect the fact that he had paid the personal property tax bill in this amount. Of course, there are no entries in the buyer's statement since his only concern is that the tax bill has been paid.

Mortgage Interest for November 1 through 15

In transactions involving the assumption by the buyer of the seller's existing mortgage, we are concerned with the interest on that mortgage for the month of closing. Mortgage loans are set up so that the interest is paid either in arrears or in advance. In this illustrated transaction, the seller's mortgage interest was paid in arrears. In other words, the mortgage payment included a payment toward the reduction of principal and a payment of interest for the preceding month.

Payment on this mortgage will be due on December 1 and with that payment, the buyer will be paying the interest for November as well as making a payment toward the reduction of principal. Since the buyer assumed the loan at closing, he is only responsible for fifteen days of interest. However, when he makes the first mortgage payment on December 1, he will be paying interest for the full month of November. Therefore, using our prorating technique, we credit the buyer with one-half of the month's interest and enter a corresponding debit to the

Settlement Date: November 15, 19XX	Buyer's Statement		Seller's Statement	
	Debit	Credit	Debit	Credit
Purchase Price	$35,000	$	$	$35,000
Earnest Money Deposit		1,500		
Insurance Premium	180			
Prorated Real Property Taxes	37.50			37.50
Assumed Mortgage		29,000	29,000	
Mortgage Interest for November 1-15		96.67	96.67	
Mortgage Assumption Fee	35			
Deed Recording	3.50			
Cost of Preparing Deed			20	
Broker's Fee			2,275	
Balance Due from Buyer		4,659.33		
Balance Due Seller			3,645.83	
Totals	$35,256.00	$35,256.00	$35,037.50	$35,037.50

Figure 9.3 *Mortgage Assumption Closing Statement*

seller. In this way, seller is paying the interest for the first half of November while he was still responsible for the mortgage.

The facts specify that the interest rate on this mortgage is 8%. The principal balance is $29,000. We simply take 8% of $29,000 and the result will give us the interest for one year. Of course, we are only interested in one month. Therefore, we can divide by 360 (using the 30 day per month proration basis), and establish the daily interest. Multiplying that times 15 days, we obtain our result of $96.67 for 15 days of interest.

Mortgage Assumption Fee

Lending institutions typically charge a small fee to transfer the mortgage record from the seller to the buyer who is assuming the seller's existing mortgage. In our example, we show a fee of $35. This is paid by the buyer who is assuming the mortgage; therefore it appears as a debit to the buyer in his closing statement.

Other Comments

If the seller has a mortgage escrow account with the lender for the purpose of accumulating the funds to pay the annual hazard insurance premium and annual tax bill when they come due, we must take this into account at closing. One way to handle this on your closing statement is to have the buyer purchase this account from the seller on a dollar for dollar basis. For example, if the seller's escrow account balance was $300 at the date of closing, the seller would receive a $300 credit in his statement for the amount of the account with a corresponding debit in the buyer's statement to pay for the account.

An alternate method for handling the escrow account would be for the buyer to establish with the lender a new escrow account for the loan that he is assuming. He would make a contribution at closing into this account equivalent to several months of payments toward the taxes and the insurance premium. This contribution would appear as a debit in the buyer's statement. The lender would then refund the seller the balance in the escrow account as of the date of closing. If this refund were to be made at closing, it would be shown in the seller's statement as a credit. If there is to be a delay in the seller obtaining the refund, it would not appear in his statement.

PRACTICE PROBLEM NO. 3

Mortgage Assumption

Use the following information to prepare statements on the worksheet. The solution to the problem is at the end of the chapter.

Settlement Date: July 10, 19XX
Purchase Price: $69,500
Earnest Money Deposit: $4,500
Insurance Premium for New Policy: $278
Real Property Taxes: $900 (Unpaid)
Personal Property Taxes: $421 (Unpaid)
Assumed Mortgage: $42,000
Mortgage Interest for July: @ 9% (Paid in advance)
Mortgage Assumption Fee: $50
Purchase Money Second Mortgage from Buyer to Seller: $9,000
Seller's Escrow Account for Taxes and Insurance on Deposit with Mortgagee: $735 (To be purchased by buyer)
Cost of Preparing Deed: $25
Cost of Preparing Second Mortgage: $30
Cost of Recording Deed and Second Mortgage: $8
Title Abstract: $320 (To be paid by seller)
Seller gives buyer an allowance of $180 for light fixture being removed by seller.
Broker's Fee: 7½%

NEW FIRST MORTGAGE STATEMENT

This is a transaction in which the purchaser is obtaining a loan from a lending institution. The security for this loan is a first mortgage given by the buyer to the lending institution.

Closing Date: August 20, 19XX
Sales Price: $48,000
Earnest Money Deposit: $2,500
Annual Premium for New Insurance: $215 (To be purchased by buyer)
New First Mortgage: $36,000
Real Property Taxes: $360 (Unpaid)
Personal Property Taxes: $180 (Unpaid)
Seller's Existing Mortgage to Be Paid Off: $26,000
Cost of Preparing Deed: $20
Cost of Preparing Mortgage: $25
Title Insurance: $90 ($2.50 per thousand dollars of loan amount)
Credit Report: $5
Survey: $50
Termite Certification: $20 (To be paid by seller)
Loan Origination Fee: $360 (1% of loan)
Title Search: $360 (1% of loan)
Cost of Recording Deed: $3.50
Cost of Recording Mortgage: $4.50
Broker's Fee 7%: $3,360

Closing Real Estate Transactions

Practice Problem No. 3—_Worksheet_

Settlement Date:	Buyer's Statement		Seller's Statement	
	Debit	Credit	Debit	Credit
Totals				

The first entry in this closing statement that we have not previously discussed is the new first mortgage. The proceeds of this new first mortgage ($36,000) appear as a credit in the buyer's statement only. This money is available to the buyer to be applied to the satisfaction of his obligations in the transaction. Now we have three sources of funds contributed to the payment of the buyer's cost instead of only two as we have had previously. These are his earnest money deposit, proceeds of the new first mortgage given to the lending institution, and the balance due from buyer that he is credited with paying at closing. Of course, he has credits from the seller, in this case for the seller's share of the taxes, but these other three items are direct cash contributions made by the buyer and available to him to satisfy his obligations at closing.

Other Costs to be Paid by Buyer

We see in the buyer's debit column a list of items of expense associated with the new first mortgage. This list starts with the cost of preparing the mortgage and goes through the appraisal fee. These are buyer's closing costs in addition to the $215 for the annual insurance premium.

Settlement Date: August 20, 19XX	Buyer's Statement		Seller's Statement	
	Debit	Credit	Debit	Credit
Purchase Price	$48,000			$48,000
Earnest Money Deposit		$2,500		
Insurance Premium	215			
Prorated Real Property Taxes		230	$230	
Personal Property Taxes		180	180	
New First Mortgage		36,000		
Cost of Preparing Mortgage	25			
Title Insurance	90			
Credit Report	5			
Survey	50			
Loan Origination Fee	360			
Title Search	360			
Cost of Recording Deed	3.50			
Cost of Recording Mortgage	4.50			
Mortgage Satisfaction			26,000	
Cost of Preparing Deed			20	
Termite Certification			20	
Broker's Fee			3,360	
Balance Due from Buyer		10,203		
Balance Due Seller			18,190	
Totals	$49,113.00	$49,113.00	$48,000.00	$48,000.00

Figure 9.4 *New First Mortgage Closing Statement*

Other Comments

The only new items that we found in this closing statement were the new first mortgage and the above mentioned list of buyer expenses in obtaining the new loan. If you prepare a reconciliation to establish the fact that the money available for disbursement to third parties and the seller is equivalent to the money available, remember that there are now three sources of funds rather than just two—the third source being the proceeds of the new first mortgage.

PRACTICE PROBLEM NO. 4

New First Mortgage

Use the following information to prepare statements on the worksheet. The solution to the problem is at the end of the chapter.

Settlement Date: July 18, 19XX
Purchase Price: $40,000
Earnest Money: $1,800
Premium for New Insurance Policy: $197
New 90% Conventional Insured First Mortgage: Calculate 4 discount points charged by mortgagee to be paid by buyer. Amount of Loan: $36,000
Real Property Taxes: $720 (Unpaid)
Seller's Personal Property Taxes: $283.75 (Unpaid)
Property Assessment for Year (Prorated): $540
Seller's Existing Mortgage To Be Satisfied: $23,760
Mortgage Guarantee Insurance: 2% of loan amount
Cost of Deed Preparation: $20
Cost of Deed of Trust Preparation: $30
Credit Report: $10
Survey: $60
Termite Certification: $50 (To be paid by seller)
Loan Service Charge: 1% of Loan Amount
Title Search: $285
Recording Fees: $12
Broker's Fee: 6%

Practice Problem No. 4—*Worksheet*

Settlement Date:	Buyer's Statement		Seller's Statement	
	Debit	Credit	Debit	Credit
Totals				

SOLUTIONS TO PRACTICE PROBLEMS

Solution to Practice Problem No. 1—*Cash Sale*

Settlement Date: May 4, 19XX	Buyer's Statement		Seller's Statement	
	Debit	Credit	Debit	Credit
Sales Price	$48,500	$	$	$48,500
Earnest Money Deposit		8,000		
Insurance Premium	294			
Prorated Real Property Taxes		558	558	
Seller's Mortgage Satisfaction			9,400	
Cost of Preparing Deed			35	
Title Abstract	485			
Recording Fee	5.50			
Transfer Taxes			97	
Broker's Fee			3,516.25	
Balance Due from Buyer		40,726.50		
Balance Due Seller			34,893.75	
Totals	$49,284.50	$49,284.50	$48,500.00	$48,500.00

Closing Real Estate Transactions

Solution to Practice Problem No. 2 *Purchase Money Mortgage*

Settlement Date: March 15, 19XX	Buyer's Statement		Seller's Statement	
	Debit	Credit	Debit	Credit
Purchase Price	$78,000	$	$	$78,000
Earnest Money Deposit		3,500		
Insurance Premium	487.50			487.50
Prorated Real Property Taxes		300	300	
Personal Property Taxes		286	286	
Transfer Taxes			117	
Purchase Money Mortgage		50,000	50,000	
Title Abstract	415			
Seller's Existing Mortgage			4,400	
Prepayment Penalty			300	
Cost of Preparing Deed			30	
Cost of Preparing Mortgage	35			
Recording Fees	8			
Broker's Fee			5,460	
Balance Due from Buyer		24,859.50		
Balance Due Seller			17,594.50	
Totals	$78,945.50	$78,945.50	$78,487.50	$78,487.50

Solution to Practice Problem No. 3— *Mortgage Assumption*

Settlement Date: July 10, 19XX	Buyer's Statement		Seller's Statement	
	Debit	Credit	Debit	Credit
Purchase Price	$69,500	$	$	$69,500
Earnest Money Deposit		4,500		
Insurance Premium	278			
Prorated Real Property Taxes		475	475	
Personal Property Taxes		421	421	
Assumed Mortgage		42,000	42,000	
Mortgage Interest	210			210
Mortgage Assumption Fee	50			
Purchase Money Second Mortgage		9,000	9,000	
Seller's Escrow Account	735			735
Cost of Preparing Deed			25	
Cost of Preparing Second Mortgage	30			
Cost of Recordings	8			
Cost of Title Abstract			320	
Light Fixture Allowance		180	180	
Broker's Fee			5,212.50	
Balance Due from Buyer		14,235		
Balance Due Séller			12,811.50	
Totals	$70,811	$70,811	$70,445	$70,445

Solution to Practice Problem No. 4 New First Mortgage

Settlement Date: July 18, 19XX	Buyer's Statement		Seller's Statement	
	Debit	Credit	Debit	Credit
Purchase Price	$40,000	$	$	$40,000
Earnest Money		1,800		
Insurance Premium	197			
New First Mortgage		36,000		
Discount Points	1,440			
Real Property Taxes		396	396	
Personal Property Taxes		283.75	283.75	
Assessment		297	297	
Seller's Mortgage Satisfaction			23,760	
Mortgage Insurance	720			
Deed Preparation			20	
Deed of Trust Preparation	30			
Credit Report	10			
Survey	60			
Termite Certification			50	
Loan Service Charge	360			
Title Search	285			
Recording Fees	12			
Broker's Fee			2,400	
Balance Due from Buyer		4,337.25		
Balance Due Seller			12,793.25	
Totals	$43,114	$43,114	$40,000	$40,000

REVIEW QUESTIONS FOR CHAPTER 9

1. The amount of an assumed mortgage appears in
   I. Seller's closing statement
   II. Buyer's closing statement

   (a) I only
   (b) II only
   (c) both I and II
   (d) neither I nor II

2. The amount of the earnest money deposit appears in
   I. Buyer's closing statement
   II. Seller's closing statement

   (a) I only
   (b) II only
   (c) both I and II
   (d) Neither I nor II

3. If property was listed for sale at $30,000 and sold for $28,500, the 6% broker's fee would appear in the seller's statement as
   I. A credit of $1,800
   II. A debit of $1,710

   (a) I only
   (b) II only
   (c) both I and II
   (d) neither I nor II

4. The cost of preparing a deed appears as
   I. A debit in the buyer's statement
   II. A credit in the seller's statement

   (a) I only
   (b) II only
   (c) both I and II
   (d) neither I nor II

5. If the closing date is June 30 and seller's personal property taxes of $132 for the year are unpaid, the appropriate entry on the buyer's closing statement would be
   I. A credit in the amount of $66
   II. A debit in the amount of $132

   (a) I only
   (b) II only
   (c) both I and II
   (d) neither I nor II

6. The proper entry on the closing statements for a transaction closed on April 15 in which the buyer is purchasing the seller's insurance policy for which the seller paid an annual premium of $156 on November 30 would be
   I. A credit to seller in the amount of $97.50
   II. A debit to the buyer in the amount of $58.50

   (a) I only
   (b) II only
   (c) both I and II
   (d) neither I nor II

7. The day of closing is
   I. Charged to the seller
   II. Charged to the buyer

   (a) I only
   (b) II only
   (c) both I and II
   (d) neither I nor II

8. In a real estate transaction, the buyer obtained an FHA insured loan in the amount of $30,000. The lending institution charged 6 discount points. The cost of these points appear as
   I. A credit to the buyer in the amount of $1,800
   II. A debit in the seller's statement of $1,800

   (a) I only
   (b) II only
   (c) both I and II
   (d) neither I nor II

9. A buyer purchased a rental property and closed the transaction on July 20. The tenant had paid rent for the month of July in the amount of $210 on July 1. The rent should be shown as
   I. A debit to seller in the amount of $70
   II. A credit to buyer in the amount of $70

   (a) I only
   (b) II only
   (c) both I and II
   (d) neither I nor II

Closing Real Estate Transactions

10. The credit column in closing statements is always
    I. To the left of the debit column
    II. To the right of the debit column

    (a) I only
    (b) II only
    (c) both I and II
    (d) neither I nor II

11. The earnest money deposit appears as
    I. A credit to the seller
    II. A debit to the buyer

    (a) I only
    (b) II only
    (c) both I and II
    (d) neither I nor II

Valuation of Real Estate

10

It is essential that real estate agents have a good knowledge and understanding of the concepts and principles of real property valuation and the methods of estimating the value of real property. In this chapter we will discuss the concepts of value, the basic valuation principles, and the various methods or approaches for estimating the value of various types of real property.

CONCEPTS OF VALUE

Value can be defined in two ways.

Market Value

This is defined by American Institute of Real Estate Appraisers and the Society of Real Estate Appraisers as follows, "The highest price in terms of money which a property will bring in a competitive and open market under all conditions requisite to a fair sale, the buyer and seller, each acting prudently, knowledgeably and assuming the price is not affected by undue stimulus."*

Implicit in this definition is the consummation of a sale as of a specified date and the passing of title from seller to buyer under conditions whereby:

1. Buyer and seller are typically motivated.
2. Both parties are well informed or well advised, and each acting in what the individual considers his or her own best interest.
3. A reasonable time is allowed for exposure in the open market.
4. Payment is made in cash or its equivalent.
5. Financing, if any, is on terms generally available in the community at the specified date and typical for the property type in its locale.
6. The price represents a normal consideration for the property sold unaffected by special financing amounts and/or terms, services, fees, costs, or credits incurred in the transaction.

Value in Use

This is defined by the American Institute of Real Estate Appraisers and the Society of Real Estate Appraisers as "The value of an economic good to its owner-user which is based on the productivity of the economic good to a specific individual; subjective value. May not necessarily represent market value." Value in use is the value of a property to its owner and this may not be the value to a typical buyer which is the basis of market value.

Necessary Property Characteristics

For a property to have value, it must have certain legal and economic characteristics. These characteristics are: (1) utility, (2) scarcity, (3) transferability, and (4) effective demand.

Utility

For the property to have value it must have the ability to satisfy a need. A property must be useful. It must be possible to use or adapt the property for some legal purpose. If a property

163

cannot be put to some beneficial use to fill a need of some kind, it will not have value.

Scarcity

The degree of scarcity is based on the supply of the property in relation to the effective demand for the property. The more abundant the supply of property in comparison to the effective demand for property at any given time, the lower the value. Conversely, the fewer properties available on the market in comparison to the effective demand or bidding for these properties at any given, the greater the value of the properties will be.

Transferability

This is a legal concept that must be present for a property to have value. It must be possible for the owner to transfer the ownership interests to a prospective buyer. These ownership interests include all of those previously discussed as expressed in the "bundle of rights" theory.

Effective Demand

Effective demand is a desire or need for property that is coupled with the financial ability to satisfy the need. In times of excessively high interest rates, many people with a strong desire and substantial need for housing are priced out of the mortgage market; therefore the demand for property is not an effective demand because individuals who want to buy do not have the financial ability to satisfy the demand.

In creating housing or other types of properties, such as office buildings, shopping malls, and hotels, a developer must take into consideration not only the need for these types of property but also the financial ability of prospective tenants or purchasers to satisfy their need.

Value, Price, and Cost Distinguished

The terms value, price, and cost do not have the same meaning. Value results from the anticipation of future benefits resulting from ownership of a particular property. Cost is a measure of expenditures of labor and materials made some time in the past. Therefore, we see that value is based on the future whereas cost is based on the past.

Price is the amount of money paid for a property. Price may be more than or less than value or cost. However, under normal market conditions, price is generally in line with value because usually the owner will not accept a price substantially less than value nor will a purchaser pay an amount significantly in excess of value. The more knowledgeable buyers and sellers are of property value, the more closely related price and value will be.

Forces Affecting Value

The forces that affect real property value are: (1) physical, (2) economic, (3) social, and (4) governmental.

Physical

The forces in this category are both natural and artificial. Natural forces are such things as topography, soil conditions, mineral resources, size, shape, climate, and location. Artificial factors include utilities, proximity to streets and highways, available public transportation, and access.

Economic

Economic forces are such things as employment levels, income levels, availability of credit, interest rates, price levels, and the amount of real property taxes.

Social

Social forces include rates or marriage, birth, divorce, and death; the rate of population growth or decline; and public attitudes toward such things as education, cultural activities, and recreation.

Governmental

Governmental forces include regulations such as zoning laws, building codes, fire regulations, city or county planning, and regulations designed to retard growth and development.

Valuation of Real Estate

Types of Value

The usual purpose of an appraisal is to estimate the market value of a particular property. However, this is not always the case as can be seen by the following discussion of assessed value, insurance value, mortgage loan value, book value, and condemnation value.

Assessed Value

The assessed value of real property is the value to which a local tax rate is applied to establish the amount of tax imposed on the property. The assessed value is normally a percentage of market value. This percentage may be up to 100 percent. Therefore, it is a combination of the rate of assessment and the tax rate applied to the property that results in the annual tax bill. Assessed value is calculated by using the following formula: Market value X assessment rate = assessed value.

Insurance Value

In estimating the value of property as a basis for arriving at the amount of insurance that should be provided to adequately protect the structure against loss by fire or other casualty, the insurance company is concerned with the cost of replacing or reproducing structures in the event of a total loss caused by an insured hazard. Therefore, insurance value is the cost of replacing or reproducing the structure in the event of a total loss. This cost is calculated by multiplying a square foot replacement cost by the number of square feet in the structure. Land value is not included in calculating insurance value.

Mortgage Loan Value

In making a mortgage loan, the lender is interested in the value of the property pledged as security for the debt. In the event of a foreclosure, the lender must recover the debt from the sale of the property. Consequently, the mortgage value is whatever the lender believes the property will bring at a foreclosure sale. Some lenders will make a conservative value estimate while others may be liberal; therefore, the mortgage loan value may be more or less than market value.

Condemnation Value

When real property is condemned under the power of emminent domain, the property owner is entitled to receive the fair market value of the property to compensate for the loss. In the case of a condemnation of an entire property, this is not difficult to estimate. However, in the case of a partial condemnation, the problem becomes more complex. In this case the property owner is entitled to be compensated for the difference in the market value of the property before and after condemnation. This amount will typically be an amount greater than the value of the amount of property condemned as a percentage of the entire property value.

Book Value or Historic Value

This is an artificial figure used for accounting or engineering purposes and results from a book depreciation. Therefore, the owner may write off a portion of the property value on the books each tax year. The book value of the property is the original value less the amount of accumulated book depreciation taken up to that time.

Original Cost	$100,000
Straight line depreciation for 10 years @ 2% per year = 20%	20,000
Present book value	$ 80,000

Competitive Market Analysis

Part of the process of listing properties for sale by real estate agents is to recommend to the owner a market price that will be the listed price if agreed to by the owner. In arriving at this price, real estate agents perform a competitive market analysis. This procedure is not an appraisal but is a presentation of the competition in the marketplace for this particular property. The analysis takes into consideration other properties currently on the market as well as properties that have sold recently.

BASIC VALUATION PRINCIPLES

Highest and Best Use

The principle of highest and best use is defined as "that possible and legal use or employment of land that will preserve its utility and yield a net income flow in the form of rent that forms, when capitalized at the proper rate of interest, the highest present value of the land." There may be a variety of uses to which land may be put at any given time; however, there is only one highest and best use for a particular property at a particular time. The highest and best use of a property will be different at different periods of time. For example, the highest and best use for land sometime in the past may have been for agricultural purposes, whereas the highest and best use at the present time may be for a shopping mall, apartment complex, or office building.

The principle of highest and best use may be illustrated by an example of the necessary activities and decisions to create an improvement on land to make the land productive. To accomplish the objective, there must be a coordinator who visualizes the investment opportunities and coordinates and employs capital and labor to create an improvement on land adhering to the principle of highest and best use. The coordinator or coordinators will typically be specialists in one or more fields of real estate such as a broker, builder, developer, and property manager. For example, let's assume that the coordinators determine that the highest and best use of a particular parcel of land at that time is to construct an apartment complex. The next decision is to determine the number of units to be constructed. Capital and labor are highly mobile whereas land has the physical characteristic of immobility; therefore, capital and labor have the top priority on the income produced by the improvement. The remaining income goes to the land that receives the residual income.

A coordinator's objective in adhering to the concept of highest and best use is to provide a residual income that when capitalized at the proper rate of interest creates the highest present value of the land. To accomplish this objective, care must be taken not to create an overimprovement or an underimprovement. If an overimprovement is created (too many apartment units are constructed), there will not be sufficient residual income for the land after the requirements of the coordinator, capital, and labor are satisfied. In other words, the investment in the improvement will exceed the ability of the improvement to provide sufficient net income to cover the priority demands and still provide a residual income that will result in the highest land value.

The same result will occur if an underimprovement is created (an insufficient number of apartment units being constructed). In this case the improvement will not produce sufficient income to result in a residual income to create maximum land value.

The creation of either an underimprovement or an overimprovement will result in depreciation of the property in the form of economic obsolescense. Therefore, in adhering to the principle of highest and best use, the coordinator must not only establish the type of use but also the capacity of the land to support a certain number of rental units to be constructed.

The income that is allocated to the land as residual income under the principle of highest and best use is defined as economic rent. This is the rent that the land is capable of producing if the most efficient use is made of the land to the optimum capacity of the land. Rent that is agreed upon in a contract between landlord and tenant is called contract rent.

The principle of highest and best use also applies to the construction of a single-family residence. For example, if a $125,000 cost is involved in constructing a home in a neighborhood of $75,000 houses, the result will be an overimprovement. Conversely, if a $50,000 house is constructed in an area of homes valued at $125,000 and up, an underimprovement will result. Consequently, as a result of economic obsolescence, the home will depreciate to the extent that the owner cannot recover the cost.

Substitution

The principle of substitution provides that the highest value of a property has a tendency to be established by the cost of purchasing or constructing another property of equal utility and desirability provided that the substitution can be made without unusual delay. Therefore, if two properties are on the market, each having the same degree of desirability and utility and one is priced at $100,000 and the other priced at $95,000, a buyer would substitute the $95,000 property instead of purchasing the $100,000 property.

Supply and Demand

This economic principle is applicable to the real estate industry just as it is applicable to other economic activities in the free enterprise system. This principle states that the greater the supply of any commodity in comparison to the demand for that commodity, the lower the value will be. Conversely, the smaller the supply and the greater the demand, the higher the value will be. Therefore, factors influencing the demand and supply of real estate will affect property values either beneficially or adversely.

Conformity

Conformity results from the homogeneous or compatible uses of land within a given area. Adherence to the principle of conformity will result in maximizing property values. Failure to adhere to the principle will result in inharmonious and incompatible uses of land within the area with the consequence of depreciating property values. In residential subdivisions, conformity is achieved through the use of restrictive convenants. In other areas, this is accomplished through zoning laws and subdivision ordinances.

Anticipation

The principle of anticipation provides that property value is based on the anticipation of the future benefits of ownership. This may also be stated as the present value of future income. Therefore, it is the future and not the past that is important in estimating the value of property. Changes in the expected demand for property can result from the creation of various improvements in an area such as schools, shopping centers, freeways, and other beneficial developments in the area. Therefore, it is important for real estate agents to be aware of plans for future development in their local market area. There may be changes that will adversely affect the expected demand for property resulting from such things as changes in surrounding land use patterns having an adverse effect on future demand. Changes causing a demand increase will increase property values whereas changes causing a reduction in demand will cause depreciation.

Contribution

The principle of contribution states that for any given part of a property its value is the result of the contribution that part makes to the total value by being present, or the amount that it subtracts from the total value as a result of its absence. This principle is utilized in the market data approach to the value estimate in making adjustments for differences between the comparable properties and the subject property (the property that is the subject of the appraisal). For example, subject property may have a fireplace whereas a comparable does not. In making the appraisal, we must estimate the value increase resulting from the presence of the fireplace in the subject property as compared with the loss in value resulting from the absence of the fireplace in the comparable.

The principle of contribution also applies to decisions regarding expenditures to modernize or improve an existing property. For example, will the addition of a garage or carport increase the value of a home sufficiently to cover the cost of constructing the improvement? This principle also applies to improving an investment property. For example, will the cost of improving the property by installing an elevator in a 4-story office building be offset by the increase in rental income resulting from the installation of the elevator? In other words, does the elevator make a sufficient contribution to value in the form of additional property income to offset all the cost associated with creating the improvement?

Competition

This principle states that when the net profit generated by a property is excessive, the result will be to create very strong competition. For example, if a growth area contains only one or two properties of a certain type such as one or two apartment complexes or office buildings, these properties will produce excess profits from rental income. The result will be to attract a number of competitors eager to participate in the profits. Competition will cause a reduction in excess profits as the supply of competing services increases until excess profits are finally eliminated.

Change

This principle states that change is continually affecting land use and therefore continually changing value. Every property and every area is constantly undergoing change. Nothing remains the same. The only constant is that change will occur. Change may cause an appreciation in value or a decrease in value. Change is constantly occurring in both the physical and economic conditions of property.

Depreciation

Depreciation is defined as a loss in value from any cause. The loss in value is estimated by the difference between the present cost of constructing a new building of equal utility and design and the market value of the depreciated property. Depreciation results from the following three causes: (1) physical deterioration, (2) functional obsolescence, and (3) economic obsolescence.

Each of these three types of depreciation are caused by forces having an adverse affect on the structure. The following are examples of these forces classified by the type of depreciation that results from the action of these forces:

Physical Deterioration

1. Unrepaired damage to the structure caused by fire, explosion, vandalism, windstorm, or other action of the elements, and damage caused by termites or other woodboring insects.
2. Wear and tear resulting from normal use of the property when adequate maintenance measures are not taken to keep the property in good condition.

Functional Obsolescence

1. Inadequacy or overadequacy of such things as wiring and plumbing, heating and cooling system, and insufficient or oversufficient number of bathrooms, closets, and other facilities.
2. Equipment that is out of date and not in keeping with current style and utility.
3. Exposed wiring or plumbing, lack of automatic controls for such things as furnaces and hot water heaters, inadequate plumbing, wiring, heating, insulation.
4. Faulty design resulting in inefficient use of floor space, poor location of various types of rooms in relation to other types such as location of bathrooms in relation to bedrooms and such things as ceilings being too high or too low.

Economic Obsolescence

1. Changes in surrounding land use patterns resulting in increased vehicular traffic, air pollution, noise pollution, inharmonious land uses, and other hazards and nuisances adversely affecting the quality of the area.
2. Failure to adhere to the principle of highest and best use and thereby creating an overimprovement or underimprovement on the land such as building a $50,000 house in a $100,000 dollar neighborhood or a $100,000 house in a $50,000 neighborhood or constructing an insufficient or excess number of rental units.
3. Changes in zoning and building regulations that adversely affect the use of property.
4. A reduction in demand for property in the area caused by local economic factors, changes in growth patterns, population shifts, other economic factors adversely affecting property value.

Depreciation in the form of physical deterioration and functional obsolescence result from forces at work within the property. These two forms of depreciation may be curable or incurable. It may be physically possible and economically practical to correct the causes of physical deterioration and functional obsolescence or it may not be possible or economically practical to effect necessary changes. In cases where it is not physically possible or economically practical to cure the depreciation, typically the structure will be torn down and replaced by a new structure.

Economic obsolescence is caused by forces outside the property. Economic obsolescence is never curable by the property owner. The owner has no control over the properties owned by others and therefore is not able to take necessary corrective measures.

Chronological Age and Economic Age

The chronological age of a structure is measured by the number of years the structure has been in existence. The economic age is based on the remaining number of years that the property will be economically useful to the owner. The economic age, therefore, is based on the number of years remaining over which the property may be put to a useful and beneficial purpose. This use may be as a family-owned dwelling or as property producing rental income, such as an apartment building, office building, warehouse, or retail complex. The economic age of a property may be considerably less than the chronological age if the property has been well maintained and modernized to keep pace with buildings currently being constructed. Conversely, the economic age may be greater than the chronological age in cases where adequate maintenance and modernization measures have not been taken.

APPROACHES TO VALUE

An appraisal is an estimate of property value based on factual data. In estimating property value, an organized and systematic program must be followed. The orderly progression of the appraisal process includes the following steps listed in chronological order:

1. Define the appraisal problem. This includes the determination of the purpose of the appraisal and the type of value to be estimated.

2. Obtain a complete and accurate description of the property that is the subject of the appraisal. The appraisal report must contain a legal description of the property to precisely locate and identify the property. The identification must specifically define the limits of the area included in the appraisal.

3. Inspect the surrounding area and the property to be appraised.

4. Determine the specific data required as the basis for the value estimate.

5. Analyze the data and arrive at a value estimate by each of the three appraisal methods: market data, cost, and income.

6. Correlate the results obtained by each of the three methods and thereby arrive at a value estimate.

7. Prepare the appraisal report.

Market Data or Comparison Approach

This appraisal method is the primary approach for estimating the value of single-family, owner-occupied dwellings and vacant land. It involves a comparison of the property that is the subject of the appraisal with other properties that offer comparable utility that have sold recently. No two properties are exactly alike; however, there are many that are comparable or similar in desirability and utility. In making the comparisons between the subject property and selected comparables, allowances are made for the differences by following the principle of contribution.

A minimum of three comparables is absolutely necessary. If available, as many as six comparables are appropriate. Comparables should be as similar as possible in all respects to subject property. Comparables may be found in real estate office files of closed sales, in the closed sales data of a multiple listing service, and from other appraisers. The more recent the date of sale of the comparable, the more valuable the comparable to the appraisal process. Also of great importance is the degree of similarity of the physical characteristics of the comparable and the location of the comparable.

In making the selection of comparables, certain property characteristics and nonproperty characteristics of each comparable must be specifically identified. Property characteristics include such things as size, type of construction, age, design, special features, and location. Nonproperty characteristics include the date of sale, verified sales price, method of financing used by the purchaser, length of time the property was on the market, and the seller's motivation in the sale.

Making the Comparisons

All of the data used in making the adjustments between the comparable properties and the subject property must be laid out in the orderly, detailed, and accurate manner as illustrated in figure 10.1. The comparison sets forth all of the property and nonproperty characteristics utilized in this particular value estimate.

As can be seen, plus and minus adjustments are made to reconcile the differences and arrive at a value estimate for subject property on the basis of the price for which each comparable was sold. A plus adjustment to a comparable is made when the comparable is deficient in a particular respect when compared to subject property. This is illustrated by the lot size adjustment of plus $500 in comparable #1 that was made because of the smaller lot size of comparable #1 in comparison to the lot size of subject property. The adjustment indicates that comparable #1 would have sold for $500 more had its lot size been as large as subject property. A minus adjustment to a comparable is made when it contains a specific feature that subject property does not contain. For example, an adjustment of minus $3,000 is made to comparable #1 because it has four bedrooms instead of three as subject property. Therefore, if comparable #1 had only the same number of bedrooms as subject property, it would have sold for $3,000 less than it did. Notice that a substantial adjustment in the amount of $4,000 is made to comparable #3 because the purchaser in that sale used a VA guaranteed loan to purchase the property whereas subject property may only be sold to a buyer using conventional financing. In identifying this nonproperty characteristic of comparable #3, it was determined that the sale price included $4,000 to cover the discount points paid by the seller to enable the purchaser to obtain that type of financing. Therefore, the adjustment is made because, had the purchaser used conventional financing, the discount points would not have been required and the seller would have been willing to accept a price $4,000 less than the $82,500 for which the property sold.

After all adjustments are made, the net adjustment amount for each comparable is calculated and the result applied to the price for which the comparable sold to arrive at an adjusted price. The adjusted price is an estimate of the price for which the comparable would have sold if all factors had been the same as subject property. The three adjusted prices are correlated to arrive at an indicated market value for subject property. This correlation is arrived at by calculating a weighted average. Comparables with a high degree of similarity are given more weight than comparables with a lesser degree of similarity. In figure 10.1, comparable #2 is given the greatest weight because it requires the fewest number of adjustments and (though this cannot be determined from the illustration) it is located in the same subdivision and just around the corner from subject property. Comparable #1, next in order of similarity is located in the same subdivision as subject property. However, comparable #1 does not have the same degree of similarity to subject property as comparable #2. Comparable #3 is given the least weight because it is located in a different subdivision and is the least similar to subject property.

Income Approach

The income approach, or appraisal by capitalization, is the primary method used to estimate the present value of properties that produce rental income. Properties included in this category are apartment complexes, single-family rental houses, office buildings, shopping malls, parking garages, leased industrial plants, and any individual properties occupied by commercial tenants.

The value of the property is estimated by capitalizing net annual income into an indication of present value by the application of a capitalization rate. This procedure is illustrated in

Date: 12-9-CY	Subject Property	Comparable No. 1		Comparable No. 2		Comparable No. 3	
Address	524 Amortization Dr.	602 Amortization Dr.		301 Acceleration Circle		12 Redemption Lane	
Sale Price		$92,000		$85,500		$82,500	
			Adjustment		Adjustment		Adjustment
Sale Date		11-10-CY	+ 600	10-20-CY	+ 1200	6-11-CY	+ 3300
Financing	Conventional	Conventional	0	Conventional	0	VA	− 4000
Location	Good	Good	0	Good	0	Fair	+ 1000
Lot Size	150 × 175 (26,250 sq.ft.)	140 × 170 (23,800)	+ 500	150 × 170 (25,500)	0	125 × 150 (18,750)	+ 1500
Age	5	6	0	7	0	8	0
Condition	Good	Good	0	Fair	+ 1000	Fair	+ 1000
Square Footage	1,800	1,900	0	1,800	0	1,650	+ 600
Total Rooms	6	6	0	6	0	6	0
Bedrooms	3	4	− 3000	3	0	3	0
Bathrooms	2½	3	− 500	2½	0	2	+ 500
Style	Ranch	Ranch	0	Ranch	0	Ranch	0
Construction	Frame	Brick & Frame	0	Frame	0	Frame	0
Air Conditioning	Central	Central	0	Central	0	None	+ 1000
Garage	Garage-2 Car	Garage-2 Car	0	Garage-2 Car	0	Carport-1 Car	+ 1000
Driveway	Paved	Paved	0	Gravel	+ 1000	Gravel	+ 1000
TOTAL ADJUSTMENT			− 2400		+ 3200		+ 6900
ADJUSTED PRICE			$89,600		$88,700		$89,300

Comparable No. 1 $89,600 × 35% = $31,360
Comparable No. 2 $88,700 × 40% = $35,480
Comparable No. 3 $89,300 × 25% = $22,325
Weighted Average = $89,165 rounded to $89,200 indicated value of subject property.

Figure 10.1 *Market Data Comparison*

figure 10.2. It shows an operating statement and the capitalization of the net annual income into an indication of value by applying the capitalization formula following the statement. A complete explanation of the income approach is presented by the analysis of the operating statement and the example of the application of the formula.

Figure 10.2 *Operating Statement*

Operating Statement

250 unit apartment complex with rent schedule of $450 per month per unit.

Potential Gross Income: 250 x $450 x 12		$1,350,000
Less Vacancy and Credit Losses (6%)		81,000
Plus Other Income		25,000
Gross Effective Income		$1,294,000
Less Expenses		
Fixed Expenses:		
Property Insurance	$24,500	
Property Taxes	95,300	
Licenses and Permits	1,200	$121,000
Operating Expenses:		
Maintenance	$106,000	
Utilities	103,200	
Supplies	16,000	
Advertising	7,500	
Legal & Accounting	15,000	
Wages & Salaries	90,000	
Property Management	64,700	$402,400
Replacement Reserve:	25,000	$ 25,000
Total Expenses		$ 548,400
Net Operating Income		$ 745,600

ANALYSIS OF OPERATING STATEMENT

INCOME

The apartment complex has a potential gross income of $1,350,000.00. This is the income that would be produced if every apartment was rented 100% of the time at $450/month for a 12-month period. It is not realistic to expect any rental property to be occupied 100% of the time on a continuing basis. Therefore, the potential gross income must be reduced by an allowance for vacancies (5%) that will inevitably occur and losses due to some tenants failing to pay their rent or paying with checks that are not collectible (1%). In the example it is anticipated that vacancy and credit losses will amount to 6% of gross potential income or $81,000.00 per year.

This apartment complex has other income generated by vending machines and laundromat facilities used by the tenants. This income is projected to be $25,000 per year. With the addition of other income, the gross effective income of $1,294,000 is projected. Gross effective income equals potential gross income minus vacancy and credit losses plus other income. This gross effective income is the amount of money the apartment complex may realistically be expected to generate in a 12-month period.

EXPENSES

To arrive at net income which is the basis for calculating the value estimate in the income approach, various expenses must be subtracted from gross income. These expenses are divided into fixed expenses, operating expenses, and the expense of the replacement reserve.

FIXED EXPENSES

These are the expenses that do not fluxuate with the operating level of the complex. The fixed expenses remain essentially the same whether the occupancy rate is 95% or 75% and include the following: An expense of $24,500 in the form of an annual premium for a hazard insurance policy to protect against financial loss caused by fire or other casualty. Real property taxes are one of the largest expense items and amount to $95,300. The $1,200 cost for licenses and permits represents fees paid to local governments as may be required for the operation of vending machines and other income producing facilities. The fixed expenses total $121,000 and are 9.27% of gross effective income.

OPERATING EXPENSES

Operating expenses in general fluctuate with the operating level or occupancy level of the property. As in the case of this apartment complex, maintenance is a major operating expense amounting to $106,000. This operating expense will vary with the level of operation and is related to a large degree to the age and condition of the property when purchased. Older properties will

Valuation of Real Estate

Figure 10.2 *Operating Statement (continued)*

naturally require a higher level of expenditures for maintenance than newer properties. The maintenance covers not only the cost of repair and maintenance to the structures but also the maintenance of grounds and parking areas. The cost of utilities for the common areas and the cost of wages and salaries paid to employees follow maintenance costs as the next largest expense.

The property manager's fee of $64,700 is a percentage of the gross effective income. The property management fee in this example is 5% of gross effective income. The smaller expense items of legal and accounting fees, advertising, and supplies round out the operating expenses which total $402,400 or 31.09% of gross effective income. Operating expenses represent the largest group in the three types of expenses.

REPLACEMENT RESERVE

This expense item of $25,000 represents an amount of money that is set aside each year to replace short-lived equipment such as hot water heaters, range and ovens, dishwashers, and disposals. Setting aside an amount of money for this purpose each year enables the project to avoid the impact of a substantial expenditure in any given year when a number of short-lived items must be replaced.

TOTAL EXPENSES AND NET INCOME

The total of the three types of expenses amounts to $548,400 which represents 42.38% of gross effective income. It should be noted that debt service (mortgage principal and interest payments) are not included in the list of expenses for appraisal purposes. For this purpose debt service is considered to be a personal obligation of the property owner. In this way, the appraisal process puts all comparable properties on the same basis by eliminating an item that will vary substantially from one property to another. Outside of the appraisal process, debt service would be deducted from gross effective income to arrive at cash flow. Cash flow is the amount of money the owner will actually receive in a given year prior to the subtraction of the income tax liability for the property. To calculate net taxable income before depreciation, the payment of mortgage interest but not principal is deductible.

Net income is arrived at by subtracting total expenses from gross effective income. The net operating income of $745,600 represents a return of 12% on an investment of $6,213,333 as illustrated by the application of the capitalization formula that follows.

$$\text{Value} = \text{Income} \div \text{Rate}$$
$$? = \$745,600 \div 12\%$$
$$\$6,213,333 = 745,600 \div .12$$

The final step in estimating property value by the income approach is the application of the capitalization formula. This involves the simple process of dividing net operating income by a capitalization rate. The difficulty lies in arriving at the proper capitalization rate. There are a number of rather complex methods for establishing this rate which are beyond the scope of this text and are not covered in pre-licensing real estate examinations. However, in essence, the appropriate rate is that rate of return investors in comparable properties are achieving on investments in the same locality at the time of the appraisal. The rate of return on any investment includes a consideration of the risk factor. The greater the risk of loss taken by the investor, the higher potential rate of return the investor is entitled to expect.

In the application of the capitalization formula to the apartment complex, we have adopted a rate of 12% as being the appropriate rate for this investment in this area at this time. By dividing the net operating income of $745,600 by .12, a value estimate of $6,213,333 (typically rounded to $6,213,000) is indicated. In other words, if an investor paid this price for the apartment complex and continued to realize a net operating income of $745,600, the investor would realize a return of 12% before deductions for debt service and income tax. As discussed in the chapter on income tax implications in real estate, the imposition of federal income tax may be eliminated or substantially reduced as a result of the deduction for depreciation or the new accelerated cost recovery.

The importance of the selection of a proper capitalization rate cannot be over-emphasized. Even a slight variation in this rate will result in a substantial change in the value estimate. For example, if a 13% rate had been used in the foregoing example, the value estimate would be $5,735,384 which represents a reduction in indicated value of $77,949 or 7.69% of the original estimate. The higher the capitalization rate, the

Figure 10.2 *Operating Statement (continued)*

lower the value estimate will be and conversely the lower the rate, the higher the resulting value estimate. Other examples of the application of the capitalization formula are found in the chapter on real estate mathematics.

Gross Rent Multiplier

Gross rent multipliers are not a part of the income approach to the value estimate, but they may be used to estimate the value of property producing rental income. There is a degree of unreliability in the use of this method because calculations are based on gross income rather than net income. If the property has been efficiently managed, the gross income will provide a reliable basis for calculating an estimate of value. However, if expenses are out of line, gross income will not fairly reflect property value.

Gross rent multipliers are calculated by dividing either the monthly or annual gross income of a property into the price for which it was sold. It does not matter whether gross annual or gross monthly income is used as long as one or the other is used consistently. The accompanying illustration provides examples of calculating gross income multipliers on both a monthly and an annual basis. As can be seen, a much lower multiplier will result from the calculations based on annual income.

In estimating the value of an income property, gross rental incomes may be established for comparable income properties that have sold recently. An average of the gross rent multipliers obtained can be used as a multiplier for the monthly gross or annual income produced by a property under consideration to provide an indication of property value. For example, if the property being considered produced a gross monthly income of $99,000, this would be multiplied by the average gross rent multiplier of 58 as shown in the illustration. This multiplication ($99,000 × 58) provides a value indication of $5,742,000. This indicated value will be as reliable as the gross monthly incomes and prices used in calculating the average gross rent multiplier.

Cost Approach or Approach by Summation

This appraisal method is used as the primary method for estimating the value of properties that are not single family dwellings or vacant land and are not properties that produce rental income. Examples of the type of structures that are appraised by this method include schools, factories occupied by the owning industry, fire stations, hospitals, government office buildings, and libraries.

The first step in the cost approach is to estimate the cost of reproducing or replacing the structure. There is a definite difference between replacement cost and reproduction cost. Reproduction cost is the cost of constructing an exact duplicate of the property when new. Replacement cost is based on constructing a building of comparable utility using modern building techniques and materials. If the subject property was constructed many years ago, it will often be impossible to estimate the cost of reproducing that property today. The materials and craftsmanship just may not be available. Therefore, the basis of the cost approach for older structures is replacement cost new. Reproduction cost new may be used for properties that have been constructed recently.

The methods of estimating reproduction or replacement costs include the quantity survey method, unit in place method, and the square foot method. Of these methods, the quantity survey method is the most accurate but is also the most complex and time consuming method. This is the method that most builders use in calculating a cost estimate for a construction job. This method involves the detailed determination

Calculating Gross Rent Multipliers

Comparable	Price	Monthly Gross	GRM	Annual Gross	GRM
No. 1	$6,213,000	$107,833	58	1,294,000	4.8
No. 2	5,865,000	101,000	58	1,212,000	4.8
No. 3	5,125,000	90,000	57	1,080,000	4.7
No. 4	6,060,000	103,000	59	1,236,000	4.9
No. 5	7,250,000	125,000	58	1,500,000	4.8
No. 6	6,588,000	111,000	59	1,332,000	4.9
Average GRM			58		4.8

of the exact quantity of each type of material to be used in the construction and the necessary material and labor costs applicable to each unit. The final estimate includes a profit to the builder. In the unit in place method, the cost of each component part of the structure is calculated including material, labor, and overhead costs plus a profit to the builder. The cost by the square foot method is calculated by multiplying the number of square feet in the structure being appraised by the cost per square foot to construct the building using the current cost per square foot. The estimated cost figures employed in any of these three methods are available through construction cost services that publish construction cost estimates for various types of structures and structural components.

The next step in the value estimate by the cost approach is to deduct from the estimated cost of replacing or reproducing the property with new construction, any observed depreciation existing and resulting from any of the three forms of depreciation. The deduction of the dollar amount of depreciation will provide the depreciated value of the structure as it presently exists. Next, the depreciated value of any other site improvements is added to the value of the structure to provide an estimate of the total depreciated value of all improvements.

The last step in the cost approach is to estimate the value of the site as though it were vacant. The site value is estimated by the market data approach which employs the use of comparable parcels of land to arrive at the value estimate. The site is compared to comparable parcels of land that have sold recently as a basis for the land value. The estimate of the land value by the market data approach is added to the estimate of the total depreciated value of the improvements to provide a value estimate for the total property by the cost approach.

The various steps and calculations employed in the cost approach are illustrated by the accompanying example of the cost approach calculations.

Cost Approach Calculations

Replacement or Reproduction Cost:
21,000 square feet @
$52.50 sq. ft. $1,102,500

Less structure depreciation:
  Physical deterioration $33,075
  Functional obsolescence 44,100
  Economic obsolescence   -0-   77,175

Depreciated value of
  structure   1,025,325

Depreciated value of other
improvements:
  Retaining walls   10,000
  Paved drive and parking 15,000
  Exterior lighting   2,000
  Fencing   1,500   28,500

Depreciated value of all
  improvements   1,053,825

Land value by market data
  approach   253,000

Total Property Value $1,306,825
Rounded to $1,306,800

Correlation and Appraisal Report

In making an appraisal, a professional appraiser will use the relevant approach to the value estimate as the primary appraisal method. Which method is most relevant depends on the type of property that is the subject of appraisal. For example, in estimating the value of a single-family owner occupied dwelling, the most relevant method is the market data approach. In addition, the qualified appraiser will also estimate the value of the property by each of the other two methods. In the case of the single-family dwelling, the appraiser would treat the property as though it were rental property and estimate the value using the income approach. Lastly, the appraiser would arrive at a value estimate by the cost approach. As a practical matter, the results obtained by these three methods will not be identical. There must be a correlation or reconciliation of the three different results to provide the most reliable estimate of value. In the correlation or reconciliation process, three factors are taken into consideration: The relevancy of each of the three methods to the subject property, the reliability of the data on which each estimate is based, and the strong points and weak points of each method.

After these considerations, the greatest weight should be given to the estimate resulting from the use of the most appropriate or relevant method for the type of property that is the subject of the appraisal. For example, if the property is an office building, the most relevant approach and the one to receive the greatest weight would be the income approach. Even though the results obtained by the different approaches will not be exactly the same, they should be reasonably close. Therefore, each approach used provides a check on the other two. If the result by one particular method is considerably out of line with the others, this indicates some calculation error or some error in the data used as a basis.

The final step in the appraisal process is the preparation of the appraisal report. The report contains the appraiser's opinion of value based on the observation of the results obtained by the three methods and the appraiser's reasons for adopting the final estimate of value. The appraisal report may be either in narrative form or may be a form report. The narrative report provides all the factual data about the property and the elements of judgment used by the appraiser in arriving at the estimate of value. When a standard form is used to report the various property data used and the appraisal method employed, it is called a form report. A form report does not contain narrative information as does the narrative report, but simply sets forth various facts and figures used in the appraisal process and the correlation of the final estimate of market value.

IMPORTANT POINTS

1. Value in exchange is the amount of money a typical buyer will give in exchange for a property. Value in exchange is market value.

2. For a property to have value, it must possess the characteristics of utility, scarcity, transferability, and there must be an effective demand.

3. Value, price, and cost are not the same.

4. The various types of value include market value, assessed value, insurance value, mortgage loan value, condemnation value, and book value.

5. The basic valuation principles are: highest and best use, substitution, supply and demand, conformity, anticipation, contribution, competition, and change.

6. Depreciation is the loss in value from any cause. In structures (land does not depreciate), the causes of depreciation are: (1) physical deterioration, (2) functional obsolescence, and (3) economic obsolescence.

7. An appraisal is an estimate (not a determination) of value based on factual data.

8. The market data or comparison approach to the value estimate is the most relevent appraisal method for estimating the value of single-family owner-occupied dwellings and vacant land.

9. The income approach or appraisal by capitalization is the most appropriate appraisal method for estimating the value of property that produces rental income.

10. The cost approach or appraisal by summation is the primary appraisal method for estimating the value of property that does not fall into the other categories.

12. A gross rent multiplier may be appropriate for estimating the value of rental property.

13. An appraisal report provides a value estimate based on a correlation of the estimates obtained by all three approaches.

Valuation of Real Estate

IMPORTANT TERMINOLOGY

Appraisal
Appraisal Process
Appraisal by Capitalization
Appraisal by Summation
Appraisal Report
Approaches to Value
Anticipation
Assessed Value
Book Value
Capitalization Formula
Cap Rate
Capitalization Rate
Cash Flow
Change
Chronological Age
Comparable
Comparison Approach
Competition
Condemnation Value
Conformity
Contract Rent
Contribution
Correlation
Cost
Cost Approach
Credit Losses
Debt Service
Depreciation
Economic Age
Economic Obsolescence
Economic Rent
Effective Demand
Fixed Expenses
Form Report
Functional Obsolescence
Gross Effective Income
GRM
Gross Rent Multiplier

Highest and Best Use
Income Approach
Insurance Value
Market Data Approach
Market Value
Mortgage Loan Value
Narrative Report
Net Operating Income
Net Taxable Income
Nonproperty Characteristics
Operating Expenses
Operating Statement
Overimprovement
Physical Deterioration
Potential Gross Income
Price
Property Characteristics
Quantity Survey Method
Rate of Return
Replacement Cost
Replacement Reserve
Reproduction Cost
Residual Income
Risk Factor
Scarcity
Square Foot Method
Substitution
Supply and Demand
Transferability
Underimprovement
Unit in Place Method
Utility
Vacancy Rate
Value
Value in Exchange
Value in Use
Weighted Average

REVIEW QUESTIONS FOR CHAPTER 10

1. The basis of market value is most typically which of the following?

    (a) Value in use
    (b) Book value
    (c) Subjective value
    (d) Value in exchange

2. All of the following characteristics must be present for a property to have value EXCEPT

    (a) Utility
    (b) Obsolescence
    (c) Transferability
    (d) Effective demand

3. Value is most closely related to which of the following?

   (a) Price
   (b) Competition
   (c) Cost
   (d) Supply

4. Adherence to the principle of conformity causes which of the following?

   (a) Depreciation
   (b) Minimizing value
   (c) Maximizing value
   (d) Competition

5. An underimprovement and an overimprovement are examples of which of the following?

   (a) Anticipation
   (b) Economic Obsolescence
   (c) Competition
   (d) Functional obsolescence

6. Physical deterioration is caused by
   I. Unrepaired damage
   II. Lack of adequate maintenance

   (a) I only
   (b) II only
   (c) both I and II
   (d) neither I nor II

7. Functional obsolescence results from
   I. Faulty design and inefficient use of space
   II. Changes in surrounding land use patterns

   (a) I only
   (b) II only
   (c) both I and II
   (d) neither I nor II

8. Which of the following causes of depreciation are not curable by the property owner?

   (a) Economic obsolescence
   (b) Functional obsolescence
   (c) Competitive obsolescence
   (d) Physical deterioration

9. The principle followed in making adjustments to comparables in an appraisal by the market data approach is which of the following?

   (a) Competition
   (b) Change
   (c) Contribution
   (d) Conformity

10. An appraisal is which of the following?

    (a) Estimate of value
    (b) Appropriation of value
    (c) Correlation of value
    (d) Determination of value

11. All of the following are approaches to value EXCEPT

    (a) Cost approach
    (b) Contribution approach
    (c) Income approach
    (d) Comparison approach

12. The primary appraisal method for estimating the value of vacant land is which of the following?

    (a) Cost approach
    (b) Market data approach
    (c) Income approach
    (d) Appraisal by capitalization

13. All of the following are important data in the selection of comparables EXCEPT

    (a) Size
    (b) Income
    (c) Location
    (d) Condition

14. The income used as a basis for estimating value is which of the following?

    (a) Monthly net
    (b) Annual gross effective
    (c) Monthly gross effective
    (d) Annual net

Valuation of Real Estate

15. If the income used in the appraisal by capitalization is $480,000 and the capitalization rate is 11%, which of the following will be the estimate of property value?

    (a) $5,280,000
    (b) $2,990,000
    (c) $4,363,636
    (d) $2,290,000

16. All of the following are deductible from gross effective income in arriving at net operating income for appraisal purposes EXCEPT

    (a) Maintenance
    (b) Legal fees
    (c) Replacement reserve
    (d) Debt service

17. In the income approach, which of the following is deducted from gross potential income to calculate gross effective income?

    (a) Fixed expense
    (b) Vacancy rate
    (c) Other income
    (d) Replacement reserve

18. If a property produced a gross income of $103,000 and the GRM was 7.5, which of the following would be the indication of value?

    (a) $1,373,333
    (b) $927,000
    (c) $137,333
    (d) $772,500

19. Which of the following would use the cost approach as the primary method for appraisal?

    (a) Shopping mall
    (b) Court house
    (c) Parking lot
    (d) Condominium apartment

20. All of the following are methods used for estimating replacement cost EXCEPT

    (a) Quantity survey
    (b) Square foot
    (c) Unit in place
    (d) Quality survey

21. Which of the following is described as the cost of constructing a building of comparable utility using modern techniques and materials?

    (a) Reproduction cost
    (b) Operating cost
    (c) Unit cost
    (d) Replacement cost

22. An appraisal report may be
    I. A narrative report
    II. A form report

    (a) I only
    (b) II only
    (c) both I and II
    (d) neither I nor II

Land Use Controls

11

Both public and private land use controls will be discussed in this chapter. Public land use controls include zoning, building codes, subdivision regulation, regulation of interstate land sales, and environmental protection laws. Private land use controls exist in the form of restrictions in individual deeds and restrictive covenants. All land use controls are encumbrances.

DEVELOPMENT OF LAND USE CONTROLS

Private control of land use was the forerunner of public controls. In 1848, the courts first recognized and enforced restrictive covenants regulating land use in residential subdivisions. However, it was not until 1926 when the United States Supreme Court upheld the validity of zoning ordinances that public land use controls became legally reliable. Prior to these two important legal events, there was no way by which a developer or governmental unit could regulate land use even though the need for such controls was readily apparent.

The increase in population density dictates the necessity for land use controls. The abuses of a few property owners in the use of their land can have a very substantial adverse affect on the rights of other property owners and depreciation of their property.

PRIVATE LAND USE CONTROLS

Individual Deed Restrictions

Individual deed restrictions exist in the form of covenants or in the form of conditions. A covenant may exist in a deed to benefit property that is sold or to benefit a property that is retained in the case of a sale of adjoining property. For example, an owner selling an adjoining property provides in the deed that a structure may not be erected in a certain area of the property sold to protect the view from the property retained or to prevent the loss of reception of light and air to the property retained. These restrictions are covenants that "run with the land" meaning that they move with the title in any subsequent conveyance. Covenants may be enforced by a suit for damages or by injunction. Restrictions that provide for a reversion of title if they are violated are called conditions. If a condition is violated, ownership reverts to the grantor.

Restrictive Covenants

These are restrictions placed on the use of land by the developer of a residential subdivision. The purpose of these covenants is to preserve and protect the quality of land in subdivisions and to maximize land values by requiring the homogenous use of land by purchasers of property in a subdivision. The covenants are promises on part of the purchasers of property in the subdivision to limit their use of their property to comply with the requirements of the restrictive covenants and therefore are negative easements. The deed conveying title to property in the subdivision will contain a reference to a recorded plat of the subdivision and a reference to the recording of the restrictive covenants; or, the restrictions may be recited in each deed of conveyance. Restrictions must be reasonable and they must be beneficial to all property owners alike.

If the subdivision is in a zoned area the restrictive covenants will have priority over the zoning ordinance to the extent that the covenants are more restrictive than the zoning requirements. For example, if the zoning permits multi-family dwellings and the restrictive covenants limit land use to single-family dwellings, the restrictive covenants will be enforced. However, if restrictive covenants are contrary to public law and public policy, they will not be enforced. For example, a restrictive covenant requiring discrimination on the basis of race, color, religion, sex, or national origin is invalid. Also, restrictive covenants are not valid unless they are recorded on the public record in the county where the land is located.

Restrictive covenants are land use limitations that provide a general plan for development of a subdivision. Prior to the start of development, the developer will establish a list of rules each lot purchaser will be required to adhere to in the use of the property. These rules controlling the use of land are then recorded in an instrument called "declaration of restrictions." The declaration is recorded simultaneously with the plat and will include a reference to the plat. Typical restrictive covenants are as follows:

1. Only single-family dwellings may be constructed in the subdivision.
2. Dwellings must contain a specified minimum number of square feet of living area.
3. Only one single-family dwelling may be constructed on a lot.
4. No lot may be subdivided.
5. Dwellings must be of a harmonious architectural style. To ensure this, a site plan and plans and specifications for the structure must be submitted to and approved by a committee prior to the start of construction.
6. Structures must be set back a specified distance from the front property line and a specified distance from interior property lines.
7. Temporary structures may not be placed on any lot.
8. Covenants may be enforced by any one property owner or several property owners of land within the subdivision by taking appropriate court action.
9. A specified time period for which the covenants will remain in effect. Also, there may be specified automatic renewal periods that may be changed by a vote of the property owners.

It is important for real estate agents to be aware of the existence of restrictive covenants in subdivisions where they are selling property. The agent should provide prospective buyers with a copy of the covenants, which may be obtained from the developer if he is still on the site or from the office of title registration in the county in which the property is located. In preparing offers to purchase in the subdivision, the real estate agent should include a provision that the offeror acknowledges the receipt of a copy of the restrictive covenants.

Termination of Covenants

Restrictive covenants may be terminated in the following ways:

1. Expiration of the time period for which the covenants were created.
2. Unanimous vote of the property owners to terminate the restrictions unless the restrictions provide for termination by vote of a smaller number of landowners.
3. Changes in the character of the subdivision that make it unsatisfactory for the type of use specified by the restrictions to continue. For example, as a result of the failure of property owners in a subdivision restricted to single-family residential use to enforce the restrictions, the area gradually changes to commercial use. Consequently, the subdivision is no longer suitable for limitation to residential use.
4. The right to enforce particular restrictions may be lost by abandonment, which occurs when the property owners have violated their restrictions and many of them have participated in the violations. As a result a court may rule that there has been an abandonment of the original general plan by the property owners and, therefore, the court will not enforce the restrictions.
5. Failure to enforce restrictions on a timely basis. An owner or owners cannot sit idly by and watch someone complete a structure in a subdivision in violation of the restrictive covenants and then attempt to enforce the restriction by court action. The court will not apply the restriction against the violator. Therefore, the

restriction is terminated by the failure of action on a timely basis by the property owners to enforce restrictive covenants.

Enforcement of Covenants

Any individual property owner (or owners) may enforce the restrictive covenants against a person acting in violation of a covenant. The enforcers apply to a court for an injunction to compel compliance to the covenants. An injunction is an order by the court instructing the violator to discontinue the violation.

Enforcement of the covenants is not limited to the original purchasers of property in the subdivision. Subsequent purchasers must abide by and may enforce the restrictive covenants until such time as the covenants may be terminated as previously discussed.

PUBLIC LAND USE CONTROLS

Private land use controls are definitely limited in scope. Only a specific area can be subject to private use controls in the form of restrictive covenants. The owners of property in subdivisions in which restrictive covenants exist have absolutely no control over surrounding land uses. Therefore, a subdivision may be very adversely affected by an uncontrolled use of an adjoining property outside the subdivision. As a result, people became aware of the need for planning and land use controls for large areas. This is provided by zoning ordinances, the first of which was enacted in 1916 and the legality of zoning laws was upheld by the United States Supreme Court in 1926.

Zoning starts with city or county planning. The zoning laws implement and enforce the plan. Violations of zoning laws can be corrected by a court injunction requiring the violation to be discontinued even to the extent of ordering an unlawful structure to be demolished.

Planning and Zoning

The purpose of planning is to provide for the orderly growth of a community that will result in the greatest social and economic benefits to the people in the community. State legislatures over the years have passed "enabling acts" that provide the legal basis for cities and counties to develop long-range plans for growth. Planning and zoning are based on the police power of government to enable it to fulfill its responsibility for the protection of the health, safety, and welfare of the people.

The first step taken in developing a master plan is to determine what the city contains by making a survey of the community's physical and economic assets. With this information as a basis, a master plan for orderly growth can be created. As a result of the plan, the various uses to which property may be put in specific areas is designated.

A zoning ordinance consists of two parts: (1) the zoning map, which divides the community into various designated districts and (2) text of the ordinance, which sets forth the type of use permitted under each zoning classification and specific requirements for compliance. The extent of authority for zoning ordinances is prescribed by the enabling acts passed by the state legislatures. These acts specify the types of uses subject to regulation and limit the geographical area subject to the ordinances to the boundaries of the government unit enacting the zoning laws. For example, city zoning ordinances may not apply into the county beyond the city limits. However, it is not unusual for a county government to authorize the extension of city zoning for some specified distance into the county and in some cases, cities have been empowered by the state to specifically extend zoning beyond the city limits.

Zoning ordinances provide for four basic types of zones: residential, commercial, industrial, and agricultural. These four basic areas of use are further subdivided into single-family and multi-family residential zones, commercial, light industrial, or heavy industrial. Also, an area may be zoned strictly single-family residential and another residential zone may permit both single-family dwellings and multi-family units. The major thrust of zoning ordinances is to definitely separate residential areas from industrial and commercial zones.

A fifth type of zoning has been added by many communities recently called multiple use or cluster zoning. This type of zoning provides for planned unit developments (PUD) and creates neighborhood communities in which various uses are permitted, including single- and multi-family residential and commercial uses such as retail establishments, offices, and other special service establishments. In this way the inhabitants of the area have ready access to markets and services within the immediate zoned area.

Zoning ordinances may provide for either exclusive-use zoning or cumulative-use zoning. In exclusive-use zoning, only the specific uses specified for that particular zone may be made of property in that zone. For example, if the zone is commercial, residential uses will not be permitted. In contrast, under cumulative zoning, uses that are not designated may be permitted in the zone. For instance, if the area were zoned commercial, a residential use could be made of the property. In cumulative zoning, uses are placed in an order of priority; therefore, a use of a higher priority may be made in an area where the zoned use has a lower priority. The priorities are in the following order: residential, commercial, industrial.

In addition to simply specifying a type of permitted use or uses within a zone, zoning laws also define certain standards and requirements that must be met for each permitted type of use. These requirements will include such things as minimum setbacks from front property line to the building line as well as setbacks from the interior property lines; lot size on which a structure may be placed; height restrictions to prevent the interference with the reception of sunlight and air to other properties; regulations against building in flood plains; requirements for off-street parking.

Nonconforming Use

A noncomforming use occurs when the use of property in a zoned area is different from that specified by the zoning code for that area. When zoning is first imposed on an area or when property is rezoned, the zoning authority cannot require the property owners to discontinue a use that does not now conform to the zoning ordinance. The nonconforming use must be permitted because it would be unconstitutional to require the property owners to terminate the nonconforming use. Therefore, in these cases, the property owner is permitted to continue a nonconforming use and this is a lawful nonconforming use. Otherwise a nonconforming use is unlawful. However, the nonconforming user is subject to certain requirements that exist to gradually eliminate the nonconforming use. Examples of these requirements are as follows:

1. If the property owner abandons the nonconforming use, the owner cannot resume that type of use at a later date but may only use the property in a manner that conforms to the zoning ordinance.
2. The property owner may not make structural changes to the property to expand the nonconforming use or change the use to a different nonconforming use. The owner is only permitted to make normal necessary repairs to the structure.
3. The nonconforming use cannot be changed from one type of nonconforming use to another type of nonconforming use.
4. If a nonconforming structure is destroyed by fire or other casualty, it cannot be replaced by another nonconforming structure.
5. Some ordinances provide for a long-term amortization period during which the nonconforming owner is permitted to continue the nonconforming use. At the end of this long-term period, the owner would have to change the use to conform with the zoning ordinance, rebuilding the structure if necessary.

Variance

A variance is a permitted deviation from specific requirements of the zoning ordinance. For example, if an owner's lot is slightly smaller than the requirements of the zoning ordinance as to the minimum lot size upon which a structure may be built, the owner may be granted a variance by petitioning the appropriate authorities.

Variances are permitted where the deviation is not substantial and where strict compliance would impose an undue hardship on the property owner. The hardship must be applicable to one property only and be a peculiar or special hardship for that property under the zoning law. The special hardship does not exist where all of the property owners in the zoned area have the same difficulty.

Spot Zoning

Spot zoning occurs when a certain property within a zoned area is rezoned to permit a use that is different from the zoning requirements for that zoned area. If the rezoning of a particular property is simply for the benefit of the property owner and has the effect of increasing the land value, the spot zoning is illegal and invalid; however, when spot zoning is used for the benefit of the community and not for the benefit of a particular property owner (or owners), the spot zoning is not illegal and is valid. Legal spot zoning may typically occur in urban development areas to permit shopping areas for the benefit of the community in locations where these uses existed previously.

Community-Based Planning

This type of land use control has its origins in the grass roots of a community. This may occur in communities located in unzoned county areas where the property owners see the need for planning for the orderly growth of the community and the enforcement of an adopted plan through zoning ordinances. The plan is created and based on a strong consensus of the property owners in the community. Along with the plan, the community will agree on certain zoning requirements. The proposal is presented to all of the property owners in the community by a referendum. If the plan and zoning are endorsed by a substantial majority of the community, the county government will adopt the plan and enact the necessary zoning ordinances to enforce the plan as conceived by the property owners.

Subdivision Regulation

States may empower local governments, cities, and counties to regulate the creation of subdivisions within their particular jurisdictions. The purpose of subdivision regulations is to protect purchasers of property within the subdivisions and to protect the taxpayers in the city or county from the imposition of significantly increased tax burdens resulting from the demands for services generated by a new subdivision.

Subdivision ordinances typically address the following requirements:

1. Streets must be of a specified width, be curbed, have storm drains, and not exceed certain maximum grade specifications.
2. Lots may not be smaller than a specified minimum size.
3. Dwellings in certain areas must be for single-family occupancy only. Specific areas may be set aside for multi-family dwellings.
4. Utilities, including water, sewer, electric, and telephone, must be available to each lot.
5. All houses must be placed on lots to meet specified minimum standards for setbacks from the front property line as well as from interior property lines.
6. There must be adequate area drainage to provide for satisfactory runoff of rainfall to avoid damage to any properties.

Once a subdivision ordinance has been adopted, subdivision developers must first obtain the approval of the appropriate officials, then the subdivision plat may be recorded on the public record and development can begin.

Building Codes

Building codes provide another form of control of land use for the protection of the public. These codes regulate such things as materials used in construction, electrical wiring, fire and safety standards, and sanitary equipment facilities.

The codes require that a permit must be obtained from the appropriate local government authority before the construction or renovation of a commercial building or residential property may be started. While construction is in progress, frequent inspections are performed by local government inspectors to make certain that the code requirements are being met.

After a satisfactory final inspection has been made, a Certificate of Occupancy will be issued. This permits the occupation of the structure by tenants or the owner. Many cities today require that a Certificate of Occupancy, based upon a satisfactory inspection of the property, be issued prior to occupancy by a new owner or tenant of any structure even though it is not new construction and/or has not been renovated. Inspection is required, to reveal any deficiencies in the structure requiring correction, before the city will issue a Certificate of Occupancy for the protection of the new purchaser or tenant.

Interstate Land Sales Full Disclosure Act

This federal regulation of the interstate (across state lines) sale of unimproved lots became effective in 1969, and was made more restrictive by an amendment in 1980. The act is administered by the Secretary of Housing and Urban Development through the office of Interstate Land Sales registration.

The purpose of the act is to prevent fraudulent marketing schemes that may occur when land is sold by misleading sales practices on a sight unseen basis. The act requires that a developer file a "Statement of Record" with HUD before offering unimproved lots in interstate commerce by telephone or through the mails. The Statement of Record requires disclosure of information about the property specified by HUD.

The developer is also required to provide each purchaser or lessee of property with a printed "Property Report," which discloses specific information about the land before a purchase contract or lease is signed by the purchaser or lessee. The property report contains specific information about the land for the protection of the purchaser or lessee. Required information includes such things as the type of title a buyer will receive, number of homes currently occupied, availability or recreation facilities, distance to nearby communities, utility services and charges, and soil or other foundation problems in construction. If the purchaser or lessee is not supplied with a copy of the Property Report prior to signing a purchase contract or lease, the purchaser may avoid the contract.

The act provides for several exemptions, the most important of which are:

1. Subdivisions in which the lots are of five acres or more,
2. Subdivisions that consist of less than fifty lots.
3. Lots that are offered for sale exclusively to building contractors.
4. Lots on which a building exists or where there is a contract which obligates the lot seller to construct a building within two years.

If a developer offers only part of the total tract owned and thereby limits the subdivision to less than fifty lots to acquire an exemption, the developer may not then sell additional lots within the tract. HUD considers these additional lots to be part of a "common plan" for development and marketing, thereby eliminating the opportunity for several exemptions for the developer as a result of a piecemeal development of a large tract in sections of less than fifty lots at a time.

The act provides severe penalties for violation by a developer or a real estate agent participating in marketing the property. The developer and/or the real estate agent can be sued for damages by a purchaser or lessee and is potentially subject to a criminal penalty by fine of up to $5,000 or imprisonment for up to five years or both. Therefore, it is extremely important for real estate agents to ascertain that a developer has complied with the law or is exempt prior to acting as an agent for the developer in marketing the property.

Environmental Protection Legislation

The purpose of this federal law is to protect the public against abuses of the environment resulting from the use or development of land. The National Environmental Policy Act of 1969 requires that an environmental impact statement be filed with the Environmental Protection Agency prior to changing or initiating a land use or development to insure that the use will not have an adverse affect on the environment. Typical subject areas regulated by the act include air, noise, and water polution as well as chemical and solid waste disposal.

Responsibility of Real Estate Agents

Real estate agents are obligated to be knowledgeable of existing public and private land use controls within their market area and must keep abreast of changes in the requirements as they occur. This knowledge is very necessary to enable real estate agents to fulfill their obligations to their principals as well as to the buying public. Lack of knowledge in these areas may subject real estate agents to civil liability to injured parties and possible criminal liability under certain federal laws.

Land Use Controls

IMPORTANT POINTS

1. Private land-use controls are in the form of deed restrictions and restrictive covenants.

2. Restrictive covenants must be reasonable and must be equally beneficial to all property owners.

3. Restrictive covenants are recorded on the public record in an instrument called a "Declaration of Restrictions." They are not legally effective and enforceable unless recorded.

4. Restrictive covenants are enforced by court injunction upon a petition by the property owners on a timely basis.

5. The purpose of planning is to provide for the orderly growth of a community that will result in the greatest social and economic benefits to the people.

6. The plan for development is enforced by zoning ordinances. Planning and zoning are an exercise of police power.

7. The types of zones include residential, commercial, planned unit developments (PUDs), industrial, and agricultural.

8. Zoning may be either exclusive-use or cumulative-use.

9. In addition to specifying permitted uses, zoning ordinances define standards and requirements that must be met for each type of use.

10. A nonconforming use is one that is different than the type of use permitted in a particular zone. The nonconforming use may be lawful or unlawful.

11. A variance is a permitted deviation from specific requirements of a zoning ordinance because a special hardship would be imposed on a property owner by strict enforcement.

12. Spot zoning occurs when a certain property within a zoned area is rezoned to permit a use that is different from the zoning requirements for that area. Spot zoning may be valid or invalid.

13. Subdivision ordinances regulate the development of residential subdivisions to protect property purchasers as well as to protect area taxpayers from increased tax burdens to provide essential services to the subdivisions.

14. Building codes require that certain standards of construction be met. The codes are primarily concerned with electrical systems, fire and safety standards, and sanitary systems and equipment.

15. The Interstate Land Sales Full Disclosure Act regulates the sale of unimproved lots in interstate commerce to prevent fraudulent schemes that may occur when land is sold on a sight unseen basis.

16. Environmental Protection Laws are a form of land-use control to protect the public against abuses of the environment.

IMPORTANT TERMINOLOGY

Building Code
Certificate of Occupancy
Cluster Zoning
Community Based Planning
Conditions
Covenants
Cumulative-Use Zoning
Declaration of Restrictions
Deed Restrictions
Enabling Act
Encumbrance
Environmental Policy Act
Environmental Protection Agency
Exclusive-Use Zoning
General Plan for Development
Interstate Land Sales Full Disclosure Act
Negative Easement

Nonconforming Use
Planned Unit Development
Police Power
Private Land Use Controls
Property Report
Public Land-Use Controls
PUD
Restrictive Covenants
Run with the Land
Setback
Spot Zoning
Statement of Record
Subdivision Ordinance
Variance
Zoning Classifications
Zoning Map
Zoning Ordinance

REVIEW QUESTIONS FOR CHAPTER 11

1. Which of the following statements about land-use controls is (are) correct?
   I. Deed restrictions are a form of private land-use control.
   II. Public land-use controls are an exercise of the police power.

   (a) I only
   (b) II only
   (c) both I and II
   (d) neither I nor II

2. Deed restrictions that run with the land are which of the following?

   (a) Conditions
   (b) Variances
   (c) Declarations
   (d) Covenants

3. All of the following statements about restrictive covenants are correct EXCEPT

   (a) They must be reasonable.
   (b) They are enforceable even though not recorded.
   (c) They are not enforceable if contrary to law.
   (d) They provide for a general plan for development.

4. The instrument used for recording restrictive covenants is called?

   (a) Plat
   (b) Master deed
   (c) Covenant
   (d) Declaration of restrictions

5. Restrictive covenants may be terminated in all of the following ways EXCEPT

   (a) Expiration
   (b) Transfer of title
   (c) Failure to enforce on a timely basis
   (d) Abandonment

6. Restrictive covenants are enforced by which of the following

   (a) Zoning
   (b) Injunction
   (c) Police Power
   (d) Condemnation

7. The type of zoning that permits a higher priority use in a lower priority zone is called?

   (a) Exclusive Use
   (b) Nonconforming use
   (c) Amortizing use
   (d) Cumulative use

Land Use Controls

8. The rezoning of a zoned area made a use by one property owner to be not in compliance with the type of use required by the new zoning ordinance. If the owner continues this use it is called which of the following?

    (a) Variance
    (b) Lawful nonconforming use
    (c) Spot zoning
    (d) Unlawful nonconforming use

9. A permitted deviation from the standards of a zoning ordinance is called?

    (a) Variance
    (b) Nonconforming use
    (c) Spot zoning
    (d) Unlawful nonconforming use

10. Rezoning a particular property for the benefit of the owner is called

    (a) Variance
    (b) Nonconforming use
    (c) Spot zoning
    (d) Unlawful nonconforming use

11. Which of the following statements about subdivision ordinances is (are) correct?
    I. The purpose is to protect taxpayers from increased taxes caused by increased demand for services to the subdivision.
    II. To protect developers during the development period from excessive costs and thereby encourage residential development.

    (a) I only
    (b) II only
    (c) both I and II
    (d) neither I nor II

12. When the initiative for zoning ordinances comes from property owners it is called?

    (a) Owner planning
    (b) Community-based planning
    (c) General planning
    (d) Exclusive use planning

13. Building codes require which of the following?

    (a) Property report
    (b) PUDs
    (c) Certificate of occupancy
    (d) Statement of record

14. Which of the following statements concerning the Interstate Land Sales Full Disclosure Act is (are) correct?
    I. The act regulates sales of unimproved lots across state lines.
    II. The act is administered by HUD.

    (a) I only
    (b) II only
    (c) both I and II
    (d) neither I nor II

15. Exemptions to the Interstate Land Sales Full Disclosure Act include all of the following EXCEPT

    (a) Subdivisions of less than 50 lots
    (b) Lots offered only to building contractors
    (c) Lots on which there is a building
    (d) Subdivisions in which the lots are four acres or more

Fair Housing   12

This chapter provides a discussion of the two federal laws prohibiting discrimination in housing. Of major importance is the Federal Fair Housing Act of 1968. The other significant law is the Civil Rights Act of 1866. The 1968 act applies specifically to housing, whereas the 1866 law prohibits discrimination only because of race in both real and personal property.

FAIR HOUSING ACT OF 1968

Originally enacted by Congress as Title VIII of the Civil Rights Act of 1968, this law prohibited discrimination in housing on the basis of race, color, religion, or national origin. An amendment in the Housing and Community Development Act of 1974 added the prohibition against discrimination on the basis of sex. As the law presently exists, it is illegal to discriminate on the basis of race, color, religion, sex, or national origin in (1) the sale or rental of housing or residential lots, (2) the advertising of the sale or rental of housing, (3) the financing of housing, and (4) the provision of real estate brokerage services. The act also makes blockbusting illegal. Following is a discussion of the various specific acts prohibited in each of these categories.

Sale or Rental of Housing

In this category there are a limited number of special exemptions available to owners in renting or selling their property. These exemptions are examined subsequently in the chapter. In the absence of an exemption, the following specific acts are prohibited:

1. Refusing to sell housing or rent, or negotiate the sale or rental of residential lots on the basis of discrimination because of race, color, religion, sex, or national origin. This includes representing to any person on discriminatory grounds "that any dwelling is not available for inspection, sale, or rental when such dwelling is in fact available." Also, it is illegal "to refuse to sell or rent after the making of a bona fide offer, or to refuse to negotiate for the sale or rental of, or otherwise make unavailable or deny, a dwelling to a person" because of race, color, religion, sex, or national origin.

    Examples of violations of these prohibited acts are (1) advising a prospective buyer that a house has been sold when it has not because of the prospect's national origin, (2) refusal to accept an offer to purchase because the offeror is a member of a particular religious faith, and (3) telling a rental applicant that an apartment is not available for inspection because the applicant is a female (or male) when the apartment is actually vacant and available for inspection.

2. The act makes it illegal "to discriminate against any person in the terms, conditions, or privileges of sale or rental of a dwelling, or in the provision of services or facilities in connection therewith, because of race, color, religion, sex, or national origin."

Examples of prohibited acts in this category are (1) the manager of an apartment complex routinely requires tenants to have a security deposit in an amount equivalent to one month's rent unless the rental applicant is a black person, in which case a deposit equivalent to two month's rent is required; (2) the manager of an apartment complex restricts use of the complex swimming pool to white tenants only; and (3) the owner of a condominium will include in the purchase of a condominium apartment a share of stock and membership in a nearby country club provided the purchaser is not from Israel.

Discriminatory Advertising

The act specifys that it is illegal "to make, print, or publish, or cause to be made, printed, or published any notice, statement, or advertisement, with respect to the sale or rental of a dwelling that indicates any preference, limitation, or discrimination based on race, color, religion, sex, or national origin, or an intention to make any such preference, limitation, or discrimination." Examples of violations are (1) an advertisement for the sale of condominium units or rental apartments that contains pictures showing owners or tenants on the property that are invariably of only one race, (2) an advertisement that states that the owner prefers tenants that are male college students, (3) a for sale sign that specifies "no Puerto Ricans," (4) a statement to prospective white tenants by a real estate agent that black tenants are not permitted.

Blockbusting

The act specifically makes blockbusting illegal and defines the practice as "for profit, to induce or attempt to induce any person to sell or rent any dwelling by representations regarding the entry or prospective entry into the neighborhood of a person or persons of a particular race, color, religion, sex, or national origin." Blockbusting describes the practice of real estate agents to induce owners to list property for sale or rent by telling them that persons of a particular race, color, religion, sex, or national origin are moving into the area.

Steering

This is another violation of the act by real estate agents. Steering may be defined as: the practice of real estate agents to direct prospective minority purchasers to integrated areas to avoid integration of nonintegrated areas. The prohibition against steering falls under the general prohibition of refusing to sell, rent, or negotiate the sale or rental of housing or residential lots. Examples of steering include (1) a real estate agent showing a white prospect only properties located in areas populated only by white people, (2) showing black prospects only properties in integrated areas or areas only populated by black persons, (3) showing Polish prospects properties only in areas populated by Poles.

Financing of Housing

"Redlining" describes violations of the Fair Housing Act by lending institutions. The term is based on the theory that some lending institutions, prior to the enactment of the act, may have circled certain local areas with a red line on the map and refused to make loans within the areas circled. The act prohibits lending institutions to refuse to make loans to purchase, construct, or repair a dwelling by discriminating on the basis of race, color, religion, sex, or national origin.

In the past, areas were redlined because they were highly integrated or populated by minorities. Today, however, the Fair Housing Act does not limit the prohibition against financial discrimination to the refusal to make loans because of the character of the neighborhood in which the property is located. The prohibition against discrimination applies to individuals by making it illegal "to deny a loan or other financial assistance to a person applying therefore for the purpose of purchasing, constructing, improving, repairing, or maintaining a dwelling," or "to discriminate against him in fixing the amount, interest rate, duration, or other terms or conditions of such loan or other financial assistance."

Real Estate Brokerage Services

The act prohibits discrimination in the provision of brokerage services and states "it shall be unlawful to deny any person access to or membership or participation in any multiple listing service, real estate brokers' organization, or other service, organization, or facility relating to the business of selling or renting dwellings, or to discriminate against him in the terms or conditions of such access, membership or participation on account of race, color, religion, sex, or national origin."

This provision of the Fair Housing Law can make the denial of membership or the imposition of special terms or conditions of membership in any real estate organization on discriminatory grounds illegal. Additionally, the refusal of a multiple listing service to accept a property for inclusion in the service or the refusal of a member broker to place a listing in the service on discriminatory grounds is illegal. The act requires real estate organizations and real estate agents to provide their services without discrimination.

Definitions

The act contains definitions of certain terms used in the Act as follows:

Dwelling—"Any building, structure, or portion thereof which is occupied as, or designed or intended for occupancy as, a residence by one or more families, and any vacant land which is offered for sale or lease for the construction or location thereon of any such building, structure or portion thereof."

Family—"includes a single individual."

Person—"includes one or more individuals, corporations, partnerships, associations, labor organizations, legal representatives, mutual companies, joint stock companies, trusts, unincorporated organizations, trustees, trustees in bankruptcy, receivers, and fiduciaries."

To rent—"includes to lease, to sublease, to let, and otherwise to grant for a consideration the right to occupy premises not owned by the occupant."

Exemptions

The Fair Housing Law provides exemptions to property owners under certain conditions. However, none of these exemptions are available if either of the following has occurred:

1. Discriminatory advertising has been used.
2. The services of a real estate broker, agent, or salesman, or any person in the business of selling or renting dwellings are used. For the purpose of the act, a person is deemed to be in the business of selling or renting dwellings if (1) the individual has, within the preceding twelve months, participated as principal in three or more transactions involving the sale or rental of any dwelling or any interest therein, or (2) the person has, within the preceding twelve months, participated as agent, other than in the sale of personal residence in providing sales or rental facilities or sales or rental services in two or more transactions involving the sale or rental of any dwelling or any interest therein, or (3) the individual is the owner of any dwelling designed or intended for occupancy by, or occupied by, five or more families.

In the absence of the occurrence of either of the preceding, exemptions are available as follows:

1. An owner who does not own more than three single-family dwellings at any one time, is exempt. Unless the owner was living in, or was the most recent occupant of the house sold, he or she is limited to only one exemption in any twenty-four month period.
2. An owner of an apartment building containing not more than four apartments is exempt in the rental of the apartments provided the owner occupies one of the apartments as a personal residence.
3. Religious organizations are exempt as to properties owned and operated for the benefit of their members only and not for commercial purposes, provided membership in the organization is not restricted on account of race, color, sex, or national origin.
4. A private club not open to the public is exempt as to properties owned by the club to provide lodging for the benefit of the membership and not for commercial purposes.

Enforcement

The Fair Housing Act may be enforced in three ways as follows:

1. By administrative procedure through the Office of Equal Opportunity of the Department of Housing and Urban Development (HUD). HUD may act on its own information and initiative. HUD must act in response to complaints. If a state or local law where the property is located is substantially equivalent, HUD must refer the complaint to the state or local authorities. Complaints must be in writing and state the facts upon which an alleged violation is based. If HUD or a state organization is unable to obtain voluntary compliance with the act within thirty days after a complaint is filed, the aggrieved party may within thirty days thereafter, file a civil lawsuit in any appropriate Federal District Court.
2. The aggrieved party, with or without filing a complaint to HUD, may bring a civil suit in Federal District Court within 180 days of the alleged violation of the act unless a complaint has been filed with HUD in which case the 180 day limitation does not apply. If the aggrieved party wins the case, the court may issue an injunction against the violator and award actual damages and punitive damages up to $1,000 to the aggrieved party.
3. The United States Attorney General may file a civil suit in any appropriate United States District Court where the Attorney General has reasonable cause to believe that any person or group is engaged in a pattern of violation of the act and as such raises an issue of general public importance. The court may issue an injunction or restraining order against the persons responsible.

CIVIL RIGHTS ACT OF 1866

This federal law prohibits discrimination because of race by providing that all citizens shall have the same right to inherit, purchase, lease, sell, hold, and convey real and personal property. There are no exemptions to this law as in the Fair Housing Act of 1968. Therefore, a property owner may qualify for an exemption under the Fair Housing Act but will be in violation of the Civil Rights Act of 1866 if he discriminates in the sale or rental of property because of race.

The Civil Rights Act of 1866 was upheld by the United States Supreme Court as recently as 1968 in the case of Jones vs. Alfred H. Mayer Company. There is only one method of enforcement of the Civil Rights Act of 1866 and that is by a private civil lawsuit in Federal District Court brought by the party who was the subject of an alleged discriminatory act on the basis of race.

Fair Housing

EQUAL HOUSING OPPORTUNITY

We Do Business in Accordance With the Federal Fair Housing Law

(Title VIII of the Civil Rights Act of 1968, as Amended by the Housing and Community Development Act of 1974)

IT IS ILLEGAL TO DISCRIMINATE AGAINST ANY PERSON BECAUSE OF RACE, COLOR, RELIGION, SEX, OR NATIONAL ORIGIN

- In the sale or rental of housing or residential lots
- In advertising the sale or rental of housing
- In the financing of housing
- In the provision of real estate brokerage services

Blockbusting is also illegal

An aggrieved person may file a complaint of a housing discrimination act with the:

U.S. DEPARTMENT OF HOUSING AND URBAN DEVELOPMENT
Assistant Secretary for Fair Housing and Equal Opportunity
Washington, D.C. 20410

HUD–928.1 (7-75) Previous editions are obsolete

Figure 12.1

IMPORTANT POINTS

1. The Civil Rights Act of 1968 prohibits discrimination in housing because of race, color, religion, sex, or national origin.

2. Discrimination is prohibited in (1) the sale or rental of housing, (2) advertising the sale or rental of housing, (3) financing of housing, and (4) the provision of real estate brokerage services. The act also makes blockbusting illegal.

3. There are four exemptions provided to owners in selling or renting housing, namely, (1) owners who do not own more than three houses, (2) owners of apartment buildings in which there are not more than four apartments and the owner occupies one of the apartments, (3) religious organizations as to properties used for the benefit of members only, and (4) private clubs as to lodging used for the benefit of members only.

4. The owners' exemptions are not available if the owner uses discriminatory advertising or the services of a real estate broker.

5. The act may be enforced in three ways: (1) by administrative procedure through HUD, (2) by civil suit in federal court, and (3) by the U.S. Attorney General who may file a suit in federal court.

6. The Civil Rights Act of 1866 prohibits discrimination only because of race. The prohibition is not limited to housing but includes all real estate transactions. The act may only be enforced by civil suit in federal court.

IMPORTANT TERMINOLOGY

Blockbusting
Brokerage Services
Civil Rights Act of 1968
Civil Rights Act of 1866
Civil Suit
Department of Housing and Urban Development (HUD)
Discriminatory Advertising

Dwelling
Family
National Origin
Person
Redlining
Steering
To Rent

Fair Housing

REVIEW QUESTIONS FOR CHAPTER 12

1. Sam Seller refused to accept an offer to purchase his home from Juan Pedro from Spain because Sam considered the $50 of earnest money insufficient. As to Sam's refusal, which of the following is (are) correct?
   I. Sam is in violation of the fair housing law because he discriminated on the ground of national origin.
   II. Since Sam refused the offer for financial reasons, he is not in violation of the 1968 act.

   (a) I only
   (b) II only
   (c) both I and II
   (d) neither I nor II

2. Which of the following is not a basis of discrimination prohibited by the 1968 act?

   (a) Race
   (b) Sex
   (c) Age
   (d) Religion

3. Larry Landlord refused to rent one of five apartments in his building to Barbara Barrister, an attorney. Which of the following statements about Larry's refusal is (are) correct?
   I. If Larry's refusal to rent to Barbara was because she is an attorney, he is not in violation of the 1968 act.
   II. If Larry's refusal to rent to Barbara was because she is a female, Larry is in violation of the 1968 act?

   (a) I only
   (b) II only
   (c) both I and II
   (d) neither I nor II

4. Seller's Town Multiple Listing Service refuses to accept a listing for inclusion in the service because the owner is Russian. Which of the following is correct?

   (a) A multiple listing service does not come under the act because it is a private nonprofit organization.
   (b) The act does not prohibit discrimination against Russians.
   (c) The listing broker's membership in the MLS may be terminated for taking the listing.
   (d) The MLS is in violation of the 1968 act for denying access to the service because of the owner's national origin.

5. A property manager refuses to rent an office because the rental applicant is a Negro. Which of the following is (are) correct?
   I. The applicant has legal recourse under the Civil Rights Act of 1968.
   II. The applicant has legal recourse under the Civil Rights Act of 1866.

   (a) I only
   (b) II only
   (c) both I and II
   (d) neither I nor II

6. In an advertisement offering her only house for sale, the owner states that she will give preference to cash buyers who are female and members of the Catholic religion. The owner subsequently refused a cash offer because the offeror was a male Presbyterian. Which of the following is (are) correct?

   (a) Since the seller only owned one house, she is exempt from the 1968 act.
   (b) Since the advertisement only stated a preference, it is not discriminatory advertising as defined by the 1968 act.
   (c) Since the seller's main purpose was to obtain cash, the refusal is not discriminatory.
   (d) Since the advertisement was in fact discriminatory, the seller's exemption is lost and she has violated the 1968 act in two ways.

7. A real estate agent only showed white prospects property in all-white areas. This discriminatory practice is called?

    (a) Redlining
    (b) Blockbusting
    (c) Steering
    (d) Directing

8. Which of the following is exempt from the provisions of the 1968 act?

    (a) An owner of four houses.
    (b) An owner occupying one of four apartments in his or her building.
    (c) A religious organization renting one of sixteen apartments it owns and operates for commercial purposes.
    (d) An owner who has listed a residential lot for sale with a real estate broker.

9. The Civil Rights Act of 1968 may be enforced by?
    I. A civil suit for damages in federal court.
    II. Administrative procedure through HUD.

    (a) I only
    (b) II only
    (c) both I and II
    (d) neither I nor II

10. A homeowner availed herself of the exemption provided by the 1968 act and refused to accept an offer because the offeror was a white person. The offeror may do which of the following?
    I. File a civil suit for damages in federal court on the basis of the 1968 act.
    II. File a civil suit for damages in federal court on the basis of the 1866 act.

    (a) I only
    (b) II only
    (c) both I and II
    (d) neither I nor II

Property Management and Insurance

13

In this chapter we will treat the topics of property management and insurance. The standard fire insurance policy, homeowners package policies, and homeowners warranty policies will be discussed.

PROPERTY MANAGEMENT

The Property Manager

Property management is one of a number of specializations within the real estate industry. A property manager is a person who manages properties for owners as an agent. In acting as an agent, the property manager is a fiduciary and, therefore, owes all the obligations imposed by the law of agency to each owner-principal. Additionally, since the property manager acts as agent in renting, leasing, and perhaps the selling of the property, the property manager must have a real estate license. The property manager must have comprehensive specialized training to be able to satisfactorily perform the functions accepted under the typical contract with the property owner. The necessary educational requirements are provided by The Institute of Real Estate Management, an affiliate of the National Association of Realtors. Upon completion of this program, the individual receives a professional designation of Certified Property Manager (CPM). In contrast to a property manager, a resident manager is a person living on the premises who is a salaried employee of the owner. Therefore, this person is not required to have a real estate license.

Expert management is often necessary for income property to be a profitable investment. Competent management can provide a comprehensive, orderly program, on a continuing basis, of analyzing all of the investment aspects of a property to insure a financially successful project.

The Functions of a Property Manager

Renting space, collecting rents, and paying expenses are important basic functions of property managers; however, their functions and responsibilities exceed these activities to a very considerable extent. In essence, the property manager's basic responsibilities are (1) to produce the best possible net operating income from the property and (2) to maintain and increase the value of the principal's investment. The property manager fulfills these responsibilities by performing the specific activities that follow.

Formulating a Management Plan

Prior to entering into a management agreement with a property owner, the property manager must formulate a long-range plan to be followed in managing the property. The management plan is included in the management proposal submitted to the owner along with a proposed management agreement. The formulation of the management plan includes the following steps:

I. **Analysis of the Owner's Objectives**
A determination of the owner's objective(s) in ownership of the property must be made.

The property manager must be satisfied that these objectives are realistic. The owner's primary objective may be either (1) income, (2) capital appreciation, or (3) tax shelter provided by depreciation for tax purposes.

II. Market Analysis

This includes a study of the national, regional, and local economic trends and the possible effect of these trends on the local rental market. Also, an analysis of the market area in which the property is located must be made, including an evaluation of the supply of and demand for comparable rental properties.

III. Property Analysis

The property analysis covers a survey of the economic and physical aspects of the property. The economic aspects are data on previous duration of leases, vacancy and credit losses, rent schedules, and operating costs. The analysis of the physical aspects includes the determination of the condition of the property, necessary repairs, and necessary or appropriate capital expenditures.

IV. Preparing Budgets

The last step in the formulation of a management plan is to establish an operating budget and a stabilized budget. The operating budget is an annual budget and as such includes only those items of income and expense expected during a particular budget year. The stabilized budget is a forecast of income and expense as may be reasonably projected over a short term of years, typically five years.

In addition to the formulation of a management plan, the property manager fulfills the basic responsibilities by performing the following specific activities.

1. Solicit tenants through advertising.
2. Show and lease space.
3. Collect rent.
4. Hire, train, and supervise employees to operate and maintain the property.
5. As the representative of the property owner, the property manager must maintain a good business relationship with all tenants in the property.
6. Provide for adequate maintenance of the property.
7. Provide for the protection of tenants by taking the necessary security precautions.
8. Maintain adequate insurance to protect the owner from loss by certain insurable risks, including policies providing coverage for fire and extended coverage, workman's compensation, general liability, and business interruption.
9. Maintain adequate records.
10. Audit and pay bills.

The Management Proposal

The first step in creating an owner-manager relationship is the submission of a management proposal by the prospective property manager to the property owner. This proposal contains the commitments of the manager if employed by the owner. A typical proposal will include the following:

1. A complete description of the land and all improvements.
2. A listing of all maintenance that is required and existing curable obsolescence.
3. Information regarding record maintenance and accounting procedures to be used by the manager.
4. Schedules of property inspections and owner conferences.
5. A thorough operating budget and stabilized budget.
6. A document citing the management fee.

The Management Agreement

The final step in forming the owner-manager relationship is the adoption of the property management agreement by the parties. This contract creates an agency relationship wherein

Property Management and Insurance

the owner is the principal and the property manager the agent for the purposes specified in the agreement. Provisions of a typical property management agreement include the following:

1. Inception date and names of the parties.
2. Property location and description of the premises.
3. Duration of the agency.
4. Method of termination by either party.
5. Agent's fee (a base fee plus a percentage of the rent actually collected).
6. Agent's authority.
7. Agent's covenants.
8. Owner's covenants.
9. Handling of security deposits by agent.
10. Execution of the agreement by owner and agent.

Property Management Report

Included in the agent's covenants is a requirement that the property manager provide a periodic (usually monthly) accounting of all funds received and disbursed. This accounting is called a *Property Management Report*. It contains detailed information of all receipts and expenditures for the period covered (plus the year-to-date) and relates each item to the operating budget for the period.

Properties Requiring Management

Properties that require management are properties that produce rental income, condominiums and cooperatives. Specific examples of income properties include: single-family rental houses, mobile home parks, office buildings, shopping malls, and industrial property.

INSURANCE

Fire Insurance Policies

Most fire insurance policies in the United States are based on the New York standard policy form as revised in 1943. The fire insurance policy indemnifies the insured against loss caused by fire. If the insured wishes to provide protection against losses resulting from other hazards, he or she must obtain an extended coverage endorsement to the fire policy. This endorsement is in the form of a rider attached to the fire policy and requires the payment of an additional premium. The extended coverage endorsement usually includes coverage from losses resulting from hail, explosion, wind storm, aircraft, civil commotion, vehicles, and smoke from friendly fires, which is a fire confined to the place where it is intended to be, such as a fireplace or furnace; otherwise it is a hostile fire.

In recent years, a package policy has become available to homeowners. This form of policy is called a "homeowner's policy," which provides coverage for the structure and contents. A homeowner's tenants policy for renters to cover their personal property is also available. The homeowner's policy provides coverage against loss caused by fire, wind storm, earthquake, hail, dust, waves, surface waters, freezing of plumbing, vandalism and industrial smoke. The policy covers not only damage to the structure but also damage to the contents. Additionally, the homeowner's policy provides personal liability coverage to the policy holder. This protects him against liability for personal injury and property damage caused by the policy holder. Homeowners policies are identified as HO-1, 2, 3, 4, 5, and 6. HO-4 is the tenant's policy and HO-6 is designed for condominiums and cooperatives. HO-1, 2, 3, and 5 cover owners of single-family dwellings.

Every hazard insurance policy must contain a description of the insured property. The street address is usually adequate; however, some insurers require a full legal description.

Insurable Interest

The insured must have an insurable interest in the property to be eligible for insurance coverage of any type. In the absence of an insurable interest, the policy is void. Examples of persons having an insurable interest include the following: buyer and seller in a contract of sale (including a contract for deed) owner, part owner, trustee, receiver, life tenant, mortgagor, and mortgagee.

Coinsurance

Every insurance policy contains a coinsurance clause. This clause requires the property owner to insure for at least 80 percent of the property value to be insured up to the face amount of the policy. Some policies require 90 percent or 100 percent, but 80 percent is the typical requirement in policies insuring an owner occupied residence. If the coverage is for less than 80 percent of value, then the policy will only pay a part of the loss in proportion to the percentage of value insured by the policy owner. For example, if a structure is worth $100,000, the coinsurance clause is 80 percent, and the insurance carried is $60,000; in the event of a partial loss ($30,000), the company's liability is only $22,500. The amount of the insurance company's liability is calculated by using the following formula:

$$\frac{\text{Insurance Carried}}{\text{Insurance Required}} \times \text{Loss} = \text{Company's Limit of Liability}$$

$$\frac{\$60,000}{\$80,000} \times \$30,000 = \$22,500$$

If there had been a loss of $80,000 or more (insurance required), then the insurance company's liability is the amount of insurance carried. If the loss equals or exceeds the amount of insurance required by the coinsurance clause, the company will pay the face amount of the policy. This is illustrated by the following example.

Value of Structure	$100,000
Insurance Required (80%)	$ 80,000
Insurance Policy Amount	$ 60,000
Loss	$ 90,000

$$\frac{\text{Insurance Carried}}{\text{Insurance Required}} \times \text{Loss} = \text{Company's Limit of Liability}$$

$$\frac{\$60,000}{\$80,000} \times \$90,000 = \$67,500 = \$60,000$$

Since the loss equals or exceeds the amount of insurance required by the coinsurance clause, the insurance company will pay the policy amount even though the requirement of the coinsurance clause is not met. However, in no event will the policy pay an amount in excess of the amount of coverage specified in the policy.

Co-owners

A hazard insurance policy covers only the person named as the insured in the policy and only to the extent of his or her interest. For example, if the title is held by two parties as tenants in common and the policy is only in the name of one of them, and a loss occurs, then the policy will only pay the person named as the insured. If the co-tenant named in the policy owned a one-half interest in the property, then the insurance company would pay up to one-half the face amount of the policy but no more than the loss sustained by the tenant in common owning the one-half interest. This is also important in the case of a married couple holding title as joint tenants or by the entireties. If the policy only names one of them as the insured and that spouse dies, the surviving spouse receives title to the deceased spouse's half interest and now owns the entire property. However, since the insurance policy did not include the surviving spouse's name as an insured, there would be no insurance protection in the event of a loss resulting from an insured hazard. Any time ownership in property is changed, the insurance coverage should also be changed to provide adequate protection for any owner or owners.

Mortgagee Insurable Interest

As previously stated, a mortgagee is an individual, group of individuals, or an insurable organization who has interest. The mortgagee usually requires, in the mortgage, that the borrower maintain adequate hazard insurance coverage on the property. In this case, the policy is issued in both the name of mortgagee and mortgagor. The policy protects the mortgagee up to the amount of principal balance owed within the coverage limits provided by the policy. In the event of a partial loss, the insurance company will pay the mortgagor so that he or she or they may make the appropriate repairs. In the event of a total loss, the mortgagee is paid first up to the amount of the mortgage debt still outstanding with any surplus going to the mortgagor.

Assignment

Insurance policies are generally assignable with the written consent of the insurance company.

It is quite usual for a seller to assign his or her interest in a hazard insurance policy to a buyer of the property as of the date of closing with the premium being prorated between buyer and seller. However, the assignment is not valid unless the written consent of the insurer is obtained. This consent is typically evidenced by the issuance by the insurance company of an endorsement to the policy changing the name of the insured.

Homeowners Warranty Policies (HOW)

This policy protects home buyers against defects in the house purchased. In the case of a new house, the policy is provided by the builder through the National Association of Home Builders. The policy provides a one-year warranty against defective workmanship, a ten-year warranty against major structural defects, and a two-year warranty against defects in mechanical and electrical systems. In the resale of an existing house, the seller may transfer the policy to the buyer if the warranty is still in effect. If the policy is no longer in force or if the house was never protected by a HOW policy, a policy is available through many real estate brokerage offices. The premium is usually paid by the listing seller who transfers the policy to the home buyer.

IMPORTANT POINTS

1. Property managers are agents engaged in the management of property for others and, therefore, must have a real estate license.

2. The property manager's basic responsibilities are (1) to produce the best possible net operating income from the property and (2) to maintain and increase the value of the principal's investment.

3. The property manager fulfills his or her basic responsibilities by formulating a management plan, soliciting tenants, leasing space, collecting rent, hiring and training employees, maintaining good tenant relations, providing for adequate maintenance, protecting tenants, maintaining adequate insurance, keeping adequate records, and auditing and paying bills.

4. The management proposal contains performance commitments on the part of the property manager, if employed by the owner.

5. The management agreement is a contract in which a property manager is employed by a property owner to act as his or her agent.

6. The property management report is a periodic accounting provided by a property manager to the property owner.

7. Properties that may require management are condominiums, cooperatives, apartments, single-family rental houses, mobile home parks, office buildings, shopping malls, and industrial property.

8. A fire insurance policy indemnifies the insured against loss by fire. Protection from losses from other hazards may be obtained by an extended coverage endorsement.

9. Packages policies, called homeowners policies, provide all the usual protections in one policy. These policies are available to both homeowners and renters.

10. To be eligible for insurance, the applicant must have an insurable interest in the property. Persons having an insurable interest include: buyer and seller in a contract, owner, part owner, trustee, receiver, life tenant, mortgagor, and mortgagee.

11. Every hazard insurance policy contains a coinsurance clause requiring the property owner to insure for at least 80 percent of the property value to be insured up to the face amount of the policy, in the event of a partial loss. However, if the loss equals or exceeds the amount of coverage required by the coinsurance clause, the insurance company will pay the policy amount even though the requirement of the coinsurance clause is not met.

12. Insurance policies are usually assignable with the written consent of the insurance company. The consent is evidenced by an endorsement to the policy.

13. Homeowners warranty policies are available to purchasers of newly constructed houses and to purchasers of existing houses. These policies insure against structural and mechanical defects.

IMPORTANT TERMINOLOGY

Coinsurance Clause
Endorsement
Extended Coverage
Face Amount
Fiduciary
Fire Insurance Policy
Friendly Fire
Homeowners Policy
Homeowners Warranty Policy (HOW)
Hostile Fire
Insurable Interest
Insurance Carried

Insurance Required
Management Agreement
Management Plan
Management Proposal
Operating Budget
Property Management
Property Management Report
Property Manager
Resident Manager
Stabilized Budget
Standard Fire Policy

REVIEW QUESTIONS FOR CHAPTER 13

1. All of the following statements about property management are correct EXCEPT

    (a) Property management is a specialized field within the real estate industry.
    (b) A property manager acts as agent of the property owner.
    (c) The terms property manager and resident manager have the same meaning.
    (d) A property manager is a fiduciary.

2. A property manager's basic responsibilities to the owner is (are) which of the following?
    I. Produce the best possible net operating income from the property.
    II. Maintain and increase the value of the owner's investment.

    (a) I only
    (b) II only
    (c) both I and II
    (d) neither I nor II

Property Management and Insurance

3. A budget that is based on a forecast of income and expense anticipated over a period of years is called a(n)

   (a) Stabilized budget
   (b) Projected budget
   (c) Anticipated budget
   (d) Operating budget

4. Which of the following creates an agency relationship between a property manager and the property owner?

   (a) Management proposal
   (b) Management report
   (c) Management agreement
   (d) Management plan

5. Properties that may require management include all of the following EXCEPT

   (a) Shopping malls
   (b) Condominiums
   (c) Single-family homes
   (d) Mobile home parks

6. A homeowner's insurance policy includes coverage for
   I. Structure and contents.
   II. Personal liability.

   (a) I only
   (b) II only
   (c) both I and II
   (d) neither I nor II

7. Which of the following statements about hazard insurance policies is not correct?

   (a) They are not assignable.
   (b) They contain a coinsurance clause.
   (c) There must be an insurable interest.
   (d) They only protect the person or persons named in the policy.

8. If a home valued at $200,000 and insured for $120,000 by a policy with an 80 percent coinsurance clause suffers a loss of $175,000 from an insured hazard, what amount will the insurance company pay?

   (a) $175,000
   (b) $120,000
   (c) $96,000
   (d) $160,000

9. Those having an insurable interest in real property include all of the following EXCEPT

   (a) Mortgagee
   (b) Life tenant
   (c) Trustee
   (d) Property manager

10. Which of the following identifies a policy insuring against loss caused by structural defects?

    (a) WOH
    (b) HOW
    (c) HO-1
    (d) WHO

Tax Implications of Real Estate Ownership and Transactions

14

It is very important that real estate agents have a basic knowledge and understanding of the federal income tax laws affecting real property. However, real estate agents may not give tax advice to buyers and sellers. Each taxpayer's situation is different. Therefore, advice should only be given by competent professional tax counsel familiar with the taxpayer's position. Real estate agents should recommend that buyers and sellers seek such counsel when appropriate.

This chapter presents the fundamentals of tax implications in the ownership and sale of a principal residence and business and investment property. The special tax benefits provided to owners and sellers of real property are illustrated and explained to enable you to achieve a good understanding of these advantages.

TAX IMPLICATIONS OF HOME OWNERSHIP

Tax Deductible Expenses

The tax deductible expenses involved in home ownership are mortgage interest (not principal) and real property taxes paid to local taxing authorities. Additionally, the fact that the taxpayer has mortgage interest as a deductible item will usually make it advantageous for him to itemize and take advantage of other tax deductible expenses not associated with home ownership. The combination of mortgage interest and other itemized expenses provide greater tax relief than available in taking the allowable standard deduction.

To put this in the form of a realistic example, let's assume a home buyer purchasing a residence for $100,000 with a $10,000 downpayment and the balance financed for thirty years at 11½ percent interest. The monthly payment of principal and interest necessary to fully amortize the remaining $90,000 over a period of thirty years is $891.27. During the first twelve months of loan payments the borrower will pay a total of $10,335.24 in interest. A proportionate amount of this interest is available as a tax deduction for the year in which the loan was created. For instance, if six payments are made during the tax year approximately half of the interest will be deductible for that particular tax year. In subsequent years the full amount of interest paid is available as a tax deduction.

In the tenth year of the loan, the borrower will pay $9,705 in interest. In fact, it is not until the twenty-fifth year of the loan that the monthly payment is allocated approximately one-half to interest and one-half to the reduction of principal.

If our homebuyer's first mortgage payment is in the first month of the tax year, there will be a tax deductible expense for that year of $10,335. Additionally, this deduction will make it beneficial for him or her to itemize and include other tax deductible items in addition to real property taxes.

Another way to look at this is to relate the taxpayer's income tax bracket to the mortgage interest rate. For instance, if our taxpayer is in a

35 percent bracket, take 35 percent of the 11½ percent interest rate, which is 4.25 percent, and deduct that amount from the mortgage interest rate. The result is an after-tax interest rate to our 35 percent bracket taxpayer of 7.475 percent.

Energy Credits Available to Homeowners and Renters

There are also tax credits available to homeowners and renters for energy conservation measures and installation of renewable energy sources.

There is a definite distinction between a tax deductible expense and a tax credit. A tax deductible expense is an amount that may be deducted from gross income in arriving at net taxable income. A tax credit is an amount that may be deducted from the tax bill to arrive at a net tax bill. For example, if a taxpayer has $5,000 taxable income and is in a 25 percent tax bracket, the tax bill will be $1,250. If the taxpayer has tax credits available in the amount of $1,000 resulting from the installation of renewable energy sources and for having taken energy conservation measures, this credit will reduce the tax bill to $250.

The federal income tax laws offer incentives to homeowners and renters in the form of tax credits for taking energy conservation measures or installing renewable energy sources. The taxpayer may take a tax credit of 15 percent of the cost of effecting conservation measures in a principal residence. The credit is limited to 15 percent of the cost not exceeding $2,000 for a maximum credit of $300. These conservation measures include: insulation, energy usage display meters, storm doors and windows, caulking, weatherstripping, energy-saving thermostats, and certain furnace improvements. Additionally, a tax credit for the installation of renewable energy sources including solar, geothermal, or wind-powered equipment is available when this equipment is installed. The tax credit for the installation of renewable energy sources is 40 percent of the first $10,000 of cost providing a maximum credit of $4,000. In addition to federal income tax credits, various states also provide tax credits for energy conservation measures and the installation of renewable energy sources.

Owners of condominium apartments and stockholders of cooperative housing corporations may claim tax credits for the cost of qualifying energy conservation measures and renewable energy source costs by the condominium association or cooperative housing corporation for the benefit of the common areas of the cooperative or condominium. Cooperative stockholders bear the cost in proportion to the stockholders' number of shares as a percentage of the total outstanding stock of the cooperative. The credit for condominium owners is based on each owner's proportionate share of ownership in the common areas of the condominium.

If a home is owned jointly by two or more owners or rented by two or more renters, the maximum credit available to each owner or renter is the amount of cost actually paid by each owner or renter. If one owner is not able to claim a portion of the credit because the owner or renter does not have sufficient tax liability, the other owners or renters are not affected insofar as their ability to claim their share of the credit.

Energy credits apply on a per-home basis. If an owner or renter occupies two different properties as a principal residence during one tax year, a new credit allowance is available for each home wherein energy conservation measures have been taken or a renewable energy source installed. Unused credits may be carried over to the following years through 1987 if the entire credit cannot be taken in the year in which the eligible energy measures were taken. In no event may the credit in any year exceed the taxpayer's tax liability for that year.

The property in which the energy conservation measures are taken or a renewable energy source installed must be a property that is owned or rented, used as a principal residence, and located in the United States. Additionally, the property must have been substantially completed prior to April 20, 1977 to qualify for energy conservation credit. To qualify for renewable energy source credits, the installation must have been made after April 19, 1977.

TAX IMPLICATIONS IN THE SALE OF A PRINCIPAL RESIDENCE

If an owner sells a principal residence and does not reinvest the proceeds of the sale in a new residence for a price equal to or greater than the adjusted sales price of the home sold within the time limits prescribed by the tax law, all or part of the proceeds of the sale are taxable for the tax year of the sale. A residence falls into the category of a capital asset. A capital asset is property used in a trade or business (other than inventory) and property held for personal use or as an investment.

The gain (profit) realized in the sale of a capital asset may be taxed in one of two ways. If the asset is held for twelve months or less prior to the sale, the gain is fully taxable as ordinary income. This is called a short-term capital gain (ordinary gain). However, if the asset is held for more than twelve months, the gain realized is a long-term capital gain. Only 40 percent of the gain realized from the sale of an asset held for more than twelve months is subject to income tax. The other 60 percent is exempt from tax. The taxable 40 percent is taxed as ordinary income at the rate applicable to the taxpayer's bracket in the year of the sale.

To qualify as a long-term capital gain, the asset must have been held for more than twelve months. In determining the holding period, the first day after the acquisition of the asset is the beginning day of the holding period. The same date of each succeeding month is the beginning of a new month regardless of the number of days in the preceding month. Also, the date on which the property is sold is included as part of the holding period. For example, in the case of a residence purchased on July 10, the holding period starts on July 11. To qualify for long-term capital gains treatment, the residence would have to be held at least until July 11 in the following year.

Long-Term Capital Loss

If the sale of a long-term capital asset results in a loss, this loss is called a long-term capital loss and is a tax deductible item for the taxpayer against other income. Only 50 percent of a capital loss is deductible. Therefore, if a taxpayer had a $10,000 loss in the sale of a long-term asset, he or she would have a $5,000 loss to offset other ordinary income. *Property held for personal use does not qualify for deduction of a capital loss. Therefore, losses in the sale of a principal residence are not tax deductible unless they were caused by theft or casualty.*

Short-Term Capital Loss

A loss incurred in the sale of a capital asset held for twelve months or less is a short-term loss and the total amount of the loss is tax deductible. This loss can be used to reduce income from any other source with a maximum allowable deduction of $3,000 for any one tax year. If the amount of the capital loss exceeds the yearly limit, the excess loss may be carried forward to the next and future years until the entire loss has been taken. *However, just as a long-term capital loss is not deductible in the sale of a principal residence, a short-term loss is also not deductible.*

Rollover Rule

The federal tax laws provide that a gain realized in the sale of a principal residence is not taxed in the year of the sale provided the seller buys or constructs another residence for a price equal to or greater than the adjusted sales price of the home sold within twenty-four months (effective 7/20/81) before or after the sale.

If the transaction qualifies under the requirements set forth above, the rollover rule is mandatory. The taxpayer does not have a choice. He or she must rollover (defer) the tax on the gain realized. The tax may be deferred indefinitely under the rollover rule. A taxpayer may be involved in a number of qualifying transactions and therefore mandatory rollovers of tax during his or her lifetime. Any gain in the sale of a residence that is not taxed under the rollover rule is used to reduce the tax basis of the new residence purchased. The basis of the new residence is reduced by the untaxed amount. This results in a lower tax basis for the new property in calculating the profit when that home is sold.

If the transaction does not qualify under the rollover rule, the gain realized in the sale of the residence is taxable for the tax year in which the sale occurs. If the residence had been held for more than twelve months, the gain will be treated as a long-term capital gain; therefore, only 40 percent of the gain will be subject to tax. However, if the residence is held for twelve months or less, any gain will be fully taxable as ordinary income under the provisions for taxation of short-term capital gains. In either case, a loss is not deductible. *Losses do not affect the tax basis of a new residence.*

Computing Taxable Gain

In computing the gain or loss in the sale of a principal residence, the first step is to establish the owner's tax basis in the property. The tax basis consists of the price paid for the property, less any gain realized in the sale of the previous residence on which the payment of tax was deferred under the rollover rule, plus expenses incurred in acquiring the property (other than those incurred in arranging financing) plus the cost of any capital improvements (not repairs) made during ownership.

Effect of Purchase and Sale Expenses

There are certain expenses for both buyer and seller in the purchase and sale of a personal residence. Listed below are examples of these expenses and their application by buyer or seller in calculating taxable gain.

1. The premium paid for a title insurance policy may be *subtracted* from the selling price if paid by the seller. It may be *added* to his or her basis if paid by the buyer.
2. Transfer taxes (ordinarily paid by the seller) may be *deducted* by the seller from the selling price. However, if the tax is paid by the buyer, then the amount is *added* to the buyer's basis.
3. Attorney's fees paid by the seller are *deductible* from the selling price. Attorney's fees paid by the buyer are *added* to the buyer's basis. However, attorney's fees incurred by the buyer to obtain financing may not be added to the buyer's basis.
4. If the seller pays the attorney's fee for the preparation of a deed, this fee may be *deducted* by the seller from the selling price. If the fee for drawing the deed is paid by the buyer, it may be *added* to the buyer's basis.
5. Buyer's closing costs that are allocable to purchasing the property may be *added* to the buyer's basis. However, expenses of borrowing the purchase price may not be added to the buyer's basis. Examples of expenses involved with obtaining the loan include such things as appraisal fees, mortgage insurance premiums, charges by the lender's attorney, and credit report cost.
6. Discount points charged by lending institutions may be *deducted* from the selling price if paid by the seller to enable the buyer to obtain a loan. These discount points are not deductible as interest by the seller because the seller has not borrowed the money and therefore has no obligation to repay. The seller usually pays the discount points charged by lending institutions in making FHA and VA loans. Therefore, these charges are not deductible as interest by the seller.

    Discount points paid by the buyer are *deductible* as interest by the buyer for the year in which the points are paid. However, if the mortgage loan was not obtained to purchase or improve a principal residence, deduction of the discount points as interest must be spread out over the life of the loan. For example, if a borrower paid $2,000 in discount points to obtain a twenty year conventional loan to purchase an apartment building, the discount points are *deductible* at the rate of $100 per year for twenty years.
7. If the borrower pays a loan origination fee or loan processing fee, typically 1 percent of the amount of the loan, the fee is *not deductible* as interest since the fee is for loan services and not for the use of the money borrowed. Also, the borrower may not add the cost of a loan origination or processing fee to the basis of the property because this is an expense of borrowing the purchase price rather than a cost for obtaining the property. Loan origination fees paid by the seller are a selling expense and may be deducted from the sales price in arriving at the amount realized.
8. Other expense items such as surveys, escrow fees, title abstracts, recording fees, and advertising costs may be *added* to the buyer's basis if paid by the buyer or *subtracted* from selling price if paid by the seller.
9. The real estate commission paid by the seller may be *deducted* from the selling price. The commission paid is not

deductible from ordinary income by the seller.
10. Fix-up expenses are costs incurred by the seller in preparing a residence for sale. To qualify as deductions from the amount realized to establish the adjusted sale price, these costs must have been incurred within ninety days prior to signing the contract of sale that results in the completed sale of the home and must be paid for within at least thirty days after the sale. Fix-up expenses are not deductible unless the seller purchases or builds a new home within the time limits specified by the rollover rule. Also, these expenses are deductions only to determine the amount of gain on which tax is to be postponed and may not be used as deductions in arriving at gain.
11. Moving expenses connected with starting work at a new job location at least thirty-five miles farther from a former residence than the old job location are tax deductible expenses. A deduction is available for both employees and self-employed taxpayers. Expenses as discussed in paragraphs 1 through 10 above may be treated as moving expenses or may be added to the basis of the new home or deducted from the selling price of the former residence. If these expenses are deducted as moving expenses, they may not also be used to reduce the amount realized on the sale of the former home and may not be added to the basis of the new home.

Other deductible moving expenses are used to calculate net taxable income. Examples of these other moving expenses include transportation of furniture and effects; expenses of transportation, meals, and lodging when traveling from the former home to the new home; house-hunting expenses, including the cost of meals, lodging, and transportation to look for a home in the new location provided a job has already been secured in the new area; and temporary living expenses for any consecutive thirty days after employment in the new job.

The tax deductible costs of moving household goods and personal effects and the tax deductible expenses incurred for travel, meals, and lodging in moving from the old residence to the new residence are not limited in dollar amount. All other costs have a limit of $3,000. Of these other costs, the costs for house-hunting trips and temporary living expenses together cannot exceed $1,500. However, if the taxpayer has expenses involved with selling and buying a home that are not deductible as moving expenses because of the $3,000 limit, these expenses may be used to reduce the gain in the sale of the old residence or to increase the basis of the new residence. There are certain exceptions to these dollar limits for married persons filing separate returns and for married persons filing joint returns and depending upon whether or not both will occupy the new residence and whether or not both will be employed in the new location.
12. A financial penalty (prepayment penalty) required by a lender for early pay-off of a mortgage loan is deductible as interest by the borrower for the year in which the prepayment penalty is paid.

Computation of Gain

Figure 14.1 illustrates the steps taken in computing taxable gain and arriving at the adjusted basis of a new residence.

As can be seen from the information in figure 14.1, the taxable gain for the year of the sale is $2,800 and not the full gain of $30,800. The taxable gain in the year of sale is incurred because the price of the new residence was not equal to or greater than the adjusted basis of the old home. The tax on the gain postponed, $28,000, is deferred indefinitely under the mandatory rollover rule. However, the gain postponed is used to reduce the tax basis of the new residence purchased and is the tax basis for the new residence when it is sold sometime in the future. Therefore, the tax basis of the new residence to the purchaser will be $33,000 ($61,000 - $28,000). Had our taxpayer purchased a new residence costing $63,800 (adjusted sale price of old home)

```
Selling Price of Old Home  $ 70,000
Less: Selling Expenses         5,600
       Amount Realized                  $ 64,400

Basis of Old Home          $ 32,400
Plus: Capital Improvements    1,200

       Adjusted Basis of
         Old Home                       $ 33,600

Gain on Old Home
  (Amount Realized Less
  Adjusted Basis) 64,400
  - 33,600                              $ 30,800

Amount Realized on Old
  Home                     $ 64,400
Less: Fix-up Expenses           600
       Adjusted Sales Price             $ 63,800
       Cost of New Home                   61,000
       *Gain Not Postponed              $  2,800

Gain Postponed (Gain
  on Old Home Less Gain
  Not Postponed) 30,800 -
  2,800                                 $ 28,000

Cost of New Home                        $ 61,000
Less: Gain Postponed                      28,000
       Basis of New Home                $ 33,000
```

*Taxable for year of sale as a long- or short-term capital gain depending on the period of ownership.

Figure 14.1 *Steps in Computation of Taxable Gain and Adjusted Basis of a New Residence*

or more, all of the gain realized would have been postponed.

The rollover rule does not require that the seller use the same funds received in the sale of his or her old principal residence to buy or build a new home. The seller may invest a lesser amount of cash and obtain a larger mortgage loan with which to purchase another qualifying residence.

Inheritance Basis

The tax basis for all real property received by heirs is the market value of the property on the date of the death of the decedent and not the market value at the time the decedent acquired the property. This provides a substantial benefit to heirs when they sell the property. As a result of this stepped-up basis, any tax on gains deferred under the rollover rule during the lifetime of the decedent is eliminated. Therefore, we see that gains deferred under the rollover rule are not taxed in the decedent's estate. The only time that these deferred taxes must be paid is in the event of a sale of property, during the lifetime of the taxpayer, that does not qualify for tax deferrment under the rollover rule and also does not qualify for the $125,000 once-in-a-lifetime exclusion.

The Age Fifty-Five-and-Over Exclusion

This is a tax exemption available to sellers of a principal residence provided the seller is age fifty-five or over. The seller may exempt from any tax up to $125,000 (effective 7/20/81) of gain in the sale of a principal residence. Another qualifying requirement is that the seller must have used the property as his or her principal residence for at least three of the five years immediately preceding the date of the sale. If the seller is age sixty-five or over at the time of the sale, the individual must have lived in the home as the principal residence for only five of the eight years preceding the date of the sale if he does not qualify on the three-of-the-last-five-years basis.

This is a once-in-a-lifetime exemption. Once it is used, it is gone. This is true even if a gain of only $40,000 was made and the exemption taken. The seller does not have an additional $85,000 to exempt in another sale of property in the future. The tax on any gain in excess of the $125,000 exemption must be deferred under the rollover rule.

Unmarried co-owners of property used as their principal residence qualify for the exemption. In this case, the exemption may be taken by the qualifying owner even though they do not both qualify. Also, if they both qualify, one may elect to take the exemption for his or her portion of the gain while the other may elect not to do so. Single owners in severalty also qualify.

If the property is owned by a married couple, only one spouse must have attained the age of fifty five for the transaction to qualify for the exemption. If the election is taken by a married couple, even though only one spouse qualifies, it is binding upon both of them. If they are divorced after the sale in which the exemption is taken, and both subsequently acquire a new spouse, the fact that each had taken the exemption in a prior marriage is binding upon the new spouse in each case as well, even though the new spouse would have qualified otherwise. Therefore, a good question to ask when considering a proposal of marriage after age fifty-five is, "Have you taken your $125,000 exemption?"

A married taxpayer filing a separate tax return may exclude a maximum of $62,500 of gain on the sale. Each spouse filing separately may exclude a maximum of $62,500.

In meeting the ownership and use tests, the taxpayer may add the time he owned and lived in a previous home that was destroyed by fire or other casualty or that was condemned under eminent domain to the time he owned and lived in the home for which he desires to exclude a gain under the age fifty-five-and-over exclusion. So we see that a seller who only owned and occupied the home being sold and wishes to exclude the gain for a period of two years, but the previous principal residence was either condemned or destroyed by fire or other casualty, had been occupied as a principal residence for a period of time that when added to the period of time of occupancy of the residence, equals a number of years sufficient to qualify under the three out of five year rule.

INSTALLMENT SALES

The subject of installment sales is included at this point because tax law applications in installment sales apply to both a personal residence and to property held for investment or for use in a trade or business. An owner may sell his or her principal residence on an installment sale basis and avoid the substantial impact of tax in one year. In situations where the seller does not plan to purchase a new residence within the time period required for the rollover rule and also does not qualify for the $125,000 maximum tax exemption, an installment sale can be used to provide tax relief.

Installment sales may be used to spread the impact of federal income taxes on profits over a period of several years or to postpone taxes to a future year or years. This enables the taxpayer to avoid the impact of tax on profit in the sale of property in a single year resulting in a substantial increase in taxpayer's tax bracket and consequently a much larger imposition of tax. In installment sales, the tax laws apply to the sale of real property, businesses, securities, and personal property.

On October 20, 1980, a new tax bill (Installment Sales Revision Act of 1980) revising the law affecting installment sales was enacted by Congress. For the most part, the revised law substantially liberalized the tax rules relating to installment sales. Some of the changes were made retroactive to January 1, 1980. One provision was made retroactive to May 14, 1980 and others became effective on October 20, 1980.

30 Percent Rule Repealed

Prior to the 1980 revisions in the tax law, if the seller received more than 30 percent of the gross sales price of the property in the calendar year of the sale, the sale would not qualify as an installment sale and therefore the taxpayer was taxed on the taxable gain in the transaction even though he or she may have only received a part of the profit in the tax year of the sale. The limit has been abolished and the taxpayer is taxed on the profit in proportion to the amount of the sales price he or she receives in a given calendar year. For example, if a seller receives 50 percent of the sales price in the calendar year of the sale, that person is taxed on 50 percent of the profit. If the gain is a long-term capital gain, only 40 percent of the gain is taxable. The repeal of the 30 percent rule is retroactive to property sales made after January 1, 1980.

Two-Payment Rule Eliminated

Prior to the 1980 revision, the tax law required an installment sale to consist of payments in at least two different calendar years. This is no longer required. In fact, a seller may receive no payment in the year of the sale and the sale will still qualify as an installment sale. The seller simply pays tax on the profits received in any given year. For example, the seller may not wish to receive any money in the calendar year of the sale but to receive all of it in another year or over several years. The seller is only taxed for any calendar year in which a portion or all of the purchase price is received. Elimination of the two-payment rule is retroactive to sales made after January 1, 1980.

Sales Price and Terms

The sale will qualify as an installment sale under the revised law even though the sales price and terms are not established precisely in the year of the sale. There may be contingencies, not resolved in the calendar year of the sale, that will affect the sales price. Even so, the contingent sales price does not disqualify the transaction as an installment sale. Prior to the 1980 change, such contingencies having an effect on the sales price would disqualify the transaction for installment sales treatment. The effective date of this revision in the tax law is October 20, 1980.

Automatic Election

Prior to the revision, the taxpayer had to elect, at the time of filing his or her tax return, that a sale be treated as an installment sale. Many taxpayers were unaware of this opportunity for tax avoidance and failed to make the election; therefore, they paid taxes unnecessarily when the sale would have qualified as an installment sale. Under the new law, the installment sale election is automatic. If the sale qualifies, it will be treated as an installment sale and tax imposed accordingly.

However, the taxpayer may make a definite election for the sale not to be treated as an installment sale. An election for the sale not to be treated as an installment sale may not be revoked without the consent of the Internal Revenue Service. Also, under an automatic election, the taxpayer cannot revoke the election or accelerate the recognition of gain after the election has been made and taxable gain reported on an installment basis.

Related Party Sales

This section of the 1980 tax law applies to almost all types of assets with the exception of marketable securities. Under this section, sales made to related parties include sales between husbands and wives and grandparents, parents, children, and grandchildren. The term "related party" also includes sales between corporations and major stockholders. Brothers and sisters are not considered to be "related parties" for this purpose.

This section of the tax law provides that if a property that was sold to a related party on an installment sale basis is resold by the purchaser within a two-year period, any gain realized from the resale is taxed to the original seller that made the sale to the related party. The original seller is taxed on the total taxable gain realized in the sale by the related purchaser in the tax year of the sale even though the purchasing seller makes an installment sale spread over a number of years. However, if the original seller dies within the two-year period, a gain on the second sale is not taxed back to the decedent's estate. This provision became effective October 20, 1980.

TAX IMPLICATIONS OF THE OWNERSHIP AND SALE OF BUSINESS AND INVESTMENT PROPERTY

As we have seen, there are special tax benefits in the ownership and sale of a principal residence. There are also special tax benefits in the ownership and sale of real property held as an investment or for use in a trade or business. These tax benefits include depreciation, deductible expenses, capital gains and losses, and tax-free exchanges of like kind property.

Depreciation

There are actually two types of depreciation, namely tax depreciation and economic depreciation. Economic depreciation results from physical deterioration of property caused by normal use of the property, damage caused by natural and other hazards, and failure to adequately maintain the property. Tax depreciation is a provision of the tax law, applicable to certain types of assets, that permits a property owner to take an ordinary business deduction for the amount of annual depreciation. This permits the owner to recover the cost or other basis of an asset over the period of the useful life of the asset. Tax depreciation is a deduction from net income in calculating taxable income.

There are two methods of tax depreciation. The method of depreciation used by taxpayers for depreciable assets placed in service by the owner prior to January 1, 1981, is based on the useful life of the asset. A new method must be used to depreciate assets placed in service after December 31, 1980. This method is called the Accelerated Cost Recovery System (ACRS). ACRS provides for the recovery of the cost of an asset over specific periods of three, five, ten, or fifteen years rather than longer periods based on the useful life of the asset. The three-and five-year periods only apply to personal property.

The next material is a discussion of the useful life method of depreciation followed by a discussion of ACRS.

Depreciable property includes such assets as buildings, equipment, machinery, and other assets that are used in business to produce income (other than inventories) or that are held as an investment. Assets held for personal use, including a personal residence, are not depreciable assets. Also, land is not a depreciable asset. Therefore, the value of the land and the value of structures on the land must be separated to arrive at a basis for determining depreciation. This basis is normally the cost of acquiring the property reduced by the estimated salvage value of the property at the end of the useful life.

When a depreciable asset is sold, the basis of the asset used to compute the taxable gain realized in the sale is the depreciated value. For example, if a depreciable asset was purchased for $100,000 and $40,000 of tax depreciation had been taken by the purchaser at the time the property was sold for $130,000, the taxable gain would be $70,000 ($130,000 sales price minus $60,000 depreciated value = $70,000 taxable gain).

Useful Life

There is no average useful life applicable to all types of property or to all property owners. The estimated useful life is the period over which the asset may reasonably be expected to be used. The useful life of an asset depends upon the length of time the owner expects to use it, the owner's policy as to maintenance repairs and replacement, and the age of the asset when it was acquired by the current owner.

The useful life of an asset establishes the period within which the basis of the asset may be written off. The Internal Revenue Service provides some guidelines for years of useful life (see table 14.1).

Table 14.1 *IRS Guidelines for Periods of Useful Life*

Structure	Years
Apartments	40
Banks	50
Dwellings	45
Factories	45
Garages	45
Grain Elevators	60
Hotels	40
Loft Buildings	50
Machine Shops	45
Office Buildings	45
Stores	50
Theatres	40
Warehouses	60

Salvage Value

This is the amount estimated by the owner that will be realized from a sale when the asset is no longer useful. Property may not be depreciated in an amount below its salvage value. The basis of the asset is reduced by the net salvage value to establish the depreciable value when using either the straight line or sum-of-the-year's digits depreciation methods. The net salvage value is the salvage value less estimated charges for removal. Net salvage value may be zero. However, a negative salvage value is not allowed. The cost of removal cannot exceed the estimated salvage value.

Depreciation Methods

The three methods used in calculating depreciation are (1) straight line, (2) declining balance, and (3) sum-of-the-year's digits. Depreciation is actually calculated on a monthly basis and taken annually. Therefore, if in the year of acquisition or the year of sale, depreciation may only be taken for the portion of the year during which the taxpayer owned the property. In using the straight line method, the basis of the property less salvage value is deducted in equal annual amounts over the period of useful life of the asset. The declining balance method of calculating depreciation enables the property owner to depreciate the asset at a rate of 125 percent, 150 percent, or 200 percent of the amount that would have been used under the straight line method. There is also a method of calculating depreciation called the sum-of-the-year's digits. Accelerated depreciation schedules are limited to certain types of property as will be subsequently discussed.

Straight Line Method

In the straight line method of calculating depreciation, the same amount of depreciation is taken each year over the useful life of the property. For example, if a building's depreciable value is $100,000 and its useful life is forty years, the annual depreciation will be $2,500. The annual rate of depreciation therefore is 2.5 percent (2.5% x 40 years = 100%).

Declining Balance Method

Under the declining balance method, the amount of depreciation taken each year is subtracted from the basis of the property before the depreciation rate is applied each year after the first year. For example, in depreciating a property with a forty-year useful life and a depreciable value of $100,000 when using the 125 percent declining balance method, the rate is 3.125 percent for the first year of ownership, 3.027 percent for the second year, 2.932 percent for the third year. Consequently the amount of depreciation taken each year gradually reduces. The 150 percent declining balance and 200 percent declining balance are calculated in the same manner as the 125 percent declining balance method except of course the rate is higher. Under the declining balance methods of depreciation, the property will not fully depreciate during the useful life. For example, at the end of forty years on the 125 percent basis, the owner will have taken only $71,900 of depreciation against $100,000 of depreciable value. Under the 150 percent and 200 percent declining balance methods, these amounts will be $78,321 and $87,149, respectively.

A change in depreciation method from declining balance or sum-of-the-year's digits to the straight line method may be made by the property owner at any time during ownership without obtaining permission from the Internal Revenue Service. It may be beneficial at some point in time for the property owner to switch from a declining balance method to the straight line method.

The Sum-of-the-Year's Digits Method

The other method of accelerated depreciation in addition to the declining balance method is the sum-of-the-year's digits method. Under this method, the property is depreciated a specified fraction each year of useful life. The fraction changes each year and also reduces each year resulting in a decreasing amount of depreciation taken each year. The fraction is established by using a denominator that remains the same over the years of useful life. The denominator is established by totaling the numbers representing the years of estimated useful life of the property. For example, if the useful life is ten years, the denominator is 1 + 2 + 3 + 4 + 5 + 6 + 7 + 8 + 9 + 10 = 55. The numerator of the fraction changes each year to a number that represents the years of useful life remaining at the beginning of the year for which the computation is made. So in our example, if the useful life is ten years, the fraction to be applied to calculate depreciation for the first year is 10/55. The second year it will be 9/55, the third year it will be 8/55, and so on for ten years.

When using the sum-of-the-year's digits method of depreciation, the salvage value is deducted from the basis to arrive at the depreciable value just as in the straight line method. However, in the declining balance method, the salvage value is not deducted to arrive at the depreciable value of the asset.

Property Qualifications

Any type of property that is qualified for depreciation may be depreciated by the straight line method. The declining balance method of 125 percent, 150 percent, 200 percent, or sum-of-the-year's digits may only be used if the property has a useful life of three years or more and was acquired after 1953. Newly constructed residential property acquired new after July 24, 1969, may be depreciated using a declining balance method at a rate not to exceed 200 percent of the straight line rate or under the sum-of-the-year's digits method.

Other types of real property newly constructed and acquired as new property after July 24, 1969 may be depreciated using only the straight line method or the 150 percent declining balance method. Used residential rental property with a

Table 14.2 *Depreciation Methods Available by Property Type*

Straight Line	125 percent Declining Balance	150 percent Declining Balance	200 percent Declining Balance	Sum-of-the-Year's Digits
(1) Any depreciable tangible personal property or real property	(1) Real and tangible personal property with a useful life of twenty years or longer	(1)* Used tangible personal property	(1)* New personal property acquired after 1953	(1) Real and tangible personal property acquired after 7/24/69 that qualifies for the 200 percent declining balance method
(2) Low-income rental housing rehabilitated or improved after 7/24/69 and before 1982 may be depreciated by this method using a useful life of five years with no deduction for salvage value		(2) Used real property acquired before 7/25/69	(2)* Tangible personal property that is put up, built or rebuilt after 1953	
		(3) New real property that is not residential rental property acquired after 7/24/69	(3) Real property that is new residential rental property	
			(4) New real property acquired after 1953 and before 7/25/69	
			(5) Real property that is put up, built, or rebuilt after 1953 and before 7/25/69	
			(6) Real property for which there was a contract to buy build, rebuild, put up, or permanently finance by 7/24/69	

NOTE: This table does not apply to ACRS. See tables 14.3, 14.4, and 14.5.

*Must be tangible property with a useful life of three years or longer.

NOTE: To qualify as residential rental property, at least 80 percent of the gross income from the property must be rental income from dwelling units. New residential property is that wherein the owner is the first user.

useful life of twenty years or more acquired after July 24, 1969, may be depreciated under the 125 percent declining balance method and the straight line method. To qualify as residential rental property, at least 80 percent of the gross rental income from the building for the year must be rental income from dwelling units. Other used real property acquired after July 24, 1969 may only be depreciated under the straight line method. Rehabilitation expenditures for low-income rental housing may be depreciated under the straight line method using a five-year useful life with no deduction for salvage value.

Personal Property

New tangible personal property with a useful life of at least three years that is held as an investment or for use in business, and acquired new after 1953, may be depreciated under the 200 percent declining balance method. Used tangible personal property purchased after 1953 and having a useful life of at least three years may be depreciated using the 150 percent declining balance method.

Recapture

When any accelerated depreciation method (any method other than straight line) is used, the depreciation in excess of the amount of depreciation that would have been taken had the straight line method been used is subject to recapture by the IRS at the time the property is sold. Excess depreciation that is recaptured is taxable as ordinary income. Any part of a gain realized in a sale that is attributable to excess depreciation is treated as ordinary income. Only that part of the gain that is not treated as ordinary income under the recapture rule is eligible for capital gain treatment. Recapture rules apply to both personal property and real property in determining what part, if any, of the gain on the sale is ordinary income. If depreciable real property is held for one year or less, all of the depreciation is excess depreciation. With this exception, gain is never excess depreciation when the straight line method of calculating depreciation is used; therefore, there is no depreciation recapture.

Component Method

The taxpayer may depreciate the entire building as one composite unit and use one useful life for the total value. The owner is also permitted the choice of using the component method with respect to any class of assets within the structure. For example, if an apartment building is purchased for $200,000 this cost may be broken down as follows:

Shell of building	$80,000
Roof	10,000
Plumbing	30,000
Elevator	20,000
Electrical	30,000
Heating	15,000
Air conditioning	15,000
TOTAL	$200,000

The components listed above have different useful lives. The shell may have a useful life of forty years, the plumbing a useful life of twelve years, the elevator a useful life of fourteen years, and so on. The use of the component method and the resulting separate calculations of useful life for each component may result in a higher total annual depreciation deduction than would be available under the composite method.

The taxpayer may use either the component method or the composite method. However, both methods may not be used with respect to the same class of asset. The government guidelines for periods of useful life for various types of structures are based on the composite method; therefore, a taxpayer using these guidelines may not use the component method with respect to particular items within the structure.

Tax Shelter

Depreciation is a deductible allowance from net income of the property when arriving at taxable income. Examples of expenses deductible from gross income include operating expenses, real estate taxes, and mortgage interest. Mortgage principal payments are not deductible in arriving at taxable income.

The deduction for depreciation can result in a negative taxable income. For example, assume that a rental property had an annual income of $200,000 and the following deductible items:

Annual Income		$200,000
Expenses		
Operating Expenses	$120,000	
Real Property Taxes	24,000	
Mortgage Interest	18,000	162,000
Taxable Income before Depreciation		38,000
Depreciation		44,000
Negative Taxable Income or Excess Depreciation		$(6,000)

The $162,000 of expense is deducted from the $200,000 of rental income to arrive at net taxable income before depreciation. The difference between the $38,000 of net income and the $44,000 of depreciation results in a tax loss of $6,000. As can be seen, the depreciation allowance provides a complete tax shelter for the net rental income produced by the building. Additionally, there is $6,000 available to the building owner to be used to shelter income derived from any other source.

Depreciation in excess of income is considered a net operating loss and as such may be carried back three years. However, the three-year provision may be waived in favor of a carryforward for seven years.

Deductible Operating Expenses

Unlike the expenses of operating property held for personal use such as a personal residence, the expenses of operating property held for use in business or as an investment may be deducted from gross income in arriving at net income. Before deducting operating expenses, losses from vacancies and credit losses are deducted from gross scheduled rental income to arrive at gross operating income. Operating expenses are deducted from gross operating income. Examples of operating expenses include the following:

Accounting and legal fees
Advertising
Property management fee
Property insurance
Licenses and permits
Wages and salaries
Services
Maintenance and repairs
Supplies
Utilities

The result obtained by deducting operating expenses is net operating income. To arrive at net taxable income, deductions for mortgage interest and real property taxes are made from net operating income. This otherwise taxable income may be completely or partially sheltered from tax liability as a result of the depreciation allowance. As a result, the building may have no taxable income and there may be surplus depreciation available to shelter other income for the owner.

Accelerated Cost Recovery System (ACRS)

Under this system (created by the Economic Tax Recovery Act of 1981) asset costs may be recovered over a predetermined period that is generally shorter than the useful life of the asset. In the accelerated cost recovery system, salvage value is not deducted and both used and new real property and personal property are included. The recovery periods are three years, five years, ten years, and fifteen years instead of the useful life of the property. As far as depreciation recapture is concerned there is no change for personal property or for residential real property. However, for nonresidential real property there is a drastic change to the effect that all depreciation in excess of straight line is recaptured to the extent that a gain is realized when the property is sold. Under the Accelerated Cost Recovery System, only the composite method of depreciation may be used—the component method may not be used.

Under this system (created by the Economic Tax Recovery Act of 1981) the cost of depreciable assets placed in service after December 31, 1980, and qualifying for ACRS is depreciated over specific periods of time designated by the tax law. For real property, these periods are ten years and fifteen years. Real property with an asset depreciation range (ADR) midpoint life of twelve and a half-years or less is ten-year real property. If the ADR midpoint life is over twelve and a half-years, it is fifteen-year real property. Tables 14.3, 14.4, and 14.5 set forth the percentage of depreciation each year for ten-year and fifteen-year real property.

Table 14.3 *Ten-Year Real Property*

Recovery Year	Depreciation (%)
1	8
2	14
3	12
4 thru 6	10
7 thru 10	9

Table 14.4 *Fifteen-Year Real Property*

Recovery Year	Depreciation (%)
1	12
2	10
3	9
4	8
5	7
6 thru 9	6
7	6
8	6
9	6
10 thru 15	5

Table 14.5 *Low-Income Housing Fifteen-Year Real Property*

Recovery Year	Depreciation (%)
1	13
2	12
3	10
4	9
5	8
6	7
7	6
8 thru 10	5
11 thru 15	4

These tables are based on the asset being placed in service the first month of the first tax year. If the asset is placed in service in a later month, the first year percentage is reduced proportionately.

These tables provide a much faster recovery of asset cost than is available under the useful life method. Using ACRS, 52 percent of an asset cost is recovered by the end of the sixth full year. For low-income housing, a 52 percent write off is achieved at the end of the fifth full year.

ACRS-Exluded Property

Special "anti-churning" rules prohibit a taxpayer from using ACRS for property placed in service prior to 1981. Such property may only be depreciated by the years of useful life method. Property is placed in service when it's ready and available for a particular use. Therefore, if a taxpayer purchased a building prior to 1981, but did not make it available for rental until 1981, ACRS would apply. However, the following rules for property transactions will exclude property acquired in 1981 or after from ACRS unless the owner and user change.

1. If the purchaser or a party related to the purchaser owned the property in 1980.

2. The purchaser leases the property back (sale and leaseback) to the seller, or someone related to the seller, who owned the property in 1980.

3. The taxpayer acquires the property in a tax-free exchange, involuntary conversion, or repossession. ACRS can be used for the portion of the property basis represented by cash or unlike property given up in exchange (see Exchanges under ACRS following).

Alternate ACRS Method

Instead of using the percentages from the ACRS tables, the taxpayer can elect to depreciate the property on a straight line basis. Owners of ten-year real property may elect recovery periods of ten, twenty-five, or thirty-five years. Owners of fifteen-year real property can elect periods of fifteen, thirty-five, or forty-five years. The straight line percentages are as follows:

Years	Depreciation
10	10
15	6.666
25	4
35	2.857
45	2.222

TAX IMPLICATIONS IN THE SALE OF PROPERTY

Capital Gains and Losses

The gain realized in the sale of an asset held for investment or personal use will be treated as a short-term capital gain if held for twelve months or less and a long-term capital gain if held for more than twelve months. Only 40 percent of a long-term capital gain is subject to taxation. The other 60 percent is tax exempt except for the possibility of a minimum tax.

Profits realized on the sale of property used in a trade or business or held for sale to customers in the course of trade or business results in ordinary income or ordinary loss. Property held for sale to customers is designated as dealer property. For example, a real estate developer is normally considered a dealer when selling lots he is developing. He is usually selling a significant number of lots each year. He is actually holding these lots for sale to others on a fairly quick turn-over basis rather than holding them as an investment. Gain realized by the developer in these sales will be treated for tax purposes as ordinary income. However, in other transactions, this same developer may not be classified as a dealer for tax purposes. For example, suppose our developer purchases an office building for rental income and not for use in a trade or business and holds it for a period of several years before selling it to someone else. The property would be regarded as investment property for tax purposes. The gain realized in the sale of the building will be taxed as a long-term capital gain.

Tax-Free Exchanges

The Internal Revenue Code provides that when a qualified exchange of properties is made, some or all of the gain on an economic basis may not have to be recognized for tax purposes. The property exchanged must be investment property or business property. If a qualified exchange occurs, the tax on the gain is postponed and the deduction of a loss must also be postponed. These requirements are not discretionary with the taxpayer or the government. If a transaction qualifies as an exchange, no gain or loss may be recognized in the year of the exchange. The property received by each exchangor is treated as if it were the same property each owned prior to the exchange.

Like-Kind Property

To qualify as an exchange, like-kind properties must be exchanged. Essentially, like-kind properties include an exchange of personal property for other personal property or the exchange of real property for other real property. Exchanges of like-kind real property include the following examples: the exchange of an office building for a shopping mall, apartment house for a tract of land, an office building for an apartment building. Examples of exchanges of personal property include: truck for a machine, an automobile for a truck.

Business or Investment Property

The property exchanged must be held for use in business or as an investment. Property held for personal use will not qualify. Therefore, an exchange of residences by homeowners will not qualify as a tax-free exchange but will be treated as a sale and a purchase.

Property Not Held for Sale

The property exchanged must not be property held for sale to customers, such as inventories of merchandise or inventories of lots held for sale by a developer.

Boot

If an exchangor receives cash or some other type of nonqualifying property in addition to like-kind property in exchange, the transaction will still qualify as a tax-deferred exchange. However, the recipient of the cash (boot) or other nonqualifying property incurs tax liability on the boot or other unlike-kind property in the calendar year of the exchange.

Basis

The basis of the property received by an exchangor is the basis of the property given up in exchange. Therefore, an exchangor does not change the basis of an asset as a result of the exchange. For example, Exchangor #1 trades a property with a market value of $100,000 and a basis of $20,000 for another property also worth $100,000. The property received by Exchangor #1 will also have a basis of $20,000 regardless of what the basis was to the other exchangor. (However, see ACRS exchanges.)

Multiple Exchange

A multiple exchange is one in which more than two properties are exchanged in one transaction. Usually, multiple exchanges are three-way exchanges. For example, A, B, and C each own like-kind real property held for investment or business purposes. In the exchange, A acquires the property owned by C, B acquires the property owned by A, and C acquires the property owned by B. Multiple exchanges qualify as tax-deferred exchanges in the same manner that two-way exchanges qualify. It is not necessary for an exchangor to receive property in exchange from the same person to whom he or she is transferring his or her property in exchange.

Starker Exchange

This type of exchange was held to qualify for tax deferrment by a United States Circuit Court of Appeals in 1979. In this case, Starker sold land to a corporation. However, the purchaser withheld the purchase price until Starker subsequently found a suitable property to be purchased with the proceeds of the sale. The court held that this procedure qualified for treatment as a tax-deferred exchange because the sale proceeds were held beyond the control of the taxpayer seeking the tax-deferred exchange. The court viewed the exchange as one continuous transaction. Therefore, if the proceeds of a sale of property are held beyond the control of the seller until the seller can locate a like-kind property in which to invest the proceeds, the transaction may constitute a tax-free exchange.

Exchanges Under Accelerated Cost Recovery System (ACRS)

The Accelerated Cost Recovery System created by the Economic Recovery Tax Act of 1981 has made significant changes in the tax-free exchange of business and investment property by creating what is called "the anti-churning rule." This rule provides that if an owner makes a tax-free exchange, not only his old basis but also the depreciation method he was using in the property he exchanged must be carried over to the property acquired in the exchange. However, the Accelerated Cost Recovery System does provide that a ten or fifteen-year period and ACRS tables may be used in depreciating the undepreciated value of the property received in exchange to the extent that value exceeds the undepreciated value in the property given up in exchange. As a result, an owner with a very low basis in the property and a corresponding large profit should exchange his or her property rather than selling it and purchasing another property and paying income tax on the gain realized in the sale. An owner with a very high basis in a property is better off to sell the property, pay a small capital gains tax, reinvest the proceeds in the sale to acquire another property by purchase for which he or she can use the more beneficial Accelerated Cost Recovery System.

To illustrate these points, a property owner with a $40,000 basis in a depreciable property valued at $200,000 would have to pay a substantial capital gains tax if the property were sold. Therefore, this owner would be in a better position taxwise if he or she exchanged the property rather than sold the property. As an exchangor, the owner would have to carry over the old $30,000 basis to the new property and continue the same depreciation method used in the old property. The advantage comes in the fact that the exchangor can use the Accelerated Cost Recovery on the increased basis in the property he or she receives in the exchange. Conversely, if an owner of a $200,000 depreciable building had a basis of $170,000, the owner would be in a better position if the property was sold, and the owner paid the capital gains tax on the $30,000 difference between the basis and the sales price and reinvested the sale proceeds in another property that can be written off under the short-term high-rate Accelerated Cost Recovery System.

IMPORTANT POINTS

1. Real estate agents must refrain from giving tax advice.

2. Homeowner's real estate property taxes and mortgage interest are deductible expenses in calculating federal income tax liability.

3. Homeowners and renters are given tax credits for taking energy conservation measures or installing renewable energy sources.

4. A short-term capital gain is realized in the sale of an asset held for twelve months or less. A long-term capital gain is realized in the sale of an asset held for *more than* twelve months.

5. All of a short-term capital gain is taxed as ordinary income. Only 40 percent of a long-term capital gain is taxed as ordinary income, the other 60 percent is tax exempt.

6. Losses incurred in the sale of a home are not tax deductible.

7. If the transaction qualifies, the rollover rule is mandatory.

8. The amount of gain on which taxes are deferred under the rollover rule is used to reduce the basis of the new home purchased.

9. The age-fifty-five-and-over exclusion enables the taxpayer to exempt up to $125,000 of gain in the sale of a principal residence occupied for at least three of the five years immediately preceding the sale. The exclusion may be taken only once.

10. The installment sale tax laws apply to a principal residence as well as to business and investment property. The requirements were substantially liberalized by the Installment Sales Revision Act of 1980 that eliminated the 30 percent rule and the two-payment rule.

11. Depreciation enables the owner of business or investment property to recover the cost or other basis of the asset. The recovery period for property put into service prior to 1981 is based on the years of useful life. For property put into service in 1981 and after the recovery period is specified by the Accelerated Cost Recovery System (ACRS) to be ten years or fifteen years depending on the type of property.

12. Land is not depreciable. Only structures on the land are depreciable real property.

13. The three methods used in calculating depreciation based on the useful life of an asset are (1) straight line, (2) declining balance, and (3) sum-of-the-year's digits.

14. When a depreciation method other than straight line is used, the depreciation in excess of straight line is recaptured by the IRS when the asset is sold and is taxed as ordinary income.

15. Under the years-of-useful-life basis, the taxpayer may use either the component method or the composite method of depreciation. ACRS requires that only the composite method be used.

16. Property placed in service after December 31, 1980, is depreciated under ACRS. For real property the periods are ten years or fifteen years. The rate of depreciation is set forth in ACRS tables. Salvage value is not deducted.

17. Antichurning rules prohibit a taxpayer from using ACRS for property placed in service before 1981.

18. ACRS provides an alternate method whereby a taxpayer can elect to depreciate real property on a straight line basis over periods of ten, fifteen, twenty-five, thirty-five, or forty-five years.

19. When a depreciable asset is sold, the basis of the asset used to compute taxable gain is the depreciated value and not the price paid for the property by the seller.

20. Depreciation is a deductible allowance from net income in arriving at taxable income. Thereby, it provides a tax shelter for the property owner.

21. Expenses of operating business or investment property are deductible expenses in arriving at taxable income.

22. To qualify as a tax-free exchange, like-kind property must be exchanged. An exchangor receiving cash (boot) or other unlike-kind property in addition to like-kind property is taxed on the value of the boot or other unlike-kind property received.

23. To qualify as a tax-free exchange, the property exchanged must have been held for use in business (other than inventory) or as an investment. Property held for personal use does not qualify.

24. ACRS provides depreciation benefits to exchangors not available under the years-of-useful-life system.

IMPORTANT TERMINOLOGY

Accelerated Cost Recovery System (ACRS)
Adjusted Basis
Age-Fifty-Five-and-Over Exclusion
Alternate ACRS Method
Antichurning Rule
Boot
Capital Asset
Capital Gain
Capital Loss
Component Method
Composite Method
Declining Balance
Depreciation
Economic Tax Recovery Act of 1981
Energy Conservation Measures
Energy Credit
Excluded Property
Fifteen-Year Property
Fixing-Up Expenses
Inheritance Basis
Installment Sale
Like-Kind Property

Long-Term Capital Gain
Multiple Exchange
Ordinary Income
Placed in Service
Recapture
Recovery Period
Renewable Energy Sources
Rollover Rule
Salvage Value
Short-Term Capital Gain
Starker Exchange
Straight Line
Sum-of-the-Year's Digits
Tax Basis
Tax Credit
Tax-Deductible Expense
Tax-Free Exchange
Tax Shelter
Ten-Year Real Property
Unlike-Kind Property
Useful Life

REVIEW QUESTIONS FOR CHAPTER 14

1. Which of the following is a tax deductible expense resulting from home ownership?

    (a) Operating expenses
    (b) Depreciation
    (c) Mortgage interest
    (d) Energy usage

2. Tax credits are available to renters and homeowners for expenditures incurred in
    I. Taking energy conservation measures
    II. Installing renewable energy sources

    (a) I only
    (b) II only
    (c) both I and II
    (d) neither I nor II

3. To qualify as a gain to be taxed as a long-term capital gain, which of the following must have occurred?
    I. The asset sold must be a capital asset.
    II. The asset must have been held for more than twelve months.

    (a) I only
    (b) II only
    (c) both I and II
    (d) neither I nor II

4. The rollover rule providing for deferment of an otherwise taxable gain makes tax deferment in qualifying transactions

    (a) Optional
    (b) Mandatory
    (c) Conditional
    (d) Flexible

5. Discount points paid by a borrower to obtain a conventional mortgage loan to purchase a principal residence
    I. Do not increase the yield on the mortgage
    II. Are not deductible by the borrower as interest

    (a) I only
    (b) II only
    (c) both I and II
    (d) neither I nor II

6. With regard to a real estate commission paid by a seller, which of the following is (are) correct?
    I. The commission may be deducted from the selling price as a selling expense in calculating the amount realized in the sale of a principal residence.
    II. The commission paid is not deductible from ordinary income by the seller when itemizing tax deductible expenses.

    (a) I only
    (b) II only
    (c) both I and II
    (d) neither I nor II

7. A mortgage prepayment penalty paid by a borrower as a requirement for early loan pay-off

    (a) May be deducted as interest in the year paid
    (b) May be deducted as interest over a five-year period
    (c) May only be deducted from selling price as a selling expense
    (d) May not be taken as a deduction for any purpose

8. The amount of gain on which tax is postponed under the rollover rule is used to

    (a) Increase the basis of the new residence
    (b) Reduce the basis of the new residence
    (c) Increase the allowable moving expenses
    (d) Reduce the inheritance basis of the new residence

9. The age-fifty-and-over exclusion provides which of the following?
    I. The choice of excluding from taxation up to $125,000 of profit resulting from the sale of a principal residence.
    II. The exclusion may be taken only once in a lifetime and if taken by a married person is binding on the other spouse even though the other spouse did not qualify.

    (a) I only
    (b) II only
    (c) both I and II
    (d) neither I nor II

10. The Installment Sales Revision Act contains which of the following provisions?
    I. The sale will not qualify as an installment sale if the seller receives more than 30 percent of the sales price in the year of the sale.
    II. Payments of the sales price must be received by the seller in at least two different calendar years.

    (a) I only
    (b) II only
    (c) both I and II
    (d) neither I nor II

11. If an asset having a depreciable value of $200,000 and a useful life of twenty-five years is depreciated by the straight-line method, what will be the amount of depreciation taken each year?

    (a) $4,000
    (b) $16,000
    (c) $8,000
    (d) $6,000

12. Which of the following is correct when taking depreciation by the declining balance method?
    I. The amount of depreciation taken each year is subtracted from the basis of the property before the depreciation rate is applied each year after the first year.
    II. A change in depreciation method from declining balance to straight line may be made at any time during the useful life of the property.

    (a) I only
    (b) II only
    (c) both I and II
    (d) neither I nor II

13. Which of the following qualifies for depreciation by the 200 percent declining balance method?

    (a) Real property that is new residential rental property
    (b) Low-income rental housing rehabilitated or improved after July 24, 1969 and before 1982
    (c) Used real property acquired before July 25, 1969
    (d) Any used real property with a useful life of twenty years or longer

14. Any accelerated depreciation is subject to which of the following when the property is sold at a profit?

    (a) Exclusion
    (b) Minimum tax
    (c) Tax credit
    (d) Recapture

15. Which of the following is a benefit provided by depreciation?

    (a) Tax credit
    (b) Tax shelter
    (c) Tax evasion
    (d) Tax deferment

16. Deductible expenses include all of the following EXCEPT

    (a) Advertising
    (b) Utilities
    (c) Mortgage principal
    (d) Insurance

17. If the owner of an apartment building sold the building seven years after purchase and realized a gain of $150,000, which of the following amounts will be taxed as ordinary income?

    (a) $60,000
    (b) $90,000
    (c) $50,000
    (d) $150,000

18. Tom Taylor and Sarah Smith traded office buildings. In the trade, Tom received $20,000 in cash in addition to Sarah's office building. With regard to this transaction, which of the following is (are) correct?
    I. The transaction qualifies as a tax free exchange.
    II. The cash Tom received is called boot and is taxable for the year in which the exchange occurred.

    (a) I only
    (b) II only
    (c) both I and II
    (d) neither I nor II

19. The basis of property received in a tax-free exchange is which of the following?

    (a) The basis as it was to the owning exchangor at the time of the exchange
    (b) the average of the difference in the basis of all properties exchanged
    (c) The same basis as the basis of the property given up in the exchange
    (d) The value of the property received in the exchange

20. Which of the following statements about the Accelerated Cost Recovery System is (are) correct?
    I. Depreciation under ACRS may only be used for property acquired after 1980.
    II. Real property may be fully depreciated in ten years or fifteen years depending on the type of property.

    (a) I only
    (b) II only
    (c) both I and II
    (d) neither I nor II

21. All of the following statements about ACRS are correct EXCEPT

    (a) The antichurning rule prevents taxpayers from using ACRS for property placed in service prior to 1981.
    (b) ACRS provides an alternate straight line method of depreciation.
    (c) ACRS can be used to depreciate the portion of the property basis represented by cash or unlike-kind property given up in exchange.
    (d) Salvage value is deducted to establish the basis for cost recovery.

22. ACRS provides for recovery of which of the following percentages of the cost of ten-year and fifteen-year real property by the end of the sixth year?

    (a) 34
    (b) 52
    (c) 72
    (d) 43

Real Estate Mathematics   15

The mathematics normally involved in real estate transactions consists of nothing more than simple arithmetic. All that is required is the ability to add, subtract, multiply, and divide. These calculations are made with whole numbers, fractions, and decimal numbers.

The difficulty that some people encounter in solving real estate mathematics problems is the conversion of word problems into the mathematical symbols illustrating the calculations to be performed. For example, the word "of" is always translated into a multiplication sign. If something is one half of something else, this means that the solution requires the multiplication of the fraction one half times the other unit.

Some people entering the field of real estate brokerage have not dealt with arithmetic problems since their school days. Consequently, they are often a little "rusty" on arithmetic. For this reason we will begin our discussion of real estate mathematics with a review of the basic fundamentals. These fundamentals merely include the addition, multiplication, and division of fractions and whole numbers.

SECTION 1—FUNDAMENTALS

Fractions

Definitions

A proper fraction is a number that is less than 1. In a proper fraction, the numerator (top number) is always smaller than the denominator. Examples of proper fractions are 1/8, 1/4, 1/2.

An improper fraction is a number that is expressed as a fraction but is equal to or larger than a whole number. In an improper fraction, the numerator is always either equal to or larger than the denominator. Examples of improper fractions are 8/8, 12/6, 25/19.

Adding Fractions

In adding fractions the denominators must be the same for each fraction to be added. Mixed fractions cannot be added. Examples of these would be 1/4 + 1/12 + 1/2. To add these fractions, they must be reduced to a common denominator. That is, each fraction must have the same denominator and this denominator should preferably be the lowest common denominator. The lowest common denominator is the smallest number that all of the denominators in the fractions to be added can be divided into evenly.

The examples that follow illustrate the addition of fractions with different denominators after having reduced them to a common denominator.

$$3/4 = 18/24$$
$$1/12 = 2/24$$
$$+ \; 1/8 = 3/24$$
$$\overline{23/24}$$

$$3/16 = 3/16$$
$$5/8 = 10/16$$
$$+ \; 1/4 = 4/16$$
$$\overline{17/16 = 1\text{-}1/16}$$

In the preceding example the selection of the denominator was done very simply by observation. There will be occasions when the selection of the denominator is not this easy. For instance, in adding 3/16, 8/24, and 5/17, the denominator cannot be readily obtained by observation. In these cases, merely multiply the denominators by each other. The result of the multiplication of the three denominators is the number that all of the denominators can be divided into evenly. In the example just stated, the denominator would be 6528. This is not the lowest common denominator, but it is a common denominator that can be used.

The comon denominator rule applies to the subtraction of fractions as well as to the addition of fractions. To subtract one fraction from another, the denominator must be the same number.

Mixed Numbers

A mixed number is a number that consists of a fraction and a whole number. For example, 1 1/2 is a mixed number. To add or subtract a mixed number, add or subtract the fractions and then add or subtract the mixed numbers in a second operation. This is shown in the following example.

$$1\text{-}1/2 = 1\text{-}12/24$$
$$2\text{-}3/8 = 2\text{-}9/24$$
$$+ \; 9\text{-}1/12 = 9\text{-}2/24$$
$$\overline{12\text{-}23/24}$$

$$12\text{-}2/3 = 12\text{-}4/6$$
$$- \; 7\text{-}1/2 = 7\text{-}3/6$$
$$\overline{5\text{-}1/6}$$

Multiplication of Fractions

The multiplication of fractions is accomplished by multiplying numerator by numerator and denominator by denominator as illustrated in the following:

$$3/4 \times 1/2 \times 5/8 \times 3/6 = \frac{45}{384}$$

To reduce the size of the numbers to be multiplied, cancel numerators into denominators by dividing numerators by the same number. The following is an example.

$$\overset{1}{\cancel{3/3}} \times \overset{3}{\cancel{24/32}} \times \overset{1}{\cancel{8/12}} = ?$$
$$1 4 4$$
$$1/1 \times 3/4 \times 1/4 = 3/16$$

Real Estate Mathematics

To multiply a fraction by a whole number, simply multiply the numerator of the fraction by the whole number and put the result of the multiplication over the denominator.

$$3/4 \times 12 = ?$$
$$3/4 \times 12/1 = 36/4 = 9$$

Division of Fractions

To divide fractions, the divisor must be inverted. The divisor is the number that you are dividing by. For example, 3/4 ÷ 1/2. The fraction 1/2 is the divisor. The fraction inverted must always be the divisor. If the other fraction is inverted, the result will be incorrect. After inverting the divisor, simply multiply the fractions. Very often the resulting fraction can be reduced to a smaller number. For example, if the result of the division is 30/45, this fraction can be reduced by dividing the same number into the numerator and into the denominator. In this case (30/45), if the numerator and denominator were each divided by 15, the resulting fraction would be 2/3. An example of the division of fractions follows.

$$5/8 \div 3/4 = ? \qquad\qquad 1/2 \div 1/6 = ?$$
$$5/8 \times 4/3 = 20/24 \qquad 1/2 \times 6/1 = 6/2 = 3$$

Working with Decimals

In every number there is a decimal point. In a whole number, the decimal point is always to the right of the last digit in the whole number. All numbers to the left of this decimal point are whole numbers and all numbers to the right of this decimal point are fractional numbers. The first place to the right of the decimal point is 10th's, second place is 100th's, third place 1,000ths, and so forth. For example, the number .10 would be 1/10, the number .25 would be 25/100, the number .025 is 25/1000.

A fraction can always be converted to its decimal equivalent by merely dividing the denominator into the numerator. The horizontal line separating the numerator and denominator means divide. For example, 1/4 is equal to .25. The result .25 is obtained by dividing 4 into 1.

Adding Decimal Numbers

Examples of adding decimal numbers follow. Notice that the decimal points must always be placed one under the other in a straight line.

6.283	.0071	487.12
0.914	.9103	96.88
86.200	.8625	33.00
14.031	.0966	74.05
22.302	.3744	6.95
129.730	2.2509	698.00

Subtraction of Decimals

The subtraction of decimals is simply the opposite of addition.

873.65	.8173	.0073
− 421.90	− .4694	− .0062
451.75	.3479	.0011

Multiplication of Decimals

To multiply one decimal number by another, simply multiply as though you were multiplying whole numbers. The decimal point in the answer is determined by the total number of decimal places in the two numbers multiplied by each other. For example, if .34 were being multiplied by 1.2 the result would be .408. Other examples of multiplying decimals follow.

```
    .06157           682.9              6.415           812.28
  × .03184         ×  13.2            ×   8.3          ×   .42
   ──────          ──────             ─────            ──────
    24628           13658              19245           162456
    49256           20487              51320           324912
     6157            6829              ─────           ──────
    18471          ──────              53.2445         341.1576
   ──────          9014.28
  .0019603888
```

Division of Decimals

To divide a decimal by a whole number, divide just as though the numbers were all whole numbers. However, before starting the division, place the decimal point in the dividend (number being divided into) immediately above the existing decimal point in the answer position. Examples of decimals follow.

```
            .154              .030
       48 /7.411         12 /.360
           48                 36
          ───                ───
           261                 0
           240
          ───
           211
           192
          ───
            19
```

In dividing a decimal into a decimal number, or a decimal number into a whole number, the decimal point in the divisor must be moved completely to the right of the divisor number. The decimal point must also be moved the same number of places to the right in the dividend. If the dividend is a whole number, remember there is always a decimal point immediately to the right of every whole number. This point would then be the starting place for moving the decimal point further to the right. Examples of decimal divisions follow.

```
          .48 /74.11            6.6 /396

            154.39                  60
         48./7411.00            66./3960.
            48                      396
           ───                     ────
            261                      0
            240
           ───
            211
            192
           ───
            190
            144
           ───
            460
            432
           ───
             28
```

Real Estate Mathematics

Percentages

In the real estate brokerage business, many arithmetic calculations involve the use of percentages. For example, a real estate broker's commission is a percentage of the sales price.

A percentage is simply a number that has been divided by 100. To use a percentage in an arithmetic calculation, the percentage must be changed to its decimal equivalent. The rule for changing a percentage to a decimal is to remove the percent sign and move the decimal point two places to the left. The decimal point, in the percentage, is always between the last whole number in the percentage and the percent sign. Examples of converting a percentage to a decimal follow.

$$98\% = .98 \qquad 1\ 1/2\% = 1.5\% = .015$$
$$1.42\% = .0142 \qquad 1\ 1/4\% = 1.25\% = .0125$$
$$.092\% = .00092 \qquad 3/4\% = .75\% = .0075$$

To change a decimal or a fraction to a percentage, simply reverse the procedure. This is done by moving the decimal point two places to the right and adding the percent sign. The following are some examples of this operation.

$$1.00 = 100\% \qquad 1/2 = 2\overline{)1.0}^{\,.5} = 50\%$$

$$.90 = 90\% \qquad 3/8 = 8\overline{)3.000}^{\,.375} = 37.5\%$$

$$.0075 = .75\% \qquad 2/3 = 3\overline{)2.000}^{\,.666} = 66.6\%$$

SECTION 2—AREA PROBLEMS

Problems involving the determination of the size of an area in square feet, cubic feet, number of acres, and so forth are quite frequent in the real estate brokerage business. In taking a listing, the broker should determine the number of square feet of heated area in the house. In establishing the lot size, the number of square feet should be determined so that it may be translated into acreage, if desired. For use in solving area problems, there is a table of measures and formulae at the end of this chapter.

Determining the Surface Area of a Rectangle or Square

The surface area of a rectangle or square is determined by simply multiplying the width times the length. In a square, the width and length are the same.

1. An acre of land has a width of 330 feet. If this acre of land were rectangular in shape, what would be its depth?

   Solution: 43,560 sq. ft. = 1 acre
   43,560 ÷ 330 = 132

   Answer: Lot depth is 132 feet

2. If a parcel of land contained 32,670 square feet, what percent of an acre would it be?

   Solution: 32,670 ÷ 43,560 = .75
   .75 = 75%

   Answer: 75%

3. A property owner's lot is 80' wide and 120' deep. The lot is rectangular. The property owner plans to have a fence constructed along both sides and across the rear boundary of his lot. The fence is to be 5' high. The property owner has determined that the labor cost in constructing the fence will be $1.25 per linear foot. The material cost will be $3.00 per square yard. What is the total cost of constructing the fence?

   Solution:

   Step 1: First determine the linear footage to establish the labor cost.

   2 × 120 ft. + 80 ft. = 320 linear feet.
   320 feet × $1.25 per linear ft. = $400 labor cost

   Step 2: Establish the number of square yards in the fence to determine material cost.

   5' × 320 ft. = 1600 sq. ft.
   1600 sq. ft. ÷ 9 (9 sq. ft. in 1 sq. yd.) = 177.78 sq. yds.
   177.78 × $3.00 per sq. yd. = $533.34 material cost

   Step 3: Total Cost
   $533.34 + $400 = $933.34

   Answer: $933.34 Total Cost

4. The property owner in the above problem plans to put a fence post every 10 linear feet for the total length of the fence. How many fence posts will be required?

   Solution: 320 linear feet ÷ 10 = 32
   32 + 1 = 33

   Answer: 33 posts

5. The property owner in the preceding two problems decides to enclose her property with a fence across the fourth side. How many fence posts will be required to enclose the entire property if the fence post interval is maintained at 10 feet?

   Solution: 2 × 80' + 2 × 120' = 400 feet
   400 ÷ 10 = 40

   Answer: Total fence posts required for 400 linear feet is 40.

6. If a rectangular map measures 10 inches × 16 inches and 1 sq. inch of map surface represents an area of 20 sq. miles, how many square miles is represented by the map in total?

   Solution: 10" × 16" = 160 sq. inches
   160 × 20 sq. mi. = 3200 sq. mi.

   Answer: 3200 sq. mi.

Real Estate Mathematics

7. A triangular lot measures 200 feet along the street and 500 feet in depth on the side that is perpendicular to the front lot line. If the lot sold for 10¢ per sq. ft., what is the selling price?

   Solution: Area of a triangle is 1/2 base × height
   1/2 × 200 × 500 = 50,000 sq. ft.
   50,000 × $.10 = $5,000

   Answer: $5,000.00

8. The plan shown is to be changed so that the garage doors are located at the east end of the garage. There is to be a new driveway installed which will be parallel to and the same width as the driveway shown and is to extend from the north end of the garage to the street. The paving cost is $.35 per square foot. What will be the minimum cost to pave the new driveway?

   Solution:
   Step 1:   Area = length × width
   A = (90 + 25) × 20
   A = 115 × 20
   A = 2300 square feet

   Step 2:   Cost = 2300 × $.35
   Cost = $805.00

   Answer: $805.00 Cost

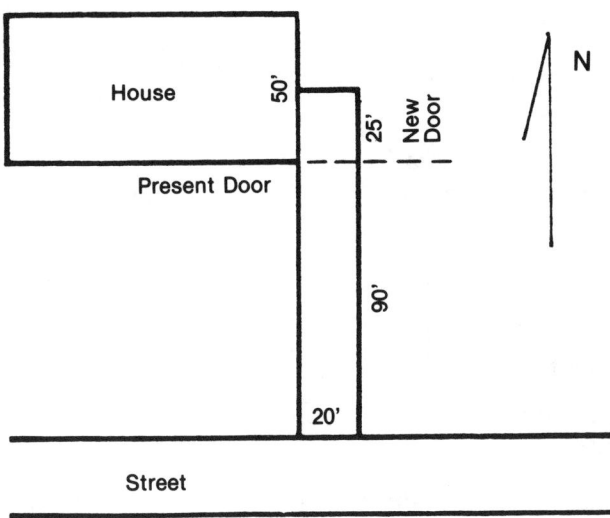

9. What percentage of the lot is occupied by the house shown in the diagram?

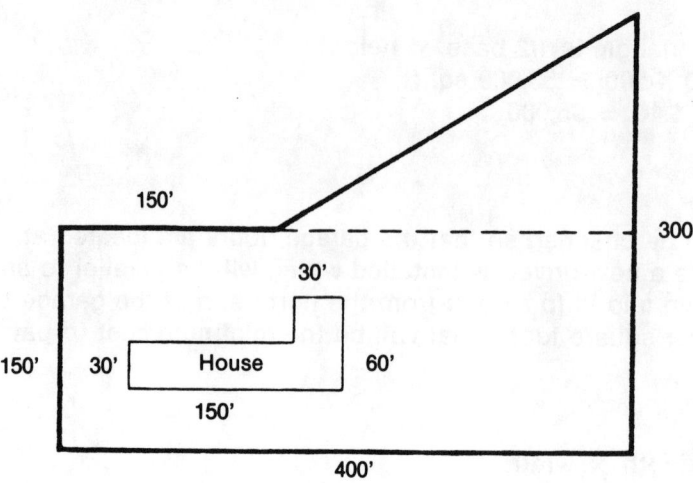

Solution:

Step 1: Divide lot into one triangle and one rectangle
Area of triangle = 1/2 base × height
A = 1/2 × 250' × 150'
A = 18,750 square feet

Area of rectangle = length × width
A = 400' × 150'
A = 60,000 square feet

Total lot area = 18,750 sq. ft. + 60,000 sq. ft.
Lot area = 78,750 square feet

Step 2: Divide house into two rectangles
Area of small rectangle = L × W
A = 30' × 30'
A = 900 square feet

Area of large rectangle = L × W
A = 150' × 30'
A = 4500 square feet

Total house area = 900 sq. ft. + 4500 sq. ft.
A = 5400 square feet

Step 3: Percentage of lot occupied by house = house footage ÷ lot footage
5400 ÷ 78,750 = .0685
.0685 = 6.85%

Answer: 6.85% of lot occupied by house

10. The diagrammed lot is sold for $14,400. What is the price per square foot?

Solution: The diagrammed lot is a trapezoid.
The formula for finding the area of a trapezoid is:

Area = $\dfrac{\text{Height}}{2}$ (Base$_1$ + Base$_2$)

$A = \dfrac{240}{2}(160 + 80)$

$A = 120(160 + 80)$
$A = 120 \times 240$
$A = 28,800$ square feet
$14,400 \div 28,800 = .50$ or 50¢ per square foot

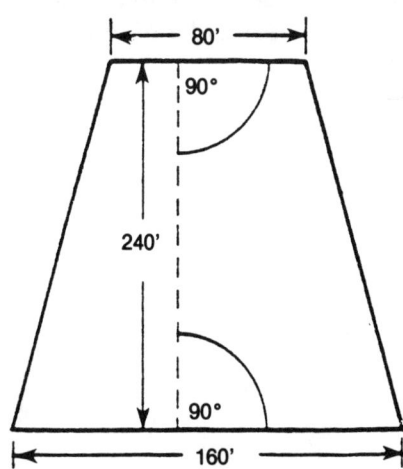

Answer: 50¢ per square foot

11. The perimeter of a rectangular lot is 1800 yards. The length is twice the width plus 6 yards. What is the length in feet?

Solution:

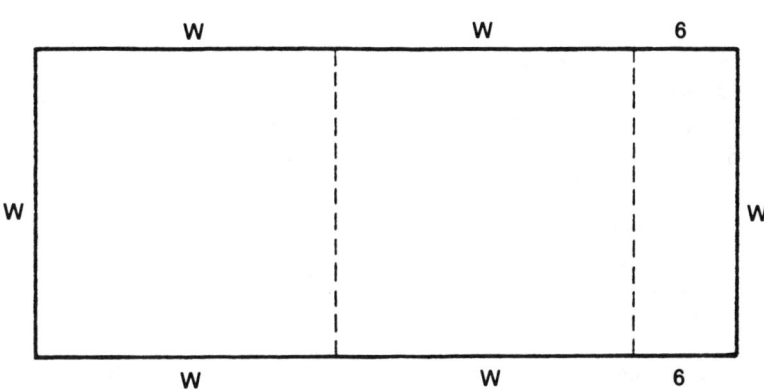

Perimeter of a rectangle = (2 × Width) + (2 × Length)
Length = 2W + 6 yards
Width = W
Therefore:
6 × Width + 12 yards = Perimeter (1800 yards)
6 × Width = 1800 − 12
6W = 1788 yards
W = 1788 ÷ 6
W = 298 yards

2 × 298 + 6 = Length
596 + 6 = 602 yards
602 × 3 = 1806 (Length in feet)

Answer: 1806 feet

12. The house with an area as shown originally cost $15 per square foot to build. If it were built today, it would cost $56,000. How much has the cost per square foot increased (in dollars)?

   Solution: Divided into 3 triangles and 1 square
   Area of a triangle = 1/2bh

   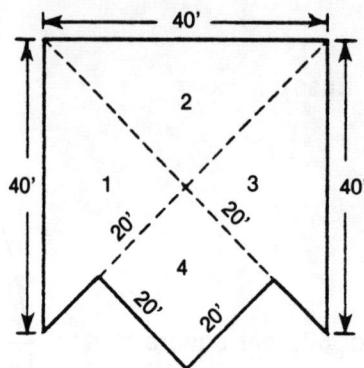

   A = 1/2 40 × 20
   A = 400 sq. ft.
   3 × 400 = 1200 sq. ft.
   Area of a square = 1 side × 1 side
   A = 20 × 20
   A = 400

   Total area = 1200 + 400
   Total area = 1600 square feet
   $56,000 ÷ 1600 = $35 cost per sq. ft. today
   $35 − 15 = $20 per sq. ft. cost increase

   Answer: $20 per square foot

Cubic Area

The next type of area problem that is to be considered involves cubic area. Cubic area is three dimensional. To determine the amount of cubic area or volume in a given space, multiply length × width × depth.

13. A house under construction contains a rectangular basement that is 20 feet wide and 30 feet long. If the basement is excavated to a uniform depth of 12 feet, how many cubic yards of dirt must be removed?

    Solution: 20 ft. × 30 ft. × 12 ft. = 7200 cu. ft.
    7200 ÷ 27 (cu. ft. in 1 cu. yd.) = 266.67 cu. yds.

    Answer: 266.67 cu. yds. of dirt must be removed.

14. A home contains a triangular attic that is 15 ft. wide, 30 ft. long, and 6 ft. high at the ridge beam of the roof. How many cubic feet of space are there in the attic?

    Solution: 1/2 × 15 × 30 × 6 = 1350

    Answer: 1350 cu. ft.

Real Estate Mathematics

15. A homeowner obtains a quotation to have his driveway paved. The driveway is to be 9 feet wide, 30 yards long, and 4 inches thick. The quotation specifies that the labor cost will be $3.00 per sq. yd. The material cost is quoted at $4.00 per cubic foot. What will be the total cost of the driveway?

   Solution: Labor cost
   3 yds. × 30 yds. = 90 sq. yds.
   90 sq. yds. × $3.00 = $270.00 labor cost
   Material Cost
   9 ft. × 90 ft. × 1/3 ft. = 270 cu. ft.
   270 cu. ft. × $4.00 per cu. ft. = $1,080 material cost

   Total Cost
   $270 labor cost + $1,080 material cost = $1,350

   Answer: $1,350 total cost of driveway construction

In the previous problems the information was given in a mixture of feet, yards, and inches. In this type problem, care must be taken to convert the dimensions to the same basis to arrive at a correct answer. In calculating the labor cost, the dimensions to obtain the surface area were all converted to yards because the labor cost was quoted at $3.00 per square yard. In calculating the material cost, the dimensions were converted to feet because the material cost was quoted at $4.00 per cubic foot. The 4" is 1/3 of a foot.

SECTION 3—PRORATION PROBLEMS

Proration is involved in the real estate brokerage business in dividing between seller and buyer the annual real property taxes and rents and in establishing the cost to the buyer of an insurance policy that is being purchased from the seller. Prorating is the process of dividing something into appropriate shares.

In prorating calculations, the best method to follow is to first determine the used portion. In calculating prorations for closing statements, the amount is figured to the day of closing. An example of this would be in prorating the real property tax for a closing to take place on May 30, where the annual real property tax is $240. In the example, the monthly tax rate would be $20. In the example, five months have transpired in the tax year from January 1 through the end of May. Therefore, five months × $20 per month = $100 for the seller's share of the real property taxes. This amount then appears in the closing statement as a debit to the seller and a credit to the buyer.

In prorating, every month is assumed to have thirty days. Therefore, in problems that require the calculation of a daily rate, the monthly rate would be divided by 30, even though the month may be February, to obtain the daily rate.

One other rule to remember in prorating various costs for the closing statements is that the day of closing is charged to the seller.

1. A house valued at $40,000 was insured for 80% of value. The cost of the insurance was 80¢ per $100 of face amount. The homeowner paid the annual premium on February 1. On August 15, the homeowner closed on the sale. The buyers are having the seller's insurance policy endorsed to them. What will be the cost of this policy to the buyers?

Solution: $40,000 × .80 = $32,000 face amount
$32,000 ÷ 100 = 320
.80 (cost per $100 of face amount) × 320 = $256 annual premium
$256 ÷ 12 mos. = $21.33 per month
6 1/2 × $21.33 = $138.65 used portion
$256 − $138.65 = $117.35

Answer: $117.35

2. In preparing a closing statement for a closing to be held on August 14, a real estate broker determined that the annual real property taxes in the amount of $360 had not been paid. What will the broker put in the buyer's statement as her entry for real property taxes?

Solution: $360 ÷ 12 = $30 per month
$30 per mo. ÷ 30 days = $1 per day
7 mos. × $30 = $210
14 days × $1 = $14
$210 + $14 = $224

Answer: Credit to buyer in the amount of $224. This is the seller's share of the real property taxes to cover the 7 months and 14 days of the tax year during which he owned the property.

3. A sale is closed on September 15th. The buyer is assuming the seller's mortgage, which has an outstanding balance of $32,000 as of the date of closing. The annual interest rate is 8% and the interest is paid in arrears. What would be the interest proration on the closing statements prepared by the broker?

Solution: $32,000 × .08 = $2,560 annual interest
$2,560 ÷ 12 = $213.33 interest for September
1/2 × $213.33 = $106.67 interest for 1/2 month
or
$2,560 ÷ 24 = $106.67 interest for 1/2 month

Answer: Credit Buyer $106.67
Debit Seller $106.67

Since the interest is paid in arrears, the buyer will be required to pay the interest for the full month of September when making the scheduled monthly payment on October 1. Therefore, the buyer is to be credited with the seller's share of 1/2 month interest for September in the amount of $106.67. The entry in the seller's closing statement will be a debit in this amount.

I/RV Formula

Problems involving commissions are readily solved by a simple formula illustrated as I/RV. In this formula, I represents income, R represents rate, and V represents value. In these problems, one of the three elements will be the unknown quantity that will be the answer to the problem. The other two will be provided. In using the formula, simply cover the letter representing the unknown quantity and perform the calculation indicated. For example, if the unknown quantity or answer sought is income, covering the I in the formula reveals that rate is to be multiplied times value (R × V). The result of this multiplication will be the income. If the known quantities are income and rate and the unknown quantity is value, covering the V results in an indicated calculation of dividing rate into income. The result of this division will be the value as the answer to the problem.

Real Estate Mathematics

To further clarify the I/RV Formula and its application in solving for any one of three possible unknowns, the following material is presented to demonstrate its use.

The formula may be written in three different ways to solve for different unknowns as follows:

Income = Rate × Value
Rate = Income ÷ Value
Value = Income ÷ Rate

Or, as discussed above, the formula may be written and applied as follows:

$$\frac{\text{Income}}{\text{Rate} \times \text{Value}} \quad \text{or} \quad \frac{I}{R \times V}$$

The horizontal line separating income from R×V indicates that in solving for rate value is to be divided into income. When value is the unknown, rate is to be divided into income. The multiplication sign between R and V, shows that rate is to be multiplied by value to solve for income when it is the unknown quantity. Simply cover up the unknown item and perform the indicated calculations.

Commission Problems

1. A real estate broker sells a property for $40,000. Her rate of commission is 6%. What was the amount of commission in dollars?

   Solution: Value = $40,000, Rate = .06, Income is unknown
   $40,000 × .06 = $2,400

   Answer: $2,400

2. A real estate broker earns a commission of $3,000 in the sale of a residential property. His rate of commission is 6%. What was the selling price of the property?

   Solution: Income = $3,000, Rate = .06
   $3,000 ÷ .06 = $50,000

   Answer: $50,000 sales price

3. A real estate broker earns a commission of $1,500 in the sale of a property for $25,000. What was her rate of commission?

   Solution: Value = $25,000. Income = $1,500
   $1,500 ÷ $25,000 = .06

   Answer: Rate = 6%

4. A real estate salesperson sells a property for $35,000. The commission on this sale to the real estate firm with whom the salesperson is associated is 6% The salesperson receives 60% of the commission paid to the real estate firm. What is the firm's share of the commission in dollars?

   Solution: Value = $35,000, Rate = .06
   $35,000 × .06 = $2,100
   100% − 60% = 40% (firm's percentage of commission)
   $2,100 × .40 = $840

   Answer: $840 firm's share of the commission

5. A broker's commission was 10% of the first $50,000 of sales price of a property and 8% on the amount of sales price over $50,000. The broker received a total commission of $7,000. What was the total selling price of the property?

Solution:
Step 1: Rate = .10, Value = $50,000
$50,000 × .10 = $5,000 commission on first $50,000 of sales price

Step 2: Total commission minus commission on first $50,000 = Commission on amount over $50,000
$7,000 − $5,000 = $2,000 commission on selling price over $50,000

Step 3: $2,000 = Income, .08 = Rate
Income ÷ Rate = Value
$2,000 ÷ .08 = $25,000

Step 4: $50,000 + $25,000 = $75,000

Answer: $75,000 total selling price

6. A seller advises a broker that he expects to net $50,000 from the sale of his property after the broker's commission of 6% is deducted from the proceeds of the sale. For what price must the property be sold to provide a $50,000 net return to the seller after paying the broker a 6% commission on the total sales price?

Solution: 100% = Gross Sales Price
100% − 6% = 94%
94% = net to owner
.94 = $50,000
$50,000 ÷ .94 = $53,191.50

Answer: $53,191.50 gross selling price

SECTION 4—CAPITALIZATION PROBLEMS

As illustrated in chapter 10, Valuation of Real Estate, the income approach to the value estimate is arrived at by capitalizing the net income. Capitalization problems revolve around rate, income, and value in which one of these is unknown. The solution to these problems is based on the use of the I/RV Formula in the same manner that the commission problems are solved.

1. An apartment building produces a net income of $4,320 per annum. The investor paid $36,000 for the apartment building. What is the owner's rate of return on investment?

    Solution: Income = $4,320, Value = $36,000
    $4,320 ÷ $36,000 = .12 or 12%

    Answer: 12% is annual rate of return on the investment

2. An investor is considering the purchase of an office building for $75,000. The investor insists upon a 14% return on investment. What must be the amount of the annual net income from this investment to return a profit to the owner at a rate of 14%?

Real Estate Mathematics

Solution: Value = $75,000, Rate = 14%
$75,000 × .14 = $10,500

Answer: Annual Net Income must be $10,500

3. In appraising a shopping center, the appraiser has established that the center produces a net income of $97,500. The appraiser has developed the capitalization rate to be 13%. What should be the appraiser's estimate of market value for this shopping center?

Solution: Income = $97,500, Rate = .13
$97,500 ÷ .13 = $750,000

Answer: Value estimate, $750,000

Interest Problems

Interest problems also use the I/RV Formula. The amount of interest is the income, the percent return on the money owed or invested is the rate, and the amount of money invested or borrowed is the value.

1. On October 1, a mortgagor makes a $300 payment on her mortgage, which is at the rate of 10%. Of the $300 total payment for principal and interest, the mortgagee allocates $200 to the payment of interest. What is the principal balance due on the mortgage on the date of payment?

Solution: $200 × 12 mo. = $2,400 annual interest income
Income ÷ Rate = Value
$2,400 ÷ .10 = $24,000

Answer: Mortgage balance on date of payment is $24,000

2. If an outstanding mortgage balance is $16,363.64 on the payment due date and the amount of the payment applied to interest is $150, what is the rate of interest charged on the loan?

Solution: $150 × 12 mos. = $1,800 annual interest
Income ÷ Value = Rate
$1,800 ÷ $16,363.64 = .11

Answer: Interest rate is 11%

3. If $27,000 is invested at 8.25%, what will be the annual income resulting from the investment?

Solution: Rate is .0825, Value is $27,000
Income = Rate × Value
$27,000 × .0825 = $2,227.50

Answer: Income is $2,227.50 annually

4. A mortgage loan of $50,000 @ 11% interest requires monthly payments of principal and interest in the amount of $516.10 to fully amortize the loan for a term of twenty years. If the loan is paid over the twenty-year term, how much interest does the borrower pay?

Solution: 20 years × 12 months per year = 240 payments
240 × $516.10 = $123,864 total amount paid
Total amount paid − principal borrowed = interest paid
$123,864 − $50,000 = $73,864

Answer: Interest paid is $73,864.

5. When making the second monthly payment of $548.85 on a $60,000 mortgage loan @ 10 1/2% interest for 30 years, how much interest does the borrower pay?

Solution: $60,000 × .105 = $6,300 annual interest
$6,300 ÷ 12 months = $525 interest first month
$548.85 − $525.00 = $23.85 principal first month
$60,000 − $23.85 = $59,976.15 principal balance after first payment
$59,976.15 × .105 = $6,297.495 annual interest
$6,297.495 ÷ 12 months = $524.79 interest second month

Answer: Borrower pays $524.79 in the second month. This same procedure can be followed to calculate interest or principal paid in third, fourth, or fifth month.

SECTION 5—DEPRECIATION AND APPRECIATION PROBLEMS

Depreciation is a loss in value from any cause. The two examples of depreciation problems that follow are representative of the types of depreciation problems that a real estate student or practitioner may encounter.

In problem one, the present value of a building is given and the requirement is to calculate the original value. Problem two provides the original value to be used in arriving at the present depreciated value. Problem three is an example of a typical appreciation problem, but it also illustrates the method of calculating the percentage of appreciation. Notice that in this problem, the house and lot appreciate at different rates and as usual have different original values. Therefore the appreciation must be calculated separately and then combined into a total appreciated or current value.

1. The value of a six-year-old building is estimated to be $45,900. What was the value when new if the building had depreciated 2% per year?

Solution: 6 yrs. × 2% = 12% depreciation
100% (new value) − 12% = 88%
88% = $45,900 (present value)
$45,900 ÷ .88 = $52,159.09

Answer: $52,159.09 was value when new

2. A 14-year-old building has a total economic life of 40 years. If the original value of the building was $75,000, what is the present undepreciated value?

Solution: 100% ÷ 40 yrs. = yearly depreciation rate
1.00 ÷ 40 = .025 or 2.5% yearly depreciation
14 yrs. × 2.5% = 35% depreciation to date
100% − 35% = 65% remaining value
Original cost × % of remaining value = remaining dollar value
$75,000 × .65 = $48,750

Answer: Present undepreciated value is $48,750

Real Estate Mathematics

3. A 10-year-old house was constructed at a cost of $20,000. The land cost was $2,000. The house has appreciated 40% and the land has appreciated 80%. What is the total percentage of appreciation for the house and the land together?

   Solution: Current Value = Original Value × Appreciation
   House CV = $20,000 × 1.40
   House CV = $28,000

   Lot CV = $2,000 × 1.80
   Lot CV = $3,600

   Total Current Value = $28,000 + $3,600
   TCV = $31,600

   Value Increase = Current Value Less Original Value
   VI = $31,600 − $22,000
   VI = $9,600

   Percentage Appreciation = Value Increase ÷ Original Value
   Percentage Appreciation = $9,600 ÷ $22,000

   Answer: 43.63%

SECTION 6—TAXATION PROBLEMS

Certain terms must be understood to solve problems involving real property taxes. "Assessed Value" is the value established by a tax assessor. The tax value or assessed value is usually a percentage of the estimated market value of the property and may be up to 100% of market value. The amount of tax is calculated by multiplying the assessed value by the tax rate which is expressed either in dollars per $100 of assessed value or in mills (one mill is one-tenth of a cent) per $1000 of assessed value.

1. If the assessed value of a property is $40,000 and the tax value is 100% of the assessed value, what is the annual tax if the rate is $1.50?

   Solution: $40,000 × 100% = $40,000 (tax value)
   $40,000 ÷ 100 = $400
   $400 × $1.50 = $6.00

   Answer: $600 annual taxes

2. A property is sold at the assessed value. The annual real property tax is $294.40 at a tax rate of $1.15 per $100 of tax value. The property is taxed at 80% of assessed value. What is the selling price?

   Solution: $294.40 ÷ $1.15 = $256.00
   $256.00 × 100 = $25,600 (tax value)
   $25,600 ÷ .80 = $32,000

   Answer: $32,000 selling price

3. If the assessed value of a property is $68,000, and the annual tax paid is $850, what is the tax rate?

   Solution: $68,000 ÷ 100 = $680
   $850 ÷ 680 = $1.25

   Answer: Tax rate, $1.25 per $100 of tax value

4. If the market value is $70,000, the tax rate is 120 mills, and the assessment is 80% what is the semiannual tax bill?

   Solution: Assessed Value = .80 × $70,000
   Assessed Value = $56,000
   Annual Tax Bill = $56,000 × .120
   Annual Tax Bill = $6,720
   Semiannual Tax Bill = $6,720 ÷ 2
   Semiannual Tax Bill = $3,360

   Answer: $3,360

5. The real property tax revenue required by a town is $140,800. The assessed valuation of the taxable property is $12,800,000. The tax value is 100% of the assessed value. What must the tax rate be per $100 of assessed valuation to generate the necessary revenue?

   Solution: Income ÷ Value = Rate
   $140,800 ÷ $12,800,000 = $.011 (rate per $1.00)
   $.011 × 100 = $1.10 per $100

   Answer: Tax rate $1.10 per $100 of assessed value

SECTION 7—PERCENTAGE LEASE PROBLEMS

1. The rental clause in a commercial lease specified a minimum monthly rental of $400 plus 2 1/2% of the gross yearly income of the tenant over $160,000. The lessee did a gross business of $240,000 during the first year of the lease. What was the annual rent paid by the lessee?

   Solution: 12 × $400 = $4,800 basic rent
   $240,000 − $160,000 = $80,000 (excess income over $160,000)
   $80,000 × .025 = $2,000 (rent on excess over $160,000)
   $4,800 + $2,000 = $6,800

   Answer: $6,800 total rent first year

2. A percentage lease specifies a minimum rent of $600 per month and 3% of the gross sales of the lessee over $130,000. The total rent paid at the end of the year was $8,300. What was the lessee's gross business income?

   Solution: 12 × $600 = $7,200 (minimum rent for one year)
   $8,300 − $7,200 = $1,100 (rent exceeding minimum)
   Income ÷ Rate = Value
   $1,100 ÷ .03 = $36,666.67 (gross over $130,000)
   $130,000 + $36,666.67 = $166,666.67

   Answer: $166,666.67 gross income

3. If a lease specifies the rent to be 2% of gross sales per annum, with a minimum annual rent of $8,000, what is the annual rent if gross sales were $1,200,000?

   Solution: $1,200,000 × .02 = $24,000

   Answer: $24,000 annual rent

Real Estate Mathematics

SECTION 8—MISCELLANEOUS PROBLEMS

1. If eighteen pumps produce 4,000 gallons of water in six hours, how many pumps would be required to pump 6,000 gallons of water in three hours?

   Solution: 18/? × 6,000/4,000 × 6/3 = 648/12 = 54

   Answer: 54 pumps

   As illustrated above, a simple method for solving this problem is to merely restate the problem and invert the gallon quantities in the restatement. The zeros in the gallon quantities can be cancelled out to reduce the size of the numbers generated. After the problem has been restated, multiply the numbers in the numerators by each other. The result of this multiplication is 648. Multiply the two numbers in the denominators by each other. The result of this multiplication is 12. Divide the denominator into the numerator to arrive at the answer: 648 ÷ 12 = 54.

2. A subdivision contained 400 lots. It a broker sold 25% of the lots and his sales force sold one-half of the remaining lots, how many lots are still unsold?

   Solution: .25 × 400 = 100
   400 − 100 = 300
   300 × 1/2 = 150

   Answer: 150 lots still unsold

3. In planning the development of a tract of land, the developer allocated one-half of the total area to single-family dwellings, one-third of the area to multi-family dwellings, and 60 acres to be used for roads and recreation areas. What is the total number of acres in the tract?

   Solution: Single family one-half = 3/6
   Multi-family one-third = 2/6
   3/6 + 2/6 = 5/6
   6/6 = entire tract
   6/6 − 5/6 = 1/6
   1/6 = 60 acres
   6 × 60 = 360 acres

   Answer: 360 acres total

4. A developer paid $1,200 per acre for a 100-acre tract. If the developer constructs 18 houses at a cost of $30,000 each and the cost for the other improvements to the land is $36,000, what would be the average sales price of the houses to insure a profit of 16% to the developer?

   Solution: 100 acres × $1,200 = $120,000
   18 houses × $30,000 = $540,000
   Improvements = $36,000
   $120,000 + $540,000 + $36,000 = $696,000 total investment
   116% of $696,000 = total sales price of 18 houses
   1.16 × $696,000 = $807,360.00
   $807,360.00 ÷ 18 = $44,853.33

   Answer: $44,853.33 average sales price per house

5. The market value of a property was estimated to be $70,000 in 1975. During 1977, the owner put it on the market for 15% above the 1975 market value. She accepted an offer for 10% less than the asking price. What was the amount of the offer?

   Solution: $70,000 × 115% = Asking Price
   $70,000 × 1.15 = $80,500
   Asking Price × 90% = offer
   $80,500 × .90 = $72,450 offer

   Answer: $72,450 amount of offer

6. An owner purchased his home at 8% below market value. He then sold the property for the original market value. What was the rate of profit?

   Solution: Market value = 100%
   100% − 8% = 92% of market value (purchase price)
   8% ÷ 92% = rate of profit
   .08 ÷ .92 = .0869 or 8.69%

   Answer: 8.69% rate of profit

Table 15.1 *Measures and Formulas*

Linear Measure
12 inches = 1 foot
3 feet = 1 yard
16 1/2 feet = 1 rod, 1 perch or 1 pole
66 feet = 1 chain
5,280 feet = 1 mile

Square Measure
144 sq. inches = 1 sq. foot
9 sq. feet = 1 sq. yard
30 1/4 sq. yards = 1 sq. rod
160 sq. rods = 1 acre
43,560 sq. ft. = 1 acre
640 acres = 1 sq. mile
1 sq. mile = 1 section
36 sections = 1 township

Cubic Measure
1,728 cubic inches = 1 cubic foot
27 cubic feet = 1 cubic yard
144 cubic inches = 1 board foot
 (12" × 12" × 1")

Circular Measure
360 degrees = circle
60 minutes = 1 degree
60 seconds = 1 minute

Formulas
1 side × 1 side = area of a square
width × depth = area of a rectangle
1/2 base × height = area of a triangle
1/2 height × (base$_1$ + base$_2$) = area of a trapezoid
1/2 × sum of the bases = distance between the other two sides at the mid-point of the height of a trapezoid
length × width × depth = volume (cubic measure) of a cube or a rectangular solid

Real Estate Mathematics

SECTION 9—REVIEW PROBLEMS FOR CHAPTER 15

1. A sale is closed on February 12. The buyer is assuming the seller's mortgage, which has an outstanding balance of $28,000 as of the date of closing. The annual interest rate is 7-3/4% and is paid in arrears. What would be the interest proration appearing in the buyer's closing statement?

    (a) $180.83 Debit
    (b) $77.52 Credit
    (c) $72.36 Credit
    (d) $253.19 Credit

2. A real estate broker earns a commission of $2,400 at a rate of 6%. What was the selling price of the property?

    (a) $25,000.00
    (b) $40,000.00
    (c) $14,400.00
    (d) $24,000.00

3. A property is sold at market value. The market value and the tax value are the same. If the tax value is 100% of assessed value, the tax rate is $1.50, and the annual tax is $540.00, what was the selling price of the property?

    (a) $24,000.00
    (b) $27,770.00
    (c) $81,000.00
    (d) $36,000.00

4. If 36 pumps produce 9,000 gallons of water in 4 hours, how many pumps would be required to pump 12,000 gallons of water in 12 hours?

    (a) 9
    (b) 8
    (c) 12
    (d) 16

5. What is the annual rent if a lease specifies the rent to be 2½% of gross sales per annum, with a minimum annual rent of $4,800.00, if the lessee's gross sales were $192,000?

    (a) $4,800.00
    (b) $12,000.00
    (c) $7,680.00
    (d) $16,000.00

6. The scale of a map is 1 inch equals 2½ miles. What would be the distance represented by 4½ inches on the map?

    (a) 18 miles
    (b) 11.25 miles
    (c) 7 miles
    (d) 180 miles

7. A rectangular lot measured 40 yards in depth and had a frontage of 80 feet. How many acres did the lot contain?

   (a) .07
   (b) .21
   (c) .22
   (d) .70

8. A real estate salesperson earns $18,000.00 per year. If she receives 60% of the 6% commissions paid to her firm on her sales, what is her monthly dollar volume of sales?

   (a) $41,666.67
   (b) $25,000.00
   (c) $33,333.33
   (d) $90,000.00

9. How many fence posts would be required in the construction of a three-sided fence if each side were 30 feet long and 5 feet high and the posts were placed at 10 foot intervals starting at one corner?

   (a) 8
   (b) 10
   (c) 15
   (d) 12

10. A parking lot containing two acres nets $12,000 per year. The owner wishes to retire and sell his parking lot for an amount that will net him $12,000 per year by investing the proceeds of the sale at 8½% per annum. What must the selling price be to accomplish the owner's objective?

    (a) $102,000
    (b) $141,176
    (c) $96,000
    (d) $120,000

11. A group of investors purchased two tracts of land. They paid $48,000 for the first tract. The first tract cost 80% of the cost of the second tract. What was the cost of the second tract?

    (a) $28,800
    (b) $125,000
    (c) $9,600
    (d) $60,000

12. A buyer obtains a commitment for an FHA loan in the amount of $27,000. If the current FHA interest rate is 7-3/4% and the lender requires sufficient discount points to increase the effective interest rate to 8%, what dollar amount will the seller have to pay for the necessary discount points?

    (a) $270
    (b) $1,080
    (c) $540
    (d) $675

Real Estate Mathematics

13. A property owner constructed a 6-foot high fence around his rectangular lot, which measured 140 feet by 265 feet. The fence cost $3 per square yard. What was the total cost of the fence?

    (a) $1,458
    (b) $1,215
    (c) $1,620
    (d) $540

14. An office building produces a gross income of $12,600 per year. The vacancy factor is 5% and the annual expenses are $3,600. What is the market value if the capitalization rate is 12%?

    (a) $69,750
    (b) $105,000
    (c) $15,120
    (d) $99,750

15. If the monthly interest payment due on a mortgage on December 1 is $570.00 and the annual interest rate is 9%, what is the outstanding mortgage balance?

    (a) $76,000.00
    (b) $61,560.00
    (c) $63,333.33
    (d) $131,158.00

16. A building has a total economic life of 50 years. The building is now five years old and has a depreciated value of $810,000. What was the value of the building when new?

    (a) $891,000
    (b) $1,234,568
    (c) $972,000
    (d) $900,000

17. If the tax value is 100% of the assessed value and the assessed value is $63,250.00, what are the annual taxes if the rate is $2.10 per $100?

    (a) $3,011.90
    (b) $1,328.25
    (c) $3,320.16
    (d) $132.83

18. If the perimeter of a rectangle is 1800 yards and the length is six yards more than twice the width, how long is the length in feet?

    (a) 298 feet
    (b) 1806 feet
    (c) 602 feet
    (d) 596 feet

19. If Jackson buys 3 parcels of land for $4,000 each and sells them as 4 separate parcels for $4,500 each, what percent profit does he make?

    (a) 150%
    (b) 33%
    (c) 50%
    (d) 60%

20. The current value of a 12-year-old house is $26,000.00. If this house has an economic life of 40 years, what was its value when new?

    (a) $31,951.22
    (b) $37,142.86
    (c) $32,527.85
    (d) $37,014.29

21. What would be the answer as a decimal of this problem?
    3/5 × 5/8 + 5/6 = ?

    (a) 1.25
    (b) .45
    (c) .313
    (d) .78

22. The outside dimensions of a rectangular house are 35 feet by 26.5 feet; if the walls are all 9 inches thick, what is the square footage of the interior?

    (a) 947.7 square feet
    (b) 927.5 square feet
    (c) 837.5 square feet
    (d) 827.5 square feet

23. A buyer is to assume a seller's existing loan with an outstanding balance of $20,000 as of the date of closing. The interest rate is 9% and payments are made in arrears. Closing is set for October 10. What will be the entry in the seller's closing statement?

    (a) $150 Debit
    (b) $150 Credit
    (c) $50 Credit
    (d) $50 Debit

24. A house is listed for $40,000. An offer was made and accepted for $38,500, if the seller agreed to pay 5½% discount points on an FHA loan of $33,000. The broker's fee was at a rate of 6%. How much will the seller net from the sale?

    (a) $34,375
    (b) $38,500
    (c) $35,875
    (d) $36,382.50

Real Estate Mathematics

25. A house and lot were assessed for 60% of market value and taxed at a rate of $3.75 per $100 of assessed value. Five years later the same tax rate and assessment rate still exist, but annual taxes have increased by $750. How much has the dollar value of the property increased?

   (a) $20,000.00
   (b) $33,333.33
   (c) $8.752.75
   (d) $38,385.82

26. What would be the sales price of an apartment complex having an annual rental of $80,000 with expenses of $8,000 annually if the purchaser receives an 8% return.

   (a) $1,000,000
   (b) $800,000
   (c) $864,000
   (d) $900,000

27. A city with rent-control guidelines says that a landlord may increase the rent on apartments by 2.25% of the cost of improvements made to the property. The landlord spent $1,200 per unit for improvements, and then raised the rent from $180 to $215. By how much has the owner exceeded the guidelines?

   (a) $35.00
   (b) $8.00
   (c) $27.00
   (d) $15.00

28. A lease specifies that there is to be a minimum monthly rental of $500 plus 3% of all business over $185,000. If the lessee did a gross business of $220,000, how much rent was paid that year?

   (a) $12,600
   (b) $6,000
   (c) $11,550
   (d) $7,050

29. A tract of land was divided up as one-half the total area for single-family dwellings, one-fourth the area for a shopping area, and one-eighth of the area for streets and parking areas. The remaining 7 acres are used for parks. What would be the total acreage of the entire tract?

   (a) 28 acres
   (b) 70 acres
   (c) 49 acres
   (d) 56 acres

30. An apartment building contains 20 units. Each unit rents for $180 per month. The vacancy rate is 5%. Annual expenses are $3,500 for maintenance, $1,200 insurance, $1,500 taxes, $900 utilities, $15,000 interest, and 10% of the gross effective income for management fee. What was the investor's net rate of return for the first year if she paid $195,000 for the property?

    (a) 8.62%
    (b) 7.61%
    (c) 22.05%
    (d) 13.43%

31. A house had an assessed value of $35,000 and the lot had an assessed value of $7,000. The property was taxed at 80% of assessed value at a rate of $2.12 per $100. If the assessed valuation is to be increased by 18%, what will be the amount of taxes to be paid on the property?

    (a) $712.32
    (b) $890.40
    (c) $840.54
    (d) $1,050.67

32. A building was valued at $110,000 four years ago. Each year since that time, it has depreciated 3% of each preceeding year's value. What is the value today?

    (a) $96,800
    (b) $77,000
    (c) $106,700
    (d) $97,382

33. An owner listed a property for sale with a broker. At what price must the property be sold to net the owner $7,000 after paying a 7% commission and satisfying the existing $18,000 mortgage?

    (a) $26,882
    (b) $26,750
    (c) $19,354
    (d) $27,750

34. A 12-year-old house was constructed at a cost of $32,000 on a lot costing $4,000. The house has appreciated 42% and the lot has appreciated 36%. What is the total percent appreciation for the house and lot combined?

    (a) 41.33%
    (b) 78.89%
    (c) 29.24%
    (d) 70.75%

35. The value of a seven-year-old building is estimated to be $63,000. What was the value when new if the building had depreciated 2½% per year?

    (a) $67,725
    (b) $114,975
    (c) $74,025
    (d) $76,363

Real Estate Mathematics

36. An investor built an office building at a cost of $320,000 on land costing $40,000. Other site improvements totaled $20,000. What must be the amount of the annual net income from the property to return a profit to the owner at an annual rate of 12%.

   (a) $31,666
   (b) $45,600
   (c) $38,400
   (d) $43,200

37. A real estate sale was closed on February 20. The real property taxes have not been paid. The assessed value of the property is $67,500 and the tax value is 80% of the assessed value. Tax rate is $1.50 per $100 of tax value. What is the proper entry on the seller's settlement statement regarding the real property taxes?

   (a) $697.50 Db
   (b) $112.50 Cr
   (c) $112.50 Db
   (d) $697.50 Cr

38. A triangular lot measures 350 feet along the street and 425 feet in depth on the side that is perpendicular to the street. If the lot was sold by a broker for 75 cents per square foot and his commission rate was 9%, what was the amount of commission earned?

   (a) $10,040.63
   (b) $6,693.75
   (c) $14,875.00
   (d) $5,020.31

39. A property owner is having a concrete patio poured at the rear of the house. The patio is to be rectangular in shape and will be 12 feet by 8 yards. The patio is to be six inches thick. The labor cost for the project is $3.50 per square yard and the material cost is $1.50 per cubic foot. What will be the total cost of the patio?

   (a) $328
   (b) $552
   (c) $112
   (d) $198

40. A broker's commission was 8% of the first $75,000 of the sales price of a house and 6% on the amount over $75,000. What was the total selling price of the property if the broker received a total commission of $9,000?

   (a) $93,000
   (b) $125,000
   (c) $79,500
   (d) $105,000

41. A buyer paid $45,000 for a home. Five years later she put it on the market for 20% more than she originally paid. The house eventually sold for 10% less than the asking price. At what price was the house sold?

    (a) $49,500
    (b) $54,000
    (c) $44,100
    (d) $48,600

42. The owner of a rectangular unimproved parcel of land measuring 600 feet in width × 145.2 feet in depth was offered $15 per front foot or $4,000 per acre. What is the amount of the higher offer?

    (a) $2,187
    (b) $8,000
    (c) $9,000
    (d) $7,680

43. The present value of an office building is $280,000. This value represents an appreciation of 35% during the 8 years since the building was purchased by the present owner. What did he pay for the building?

    (a) $182,000
    (b) $430,769
    (c) $207,407
    (d) $198,000

44. $150 is 2½% of what amount?

    (a) $600
    (b) $6,000
    (c) $375
    (d) $1,666

45. After purchasing a home containing 2300 square feet on a rectangular lot 150 feet × 210 feet, the owner added a two-car garage with interior dimensions of 23 feet by 22 feet. The house is valued at $26 per square foot, the lot at 25 cents per square foot, and the garage at $12 per square foot. What was the percentage of increase in value of the property resulting from the addition of the garage?

    (a) 8.23%
    (b) 11.15%
    (c) 10.15%
    (d) 8.97%

46. A broker negotiated the sale of the north east ¼ of the north east ¼ of the north east ¼; section 25, township 2, south; range 1 east for $700 per acre. The listing agreement with the owner specified a 12% commission. How much did the broker earn?

    (a) $840
    (b) $3,360
    (c) $8,400
    (d) $480

Real Estate Mathematics

47. A tract of land containing 560 square rods was sold for 12 cents per square foot. What was the total selling price?

   (a) $6,720
   (b) $20,160
   (c) $11,088
   (d) $18,295

48. A property owner plans to fence his land, which is rectangular in shape and measures 300 feet × 150 feet. How many fence posts will be required if there is to be a post every 15 feet?

   (a) 61
   (b) 60
   (c) 45
   (d) 450

49. A triangular tract is 4000 feet deep and has 900 feet of highway frontage which is perpendicular to the 4,000 foot boundary. How many square yards does the tract contain?

   (a) 1,800,000
   (b) 400,000
   (c) 300,000
   (d) 200,000

50. The owner of an apartment building earns a net income of $10,200 per year. The annual operating cost is $3,400. The owner is realizing a gross return of 14% on investment. What was the price paid for the building?

   (a) $48,572
   (b) $72,857
   (c) $97,143
   (d) $142,800

51. A percentage lease stipulates a minimum rent of $1,200 per month and 3% of the annual gross sales of the lessee over $260,000. The total rent paid by the end of the year was $16,600. What was the lessee's gross business income for the year?

   (a) $73,333.33
   (b) $333,333.33
   (c) $260,000.00
   (d) $553,333.33

52. A building now 14 years old has a total economic life of 40 years. If the original value of the building was $150,000, what is the present undepreciated value?

   (a) $52,500
   (b) $202,500
   (c) $60,000
   (d) $97,500

53. On February 1, a mortgagor makes a $638 payment on her mortgage, which is at the rate of 10%. The mortgagee allocates $500 to the payment of interest. What is the principal balance due on the mortgage on February 1?

    (a) $60,000
    (b) $79,750
    (c) $95,700
    (d) $38,400

54. A house under construction contains a rectangular basement that is 30 feet wide, 90 feet long, and is to be excavated to a uniform depth of 14 feet. A subcontractor received 25 cents per cubic yard for the excavating work. How much did the subcontractor receive?

    (a) $1,400
    (b) $1,050
    (c) $350
    (d) $315

55. A house valued at $60,000 was insured for 85% of value. The annual premium was 60 cents per $100 of the face amount of the policy. The homeowner paid a three-year premium on February 28. On April 30 the following year she closed the sale of the home. The buyer is having this policy endorsed to him. What will be the cost to the buyer?

    (a) $357
    (b) $306
    (c) $510
    (d) $561

56. The perimeter of a rectangular lot is 120 yards. The length is twice the width plus 8 yards. What is the length in feet?

    (a) 128
    (b) 52
    (c) 76
    (d) 188

57. In planning the development of a tract of land, the developer allocated one-half of the total area to single-family dwellings, one-third to multi-family dwellings, and 20 acres for roads and recreation areas. What is the total number of acres in the tract?

    (a) 120
    (b) 36.67
    (c) 320
    (d) 56.67

Real Estate Mathematics

58. A developer paid $450 per acre for a $125-acre tract. His costs for grading, paving, and surveying totalled $125,000. He constructed 200 houses at an average cost of $45,000 each. What was the average sales price per house if the developer realized a net return of 14% on his total investment?

(a) $64,267.00
(b) $54,062.50
(c) $52,333.13
(d) $45,906.25

59. A tract of land one and one-quarter miles square was sold by Action Realty Company for $200 per acre. Action Realty received a commission of 9% on the sale. They paid 45% of the commission to the selling associate. How much did Action Realty net?

(a) $9,900
(b) $8,100
(c) $18,000
(d) $4,950

60. A farm earns $3,600 net after allowing $24 a month for all expenses. A buyer wants 6 percent return on investments. What would she have to pay for the farm so as to gross 6 percent?

(a) $60,000
(b) $64,800
(c) $60,600
(d) $59,800

61. If a shopping center had an annual rental of $50,000 and total annual expenses of $5,000, and if you desired a net profit of 9 percent per annum, what would be the purchase price?

(a) $555,000
(b) $500,000
(c) $494,505
(d) $490,500

62. A broker sold a lot 125 feet wide and 160 feet deep for 17 cents per square foot, but the purchaser assumed a paving lien of $2.25 per front foot. What total amount would the purchaser have to ask for the property if he expected to make a profit of $295 and give a clear title to the property?

(a) $48,695.00
(b) $4,869.50
(c) $44,212.00
(d) $3,976.25

63. An office building has a total income of $53,200 per year. The yearly expenses are: taxes—$8,925.25, insurance—$1,510.60, heating and air-conditioning—$4,920.05, miscellaneous expense—$3,644.10. If a buyer pays $360,000 for the building, what will be the net return?

(a) $53,200
(b) $19,000
(c) $34,200
(d) $5,420

64. An enterprise earns $14,000 per year net after allowing $500 per month for all expenses. Assuming that these figures will hold constant, what price could a buyer afford to pay for the enterprise in order to gross 25% annually on the investment?

    (a) $5,000
    (b) $80,000
    (c) $6,000
    (d) $320,000

65. On the following diagram: It cost $15 per square foot to build this house. If it had to be built today, it would cost $56,000. How much has the cost per square foot increased?

    (a) $15
    (b) $13
    (c) $20
    (d) $35

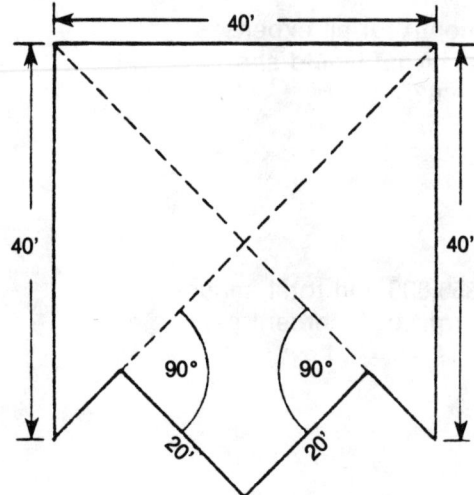

66. If a man has a $325 weekly gross income from his property and a monthly expense of $845, what is the net annual percent of interest return on his investment of $84,500?

    (a) 67.5%
    (b) 8.0%
    (c) 2.75%
    (d) 6%

67. A broker has a problem of subdividing a ten-acre tract into 50 × 100 foot lots; after allowing 85,600 square feet for the necessary streets, how many lots will the broker realize from this subdivision?

    (a) 70
    (b) 87
    (c) 116
    (d) 92

Real Estate Mathematics

68. The tax valuation of a property being sold at $50,000 is 75 percent of the sales price. If the tax rate is $4.50 per $100, what is the semiannual payment for taxes?

    (a) $843.75
    (b) $750.25
    (c) $1,687.50
    (d) $1,500.50

69. A lot has 50 feet of frontage by 180 feet deep. The buyer had only $5,000 cash. The lot cost $63 per front foot, and the house cost was $9,216. He secured a mortgage for the balance. If his interest was 5½ percent per annum, payable semiannually, what was the amount of his first semiannual interest payment?

    (a) $101.26
    (b) $405.13
    (c) $202.57
    (d) $7,366.00

70. A broker bought a three-story office building. Each story is 80 feet by 75 feet. He paid $300 per front foot for the lot, which is 100 feet of frontage by 200 feet. He estimated the building cost at $25 per square foot and paving the lot exclusive of the building would be $3 per square foot. What would the total cost of the lot and construction be?

    (a) $480,000
    (b) $522,000
    (c) $492,000
    (d) $552,000

71. See the following diagram. If the house costs $21 per square foot to build and the lot costs $4,000 per acre, what would the selling price be if you wanted to make 10 percent gross profit on the finished house and lot?

    (a) $54,000
    (b) $53,460
    (c) $44,180
    (d) $48,000

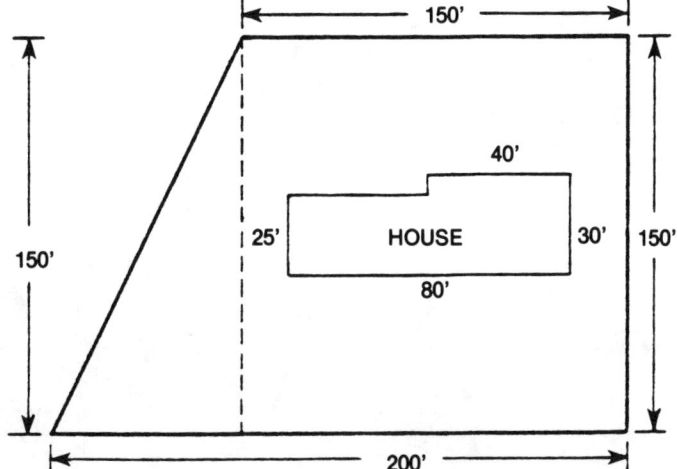

72. An investor wishes to build a flat-roofed building 130 feet long, 30 feet wide, and 24 feet high. Champion Construction Company offers to build such a structure for $18.90 per square foot. Action Construction Company offers to build the building for 80 cents per cubic foot. How much will the investor save by giving the building contract to Champion?

    (a) $3,900
    (b) $9,360
    (c) $1,769
    (d) $1,170

73. The house below occupies what percent of the lot?

    (a) 9%
    (b) 15%
    (c) 10%
    (d) 18%

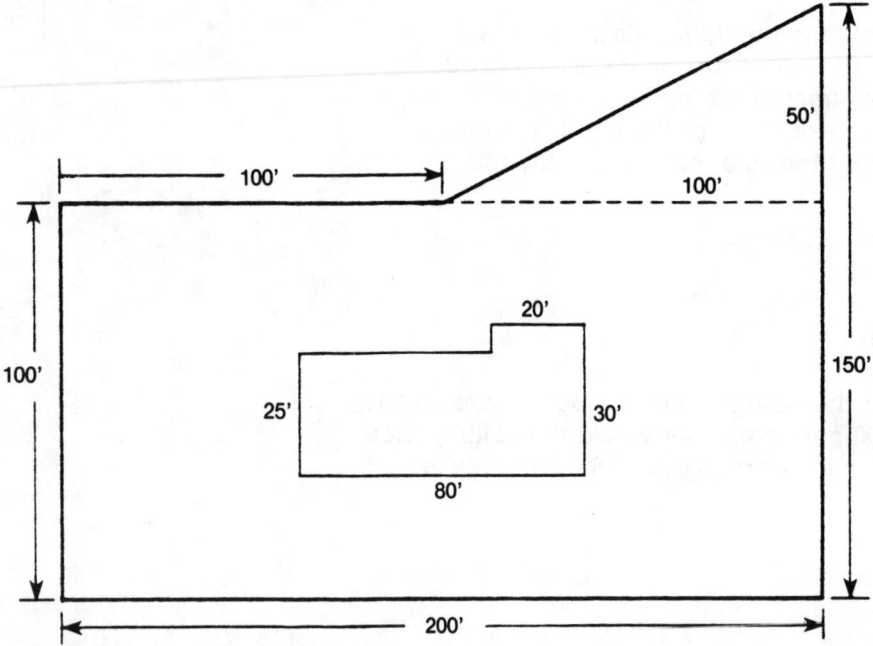

74. A new house and lot cost $14,000. Of the total price, it was estimated that the lot was worth $2,000. The owner had the property for six years. Assuming an annual depreciation of 2½ percent on the house and an annual increase in value of 8 percent on the lot, what was the total value of the property at the end of six years?

    (a) $10,200
    (b) $12,960
    (c) $13,160
    (d) $10,434

Real Estate Mathematics

75. The commission schedule for negotiating a 20-year ground lease was 6% for the first year, 5½% for each of the next two years, 5% for each of the next three years, 4½% for each of the next four years, and 2% for each year thereafter. What was the total commission earned if the annual rental was $8,500?

   (a) $5,950
   (b) $10,000
   (c) $4,415
   (d) $8,500

76. The diagrammed tract of land was sold for $25,380. What was the price per acre?

   (a) $1,042
   (b) $982.58
   (c) $1,333
   (d) $1,200

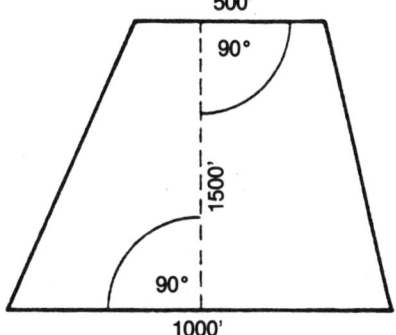

77. A rectangular acre of land has a width of 165 feet. What is the depth of the property?

   (a) 379 feet
   (b) 275 feet
   (c) 718.74 feet
   (d) 264 feet

78. If the assessed value of a property is $136,000 and the annual tax paid is $1,700, what is the tax rate per $100 of assessed value?

   (a) $1.25
   (b) $125.00
   (c) $0.80
   (d) $2.31

79. If a lease specifies the rent to be 2% of gross sales per annum with a minimum annual rent of $12,000, what is the annual rent if gross sales are $400,000?

   (a) $12,000
   (b) $8,000
   (c) $14,000
   (d) $8,240

80. Ms. Jones paid fair market value of $60,000 for a new home. The property is assessed at 80% of market value. If the semiannual tax bill is $900, what is the tax rate per $100?

    (a) $3.00
    (b) $1.88
    (c) $2.40
    (d) $3.75

81. A tract 300 feet square was sold by a broker for $2,750 per acre. If the commission rate was 9%, how much did the broker earn?

    (a) $1,893.93
    (b) $511.34
    (c) $568.15
    (d) $2,066.00

82. What is the area of the shaded portion?

    (a) 14,750 sq. ft.
    (b) 15,000 sq. ft.
    (c) 18,500 sq. ft.
    (d) 16,400 sq. ft.

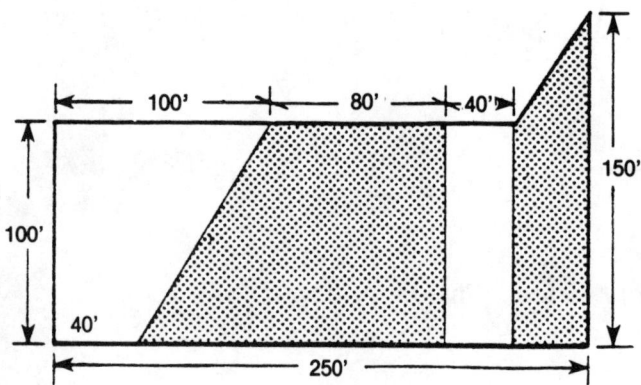

83. A broker's average sale during one year was $41,500. His commission schedule is 7%. If he averaged one sale for every 16.5 showings of properties, how many showings did he accomplish to earn $46,480 in that year?

    (a) 264
    (b) 176
    (c) 247
    (d) 237

84. An investor purchased a building at 15% below market value. Ten days later she sold it at the originally quoted market value price. What was her rate of profit?

    (a) 15.00%
    (b) 12.75%
    (c) 5.67%
    (d) 17.65%

Real Estate Mathematics 265

85. A tract of land contained 14,520 square yards. If the tract was valued at $27,000, what would be the value of a rectangular lot 150 feet by 300 feet?

   (a) $9,680
   (b) $9,297
   (c) $9,000
   (d) $3,099

86. The value of a building now 26 years old is $54,000. What was the value when new, if the building had an economic life of 50 years?

   (a) $112,500
   (b) $79,920
   (c) $82,080
   (d) $103,846

87. If a property sold at tax value and the annual tax was $588.80 at a tax rate of $2.30 per $100, what was the selling price?

   (a) $13,542
   (b) $17,664
   (c) $51,200
   (d) $25,600

88. If a real estate broker earned a commission of $5,600 at a commission rate of 7%, at what price was the property sold?

   (a) $39,200
   (b) $68,000
   (c) $125,000
   (d) $80,000

89. A purchaser negotiates a loan for 80% of the purchase price of her new home. If the interest rate is 9% and the first monthly payment on the loan includes $337.50 for interest, what did the woman pay for the home?

   (a) $37,500
   (b) $56,250
   (c) $46,875
   (d) $50,625

90. A broker was paid a commission of 9% for negotiating the sale of the tract illustrated. If the sale price was $1,200 per acre, what was the amount of the broker's commission?

   (a) $2,008.26
   (b) $1,928.88
   (c) $1,673.55
   (d) $2,333.33

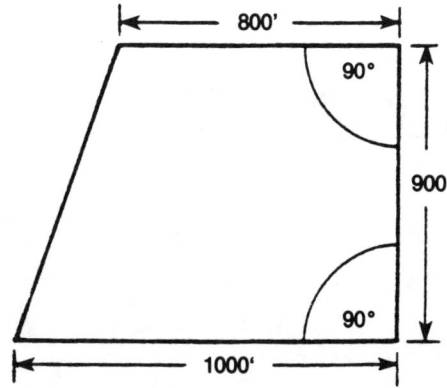

91. An owner sold three houses for an average price of $32,000. He made a profit of 12% on his original investment. What amount did he have invested in all three houses?

    (a) $84,480.00
    (b) $85,714.29
    (c) $28,571.43
    (d) $96,000.00

92. What is the cost, at $12 per square yard, to put a 3 foot wide concrete walk around the garden?

    (a) $1,133.28
    (b) $425.97
    (c) $567.96
    (d) $5,112.00

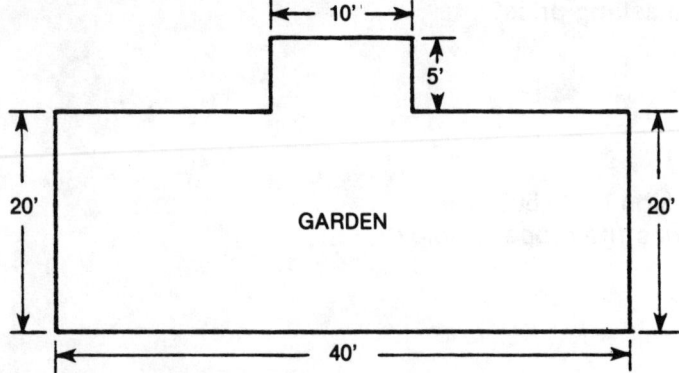

93. If a building sold for $200,000, which represented a profit of 25%, what was the seller's original cost?

    (a) $160,000
    (b) $184,000
    (c) $187,500
    (d) $150,000

94. An investor had a net return of $12,500 in the first year of operation of an office building. If her expenses totalled $7,000 and the investment in the building is capitalized at 12%, what did she pay for the property?

    (a) $45,833
    (b) $150,000
    (c) $104,167
    (d) $58,333

95. A broker received a commission of $64,000 at a rate of 10% in the sale of a tract of land one mile square. What was the price per acre at which the property sold?

    (a) $1,000
    (b) $6,400
    (c) $10,000
    (d) $640

Real Estate Mathematics

96. A broker sold ¼ of the Southwest ¼ of the Southwest ¼, and ½ of the Northwest ¼ of Section 20, Township 3, Range 2, East. How many acres are included in the sale?

   (a) 160
   (b) 340
   (c) 80
   (d) 90

97. An owner sold a building for $98,000. Later she sold a second building. The first building sold for 70% of the amount received for the second building. What was the sale price of the second building?

   (a) $166,600
   (b) $140,000
   (c) $68,600
   (d) $169,428

98. If one month's interest paid on a mortgage is $200 and the principal balance is $30,000, what is the rate of interest?

   (a) 6%
   (b) 6.67%
   (c) 7.25%
   (d) 8%

99. A house valued at $80,000 was insured for 85% of value. The cost of the insurance was 70 cents per $100 of face amount of the policy. The owner paid an annual premium on March 15. On September 30 of the same year, the sale of the home was closed. The unused value of the policy was purchased by the buyer. What was the buyer's cost?

   (a) $260.81
   (b) $257.86
   (c) $476.00
   (d) $218.14

100. An apple orchard nets the owners $28,000 per year. If they decide to sell the orchard for $400,000 and retire, at what rate of interest must they invest the sale proceeds to receive $24,000 per year?

   (a) 6%
   (b) 8%
   (c) 11.2%
   (d) 9.6%

SECTION 10—SOLUTIONS AND ANSWERS TO MATH REVIEW PROBLEMS

1. $28,000 × .0775 = $2170/yr
   $2170 ÷ 12 mos = $180.83/mo
   $180.83 ÷ 30 days = $6.03/day
   $6.03 × 12 days = $72.36 used portion
   Since payments are made in arrears, this amount will be a credit to the buyer.

2. Value = Income ÷ Rate
   V = $2400 ÷ .06
   V = $40,000

3. $540 ÷ $1.50 = 360
   360 × $100 = $36,000

4. 9000 gal ÷ 4 hrs = 2250 gal/hr by 36 pumps
   2250 gal/hr ÷ 36 pumps = 62.5 gal/hr per pump
   12000 gal ÷ 12 hrs = 1000 gal/hr by ? pumps
   1000 gal/hr ÷ 62.5 gal/hr/pump = 16 pumps

   or

   $$\underset{\text{pumps}}{\frac{36}{?}} \times \underset{\text{gals}}{\frac{12000}{9000}} \times \underset{\text{hrs}}{\frac{4}{12}} = 16 \text{ pumps}$$

5. $4,800 minimum
   $192,000 × .025 = $4800

6. 4½" × 2½ miles = ?

   $$\frac{9''}{2} \times \frac{5 \text{ miles}}{2} = \frac{45}{4} = 11¼ \text{ miles}$$

   11¼ miles = 11.25 miles

7. 40 yds × 3 ft/yd = 120 ft
   120 ft × 80 ft = 9600 sq ft
   9600 sq ft ÷ 43,560 sq ft = .22 acres

8. Value = Income ÷ Rate
   R = 60% of 6% = .6 × .06 = .036
   V = $18,000 ÷ .036 = $500,000 per year
   $500,000/yr ÷ 12 mos = $41,666.67

9. 30 ft X 3 sides = 90 ft
   90 ft ÷ 10 ft interval = 9 posts
   9 posts + 1 (starting post) = 10 posts

10. Value = Income ÷ Rate
    V = $12000/yr ÷ .085
    V = $141,176 (rounded)

Real Estate Mathematics

11. 80% of 2nd tract = 1st tract
    .8 × ? (2nd tract) = $48,000
    2nd tract = $48,000 ÷ .8
    2nd tract = $60,000

12. One point raises the effective interest rate 1/8 of 1%.
    One point costs 1% of the amount of the loan.

    8% − 7 3/4% = 1/4% = 2 pts = 2% of loan
    $27,000 × .02 = $540

13. 140 ft × 2 = 280 ft
    265 ft × 2 = 530 ft
    280 ft + 530 ft = 810 ft
    810 ft × 6 ft = 4860 sq ft
    4860 sq ft ÷ 9 sq ft/sq yd = 540 sq yds
    540 sq yds × $3 = $1620

14. $12,600 = gross income
    $12,600 × .05 = $630 (vacancy factor)
    $12,600 − $630 = $11,970 (gross effective income)
    $11,970 − $3600 = $8370 (net income)
    Value = Income ÷ Rate
    V = $8370 ÷ .12
    V = $69,750

15. $570/mo × 12 mos = $6840/yr
    Value = Income ÷ Rate
    V = $6840 ÷ .09
    V = $76,000

16. 100% ÷ 50 years = 2%/yr
    2% × 5 yrs = 10% (depreciation to date)
    100% − 10% = 90% (remaining value)
    Original Value = Current Value ÷ % of Remaining Value
    OV = $810,000 ÷ .9
    OV = $900,000

17. $63,250 × 100% = $63,250 (tax value)
    $63,250 ÷ $100/unit = 632.5 ($100 units)
    632.5 units × $2.10 (per $100 units) = $1328.25

18. Perimeter = (2 × width) + (2 × length)
    Width = W
    Length = 2W + 6 yds
    2(2W + 6yds) + 2W = 1800 yds
    6W + 12 yds = 1800 yds
    6W = 1788 yds
    W = 298 yds

    2(298) + 6 = length
    602 yds = length
    602 yds × 3 ft/yd = 1806 ft

19. $4000 × 3 = $12000
    $4500 × 4 = $18000
    $18000 − $12000 = $6000
    n% of $12000 = $6000
    n = $6000 ÷ $12000
    n = .5 or 50%

20. 100% ÷ 40 yrs = yearly depreciation rate
    1.00 ÷ 40 = .025 or 2.5% yearly depreciation
    12 yrs × 2.5% = 30% depreciation to date
    100% − 30% = 70% remaining value
    70% of original value = $26,000
    Original Value = $26,000 ÷ .70
    OV = $37,142.86

21. $\frac{3}{5} \times \frac{5}{8} \div \frac{5}{6} = ?$

    $\frac{3}{5} \times \frac{5}{8} \times \frac{6}{5} = ?$

    $\frac{3}{\cancel{5}_1} \times \frac{\cancel{5}^1}{\cancel{8}_4} \times \frac{\cancel{6}^3}{5} = \frac{9}{20}$

    9 ÷ 20 = .45

22. 9 inches thick on each of two ends = 1.5 ft
    35 ft − 1.5 ft = 33.5 ft
    26.5 ft − 1.5 ft = 25 ft
    33.5 ft × 25 ft = 837.5 sq ft

23. $20,000 × .09 = $1800 annual interest
    $1800 ÷ 12 mos = $150/mo
    $150 ÷ 30 days = $5/day
    $5 × 10 days = $50 Debit

24. $38,500 × .06 = $2310 brokers fee
    $33,000 × .055 = $1815 discount points
    $2310 + $1815 = $4125 total expenses
    $38,500 − $4125 = $34,375 Net

25. $750 incr ÷ $3.75 = 200 ($100 units)
    200 ($100 units) × $100/unit = $20,000 tax value
    $20,000 ÷ .60 = $33,333.33

26. Gross Income − Expenses = Net Income
    $80,000 − $8000 = $72,000
    Income ÷ Rate = Value
    $72,000 ÷ .08 = $900,000

27. $1200 × .0225 = $27
    $215 − $180 = $35
    $35 − $27 = $8

Real Estate Mathematics

28. $500/mo × 12 mo = $6000/year base rent
    $220,000 − $185,000 = $35,000 (earnings over $185,000)
    $35,000 × .03 = $1050
    $6000 + $1050 = $7050

29. 1/2 + 1/4 + 1/8 = Unknown Area
    4/8 + 2/8 + 1/8 = 7/8
    8/8 − 7/8 = 1/8 remaining
    Remaining Area = 7 acres = 1/8
    1/8 of Total = 7 acres
    Total = 7 acres × 8/1 = 56 acres

30. 20 units × $180/mo × 12 mos = $43,200 gross rent
    $43,200 − $2160 (vacancy @ 5%) = $41,040 gross effective income
    $41,040 − $26,204 (expenses) = $14,836 net income
    Income ÷ Value = Rate
    $14,836 ÷ $195,000 = .07608 = 7.61%

31. $35,000 + $7000 = $42,000 total assessed value
    $42,000 × 1.18 = $49,560 increased valuation
    $49,560 × .80 = $39,648 new tax basis
    $39,648 ÷ $100/unit = 396.48 ($100 units)
    396.48 ($100 units) × $2.12 (rate/$100 unit) = $840.54

32. $110,000 × .97 = $106,700
    $106,700 × .97 = $103,499
    $103,499 × .97 = $100,394
    $100,394 × .97 = $97,382

33. $7000 + $18,000 = $25,000
    100% − 7% commission = 93%
    $25,000 ÷ .93 = $26,882 (rounded)

34. Current Value = Original Value × Appreciation
    $32,000 × 1.42 (142%) = $45,440
    $4,000 × 1.36 (136%) = $5440
    $45,440 + $5440 = $50,880 (total appreciated value)
    $32,000 + $4000 = $36,000 (total original value)
    $50,880 − $36,000 = $14,880 (amount of appreciation)
    $14,880 ÷ $36,000 = 41.33%

35. 7 yrs × .025 = .175 or 17.5% depreciation to date
    100% − 17.5% = 82.5% remaining value
    Current Value ÷ % Remaining Value = Original Value
    $63,000 ÷ .825 = $76,363

36. $320,000 + $40,000 + $20,000 = $380,000 total investment
    Rate × Value = Income
    .12 × $380,000 = $45,600

37. $67,500 × .80 = $54,000 tax value
    $54,000 ÷ $100/unit = 540 ($100 units)
    540 ($100 units) × $1.50 (per $100 unit) = $810 tax bill
    $810 ÷ 12 mos = $67.50 monthly rate
    $67.50 ÷ 30 days = $2.25 daily rate
    $67.50 × 1 month = $67.50
    $2.25 X 20 days = $45.00
    $67.50 + $45.00 = $112.50 Debit

38. Area of a triangle = 1/2 × base × height
    1/2 × 350 ft × 425 ft = 74,375 sq ft
    74,375 sq ft × .75/sq ft = $55,781.25 sales price
    $55,781.25 × .09 = $5020.31

39. 4 yards × 8 yards = 32 square yards
    32 sq yds × $3.50/sq yd = $112 labor cost

    1/2 ft × 12 ft × 24 ft = 144 cubic feet
    144 cu ft × $1.50 = $216 material cost

    $112 + $216 = $328

40. $75,000 × .08 = $6000 commission on 1st $75,000
    $9000 − $6000 = $3000 commission on price over $75,000

    Income ÷ Rate = Value
    $3000 ÷ .06 = $50,000
    $75,000 + $50,000 = $125,000

41. $45,000 × 1.20 (120%) = $54,000 asking price
    $54,000 × .90 = $48,600 Sold Price

42. 600 ft × 145.2 ft = 87,120 sq ft
    87,120 sq ft ÷ 43,560 sq ft/acre = 2 acres
    2 acres × $4000 = $8000 acreage basis
    $15 × 600 ft = $9000 Front Foot Basis

43. Current Value = 100% Original Value + 35% of Original Value
    $280,000 ÷ 1.35 = $207,407 (rounded)

44. Income ÷ Rate = Value
    $150 ÷ .025 = $6000

45. 2300 sq ft × $26 = $59,800 house value
    150 ft × 210 ft = 31,500 sq ft lot area
    31,500 sq ft × $.25 = $7875 lot value
    $59,800 + $7875 = $67,675 value house & lot

    23 ft × 22 ft = 506 sq ft interior of garage
    506 sq ft × $12 = $6072 garage value

    Value Increase ÷ Original Value = Percentage of Increase
    $6072 ÷ $67,675 = .0897 or 8.97%

46. $1/4 \times 1/4 \times 1/4 \times \dfrac{640 \text{ acres}}{1 \text{ section}}$ = total acres sold

Real Estate Mathematics

$\frac{1}{64} \times \frac{640 \text{ acres}}{1 \text{ section}} = 10$ acres sold

10 acres × $700 = $7000
Rate × Value = Income
.12 × $7000 = $840 ANSWER

1 Section = 640 Acres

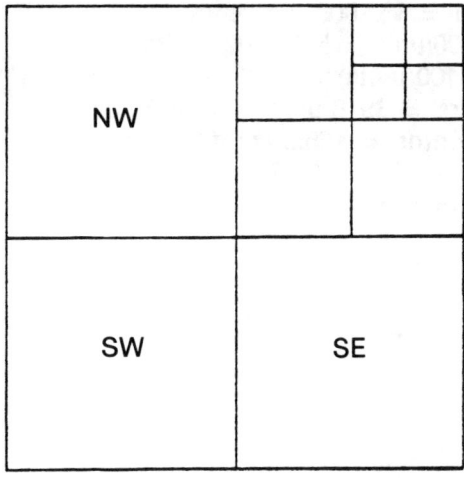

47. 160 Square Rods = 1 Acre (43,560 sq ft)
    560 sq rods ÷ 160 sq rods/acre = 3.5 acres
    3.5 acres × 43,560 sq ft/acre = 152,460 sq ft
    152,460 sq ft × $.12 = $18,295

48. (2 × 300 ft) + (2 × 150 ft) = 900 feet
    900 ft ÷ 15 ft/post = 60 posts

49. 1/2 × base × height = Area of a Right Triangle
    1/2 × 900 ft × 4000 ft = 1,800,000 square feet
    1,800,000 sq ft ÷ 9 sq ft/sq yd = 200,000 sq yards

50. $10,200 + $3,400 = $13,600 gross income
    Income ÷ Rate = Value
    $13,600 ÷ .14 (gross return) = $97,143 (rounded)

51. 12 mos × $1200 = $14,400 minimum annual rent
    $16,600 − $14,400 = $2200 rent above minimum

    Income ÷ Rate = Value
    $2200 ÷ .03 = $73,333.33 sales over $260,000
    $260,000.00 + $73,333.33 = $333,333.33

52. 100% ÷ 40 years = 2 1/2% per year depreciation
    14 years × 2.5%/yr = 35% depreciation to date
    100% − 35% = 65% remaining value

    Original Value × % Remaining Value = Current Value
    $150,000 × .65 = $97,500

53. $500 × 12 months = $6000 annual interest
    Income ÷ Rate = Value
    $6000 ÷ .10 = $60,000

54. Length × Width × Depth = Volume (Cubic Measure)
    90 ft × 30 ft × 14 ft = 37,800 cu ft
    37,800 cu ft ÷ 27 cu ft/cu yd = 1400 cubic yards
    1400 cu yds × $.25 = $350

55. $60,000 × .85 = $51,000 face amount
    $51,000 ÷ $100/unit = 510 ($100 units)
    $.60 × 510 ($100 units) = $306 annual premium
    $306 × 3 years = $918 premium for 3 years
    $918 ÷ 36 months = $25.50 monthly rate
    $25.50 × 14 months = $357 value used
    $918 − $357 = $561

56.

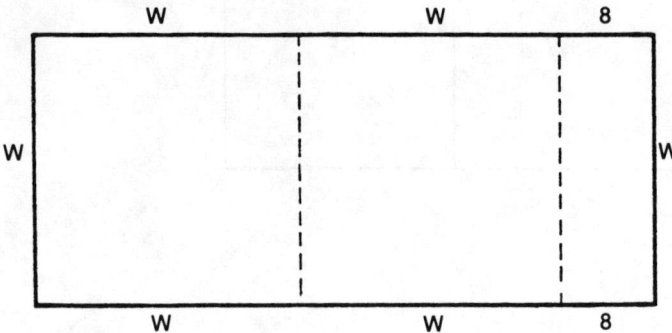

Perimeter = (2 × Length) + (2 × Width)
Length = (2 × Width) + 8 yards
2(2W + 8) + 2W = 120 yards
6 × Width + 16 yds = 120 yards
6W = 120 yds + 16 yds
6W = 104 yds
W = 104 yds ÷ 6
W = 17 1/3 yards
W = 17 1/3 yds × 3 ft/yd = 52 feet
Length = 2 × Width + 24 feet
L = 2 × 52 ft + 24 ft
L = 128 feet

57. 1/2 + 1/3 = Unknown Area
    3/6 + 2/6 = 5/6
    6/6 (entire area) − 5/6 = 1/6
    Remainder = 20 acres
    1/6 of entire tract = 20 acres
    Entire tract = 20 acres × 6 = 120 acres

58. 125 acres × $450 = $56,250
    200 houses × $45,000 = $9,000,000
    Other costs = $125,000
    $56,250 + $9,000,000 + $125,000 = $9,181,250 investment
    1.14 (114%) × $9,181,250 = $10,466,625 gross sales
    $10,466,625 ÷ 200 houses = $52,333.13

59. 5,280 ft × 1.25 = 6600 feet
    6600 ft × 6600 ft = 43,560,000 square feet
    43,560,000 sq ft ÷ 43,560 sq ft/acre = 1000 acres
    1000 acres × $200 = $200,000

    Value × Rate = Income
    $200,000 × .09 = $18,000 total commission
    100% − 45% = 55% retained net
    .55 × $18,000 = $9,900

60. $24 × 12 months = $288 annual expenses
    $3600 + $288 = $3888 gross income
    Income ÷ Rate = Value
    $3888 ÷ .06 = $64,800

61. $50,000 − $5,000 = $45,000 net income
    Income ÷ Rate = Value
    $45,000 ÷ .09 = $500,000

62. 125 ft × 160 ft = 20,000 square feet
    20,000 sq ft × .17 = $3400 purchase price
    $2.25 × 125 ft = $281.25 paving lien
    $3400 + $281.25 = $3681.25 total investment
    $3681.25 + $295.00 = $3976.25

63. $8925.25 + $1510.60 + $4920.05 + $3644.10 = $19,000
    Gross Annual Income − Annual Expenses = Net Return
    $53,200 − $19,000 = $34,200

64. $500 × 12 months = $6000 annual expenses
    $14,000 + $6000 = $20,000 gross income
    Income ÷ Rate = Value
    $20,000 ÷ .25 = $80,000

65. Divide house diagram into 3 triangles and 1 square.
    1/2 × base × height = Area of Triangle
    Height = 20 ft since the two diagonal lines intersect in the center
    1/2 × 40 ft × 20 ft = 400 square feet
    3 × 400 sq ft = 1200 sq ft (area of 3 triangles)
    20 ft × 20 ft = 400 sq ft (area of square)
    1200 sq ft + 400 sq ft = 1600 sq ft (area of house)
    $56,000 ÷ 1600 sq ft = $35 present cost per square foot
    $35 − $15 = $20

66. $325 × 52 weeks = $16,900 annual gross income
    $845 × 12 months = $10,140 annual expense
    $16,900 − $10,140 = $6,760 net annual income
    Income ÷ Value = Rate
    $6,760 ÷ $84,500 = .08 or 8%

67. 10 × 43,560 sq ft (1 acre) = 435,600 square feet
    435,600 sq ft − 85,600 sq ft = 350,000 sq ft available for lots
    50 ft × 100 ft = 5000 square feet per lot
    350,000 sq ft ÷ 5000 sq ft = 70 lots

68. $50,000 × .75 = $37,500 (tax value)
    $37,500 ÷ $100/unit = 375 ($100 units)
    375 ($100 units) × $4.50 (per $100 unit) = $1687.50 annually
    $1687.50 ÷ 2 = $843.75 Semi-Annual

69. 50 ft × $63 = $3150 lot cost
    $3150 + $9216 = $12,366 total cost
    $12,366 − $5,000 = $7,366 mortgage amount
    $7,366 × .055 = $405.13 annual interest
    $405.13 ÷ 2 = $202.57

70. 3 × 80 ft × 75 ft = 18,000 square feet in building
    $25 × 18,000 sq ft = $450,000 building cost
    $300 × 100 = $30,000 cost of lot
    100 × 200 = 20,000 sq ft lot size
    20,000 sq ft − (80 ft × 75 ft) = 14,000 sq ft to be paved
    14,000 sq ft × $3 = $42,000 paving cost
    $450,000 + $30,000 + $42,000 = $522,000

71. Divide lot into 1 triangle and 1 square
    1/2 × base × height = Area of Right Triangle
    1/2 × 50 ft × 150 ft = 3750 square feet in triangle
    150 ft × 150 ft = 22,500 square feet in square
    3750 sq ft + 22,500 sq ft = 26,250 sq ft lot size
    26,250 sq ft ÷ 43,560 sq ft/acre = .60 acre
    .60 acres × $4000 = $2400 lot cost
    Divide house into 2 rectangles
    80 ft × 25 ft = 2000 square feet
    5 ft × 40 ft = 200 square feet
    2000 sq ft + 200 sq ft = 2200 sq ft house size
    2200 sq ft × $21 = $46,200 house cost

    $2400 + $46,200 = $48,600 total cost
    $48,600 × 1.10 = $53,460

72. 130 ft × 30 ft = 3900 square feet
    3900 sq ft × $18.90 = $73,710 cost on square foot basis

    130 ft × 30 ft × 24 ft = 93,600 cubic feet
    93,600 cu ft × $.80 = $74,880 cost on cubic foot basis
    $74,880 − $73,710 = $1,170

73. Divide house into 2 rectangles
    5 ft × 20 ft = 100 sq ft
    25 ft × 80 ft = 2000 sq ft
    2000 sq ft + 100 sq ft = 2100 square feet in house

    Divide lot into 1 rectangle and 1 triangle
    100 ft × 200 ft = 20,000 square feet (rectangle)
    1/2 × 50 ft × 100 ft = 2500 square feet
    20,000 sq ft + 2500 sq ft = 22,500 sq ft in lot

    Area of House + Area of Lot = Percentage of Lot Occupied by House
    2100 sq ft ÷ 22,500 sq ft = .0933 rounded to 9%

Real Estate Mathematics

74. $14,000 − $2000 = $12,000 original house value
.025 × 6 yrs = .15 or 15% depreciation
$12,000 × .15 = $1800 depreciation
$12,000 − $1800 = $10,200 house value at end of 6 years

.08 × 6 yrs = .48 or 48% lot appreciation
$2000 × 1.48 (148%) = $2960 lot value at end of 6 years
$10,200 + $2960 = $13,160

75. .06 × $8500 = $ 510
    .055 × (2 yrs × $8500) =   935
    .05 × (3 yrs × $8500) =   1275
    .045 × (4 yrs × $8500) =   1530
    .02 × (10 yrs × $8500) =   1700
                                 $5950

76. Area of Trapezoid = 1/2 × height × (base$_1$ + base$_2$)
Area = 1/2 × 1500 ft × (500 ft + 1000 ft)
Area = 750 ft × 1500 ft
Area = 1,125,000 square feet
1,125,000 sq ft ÷ 43,560 sq ft/acre = 25.83 acres
$25,380 ÷ 25.83 = $982.58

77. 43,560 sq ft (1 acre) ÷ 165 ft = 264 feet

78. $136,000 ÷ $100/unit = 1360 ($100 units)
$1700 ÷ 1360 ($100 units) = $1.25

79. $400,000 × .02 = $8,000
Therefore: Annual Rent = $12,000 Minimum

80. $60,000 × .80 = $48,000 assessed value
$48,000 ÷ $100/unit = 480 ($100 units)
$900 × 2 = $1800 annual taxes
$1800 ÷ 480 ($100 units) = $3.75 Rate

81. 300 ft × 300 ft = 90,000 square feet
90,000 sq ft ÷ 43,560 sq ft/acre = 2.066 acres
2.066 acres × $2750 = $5,681.50 sales price

Value × Rate = Income
$5,681.50 × .09 = $511.34

82.

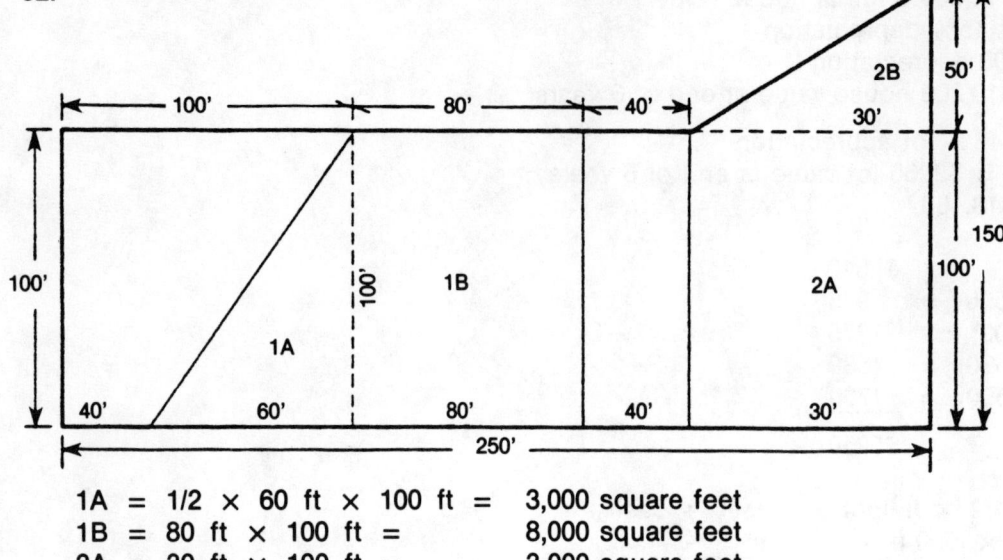

1A = 1/2 × 60 ft × 100 ft = 3,000 square feet
1B = 80 ft × 100 ft = 8,000 square feet
2A = 30 ft × 100 ft = 3,000 square feet
2B = 1/2 × 30 ft × 50 ft =   750 square feet
                                        14,750 square feet

83. $41,500 × .07 = $2905 earnings per sale
$46,480 ÷ $2905 = 16 sales
16 sales × 16.5 = 264 showings

84. Market Value = 100%
100% − 15% = 85% of MV (purchase price)

Percentage Increase ÷ Original Value = Rate of Profit
15% ÷ 85% = Rate of Profit
.15 ÷ .85 = .1765 or 17.65%

85. 14,520 sq yds × 9 sq ft/yd^2 = 130,680 square feet
$27,000 ÷ 130,680 sq ft = $.2066 per square feet
150 ft × 300 ft = 45,000 square feet
45,000 sq ft × $.2066 = $9,297

86. 100% ÷ 50 years = 2% depreciation per year
26 years × 2% = 52% depreciation to date
100% − 52% = 48% remaining value

Current Value ÷ % Remaining Value = Original Value
$54,000 ÷ .48 = $112,500

87. $588.80 ÷ $2.30 = 256 ($100 units)
256 ($100 units) × $100/unit = $25,600

88. Income ÷ Rate = Value
$5600 ÷ .07 = $80,000

89. $337.50 × 12 months = $4050 annual interest
Income ÷ Rate = Value
$4050 ÷ .09 = $45,000 loan amount
$45,000 ÷ .80 = $56,250

90. Area of Trapezoid = 1/2 × height × (base$_1$ + base$_2$)
    A = 1/2 × 900 ft × (1000 ft + 800 ft)
    A = 810,000 square feet
    810,000 sq ft ÷ 43,560 sq ft/acre = 18.595 acres
    18.595 acres × $1200 = $22,314

    Value × Rate = Income
    $22,314 × .09 = $2008.26

91. $32,000 × 3 = $96,000 total sale price
    $96,000 ÷ 1.12 (112%) = $85,714.29

92.

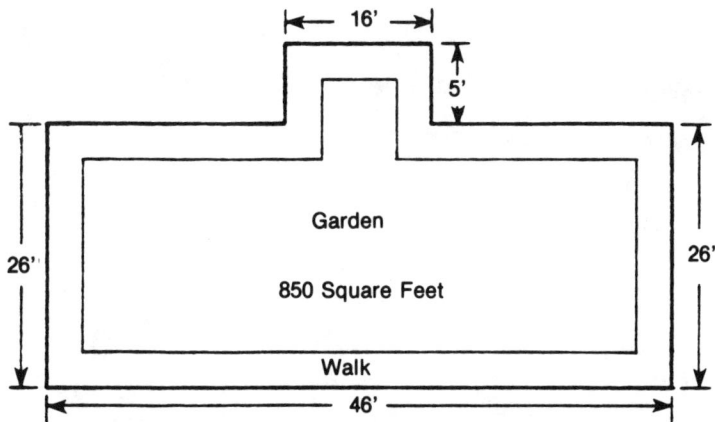

- *Step 1:* Divide garden into 2 rectangles
    20 ft × 40 ft = 800 square feet
    5 ft × 10 ft = 50 square feet
    800 sq ft + 50 sq ft = 850 sq ft garden area

- *Step 2:* Calculate total area including walk
    46 ft × 26 ft = 1196 square feet
    16 ft × 5 ft = 80 square feet
    1196 sq ft + 80 sq ft = 1276 sq ft total area

- *Step 3:* Determine square yards in walk and calculate cost
    1276 sq ft − 850 sq ft = 426 sq ft walk area
    426 sq ft ÷ 9 sq ft/sq yd = 47.33 square yards
    47.33 sq yd × $12 = $567.96

93. Current Value = 100% Original Value + 25% of Original Value
    $200,000 ÷ 1.25 = $160,000

94. Income ÷ Rate = Value
    $12,500 ÷ .12 = $104,167
    (Note: Net income is used with cap. rate)

95. 5280 ft × 5280 ft = 27,878,400 square feet
    27,878,400 sq ft ÷ 43,560 sq ft/acre = 640 acres

    Income ÷ Rate = Value
    $64,000 ÷ .10 = $640,000 total sale price
    $640,000 ÷ 640 acres = $1000

96.

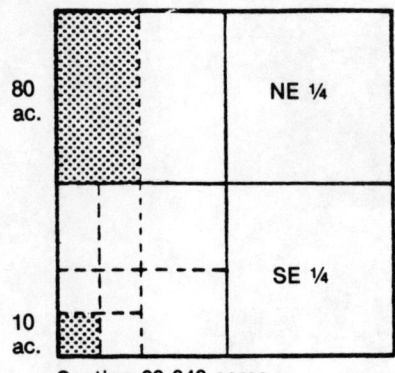

$$1/4 \times 1/4 \times 1/4 \times \frac{640 \text{ acres}}{1 \text{ section}} = 10 \text{ acres}$$

$$1/2 \times 1/4 \times \frac{640 \text{ acres}}{1 \text{ section}} = 80 \text{ acres}$$

10 acres + 80 acres = 90 acres

97. 1st Building = 70% of 2nd Building
$98,000 ÷ .70 = $140,000

98. $200 × 12 months = $2400 annualized interest
Income ÷ Value = Rate
$2400 ÷ $30,000 = .08 or 8%

99. $80,000 × .85 = $68,000 face amount
$68,000 ÷ $100/unit = 680 ($100 units)
680 ($100 units) × $.70 = $476 annual premium
$476 ÷ 12 = $39.67 premium per month
6.5 months × $39.67 = $257.86 value used
$476.00 − $257.86 = $218.14

100. Income ÷ Value = Rate
$24,000 ÷ $400,000 = .06 or 6%

The Language of Real Estate: A Glossary of Real Estate Terminology

16

This chapter presents definitions of all real estate terms appearing in the text. At the end of each of these definitions you will find the chapter number where the term defined is fully discussed. In this way you are directed to the text material for additional reading if the definition does not provide a complete understanding. Also, there are definitions of some terms that are not specifically discussed in the text but may possibly be included in the license examinations.

It is absolutely necessary that you recognize and understand the terminology in this chapter to be successful in taking the license examinations.

Abandonment—The surrender or release of a right, claim, or interest in real property. (5)

Abstract Continuation—An update of an abstract of title by a memorandum of a new transfer of title. (7)

Abstract of Title—A history of a title and the current status of a title based on a title examination. (7)

Accelerated Cost Recovery System (ACRS)—A method of depreciation created by the Economic Tax Recovery Act of 1981. (14)

Accelerated Depreciation—A method of depreciating structures for tax purposes at a rate in excess of straight line. (14)

Acceleration Clause—A provision in a mortgage or deed of trust that permits the lender to declare the entire principal balance of the debt immediately due and payable if the borrower is in default. (8)

Access—The right to go onto and leave a property. (5)

Accord and Satisfaction—A new agreement by contracting parties that is satisfied by full performance, thereby terminating at prior contract as well. (6)

Accrued—Accumulated. (14)

Accrued Depreciation—The amount of depreciation taken, as of a given date, for tax purposes. (14)

(2) The loss in value in a structure measured by the cost of a new replacement. (10)

Acknowledgement—A formal statement before an authorized official (e.g., notary public) by a person who executed a deed, contract, or other document that it was (is) his free act. (6, 7)

Acquisition—The act of acquiring a property. (8)

Acquisition Cost—The basis used by the FHA in calculating the loan amount. (8)

Acre—A land area containing 43,560 square feet. (15)

Action to Quiet Title—A lawsuit to clear a title to real property. (5, 7)

Actual Age—Chronological age. (10)

Actual Eviction—The removal of a tenant by the landlord because the tenant breached a condition of a lease or other rental contract. (6)

Actual Notice—The knowledge that a person has of a fact. (7)

Adjoining Lands—Lands sharing a common boundary line. (5)

Adjustable Rate Mortgage (ARM)—One in which the interest rate changes according to changes in a predetermined index. (8)

Adjusted Sales Price—The amount realized reduced by the cost of fixing up expenses. (14)

Adjustments—Additions or subtractions of dollar amounts to equalize comparables to subject property in the market data approach to the value estimate. (10)

Administrator—A man appointed by a court to administer the estate of one who has died intestate. (7)

Administratrix—A woman appointed by a court to administer the estate of one who has died intestate. (17)

Administrators Deed—One executed by an administrator to convey title to estate property. (7)

Ad Valorem—Latin meaning "according to value." Real property is taxed on an *ad valorem* basis. (5)

Adverse Possession—A method of acquiring title to real property by conforming to statutory requirement. A form of involuntary alienation of title. (7)

Affirmative Easement—A legal requirement that a servient owner permit a right of use in the servient land by the dominant owner. (5)

Age 55-and-over Exclusion—A tax exemption available to sellers of a principal residence who are age 55 or over. (14)

Agency—The fiduciary relationship existing between a principal and agent. (6)

Agent—A person authorized by another to act on his or her behalf. (6)

Agreement—A contract. Mutual assent between two or more parties. (6)

Air Rights—Rights in the air space above the surface of land. (5)

Alienation—Transfer of title to real property. (7)

Alienation Clause—A clause in a mortgage or deed of trust that entitles the lender to declare the entire principal balance of the debt immediately due and payable if the borrower sells the property during the mortgage term. (8)

Allodial System—The type of land ownership existing in the United States whereby title to real property may be held absolutely by individuals. (5)

Alternate ACRS Method—An ACRS Provision that permits a taxpayer to depreciate property on a straight line basis instead of using ACRS for property placed in service in 1981 and subsequent years. (14)

Amenities—Benefits resulting from the ownership of a particular property. (5)

Amortization Schedule—A designation of periodic payments of principal and interest over a specific term to satisfy a mortgage loan. (8)

Amortizing Mortgage—One in which uniform installment payments include the payment of both principal and interest. (8)

Annexation—The addition of an area into a city. (10)

Annual—Yearly.

Annual Percentage Rate (APR)—The yearly rate of interest charged on a loan. (8)

Antichurning Rule—An ACRS Rule prohibiting a taxpayer from using ACRS for property placed in service prior to 1981. (14)

Anticipation—The principle that property value is based on the anticipation of the future benefits of ownership. (10)

Appraisal—An estimate of property value based on factual data. (10)

Appraisal Process—An organized and systematic program for estimating real property value. (10)

Appraisal Report—A report containing an estimate of property value and the data on which the estimate is based. (10)

Appreciation—An increase in property value. (10, 15)

Approaches to Value—Methods of estimating real property value. (10)

Appurtenance—All rights or privileges that result from ownership of a particular property and move with the title. (5)

Appurtenant Easement—A right of use in the adjoining land of another that moves with the title to the property benefiting from the easement. (5)

Arrears—Deliquent in meeting an obligation. The payment of interest for a prior period as scheduled. (9, 15)

Artificial Person—A corporation or other legally recognized entity. (5)

Asking Price—The price specified in a listing contract. (6)

Assessed Value—The value to which a local tax rate is applied to calculate the amount of real property tax. (10)

Assessment—A levy against property. (5)

Assessor—An official of local government who has the responsibility for establishing the value of property for tax purposes. (5)

Assignee—One to whom contractual rights and obligations are transferred. (6)

Assignment—A transfer of legal rights and obligations by one party to another. (6)

Assignment of a Lease—The transfer by a lessee of the entire remaining term of a lease without any reversion of interest to the lessee. (6)

Assignor—One transferring contractual rights and obligations to another. (6)

Assumable Mortgage—One that does not contain an alienation clause. (8)

Attestation—Witnessing a document. (7)

Attorney-at-Law—A person licensed by a state to engage in the practice of law. (4)

Attorney-in-Fact—A person appointed to perform legal acts for another under a power-of-attorney. (4)

Auction—A form of property sale in which people are bidding against each other. (5, 8)

Availability—An economic characteristic of land describing that land is a commodity having a fixed supply base. (3)

Bail Bond—A bond given by a defendant under criminal charges to obtain release from custody. (5)

Balloon Mortgage—One in which the scheduled payment will not fully amortize the loan over the mortgage term. Therefore, it requires a final pay called a balloon payment, larger than the uniform payments, to fully satisfy the debt. (8)

Bargain and Sale Deed—A form of deed with or without covenants of title. (7)

Base Lines—East-West lines in the rectangular method of property description. (7)

Base Rent—The fixed or minimum rent portion in a percentage lease. (6, 15)

Basis—The value of property for income tax purposes. It is original cost, plus capital improvements, less accrued depreciation.

Beneficial Title—The equitable title to real property retained by a mortgagor or trustor conveying the legal title to secure a mortgage debt. (8)

Beneficiary—(1) The recipient of a gift of personal property by will. (7)

(2) The lender in a deed of trust. (8)

Bequest—A gift of personal property by will. (7)

Bilateral Contract—An agreement based on mutual promises that provide the consideration. (6)

Bill of Sale—An instrument transferring ownership of personal property.

Blanket Mortgage—One in which two or more parcels of real property are pledged to secure the payment of the note. (8)

Blockbusting—For profit, to induce or attempt to induce any person to sell or rent any dwelling by representations regarding the entry or prospective entry into the neighborhood of a person or persons of a particular race, color, religion, sex, or national origin. (12)

Bona Fide—Latin meaning "in good faith." (7)

Book Value—The value as it appears on the books of the owner. (10)

Boot—Cash received in a tax-free exchange. (14)

Breach of Contract—Failure, without legal excuse, to perform any promise that forms the whole or part of a contract. (6)

Broker—A person or organization acting as agent for others in negotiating the purchase and sale of real property or other commodities for a fee. (4, 6)

Bundle of Rights—The rights of an owner of a freehold estate to possession, enjoyment, control, and disposition of real property. (5)

Building Codes—Public controls regulating construction. (11)

Capital Asset—Property held for personal use or as an investment. (14)

Capital Gain—The profit realized in the sale of an asset. (14)

Capital Gains Tax—Tax imposed on the gain realized in the sale of a capital asset. (14)

Capital Improvement—An item that adds value to the property, adapts the property to new uses, or prolongs the life of property. Maintenance is NOT a capital improvement. (14)

Capital Loss—A loss incurred in the sale of a capital asset. (14)

Capitalization—The process of converting future income into an indication of the present value of a property by applying a capitalization rate to net annual income. (10)

Capitalization Rate—The rate of interest appropriate to the investment risk as a return on the investment. (10)

Carry-Over Clause—A clause in a listing contract protecting the broker's commission entitlement for a specified period of time after expiration of the contract. Also called extender clause. (6)

Cash Flow—The income produced by a rental property after deducting operating expenses and debt service. (10)

Caveat Emptor—Latin meaning "let the buyer beware." Applies to "sales talk" and not to statements of material facts. (6)

Certificate of Eligibility—A statement provided to veterans of military service setting forth the amount of loan guarantee to which they are entitled at that time. (8)

Certificate of Occupancy—A document issued by a local government agency, after a satisfactory inspection of a structure, authorizing the occupancy of the structure. (11)

Certificate of Reasonable Value—A document setting for the value of a property as the basis for the loan guarantee by the Veterans Administration to the lender. (8)

Certificate of Title Opinion—A report, based on a title examination, setting for the examiner's opinion of the quality of a title to real property. (7)

Chain—In land measurement, a distance of 66 feet. (7)

Chain of Title—The successive conveyances of title to a particular parcel of land. (7)

Change—The principle stating that change is continually affecting land use and therefore continually altering value. (10)

Chattel—Personal property. (5)

Chattel Mortgage—One in which personal property is pledged to secure the payment of a debt.

Chattel Real—Nonfreehold interests in real property. Also includes fixtures. (5)

Civil Action—A lawsuit between private parties. (12)

Civil Rights Act of 1866—A federal law that prohibits all discrimination on the basis of race. (12)

Closed-End Mortgage—One that cannot be refinanced. (8)

Closed Mortgage—One that imposes a prepayment penalty. (8)

Closing—The consumation of a real estate contract. Also called settlement. (9)

Closing Costs—Expenses incurred in the purchase and sale of real property paid at the time of settlement or closing. (9)

Closing (or Settlement) Statement—An accounting of the funds received and disbursed in a real estate transaction. (9)

Cloud on a Title—A claim against a title to real property. (7)

Cluster Zoning—A form of zoning providing for several different types of land use within a zoned area. (11)

Code of Ethics—A standard of conduct required by license laws and by the National Association of REALTORS®. (4)

Coinsurance Clause—A requirement of hazard insurance policies that property be insured for a certain percent of value to obtain the full amount of loss. (13)

Collateral—Property pledged as security for the payment of a debt. (8)

Color of Title—A defective claim to a title. (7)

Commercial Property—Property producing rental income or used in business. (8, 14)

Comingling—Mixing the money or property of others by an agent with the agent's personal or business funds or other property. (4)

Commission—A fee paid for the performance of services, such as a broker's commission. (6)

Commissioner's Deed—A form of judicial deed executed by a commissioner. (7)

Commitment—A promise, such as a promise by a lending institution to make a certain mortgage loan. (6)

Common Areas—Property to which title is held by co-owners as a result of ownership of a condominium unit. (5)

Community-Based Planning—A form of land-use control originating in the grassroots of a community. (11)

Community Planning—A plan for the orderly growth of a city or county to result in the greatest social and economic benefits to the people. (11)

Community Property—A form of co-ownership limited to husband and wife. Does not include the right of survivorship. (5)

Comparable—A property that is similar to a property being appraised by the market data approach. (10)

Comparison Approach—See Market Data Approach. (10)

Competent Parties—Persons and organizations legally qualified to manage their own affairs, including entering into contracts. (6)

Competition—The principle stating that when the net profit generated by a property is excessive, the result will be to create very strong competition. (10)

Component Depreciation—The method of depreciating the various parts of a structure over different periods of useful life. (14)

Composite Depreciation—The adoption of one period of useful life for an entire structure as a basis for calculating depreciation. (14)

Condemnation—The exercise of the power of eminent domain. The taking of private property for public use. (5)

Condemnation Value—Market value of property condemned. (10)

Condominium—A form of ownership of real property recognized in all states that consists of individual ownership of some aspects and co-ownership in other aspects of the property. (5)

Condominium Declaration—The document which, when recorded, creates a condominium. Also called a master deed. (5)

Conformity—The homogeneous uses of land within a given area results in maximizing land value. (10)

Consideration—Anything of value as recognized by law offered as an inducement to contract. (6)

Construction Loan—A short-term loan, secured by a mortgage, to obtain the funds to construct an improvement on land. (8)

Construction Mortgage—A temporary mortgage used to borrow the money to construct an improvement on land. (8)

Constructive Eviction—Results from some action or inaction by the landlord that renders the premises unsuitable for the use agreed to in a lease or other rental contract. (6)

Constructive Notice—Everyone is bound by the knowledge of a fact even though they have not been actually notified of such fact. (7)

Consumer Price Index (CPI)—An index of the change in prices of various commodities and services that provides a measure of the rate of inflation. (6)

Contingency—A condition in a contract relieving a party of liability if a certain event occurs. (6)

Contract—An agreement between competent parties upon legal consideration to do, or abstain from doing, some legal act. (6)

Contract for Deed—A contract of sale and a financing instrument wherein the seller agrees to convey title when the buyer completes the purchase price installment payments. Also called installment land contract, land contract, and conditional sales contract. (6)

Contract Rent—The amount of rent agreed to in a lease. (10)

Contribution—The principle that for any given part of a property, its value is the result of the contribution that part makes to the total value by being present, or the amount that it subtracts from total value as a result of its absence. (10)

Cooperative—A form of ownership in which stockholders in a corporation occupy property owned by the corporation under a lease. (5)

Cooperating Broker—One who participates in the sale of a property through the listing broker. (6)

Co-ownership—Title to real property held by two or more persons at the same time. Also called concurrent ownership. (5)

Corporation—A form of organization existing as an entity. (5)

Corporeal—Tangible things. (5)

Cost Approach—An appraisal method whereby the cost of constructing a substitute structure is calculated depreciation is deducted, and land value is added. (10)

Counteroffer—A new offer made by one rejecting an offer. (6)

Covenant—A promise in writing. (7)

Covenant against Encumbrances—A promise in a deed that there are no encumbrances against the title except those set forth in the deed. (7)

Covenant for Further Assurances—A promise in a deed that the grantor will execute such further assurances as may be reasonable or necessary to perfect the title in the grantee. (7)

Covenant of Quiet Enjoyment—A promise in a deed (or lease) that the grantee (or lessee) will not be disturbed in his or her use of the property because of a defect in the grantor's (or lessor's) title. (7)

Covenant of Right to Convey—A promise in a deed that the grantor has the legal capacity to convey the title. (7)

Covenant of Seisin—A promise in a deed assuring to the grantee that the grantor has the title being conveyed. (7)

Covenant of Warranty—A promise in a deed that the grantor will guarantee and defend the title against lawful claimants. (7)

Conventional Life Estates—Those created intentional act of the parties. (5)

Conventional Loan—One in which the federal government does not insure or guarantee the payment to the lender. (8)

Conversion—Change in a form of ownership, such as changing rental apartments to condominium ownership. (5)

Conveyance—Transfer of title to real property. (5)

Credit—In a closing statement, money to be received or credit given for money or an obligation given. (9)

Creditor—One to whom a debt is owed. (5)

Cul-de-Sac—A dead-end street with a circular turnaround at the dead end. (7)

Cumulative-Use Zoning—A type of zoning permitting a higher priority use even though different from the type of use designated for the area. (11)

Curable Depreciation—A condition of property that exists when correction is physically possible and the cost of correction is less than the value increase. (10)

Curtesy—A husband's interest in the real property of his wife. (5)

Damages—The amount of financial loss incurred as a result of the action of another. (6)

Debit—In a closing statement, an expense or money received against a credit. (9)

Debt Service—Principal and interest payments on a debt. (10)

Decedent—A dead person. (7)

Declaration of Restrictions—The instrument used to record restrictive covenants on the public record. (11)

Declining Balance Depreciation—A method of accelerated depreciation in which the property value is reduced annually by previous depreciation to be used as the basis for applying the annual rate of depreciation. (14)

Decree—An order of a court. (6)

Dedication—An appropriation of land or an easement therein by the owner to the public. (5)

Deed—A written instrument that transfers an interest in real property when delivered to the grantee. (7)

Deed in Lieu of Foreclosure—A conveyance of title to the mortgagee by a mortgagor in default to avoid a record of foreclosure. Also called friendly foreclosure. (8)

Deed in Trust—A deed used to transfer title to a trustee in a land trust. (5)

Deed of Bargain and Sale—A deed with or without warranties except an implied convenant that the grantor has title and possession. (7)

Deed of Confirmation—A deed executed to correct an error in a prior deed. Also called a deed of correction. (7)

Deed of Gift—A warranty or quit claim deed conveying title as a gift to the grantee. (7)

Deed of Release—A deed executed by a mortgage lender to release a title from the lien of a mortgage when the debt has been satisfied. Also used to release a dower right. (7)

Deed of Surrender—A deed executed by a life tenant to convey his or her estate to the remainder or reversionary interest. (7)

Deed of Trust—A form of mortgage wherein there is a third party, who is called a trustee. (8)

Deed Restrictions—Limitations on land use appearing in deeds. (11)

Default—Failure to perform an obligation. (6)

Defeasance Clause—The clause in a mortgage or deed of trust giving the borrower the right to redeem the title and have the mortgage lien released at any time prior to default by paying the debt in full. (8)

Defeasible—Subject to being defeated by the occurrance of a certain event. (5)

Defeasible Fee—A title that is subject to being lost if certain conditions occur. (5)

Deficiency Judgment—A judgment obtained by a mortgagee for the amount of money a foreclosure sale proceeds were deficient in fully satisfying the mortgage debt. (8)

Demise—To convey an estate for years. Synonymous with lease or let. (5)

Density—The number of persons or structures per acre. (11)

Department of Housing and Urban Development (HUD)—A federal agency involved with housing. (12)

Depreciation—Loss in value from any cause. (10)

Depreciation—For tax purposes, the write-off of the cost of an asset over the useful life of the asset or over the time periods specified by the Economic Tax Recovery Act of 1981. It thereby, creates a tax shelter. (14)

Depreciable Asset—Property other than land, held as an investment or for use in a business. (14)

Depreciation Methods—The methods used in calculating depreciation. They are: straight line, declining balance, sum-of-the-year's digits, and the method authorized by the Economic Recovery Tax Act of 1981. (14)

Depreciated Value—The original basis of a property less the amount of depreciation taken at any point in time. (14)

Descent—The distribution of property of one who has died intestate to legally qualified heirs. (7)

Devise—A gift of real property by will. (7)

Devisee—The recipient of a gift of real property by will. (7)

Disclosure Statement—An accounting of all financial aspects of a mortgage loan required of lenders to borrowers in residential mortgage loans by Regulation Z of the Federal Reserve Board. (8)

Discount Points—A percentage of the loan amount required by the lender for making a mortgage loan. (8)

Discriminatory Advertising—Any advertising that states or indicates a preference, limitation, or discrimination on the basis of race, color, religion, sex, or national origin in offering housing for sale or rent. (12)

Disintermediation—The loss of funds available to lending institutions for making mortgage loans caused by the withdrawal of funds by depositors for making investments providing greater yields. (8)

Dominant Tenement—Land benefiting from an appurtenant easement. (5)

Dower—A wife's interest in the real property of her husband. (5)

Due-on-Sale Clause—See Alienation Clause. (8)

Duress—The inability of a party to exercise his or her free will because of fear of another party. (6)

Earnest Money—A deposit of money made by a buyer at the time of making an offer to demonstrate the earnest intent to purchase. Also called binder, good faith deposit, or escrow deposit. (6)

Easement—A nonpossessory right of use in the land of another. (5)

Easement in Gross—A personal right of use in the land of another without the requirement that the holder of the right own adjoining land. (5)

Economic Life—The period of time during which a property is economically beneficial to the owner. (10)

Economic Obsolescence—A loss in value caused by such things as changes in surrounding land-use patterns and failure to adhere to the principle of highest and best use. (10)

Economic Rent—The amount of rent established by the market value of a property. (10)

Economic Tax Recovery Act—A revision to the tax law enacted by Congress in 1981. (14)

Effective Age—The age of a property based on the remaining economic life. (10)

Effective Demand—A desire for property accompanied by the financial ability to satisfy the desire by purchasing the property. (10)

Effective Interest Rate—The actual rate of interest being paid. (8)

Ejectment—A legal action to evict a tenant from property. (6)

Emblements—Personal property growing in the soil requiring planting and cultivation. Annual crops. (5)

Eminent Domain—The power of government to take private property for public use. (5)

Enabling Acts—Laws passed by state legislatures authorizing cities and counties to regulate land use within their jurisdictions. (11)

Encroachment—A tresspass on the land of another as a result of an intrusion by some structure or other object. (5)

Encumbrance—A claim, lien, charge, or liability attached to and binding upon real property. (5)

Enforceable—A contract in which the parties may legally be required to perform. (6)

Environmental Impact Statement—A requirement of National Environmental Policy Act prior to initiating or changing a land use that may have an adverse affect on the environment. (11)

Equal Credit Opportunity Act (ECOA)—A federal law prohibition discrimination in consumer loans. (8)

Equity of Redemption—The borrower's right to redeem the title pledged or conveyed in a mortgage or deed of trust after default and prior to a foreclosure sale by paying the debt in full, accrued interest, and lender's costs. (8)

Escalation Clause—A clause in a lease permitting the lessor to increase the rent. (6)

Escalated Lease—One in which the rental amount changes in proportion to the lessor's costs of ownership and operation of the property. (6)

Escheat—The power of government to take title to property left by a person who has died without leaving a will or qualified heirs. (5)

Escrow Account—An account maintained by the borrower with the lender in certain mortgage loans to accumulate the funds to pay an annual insurance premium, real property tax, and/or Homeowner's Association assessment. (8)

Escrow Account—An account maintained by a real estate broker in an insured bank for the deposit of other people's money. Also called trust account. (6)

Escrow Agent—A neutral third party named to carry out the provisions of an escrow agreement. (6)

Estate in Real Property—An interest sufficient to provide the right to use, possession, and control of land and establishes the degree and duration of ownership. (5)

Estate at Sufferance—Describes the situation of someone continuing to occupy property after lawful authorization has expired. A form of leasehold estate. (5)

Estate at Will—A leasehold estate that may be terminated at the will of either party. (5)

Estate for Years—A leasehold estate of definite duration. (5)

Estate from Year-to-Year—A leasehold estate that automatically renews itself for consecutive periods until terminated by notice given by either party. Also called estate from period-to-period or periodic tenancy. (5)

Estate in Fee—An estate in fee simple absolute. (5)

Estoppel—The prevention of a person from making a statement contrary to a previous statement.

Estoppel Certificate—A document executed by a mortgagor or mortgagee setting forth the principal amount. Executing parties are bound by the amount specified.

Estovers—The right of a life tenant or lessee to cut timber on the property for fuel or to use in making repairs. (5)

et al—Latin for "and another."

et ux—Latin for "and wife."

Eviction—A landlord's action that interferes with the tenant's use or possession of the property. Eviction may be actual or constructive. (6)

Excluded Property—Under ACRS, property placed in service prior to 1981. (14)

Exclusive Agency Listing—A listing given to one broker only (exclusive) who is entitled to the commission if a sale is effected by the broker or any agent of the listing broker, but imposes no commission obligation on the owner who sells the property to a person who was not interested in the property by the listing broker or an agent of the listing broker. (6)

Exclusive-Right-to-Sell Listing—A listing given to one broker only who is entitled to the commission if the property is sold by anyone during the term of the listing contract. (6)

Exclusive-Use Zoning—A type of zoning in which only the specified use may be made of property within the zoned district. (11)

Executed Contract—An agreement that has been fully performed. (6)

Execution—The signing of a contract or other legal document. (6)

Executor—A man appointed in a will to see that the terms of the will are carried out. (7)

Executory Contract—An agreement that has not been fully performed. (6)

Executrix—A woman appointed in a will to see that the terms of the will are carried out. (7)

Exempt—Relieved of liability.

Exercise of Option—The purchase of optioned property by the optionee. (6)

Express Contract—One created verbally or in writing by the parties. (6)

Extender Clause—*See* Carry-Over Clause

Fair Market Value—A price for property agreed upon between buyer and seller in a competitive market with neither party being undue pressure. (10)

Fannie Mae—The shortened name for the Federal National Mortgage Association. (8)

Fair Housing Act of 1968—A federal prohibition on discrimination in the sale, rental, or financing of housing on the basis of race, color, religion, sex, or national origin. (12)

Federal Home Loan Bank System—The federal agency that regulates federally chartered savings and loan associations. (8)

Federal Home Loan Mortgage Corporation (Freddie Mac)—A corporation that is wholly owned by the Federal Home Loan Bank System that purchases FHA, VA, and conventional mortgages. (8)

Federal Housing Administration (FHA)—The federal agency that insures mortgage loans to protect lending institutions. (8)

Federal National Mortgage Association (Fannie Mae)—A privately owned corporation that purchases FHA, VA, and conventional mortgages. (8)

Federal Reserve System—The federal agency that regulates monetary policy and, thereby, the money supply and interest rates. (8)

Fee Simple Absolute—An inheritable estate in land providing the greatest interest of any form of title. (5)

Fee Simple Determinable—A defeasible fee (title). (5)

Fee Simple Subject to a Condition Subsequent—A defeasible fee (title). (5)

Feudal System—A type of land ownership previously existing in England whereby only the King could hold absolute title to real property. (5)

FHA—The Federal Housing Administration that was existing in England and whereby only the King could hold absolute title to real property. (5)

FHA Loan—A mortgage loan in which the payments an insured by the Federal Housing Administration. (8)

FHA Mutual Mortgage Insurance—The insurance in FHA loans to protect the lender with the premiums being paid by the borrower. (8)

Fiduciary—A person, such as an agent, who is placed in a position of trust in relation to the person for whose benefit the relationship is created. Essentially the same as a trustee. (6)

Fifteen-Year Property—Property with an asset depreciation range (ADR) midpoint life exceeding twelve and a half years. (14)

First Mortgage—One that is superior to later recorded mortgages. (8)

Final Settlement—Consumation of a contract to buy and sell real property. (6)

Finance Charge—A charge imposed on the borrower in a mortgage loan consisting of origination fee, service charges, discount points, interest, credit report fees, and finders' fees. (8)

Fixed Lease—One in which the rental amount remains the same for the entire lease term. Also called flat, straight, or gross lease. (6)

Fixed-Rate Mortgage—One in which the interest does not change. (8)

Fixing Up Expenses—Costs incurred by the seller of a principal residence in preparing it for sale. (14)

Fixture—Personal property that has become real property by having been permanently attached to real property. (5)

Flat Lease—One in which the rental amount does not change during the lease term. (6)

Flexible Loan Insurance Program (FLIP Mortgage)—A form of graduated payment mortgage in which part of each monthly payment is made from current income and the remainder from an account on deposit with the lender. (8)

Foreclosure—The legal procedure of enforcing payment of a debt secured by a mortgage or any other lien. (8)

Forfeiture Clause—A clause in a contract for deed providing for forfeiture of all payments by a buyer in default. (6)

Fraud—An intentional false statement of a material fact. (6)

Freehold Estate—A right of title to land. (5)

Friendly Foreclosure—An absolute conveyance of title to the lender by the mortgagor in default to avoid a record of foreclosure. Also called a deed in lieu of foreclosure. (8)

Front Foot—A linear foot of property frontage on a street or highway.

Fully Amortizing Mortgage—One in which the scheduled uniform payments will pay off the loan completely over the mortgage term. (8)

Functional Obsolescence—A loss in value resulting from such things as faulty design, inadequacies, overadequacies, and equipment being out-of-date. (10)

Future Interest—An owner of an estate who will vest at some time in the future. (5)

Gain Realized—The excess of the Amount Realized over the adjusted basis. (14)

General Lien—One that attaches to all of the property of the license within the jurisdiction of the court. (5)

General Warranty Deed—A deed in which there is an unlimited warranty of title. (7)

Good Faith Estimate—The lender's estimate of a borrower's settlement costs that is required by RESPA to be furnished to borrowers at time of loan application. (8)

Government National Mortgage Association (Ginnie Mae)—A government Agency that purchases FHA and VA mortgages. (8)

Government Survey System—A type of land description by townships and sections. (7)

Graduated Lease—One in which the rental amount changes in specified amounts over the lease term. (6)

Graduated Payment Adjustable Mortgage (GPAM)—One combining the features of a graduated payment mortgage and an adjustable or variable rate mortgage. (8)

Graduated Payment Mortgage (GPM)—One in which the payments are lower in the early years but increase on a scheduled basis until they reach an amortizing level. (8)

Grant—A transfer of title to real property by deed. (7)

Grant Deed—A statutory form of deed where the warranties are implied from the statute rather than being spelled out in the deed. (7)

Grantee—One who receives title to real property by deed. (7)

Granting Clause—The clause in a deed containing words of conveyance. (7)

Grantor—One who conveys title to real property by deed. (7)

Gross Effective Income—Gross potential income less deductions for vacancy and credit losses plus other income. (10)

Gross Income—Income received without the subtraction of expenses. (10, 15)

Gross Lease—One in which the lessor pays all costs of operating and maintaining the property and real property taxes. (6)

Gross Potential Income—The amount of rental income that would be received if all units were rented 100 percent of the time and there were no credit losses. (10)

Gross Rent Multiplier—A method of estimating the value of income property. Also called Gross Income Multiplier. (10)

Ground Lease—A lease of unimproved land. (6)

Ground Rent—Lessee's payment under a ground lease. (6)

Habendum Clause—The clause in a deed beginning with the words "to have and to hold" and describing the estate granted. (7)

Habitable—Suitable for the type of occupancy intended.

Heirs—Persons legally eligible to receive property of a decedent. (7)

Heterogeneous—A variety of dissimilar uses of property. Nonhomogeneous. (3)

Highest and Best Use—The use of land that will preserve its utility and yield a net income flow in the form of rent that forms, when capitalized at the proper rate of interest, the highest present value of the land. (10)

Holding Over—The act of a tenant remaining in possession of property after the termination of a lease.

Holding Period—The length of time a property is owned. (14)

Holographic Will—One hand written by the testator.

Homeowner's Association—The organization of owners having the responsibility of providing for the operation and maintenance of the common areas of a condominium or residential subdivision. Also called Property Owner's Association. (5)

Homeowner's Policy—An insurance policy protecting against a variety of hazards. (13)

Homeowner's Warranty (HOW)—An insurance policy protecting against loss caused by structural and other defects in a dwelling. (13)

Home Buyer's Guide—A booklet explaining aspects of loan settlement required by RESPA. (8)

Homestead—The land and dwelling of a homeowner.

Homestead Exemption—An exemption of a specified amount of value of a homestead from the claims of creditors provided by state statute.

Homogeneous—Similar and compatible land uses. (11)

Horizontal Property Act—The title of condominium statutes in some states. (5)

Housing and Urban Development (HUD)—An agency of the federal government concerned with housing programs and laws. (12)

HUD Form No. 1—A standard settlement form required by RESPA. (8)

Hypothecate—Pledging property as security for the payment of a debt without giving up possession. (8)

Illusory Offer—One that does not obligate the offeror. (6)

Implied Contract—One created by deduction from the conduct of the parties rather than from the direct words of the parties. Opposite of an express contract. (6)

Implied Warranty—One presumed by law to exist in a deed though not expressly stated. (7)

Improved Land—Land on which structures or roads exist.

Improvements—Structures, walls, roads, etc.

Immobility—The physical characteristic of real property describing that land cannot be moved from one location to another. (3)

Inchoate—In suspension or pending, possibly occurring at some future time. (5)

Income Approach—The primary method of estimating the value of properties that produce rental income. Also called appraisal by capitalization. (10)

Income Property—One that produces rental income. (10)

Incompetent—A person who is not capable of managing his or her own affairs. (6)

Incorporeal—Intangible things such as rights. (5)

Incurable Depreciation—That which is not physically correctible or not economically practical to correct. (10)

Index Lease—One in which the rental amount is changed in proportion to changes in the Consumer Price Index. (6)

Indestructibility—A physical characteristic of land describing that land is a permanent commodity and cannot be destroyed. (3)

Ingress and Egress—The right to enter (ingress) and to and return (egress) from a parcel of land. (5)

Injunction—An instruction of a court to discontinue a specified activity. (11)

Installment Land Contract—See Contract for Deed.

Installment Sale—A transaction in which the seller does not receive all of the sale price in the calendar year of the sale. (14)

Instrument—A written legal document such as a contract, note, and mortgage. (8)

Insurable Interest—The degree of interest qualifying for insurance. (5, 13)

Insurance Value—The cost of replacing a structure completely destroyed by an insured hazard. (10)

Insured Conventional Loan—One in which the loan payment is insured by private mortgage insurance to protect the lender. (8)

Interest—Money paid for the use of money. Also an ownership or right. (5, 8)

Interim Financing—Short-term or temporary financing such as a construction loan. (8)

Intermediate Theory—The legal theory followed in some states that a conveyance of the title pledged in a mortgage occurs if the mortgagor is in default. (8)

Interstate Land Sales Full Disclosure Act—A federal law regulating the interstate sale of land under certain conditions. (11)

Intestate—A person who has died without leaving a valid will. (7)

Intestate Succession—Distribution of property by descent as provided by statute. (5)

Invalid—Not legally enforceable. (6)

Irrevocable—That which cannot be changed or cancelled.

Joint Tenancy—A form of co-ownership that includes the right of survivorship. (5)

Joint Venture—Participation by two or more parties in a single undertaking. (6)

Judgment—A court determination of the rights and obligations of parties to a lawsuit. (5)

Judgment Lien—A general lien resulting from a court decree. (5)

Judicial Deed—One executed by an official with court authorization. (7)

Judicial Foreclosure—A court proceeding to require that property be sold to satisfy a mortgage lien. (8)

Junior Mortgage—One that is subordinant to a prior mortgage. (8)

The Language of Real Estate: A Glossary of Real Estate Terminology

Jurisdiction—The extent of the authority of a court. (5)

Laches—The loss of legal rights because of failure to assert them on a timely basis.

Land—The surface of the earth, the area above and below the surface, and everything permanently attached thereto. (5)

Land Capacity—The degree to which land can sustain improvements created to make the land productive. (10)

Land Contract—*See* Contract for Deed.

Land Grant—The conveyance of, as a gift for the benefit of the public.

Land-Use Regulations—Governmental controls over land use (e.g. zoning laws and building codes). (11)

Landlocked—An adjective to describe property with no access to a public road. (5)

Land Trust—The condition of a title to land being held by a trustee for the benefit of others. (5)

Lawful—Legal, not prohibited by law. (5, 6)

Lease—A contract wherein a landlord gives a tenant the right of use and possession of property for a limited period of time in return for rent. (5, 6)

Leased Fee—The lessor's interest in the leased property. (5, 6)

Leasehold Estates—Nonfreehold estates. All are of limited duration and provide the right of possession and control but not title. (5)

Leasehold Mortgage—One in which a leasehold (nonfreehold) estate is pledged to secure the payment of the note. (8)

Leasehold Title Insurance Policy—A policy insuring a lessee against defects in the lessor's title. (7)

Legal Capacity—The ability to contract. (6)

Legal Description—A description of land recognized by law. (7)

Legal Entity—A person or organization with legal capacity. (6)

Legal Life Estates—Those created by the exercise of the right of dower, curtesy, or a statutory substitute. (5)

Legal Rate of Interest—The maximum rate permitted by law.

Lessee—A tenant under a lease. (6)

Lessor—A landlord under a lease. (6)

Leverage—The use of borrowed funds. The larger the percentage of borrowed money, the greater the leverage.

Levy—Imposition of a tax, executing a lien. (5)

License—A personal privilege to do a particular act or series of acts on the land of another. (5)

Lien—A claim that one person has against the property of another for some debt or charge which entitles the lienholder to have the claim satisfied from the property of the debtor. (5)

Lienee—One whose property is subject to a lien.

Lienor—The one holding a lien against another.

Lien Theory—The legal theory that a mortgage creates a lien against the real property pledged in the mortgage to secure the payment of a debt. (8)

Life Estate—A freehold estate created for the duration of the life or lives of certain named persons. A noninheritable estate. (5)

Life Estate in Remainder—A form of life estate in which certain persons called remaindermen are designated to receive the title upon termination of the life tenancy. (5)

Life Estate in Reversion—A form of life estate that reverts to the creator of the estate in fee simple upon termination. (5)

Life Estate Per Autre Vie—A life estate in which the duration is measured by the life of someone other than the life tenant. *See also* pur autre vie. (5)

Life Tenant—One holding a life estate. (5)

Like-Kind Property—Real or personal property that qualifies for tax treatment as a tax-free exchange. (14)

Limited Partnership—An organization consisting of one or more general partners and several limited partners. (5)

Liquidated Damages—An amount of money to be paid and received as compensation for a breach of contract.

Liquidity—The fact that an asset can be converted to cash. (8)

Lis Pendens—Latin meaning "a lawsuit pending." (5)

Listing Contract—A contract whereby a property owner employs a real estate broker to market the property described in the contract. (6)

Litigation—A lawsuit.

Loan Commitment—The obligation of a lending institution to make a certain mortgage loan. (6)

Loan-to-Value Ratio—The relationship between the amount of a mortgage loan and the lender's opinion of the value of the property pledged to secure the payment of the loan. (8)

Location (Situs)—An economic characteristic of land having the greatest effect on value of any other characteristic. (3)

Long-Term Capital Gain—The gain realized in the sale of a capital asset held for more than twelve months. (14)

Long-Term Capital Gain Tax—Only 40 percent of the gain is tax as ordinary income; 60 percent of the gain is exempt from tax. (14)

L.S.—Letter standing for **Locus Sigilli**-a Latin term meaning the "place of the seal." (7)

Management Agreement—A contract wherein an owner employs a property manager. (13)

Management Plan—A long-range program for the management of a property that is prepared by a property manager. (13)

Management Proposal—A program for operating a property submitted to the owner by a property manager. (13)

Marketable Title—One that is free from reasonable doubt and that a court would require a purchaser to accept. (7)

Market Data Approach—The primary method of estimating the value of vacant land and single-family owner-occupied dwellings. Also called comparable approach. (10)

Market Value—The value in terms of price agreed upon by a willing buyer and seller with neither being under any undue pressure and each being knowledgeable of market conditions at the time. (10)

Master Deed—The instrument that legally establishes a condominium. Also called condominium declaration. (5)

Material Fact—An important fact that may affect a person's judgment. (6)

Mechanics Lien—A statutory lien available to persons supplying labor (mechanic) or material (materialmen) to the construction of an improvement on land if they are not paid. (5)

Metes and Bounds—A system of land description by distances and directions. (7)

Mill—One tenth of a cent. (15)

Mineral Lease—A nonfreehold (leasehold) estate in the area below the surface of land. (5)

Mineral Rights—The right of the landowner to take minerals from the earth or to sell or lease this right to others. (5)

Minor—A person who has not attained the statutory age of majority. (6)

Misrepresentation—A false statement of a material fact. (6)

Modification by Improvement—An economic characteristic of land providing that the economic supply of land is increased by improvements made to land and on land. (3)

Mortgage—A written instrument used to pledge a title to real property to secure the payment of a promissory note. (9)

Mortgage Assumption—The transfer of mortgage obligations to a purchaser of the mortgaged property. (8)

Mortgage Banker—A form of organization that makes and services mortgage loans. (8)

Mortgage Broker—One who arranges a mortgage loan between a lender and borrower for a fee. (8)

Mortgage Guarantee Insurance Corporation (Maggie Mae)—A privately owned corporation that insures conventional mortgages and also purchases conventional mortgages that it has insured. (8)

Mortgage Loan Value—The value sufficient to secure the payment of a mortgage loan. (10)

Mortgage Satisfaction—Full payment of a mortgage loan. (8)

Mortgagee—The lender in a mortgage loan receiving a mortgage from the borrower mortgagor. (8)

Mortgagee's Title Insurance Policy—A policy that insures a mortgagee against defects in a title pledged by a mortgagor to secure payment of a mortgage loan. (7)

Mortgaging Clause—The clause in a mortgage or deed of trust that demonstrates the intention of the mortgagor to mortgage the property to the mortgagee. (8)

Mortgagor—The borrower in a mortgage loan who executes and delivers a mortgage to the lender. (8)

Multiple Exchange—One in which more than two like-kind properties are exchanged. (14)

Multiple Listing—A type of listing by an organized method of sharing or pooling listings by member brokers. (6)

Mutual Assent—The voluntary agreement of all parties to a contract as evidenced by an offer and acceptance. (6)

Mutual Rescission—The agreement of all parties to an executory contract to release each other. (6)

Mutual Savings Banks—Similar to savings and loan associations. These banks provide a substantial source of financing for housing. (8)

Narrative Appraisal Report—A statement of an opinion of value containing the elements of judgment as well as the data used in arriving at the value estimate. (10)

NARELLO—The abbreviation for the National Association of Real Estate License Law Officials. (4)

National Association of REALTORS®—The largest and most prominent trade organization of real estate licensees. (4)

Negative Covenants—See Restrictive Covenants.

Negative Easement—A right in the land of another prohibiting the servient owner from doing something on the servient land because it will affect the dominant land. (5)

Net Income—Gross income less operating expenses. Also called net operating income. (10)

Net Lease—One in which the lessee pays a fixed amount of rent plus the costs of operation of the property. (6)

Net Listing—Not a type of listing but a method of establishing the listing broker's commission as all money above a specified net amount to the seller. (6)

Net Salvage Value—The salvage value less the cost of removal. (14)

Nonconforming Use—A use of land that does not conform to the use permitted by a zoning ordinance for the area. It may be lawful or unlawful. (11)

Nonjudicial Foreclosure—A form of foreclosure that does not require court action to conduct a foreclosure sale. Also called foreclosure under power of sale. (8)

Nonrecourse Note—A note in which the borrower has no personal liability for payment. (8)

Notary Public—A person authorized by a state to take oaths and acknowledgements. (10)

Nonhomogeneity—A physical characteristic of land describing that land is a unique commodity. (3)

Notice of Lis Pendens—A notice on the public record warning all persons that a title to real property is the subject of a lawsuit and any lien resulting from the suit will attach to the title held by a purchaser from the defendant. (5)

Novation—The substitution of a new contract for a prior contract. (6)

Null and Void—Invalid, without legal force or effect. (6)

Obligee—One to whom an obligation is owed.

Obligor—One who owes an obligation to another.

Obsolescense—A loss in property value caused by economic or functional factors. (10)

Occupancy—Physical possession of property. (5)

Offer—A promise made to another conditional upon acceptance by a promise or act made in return. (6)

Offeree—One to whom an offer is made. (6)

Offeror—One making an offer. (6)

Offer and Acceptance—Necessary elements for the creation of a contract. (6)

Open-End Mortgage—One that may be refinanced without rewriting the mortgage. (8)

Open-Ended Listing Contract—One without a termination date. (6)

Open Listing—A listing given to one or more brokers wherein the broker procuring a sale is entitled to the commission but imposes no commission obligation on the owner in the event the owner sells the property to a person who was not interested in the property by one of the listing brokers. (6)

Open Mortgage—One that does not impose a prepayment penalty. (8)

Operating Budget—A yearly budget of income and expense for a particular property prepared by a property manager. (13)

Operating Expenses—The costs of operating a property held as an investment. (14)

Operating Statement—A report of receipts and disbursements with resulting in net income of rental property. (10)

Operation of Law—The manner in which the rights and/or liabilities of parties may be changed by the application of law without the act or cooperation of the parties. (6)

Opinion of Title—See Certificate of Title Opinion.

Option to Purchase—A contract whereby a property owner (optionor) sells a right to purchase his or her property to a prospective buyer (optionee). (6)

Optionee—One who receives an option. (6)

Optionor—One who gives an option. (6)

Ordinance—A law enacted by a local government. (11)

Origination—A service charge made by a lending institution for making a mortgage loan. (8)

Ownership—The right to use, control, possess, and dispose of property. (5)

Ownership in Severalty—Title to real property held in the name of one person only. (5)

Owner's Title Insurance Policy—A policy insuring an owner of real property against a financial loss resulting from a title defect. (7)

Package Mortgage—One in which personal property as well as real property is pledged to secure the payment of the note. (8)

Parol—Verbal.

Participation Mortgage— (1) One in which two or more lenders share in making the loan.

(2) One in which a lender shares in the profit produced by an income property pledged to secure the loan payment in addition to receiving interest and principal payments. (8)

Partially Amortizing Mortgage—One in which the schedule of uniform payments will not completely satisfy the debt over the mortgage term and will therefore require a final payment larger than the uniform payments to completely satisfy the debt. The final payment is called a balloon payment. (8)

Partition—A legal proceeding dividing property of coowners so that each holds title in severalty. (5)

Party Wall—A common wall used by two adjoining structures. (5)

Per Autre Vie—Latin meaning "for the life of another." A life estate measured by the life of someone other than the life tenant. *See also* pur autre vie. (5)

Percentage Lease—One in which the rental amount is a combination of a fixed amount plus a percentage of the lessee's gross sales. (6)

Perch—A surveyor's measure 16½ feet in length. (15)

Percolation Test—A test of soil to determine if it is sufficiently porous for the installation of a septic tank.

Periodic Tenancy—A lease that automatically renews for successive periods unless terminated by either party. Also called an estate from year to year. (5)

Personal Property—All property that is not land and is not permanently attached to land. Everything that is moveable. (3)

Physical Deterioration—A loss in value caused by unrepaired damage or inadequate maintenance. (10)

PITI—Letters following the amount of a mortgage payment designating that the payment includes principal, interest, taxes, and insurance.

Placed In Service—The date when an asset is ready and available for a particular use. (14)

Planned Unit Development (PUD)—A form of cluster zoning providing for both residential and commercial land uses within a zoned area. (11)

Planning—A program for the development of a city or county designed to provide for orderly growth. (11)

Plat—A property map. (7)

Plat Books—Books wherein plats are recorded on the public record. (7)

Pledge—To provide property as security for the payment of a debt or for the performance of a promise. (8)

Plottage—Combining two or more parcels of land into one tract having a value exceeding the total value of the individual parcels.

Points—*See* Discount Points

Police Power—The power of government to regulate the use of real property for the benefit of the public interest. (5)

Population Density—The relationship of the number of people to a given land area. (11)

Potential Income—*See* Gross Potential Income

Power of Attorney—An instrument appointing an attorney-in-fact. (4)

Prepaid Items—Funds paid at closing to start an escrow account required in certain mortgage loans. Also called prepaids. (8)

Prepayment Penalty—A financial penalty imposed on a borrower for paying a mortgage prior to the expiration of the full mortgage term. (8)

Prescription—A method of acquiring an easement by continuous and uninterrupted use without permission. (5)

Prescriptive Easement—One obtained by prescription. (5)

Prima Facie—Latin meaning "on the face of it." A fact presumed to be true unless disproved by contrary evidence.

Prima Facie Case—One that is sufficiently strong that it can only be defeated by contrary evidence.

Price Level Adjusted Mortgage (PLAM)—One in which the interest rate is fixed but the principal changes according to changes in the Consumer Price Index. (8)

Primary Financing—The loan with the highest priority.

Primary Mortgage Market—The activity of lenders making mortgage loans to individual borrowers. (8)

Prime Rate—The interest rate a lender charges the most creditworthy customers.

Principal—In the law of agency, one who appoints an agent to represent him or her. (6)

Principal Residence—The home the owner or renter occupies most of the time. (14)

Private Land-Use Control—The regulations of land use by individuals or nongovernment organizations in the form of deed restrictions and restrictive covenants. (11)

Private Mortgage Insurance (PMI)—A form of insurance coverage required in high loan-to-value ratio conventional loans to protect the lender in case of borrower default in loan payment. (8)

Private Property—That which is not owned by government.

Probate—The procedure for proving a will. (7)

Profit à Prendre—The right to participate in the profits of the land of another. (5)

Promissory Note—A written promise to pay a debt as set forth in the writing. (8)

Promulgate—To put in effect by public announcement.

Property Management Report—A periodic financial report prepared by a property manager for the owner. (13)

Property Manager—One who manages properties for an owner(s) as the owner's agent. (13)

Proration—Division of certain settlement costs between buyer and seller. (9, 15)

Proprietary Lease—A lease in a cooperative apartment. (5)

Public Land-Use Control—The regulation of land use by government organizations in the form of zoning laws, building codes, subdivision ordinances, and environmental protection laws. (11)

Public Property—That which is owned by government.

Public Record—Record providing constructive notice of real property conveyances and other matters. (5, 7)

Purchase Money Mortgage—A mortgage given by a buyer to a seller to secure the payment of all or part of the purchase price. (8)

Quantity Survey—A method for estimating replacement or reproduction cost. (10)

Quarter Section—One-fourth of a section containing 160 acres. (7)

Quiet Enjoyment—The use or possession of property that is undisturbed by an enforceable claim of superior title. (7)

Quiet Title Action—A lawsuit to remove a cloud on a title. (7)

Quit Claim—To relinquish or release a claim to real property. (7)

Quit Claim Deed—A deed of release that contains no warranty of title. It is used to remove a cloud on a title. (7)

Range—An area of land defined by the rectangular survey system of land description. (7)

Radius—The distance from the center of a circle to the perimeter. A part of a metes and bounds description. (7)

Rate of Return—The percentage of the net income produced by a property or other investment. (10, 15)

Ratify—To reaffirm a previous action. (6)

Ready, Willing and Able—Describes a buyer who is ready to buy, willing to buy, and financially able to pay the asking price. (6)

Real Estate—Land and everything that is permanently attached to land. Interchangeable with the terms real property and realty. (5)

Real Estate Broker—A person or organization who negotiates real estate sales, exchanges, or rentals for others for compensation or a promise of compensation. (4)

Real Estate Commission—A state agency charged with the obligation of enforcing real estate license laws. (4)

Real Estate Investment Trust (REIT)—A form of business trust owned by shareholders making mortgage loans. (5, 8)

Real Estate Market—A local activity in which real property is sold, exchanged, leased, or rented at prices set by competing forces. (3)

Real Estate Salesperson—Any person performing any of the acts included in the definition of real estate broker but does so while associated with and supervised by a broker. (4)

Real Estate Settlement Procedures Act (RESPA)—A federal law regulating activities of lending institutions in making mortgage loans for housing. (8)

Real Property—Land and everything permanently attached to land. (5)

Realty—Land and everything permanently attached to land. (3)

Realized Gain—Actual profit resulting in a sale. (14)

Reappraisal Lease—One in which changes in rental amount are based on changes in property value as demonstrated by periodic reappraisals of the property. (6)

REALTOR®—A registered trademark of the National Association of Realtors. Its use is limited to members only. (4)

Recapture—Taxation of any part of a gain realized in the sale of a depreciable asset that is attributable to accelerated depreciation. (14)

Reciprocity—The mutual agreement by states to extend licensing privileges to licensees in each state. (4)

Recognized Gain—The amount of profit that is taxable. (14)

Recording—The registration of a document on the public record. (7)

Rectangular Survey—*See* Government Survey System

Redemption—*See* Equity of Redemption

Redlining—The refusal of lending institutions to make loans for the purchase, construction, or repair of a dwelling because the area in which the dwelling is located is integrated or populated by minorities. (12)

Reentry—The right of the owner to regain possession of real property. (5, 6)

Refinancing—Obtaining a new mortgage loan to pay and replace an existing mortgage. (8)

Referral Fee—A percentage of a broker's commission paid to another broker for referring a buyer or seller. (6)

Regulation Z—Requirements issued by the Federal Reserve Board in implementing the Truth-in-Lending Law, which is a part of the Federal Consumer Credit Protection Act. (8)

Reject—To refuse to accept an offer. (6)

Release Clause—A provision in a mortgage to release certain properties from the mortgage lien when the principal is reduced by a specified amount. (8)

Remainder—A future interest in a life estate. (5)

Remainderman—One having a future interest in a life estate. (5)

Remise—To release or give up. (7)

Renegotiable Rate Mortgage—One in which the interest rate is changed every three or five years in relation to changes occurring in a specified index. (8)

Replacement Cost—The amount of money required to replace a structure with another structure of comparable utility. (10)

Repossession—Regaining possession of property as a result of a breach of contract by another. (6)

Reproduction Cost—The amount of money required to build an exact duplicate of a structure. (10)

Rescission—Cancellation of a contract when another party is in default. (6)

Residual Income—The income allocated to the land under the principle of highest and best use. (10)

Restrictive Covenants—Limitations on land use binding on all property owners. A form of private land-use control. (11)

Reversion—A return of title to the holder of a future interest, such as the grantor in a life estate not in remainder. (5)

Revocation—The withdrawal of an offer. (6)

Right of First Refusal Clause—A clause in a lease or condominium articles of association that provides for a lessee or an association to have the first opportunity to purchase the property before it is offered to anyone else. (6)

Right of Survivorship—The right of an owner to receive the title to a co-owner's share upon death of the co-owner, as in the case of joint tenancy and tenancy by the entirety. (5)

Right to Emblements—The right of a former owner or former tenant to reenter property to cultivate and harvest annual crops that were planted by them. (5)

Riparian Rights—The right of an owner to use water flowing by the property.

Rollover Rule—A mandator provision in the tax law providing that the tax on any gain realized in the sale of a principal residence must be postponed if the sale and purchase qualifies. (14)

Run-with-the-Land—Rights that move from grantor to grantee along with a title. (5, 11)

Sales and Leaseback—A transaction whereby an owner sells his/her property to an investor who immediately leases the property to the seller as agreed in the sales contract. (6)

Sales Contract—An agreement between buyer and seller on the price and other terms and conditions of the sale of property. (6)

Salvage Value—The amount estimated by an owner that will be realized from the sale of an asset at the end of the useful life of the asset. (14)

Savings and Loan Associations—A major source of funds for financing residential real estate. (8)

Scarcity—In short supply in comparison to demand. (10)

Second Mortgage—One first in priority after a first mortgage. (8)

Secondary Mortgage Market—The market in which mortgages are sold by lenders. (8)

Section—An area of land described by the rectangular survey system consisting of 640 acres and being one mile square. (7)

Seisin—Possession of a freehold estate in land. (7)

Seizin—An alternate spelling for Seisin. (7)

Separate Ownership—Ownership in severalty by one spouse. (5)

Servient Tenement—Land encumbered by an easement. (5)

Setback—The distance from a front or interior property line to the point where a structure can be located. (11)

Settlement—The consumation of a real estate contract. Also called closing. (9)

Settlement Costs—Expenses paid by buyers and sellers at the time of consumation of a real estate sales contract. Also called closing costs. (8, 9)

Severalty Ownership—Ownership by only one person. (5)

Shared Appreciation Mortgage (SAM)—One in which the lender shares in the appreciation in property value in return for making the loan at a fixed rate lower than the rate in effect at the time the loan is made. (8)

Short Term Capital Gain—A gain realized in the sale of a capital asset held for 12 months or less. (14)

Short Term Capital Gain Tax—Entire gain is taxed as ordinary income. (14)

Situs—Location of land. (3)

Special Assessment—A levy by a local government against real property for part of the cost of making an improvement to the property such as street paving, installing water lines, or making side walks. (5)

Special Warranty Deed—A deed containing a limited warranty of title. (7)

Specific Lien—One that attaches to one particular property only. (5)

Specific Performance—An instruction of a court requiring a defaulting party to a contract to buy and sell real property to specifically perform his/her obligations under the contract. (6)

Spot Zoning—Rezoning of a particular property in a zoned area to permit a different type of use than that authorized for the rest of the area. May be valid or invalid. (11)

Stabilized Budget—A forecast of income and expense as may be reasonably projected over a period of several years prepared by a property manager. (13)

Statute of Frauds—A law in effect in all states requiring certain contracts to be in writing to be valid. (6)

Statute of Limitations—State laws establishing the time period within which certain lawsuits may be brought. (6)

Statutory Foreclosure—A statutory time period after a foreclosure sale during which the borrower may still redeem the title. (8)

Steering—The practice of directing prospective minority purchasers to integrated areas to avoid integration of non-integrated areas. (12)

Strict Foreclosure—A proceeding in which a court gives a mortgagor in default a specified time period to satisfy the debt to prevent transfer of the title to the mortgaged property to the lender. (8)

Straight Line Depreciation—A depreciation method whereby the property is depreciated in equal annual installments over the years of useful life. (14)

Subdivision Regulation (Ordinance)—Public control of the development of residential subdivisions. (11)

Sublet—The transfer of only part of a lease term with reversion to the lessee. (6)

Subordinate—Lower in priority. (8)

Substitution—The principle providing that the highest value of a property has a tendency to be established by the cost of purchasing or constructing another property of equal utility and desirability provided that the substitution can be made without unusual delay. (10)

Supply and Demand—The principle stating that the greater the supply of any comodity in comparison to demand the lower the value. Conversely, the smaller the supply and the greater the demand, the higher the value. (10)

Survivorship—The right of the surviving co-owner(s) to automatically receive the title of a deceased co-owner immediately without probate. (5)

Taking Title Subject to a Mortgage—Accepting a title pledged to secure a mortgage and with no personal liability for the payment of the note. (8)

Tax Credit—An amount of money that may be deducted from a tax bill to arrive at the net amount of tax due. (14)

Tax Deductible Expense—An amount of money that may be deducted from gross income in arriving at net taxable income before depreciation, if any. (14)

Tax Free Exchange—Trading of like kind properties held as an investment or for use in business. (14)

Tax Shelter—A method of tax avoidance such as protecting income from taxation by allowable depreciation. (14)

Taxable Gain—The amount of profit subject to tax (recognized gain). (14)

Taxation—One of the four powers of government. The power of government to tax, among other things, real property. (5)

Tenancy by the Entirety—A form of co-ownership limited to husband and wife with the right of survivorship. (5)

Tenancy In Common—A form of co-ownership that does not include the right of survivorship. (5)

Term Mortgage—One that requires the mortgagor to pay interest only during the mortgage term with the principal due at the end of the term. (8)

Testate—To have died leaving a valid will. (7)

Testator—A man who has died and left a valid will. (7)

Testatrix—A woman who has died and left a valid will. (7)

Title—Evidence of the right to possess property. (5)

Title Examination—A search of the public record to determine the quality of a title to real property. (7)

Title Insurance—An insurance policy protecting the insured from a financial loss caused by a defect in a title to real property. (7)

Title Theory—The legal theory followed in some states that a mortgage conveys a title to real property to secure the payment of a debt. (8)

Title Transfer Tax—A tax imposed on the conveyance of title to real property by deed. (7)

Torrens System—A system of title recordation. (7)

Tract—An area of land.

Trade Fixtures—Items installed by a commercial tenant which are removable upon termination of the tenancy. (5)

Transferability—The ability to transfer property ownership from seller to buyer. (10)

Trespass—Unlawful entry on the land of another. (5)

Trust Deed—See deed of trust.

Trustee—One who holds title to property for the benefit of another called a beneficiary. (5, 8)

Trustor—One who conveys title to a trustee. (5, 8)

Trapezoid—An area with two parallel sides and two non-parallel sides. (15)

Truth in Lending Law—*See* Regulation Z.

Undisclosed Principal—A principal whose identity may not be disclosed by an agent. (6)

Undivided Interest—Ownership of fractional parts not physically divided. (5)

Undue Influence—Any improper or wrongful influence by one party over another whereby the will of a person is overpowered so that he or she is induced to act or prevented from acting on free will. (6)

Unencumbered Property—One that is free of any lien. (5)

Uniform Commercial Code (U.C.C.)—A standardized and comprehensive set of commercial law regulating security interests in personal property. (5)

Unilateral Contract—An agreement wherein there is a promise in return for a specific action which together supply the consideration. (6)

Uninsured Conventional Loan—One in which the loan payment is not insured to protect the lender. (8)

Unintentional Misrepresentation—An innocent false statement of a material fact. (6)

Unities of Title—Time, title, interest, and possession. (5)

Useful Life—The period of time that a property is expected to be economically useful. (14)

Usury—Charging a rate of interest higher than the rate allowed by law.

Utility—Capable of serving a useful purpose. (10)

VA Loan—A mortgage loan in which the loan payment is guaranteed to the lender by the Veteran's Administration. (8)

Vacancy Rate—A projected rate of the percentage of rental unit vacancies that will occur in a given year. (10)

Valid Contract—An agreement that is legally binding and enforceable. (6)

Value in Exchange—The amount of money a property may command for its exchange. This is the market value. (10)

Value in Use—The present worth of the future benefits of ownership. A subjective value that is not market value. (10)

Valuable Consideration—Anything of value agreed upon by parties to a contract. (6)

Variable Rate Mortgage (VRM)—One in which the interest rate changes according to changes in a predetermined index. (8)

Variance—A permitted deviation from specific requirements of a zoning ordinance because of the special hardship to a particular property owner. (11)

Vendee—Purchaser.

Vendor—Seller.

Void Contract—An agreement that has no legal force or effect. (6)

Voidable Contract—An agreement that may be avoided by the parties without legal consequences. (6)

Voluntary Alienation—The transfer of title freely by the owner. (7)

Waste—A violation of the right of estovers. (5)

Words of Conveyance—Wording in a deed demonstrating the definite intention to convey a particular title to real property to a named grantee. (7)

Wrap Around Mortgage—A junior mortgage that is in an amount exceeding a first mortgage against the property. (8)

Yield—The return on an investment. (8)

Zoning—A public law regulating land use. (11)

Diagnostic Practice Test

17

INTRODUCTION

This test is to be taken after the study of all the preceding chapters has been completed. The diagnostic test enables you to make a self-diagnosis of your comprehension of the subject matter and your ability to apply knowledge in answering questions. The questions are in groups by chapters as indicated, so that you may more readily identify weak subject areas for further and more intensive study.

A passing score of 80% for each chapter group will indicate that you have a good understanding and retention of the information. Filling out the score card (figure 17.1) will reveal your strong and weak subject areas.

Chapter Number	Subject	Number of Questions	Number Correct	Percent Correct
3	Introduction	10		
4	Licensing	10		
5	Ownership	15		
6	Contracts	15		
7	Transfer of title	10		
8	Finance	15		
9	Closing	5		
10	Valuation	10		
11	Land use controls	8		
12	Fair housing	5		
13	Mgmt. and insurance	5		
14	Tax implications	10		
15	Mathematics	12		
	TOTALS	130		

Figure 17.1 *Score Card for Chapters 3-15*

CHAPTER 3 — INTRODUCTION

1. The characteristic of land that specifies that it is a unique commodity is which of the following?

    (a) Nonhomogeneity
    (b) Availability
    (c) Situs
    (d) Indestructibility

2. Ownership of land includes all of the following EXCEPT

    (a) Surface of the land
    (b) Area below surface of the land
    (c) Personal property on the land
    (d) Area above the surface of the land

3. The characteristic of land that has the greatest affect on land value is

    (a) Nonhomogeneity
    (b) Location
    (c) Indestructibility
    (d) Immobility

4. Such things as wage and employment levels, interest rates, and real property tax rates are described as

    (a) Physical factors affecting land use
    (b) Artificial factors affecting land use
    (c) Natural factors affecting land use
    (d) Economic factors affecting land use

5. The percentage of wealth in the United States represented by real estate is which of the following?

    (a) 40%
    (b) 78%
    (c) 65%
    (d) 55%

6. The real estate market is
    I. Local in character.
    II. A free market.

    (a) I only
    (b) II only
    (c) both I and II
    (d) neither I nor II

7. A listing contract authorizes a real estate agent to act as a

    (a) Principal
    (b) Negotiator
    (c) Legal advisor
    (d) Settlement agent

8. Factors affecting supply and demand in the real estate market include all of the following EXCEPT

    (a) Population migrations
    (b) Interest rates
    (c) Availability of construction materials
    (d) Brokerage specializations

9. All of the following are examples of public land-use controls EXCEPT

    (a) Deed restrictions
    (b) Building codes
    (c) Zoning
    (d) Environmental control laws

10. The real estate market is
    I. Subject to recurring economic cycles.
    II. Slow to react to changes in supply and demand.

    (a) I only
    (b) II only
    (c) both I and II
    (d) neither I nor II

CHAPTER 4 — LICENSING

1. Which of the following statements about license laws is (are) correct?
    I. License laws are an exercise of the police power of a state.
    II. The purpose of license laws is to protect the general public.

    (a) I only
    (b) II only
    (c) both I and II
    (d) neither I nor II

2. A violation of a state license law may also be a violation of which of the following?

   (a) Law of supply and demand
   (b) Law of agency
   (c) Law of arbitration
   (d) Law of nature

3. A salesperson licensee may receive commissions from which of the following?

   (a) Cooperating broker
   (b) Buyer
   (c) Seller
   (d) Employing broker

4. A real estate license may be revoked or suspended if a licensee
   I. Fails to submit all written offers to the listing seller.
   II. Advises a prospective buyer that the seller will take a certain price for the property that is less than the listed price.

   (a) I only
   (b) II only
   (c) both I and II
   (d) neither I nor II

5. Licensing commissions are authorized by statute to do which of the following?
   I. Issue, revoke, and suspend licenses.
   II. Promulgate rules and regulations.

   (a) I only
   (b) II only
   (c) both I and II
   (d) neither I nor II

6. All funds received for the benefit of others by a real estate broker acting in his or her fiduciary capacity
   I. Must be deposited in a trust or escrow account.
   II. May not be commingled with the broker's business or personal funds.

   (a) I only
   (b) II only
   (c) both I and II
   (d) neither I nor II

7. To legally receive a commission in a real estate transaction, a person acting as attorney-in-fact for this purpose must have which of the following?
   I. A real estate broker's license.
   II. A real estate salesperson's license.

   (a) I only
   (b) II only
   (c) both I and II
   (d) neither I nor II

8. A broker may do all of the following without violating the license law EXCEPT

   (a) Prepare and deliver a certificate of title opinion to a prospective buyer
   (b) Witness a deed
   (c) Market personally owned property through another broker
   (d) Act as a property manager

9. For a person to legally receive compensation for negotiating the sale of a friend's real property located in a state other than the negotiating party's state of residence, which of the following is (are) required?
   I. The negotiating party must be licensed in his or her state of residence.
   II. The negotiating party must possess a nonresident license in the state in which the property is located.

   (a) I only
   (b) II only
   (c) both I and II
   (d) neither I nor II

10. A salesperson's license
    I. Is issued to and maintained in the custody of the broker with whom the salesperson is associated.
    II. Must be displayed prominently in the office of the broker with whom the salesperson is associated.

    (a) I only
    (b) II only
    (c) both I and II
    (d) neither I nor II

CHAPTER 5 — OWNERSHIP AND INTERESTS IN PROPERTY

1. Annual crops such as wheat and corn are

   (a) Easements
   (b) Emblements
   (c) Encroachments
   (d) Encumbrances

2. Which of the following is a right in the land of another requiring ownership of adjoining land?

   (a) Profit
   (b) Appurtenant easement
   (c) License
   (d) Easement-in-gross

3. Prescription is a method of creating which of the following?

   (a) License
   (b) Encroachment
   (c) Lien
   (d) Easement

4. An estate created for the life of a person other than the life tenant is called a life estate

   (a) *Per Autre Vie*
   (b) In remainder
   (c) By dower
   (d) In reversion

5. A title in fee simple absolute provides all of the following rights EXCEPT

   (a) Possession
   (b) Condemnation
   (c) Control
   (d) Quiet enjoyment

6. All of the following are powers of government EXCEPT

   (a) Police power
   (b) Escheat
   (c) Estovers
   (d) Taxation

7. Freehold estates that are not inheritable are called

   (a) Life estates
   (b) Leasehold estates
   (c) Defeasible estates
   (d) Fee simple estates

8. The owner of a condominium apartment holds title to the common areas as a

   (a) Joint tenant
   (b) Community property
   (c) Tenant in common
   (d) Tenant by the entirety

9. The instrument used to place a title to real property in trust is called

   (a) Trust deed
   (b) Deed in trust
   (c) Deed of trust
   (d) Trustee's deed

10. A trespass on the land of another as a result of an intrusion by some structure or other object is an

    (a) Encroachment
    (b) Easement
    (c) Estate
    (d) Emblement

11. An estate created by a demise is called

    (a) Fee simple
    (b) Community property
    (c) Freehold
    (d) Leasehold

12. The right to take minerals, soil, or timber from another's land is called

    (a) Periodic tenancy
    (b) Trust
    (c) Lien
    (d) Profit

13. Easements may be created in all of the following ways EXCEPT

    (a) Prescription
    (b) Lis pendens
    (c) Condemnation
    (d) Dedication

14. Liens that are given the highest priority are

    (a) Income tax liens
    (b) Judgment liens
    (c) Real property tax liens
    (d) Mortgage liens

15. Estates of limited duration are

    (a) Freehold estates
    (b) Licenses
    (c) Easements
    (d) Leasehold estates

CHAPTER 6 — CONTRACTS AND AGENCY

1. A contract in which one party makes a promise and in return another party renders a service is which of the following

    (a) Unilateral
    (b) Multilateral
    (c) Trilateral
    (d) Bilateral

2. Mutual promises supply which of the following

    (a) Competency
    (b) Consideration
    (c) Contingency
    (d) Collateral

3. An agent is a

    (a) Principal
    (b) Fiduciary
    (c) Consideration
    (d) Contract

4. Which of the following statements about offers is (are) correct?
    I. They must not be illusory.
    II. They may not be revoked.

    (a) I only
    (b) II only
    (c) both I and II
    (d) neither I nor II

5. An owner listed her property with three brokerage firms. In each case she retained the right to sell the property herself without being obligated to pay a commission to any of the brokers. The type of listing contract given to each broker is called

    (a) Exclusive
    (b) Net
    (c) Multiple
    (d) Open

6. A listing contract creates an agency relationship in which
    I. The broker is a general agent.
    II. The seller is principal.

    (a) I only
    (b) II only
    (c) both I and II
    (d) neither I nor II

7. As a result of a salesperson's negligence in filling in the provisions in a contract of sale, the seller incurred a financial loss. Liability for this loss may be imposed on
    I. The salesperson.
    II. The salesperson's employing broker.

    (a) I only
    (b) II only
    (c) both I and II
    (d) neither I nor II

8. A contract for deed or installment land contract is which of the following
    I. A financing instrument.
    II. A contract of sale.

    (a) I only
    (b) II only
    (c) both I and II
    (d) neither I nor II

9. A verbal option is which of the following

    (a) Void
    (b) Valid
    (c) Enforceable
    (d) Voidable

10. A party to a contract to buy and sell real property may pursue which of the following legal remedies against the other party in default?
    I. Action for breach of contract *and* specific performance.
    II. Action for breach of contract *or* specific performance.

    (a) I only
    (b) II only
    (c) both I and II
    (d) neither I nor II

11. A lease provides the lessee with which of the following?
    I. Exclusive right to possession and control of the property.
    II. Title to the property for the duration of the lease term.

    (a) I only
    (b) II only
    (c) both I and II
    (d) neither I nor II

12. To create a leasehold estate for ten years, which of the following is (are) necessary?
    I. The contract must be in writing.
    II. The contract must be executed by the lessor and delivered to and accepted by the lessee.

    (a) I only
    (b) II only
    (c) both I and II
    (d) neither I nor II

13. An action or inaction by the lessor results in the property being unusable is which of the following?

    (a) Actual eviction
    (b) Constructive eviction
    (c) Sandwich lease
    (d) Assignment

14. A lease is which of the following?
    I. A contract.
    II. An estate.

    (a) I only
    (b) II only
    (c) both I and II
    (d) neither I nor II

15. Subletting creates which of the following?

    (a) Assignment
    (b) Sandwich lease
    (c) Abandonment
    (d) Actual eviction

CHAPTER 7 — TRANSFER OF TITLE

1. A gift of real property by will is which of the following?

   (a) Demise
   (b) Bequest
   (c) Escheat
   (d) Devise

2. Of the following types of deeds, which provides the grantee with the least assurance of title?

   (a) Quit claim
   (b) Bargain and sale
   (c) Grant
   (d) Special warranty

3. Which of the following is (are) required to effect voluntary alienation of title during life?
   I. Delivery of a valid deed to the grantee.
   II. Acceptance of delivery by the grantee.

   (a) I only
   (b) II only
   (c) both I and II
   (d) neither I nor II

4. Placing a deed on the public record provides which of the following?

   (a) Public notice
   (b) Constructive notice
   (c) Actual notice
   (d) Effective notice

5. Recording protects the grantee against
   I. Subsequent purchasers from the grantor.
   II. Creditors of the grantor.

   (a) I only
   (b) II only
   (c) both I and II
   (d) neither I nor II

6. The wording *seised of said premise in fee* means
   I. The grantor has a fee simple title to the property.
   II. That the title is free from encumbrances.

   (a) I only
   (b) II only
   (c) both I and II
   (d) neither I nor II

7. The statement made by a grantor to a qualified public official that the signing of a deed (or other instrument) was done by him or her and was a voluntary act is called

   (a) An abstract
   (b) A conveyance
   (c) A covenant
   (d) An acknowledgement

8. Which of the following statements about title insurance policies is (are) correct?
   I. A title acceptable to a title insurance company is called an insurable title.
   II. A title insurance premium is paid only once.

   (a) I only
   (b) II only
   (c) both I and II
   (d) neither I nor II

9. Which of the following may lawfully give an opinion as to the quality of a title

   (a) Attorney-in-fact
   (b) Escrow agent
   (c) Real estate broker
   (d) Attorney-at-law

10. A property description reading "one quarter of the northeast quarter of section 10" describes how many acres?

    (a) 160
    (b) 20
    (c) 240
    (d) 40

CHAPTER 8 — REAL ESTATE FINANCE

1. All of the following are requirements for mortgage validity EXCEPT

   (a) Granting clause
   (b) Mortgaging clause
   (c) Execution by mortgagor
   (d) Valid debt

2. All of the following are rights of a mortgagor EXCEPT

   (a) Defeasance
   (b) Foreclosure
   (c) Equity of redemption
   (d) Possession

3. Which of the following gives the mortgagee the right to declare the entire principal balance immediately due and payable if the mortgagor is in default?

   (a) Acceleration clause
   (b) Alienation clause
   (c) Statutory foreclosure clause
   (d) Assignment clause

4. Which of the following enables the mortgagee to sell the mortgage in the secondary mortgage market?

   (a) Assignment clause
   (b) Due-on-sale clause
   (c) Mortgaging clause
   (d) Power-of-sale clause

5. Friendly foreclosure is also called

   (a) Beneficial foreclosure
   (b) Statutory foreclosure
   (c) Strict foreclosure
   (d) Deed in lieu of foreclosure

6. The process of liquidating a financial obligation by installment payments of principal and interest is described as

   (a) Amortization
   (b) Acceleration
   (c) Alienation
   (d) Acquisition

7. Using the amortization schedule in chapter 8, determine which of the following is the monthly payment of principal and interest required to fully amortize a $50,000, twenty-year mortgage loan at 14% interest.

    (a) $592.50
    (b) $622.00
    (c) $357.14
    (d) $512.18

8. A lending institution making an FHA-insured loan at 12% interest increases the yield to 12¾% by charging which of the following number of discount points?

    (a) 8
    (b) 6
    (c) 12
    (d) 4

9. Which of the following provides the highest loan-to-value ratio?

    (a) Conventional
    (b) FHA 245
    (c) 95% insured conventional
    (d) FHA 203B

10. Leverage is defined as the use of borrowed money. The more borrowed funds and the less personal funds, the greater the leverage. Which of the following mortgage loan programs provides the greatest leverage?

    (a) FHA 203B
    (b) Conventional
    (c) VA
    (d) 95% insured conventional

11. Which of the following regulates a maximum loan amount?

    (a) RESPA
    (b) VA
    (c) FHA
    (d) Regulation Z

12. Which of the following provides for a three-day right of recission?

    (a) RESPA
    (b) VA
    (c) FHA
    (d) Regulation Z

13. Which of the following purchases mortgages that it has insured?

    (a) Ginnie Mae
    (b) Fannie Mae
    (c) Maggie Mae
    (d) Freddie Mac

14. The loss of funds by lending institutions for making mortgage loans because of depositor withdrawals is called

    (a) Disintermediation
    (b) Liquidation
    (c) Discrimination
    (d) Amortization

15. Brantley Buyer obtained an FHA-insured loan to purchase a home. The difference between the purchase price and the loan amount was $3,100. Which of the following statements about the $3,100 is correct?

    (a) Brantley must pay this amount from his existing assets.
    (b) Brantley may satisfy this amount by giving the seller a purchase money second mortgage.
    (c) Brantley may borrow the $3,100 from a relative at 6% interest.
    (d) Brantley may obtain the money by giving a lending institution a second mortgage.

CHAPTER 9 — CLOSING REAL ESTATE TRANSACTIONS

1. On June 16, 19CY, a seller closed on the sale of her home. The annual taxes of $775 and the water bill of $86 for the current year had been paid in full by the seller prior to the sale. If these payments are prorated, which of the following amounts would be returned to the seller? (Answers are rounded).

    (a) $357
    (b) $464
    (c) $430
    (d) $397

2. The tax year in Sellerstown begins each July 1, at which time Charles Conveyor paid $745 to satisfy his tax bill through June 30 of the next year. On January 1, of the same year, Charles paid a three-year fire insurance premium of $126 for a policy effective that date. What was the prorated amount returned to Charles when he closed the sale of his home on October 28? (Answers are rounded).

   (a) $592
   (b) $244
   (c) $279
   (d) $220

3. On April 1, Chuck and Sara Vollaro made the mortgage payment of principal and interest for April on their home in the amount of $402.50. On April 20, the Vollaro's closed on the sale of their home to Harry and Helen Hudson. The Hudsons assumed the Vollaro's mortgage with a principal balance of $42,000 and an interest rate of 9%. Which of the following is the correct closing statement entry for interest?

   (a) Seller's credit—$210
   (b) Buyer's credit—$105
   (c) Buyer's debit—$105
   (d) Seller's debit—$315

4. The sale of a rental property was closed on December 12. On December 1, the tenant had paid December rent in the amount of $510. A correct closing statement entry for this transaction would be

   (a) Seller's debit—$204
   (b) Buyer's credit—$306
   (c) Seller's credit—$204
   (d) Buyer's credit—$204

5. If the real property tax year is January 1 through December 31 and a homeowner made the semi-annual payment on July 1, which of the following would be the correct closing statement entry if a sale is closed on September 19, and the annual tax bill is $1,440?

   (a) Buyer's credit—$316
   (b) Seller's debit—$404
   (c) Buyer's credit—$404
   (d) Seller's credit—$404

CHAPTER 10 — VALUATION OF REAL ESTATE

1. The type of demand that has an affect on market value is which of the following

   (a) Urgent
   (b) Unlimited
   (c) Restrictive
   (d) Effective

2. In arriving at a price for listing purposes, real estate agents perform which of the following?

   (a) A competitive market analysis
   (b) Market surveys
   (c) Appraisals
   (d) Assessments

3. If the GRM is 7.5 and the annual gross income is $250,000, what is the estimated property value?

   (a) $1,875,000
   (b) $3,333,000
   (c) $3,000,000
   (d) $2,500,000

4. Which of the following statements about the principle of highest and best use is (are) correct?
   I. It applies to the construction of a single-family dwelling.
   II. It applies to the construction of a shopping mall.

   (a) I only
   (b) II only
   (c) both I and II
   (d) neither I nor II

5. An owner whose property is condemned is entitled to be compensated for which of the following?

   (a) Book value
   (b) Assessed value
   (c) Market value
   (d) Mortgage value

6. The age of a property based on the remaining years of useful life is described as

    (a) Economic
    (b) Useful
    (c) Chronological
    (d) Physical

7. Historic value is the same as which of the following?

    (a) Book value
    (b) Condemnation value
    (c) Assessed value
    (d) Reproduction cost

8. An appraisal by summation is based on which of the following?

    (a) Replacement cost
    (b) Comparables
    (c) Annual income
    (d) Rate of return

9. The unit-in-place method is used in which of the following?

    (a) Cost approach
    (b) Income approach
    (c) Comparable approach
    (d) Market data approach

10. Which of the following is (are) correct?
    I. Land does not depreciate.
    II. Structures depreciate.

    (a) I only
    (b) II only
    (c) both I and II
    (d) neither I nor II

CHAPTER 11 — LAND-USE CONTROLS

1. Restrictive covenants are which of the following?

    (a) Public land-use controls
    (b) Negative easements
    (c) Variances
    (d) Statements of record

2. Deed restrictions that provide for a reversion of title are called

    (a) Certificates
    (b) Conditions
    (c) Clusters
    (d) Covenants

3. Which of the following statements about a lawful nonconforming use is (are) correct?
    I. If abandoned, it cannot be returned.
    II. Cannot be changed to a conforming use.

    (a) I only
    (b) II only
    (c) both I and II
    (d) neither I nor II

4. A property owner subject to a special hardship by strict compliance with a zoning standard may apply for

    (a) Spot zoning
    (b) Variance
    (c) Nonconforming use
    (d) Cumulative zoning

5. Zoning laws are enforced by which of the following?

    (a) Escheat
    (b) Conditions
    (c) Police power
    (d) Exclusive use

6. Cluster zoning provides for which of the following?

    (a) Deed restrictions
    (b) HUDs
    (c) PUDs
    (d) Interstate land sales

7. The Interstate Land Sales Full Disclosure Act requires which of the following?

    (a) Property report
    (b) Enabling act
    (c) Zoning
    (d) Cumulative use

8. Zoning ordinances regulate all of the following EXCEPT

    (a) Setbacks
    (b) Lot size for construction
    (c) Construction cost
    (d) Building height

CHAPTER 12 — FAIR HOUSING

1. An owner's exemptions from the Fair Housing Act of 1968 are lost if
   I. The owner uses discriminatory advertising.
   II. The owner lists the property with a real estate broker.

   (a) I only
   (b) II only
   (c) both I and II
   (d) neither I nor II

2. The term *redlining* applies to which of the following?

   (a) Brokers
   (b) Developers
   (c) Landlords
   (d) Lenders

3. The act of real estate agents to induce property owners to enter listing contracts by telling them that persons of a particular race, color, religion, sex, or national origin are moving into their neighborhood thereby causing property values to depreciate is called

   (a) Blockbusting
   (b) Steering
   (c) Redlining
   (d) Integration

4. The act of real estate agents to direct prospective purchasers to integrated areas to avoid integration of nonintegrated areas is called

   (a) Redlining
   (b) Blockbusting
   (c) Steering
   (d) Directing

5. The Civil Rights Act of 1968 applies to all of the following EXCEPT

   (a) Residential lot
   (b) Office space
   (c) Apartments
   (d) Residential condominium units

CHAPTER 13 — PROPERTY MANAGEMENT AND INSURANCE

1. The first step in creating an owner-manager relationship is which of the following?

   (a) Management proposal
   (b) Management report
   (c) Management agreement
   (d) Management fee

2. All of the following titles apply to property managers EXCEPT

   (a) Fiduciary
   (b) Agent
   (c) Licensee
   (d) Resident

3. A property manager's fee is a combination of a base fee and a percentage of which of the following?

   (a) Gross potential income
   (b) Gross operating income
   (c) Gross effective income
   (d) Net operating income

4. Periodic financial reports provided to the owner are called

   (a) Stabilized budgets
   (b) Operating reports
   (c) Management statements
   (d) Property management reports

5. The clause in a fire insurance policy requiring the property owner to insure for a stated minimum percentage of property value is called

   (a) Fire clause
   (b) Coinsurance clause
   (c) Extended coverage clause
   (d) Insurable interest clause

CHAPTER 14 — TAX IMPLICATIONS

1. Which of the following are required to qualify for tax deferrment under the Rollover Rule?

    (a) Owner must be age fifty-five or over
    (b) Owner must have occupied the house for three years.
    (c) Owner must purchase another home within twenty-four months.
    (d) The sale must qualify as an installment sale.

2. An amount of money deductible from a tax bill in arriving at tax liability is most accurately described as

    (a) Tax deductible expense
    (b) Capital gain
    (c) Tax credit
    (d) Tax basis

3. Which of the following is a deductible expense for homeowners?

    (a) Real property taxes
    (b) Maintenance
    (c) Mortgage principal payments
    (d) Energy usage

4. Which of the following is used to reduce the basis of a new residence?

    (a) Depreciation
    (b) Energy credits
    (c) Gain on which tax is postponed
    (d) Installment sale

5. All of the following statements about the age-55-and-over exclusion are correct EXCEPT

    (a) It may be taken only once in lifetime
    (b) It is available to coowners
    (c) It is up to $125,000.
    (d) It is available for commercial property.

6. Which of the following is (are) correct regarding installment sales?
    I. They enable the seller to reduce tax liability.
    II. The seller is taxed only on the amount of gain received in any given year.

    (a) I only
    (b) II only
    (c) both I and II
    (d) neither I nor II

7. An investment property is purchased for $100,000 and sold for $250,000 after being depreciated by the straight line method to a basis of $60,000. Which of the following represents the taxable gain in the sale?

    (a) $150,000
    (b) $190,000
    (c) $60,000
    (d) $140,000

8. Which of the following statements about the sum-of-the-year's digits method of depreciation is (are) correct?
    I. The denominator does not change and represents the total years of useful life.
    II. The numerator changes each year and represents the years of useful life remaining.

    (a) I only
    (b) II only
    (c) both I and II
    (d) neither I nor II

9. In a tax-free exchange, which of the following is taxable?

    (a) Like-kind property
    (b) Boot
    (c) Personal property
    (d) Salvage value

10. All of the following statements about the Accelerated Cost Recovery System (ACRS) are correct EXCEPT

    (a) Excluded property includes property placed in service prior to 1981.
    (b) Recovery of the cost of an asset is not based on years of useful life.
    (c) ACRS provides an alternate method of cost recovery based on straight line.
    (d) Under ACRS there is no recapture.

CHAPTER 15 — REAL ESTATE MATHEMATICS

1. What would the selling price of a property have to be to net the owner $68,000 after paying a 6 percent broker's fee and satisfying a mortgage of $16,000?

   (a) $72,080
   (b) $89,040
   (c) $88,080
   (d) $89,362

2. A salesperson with Action Realty sold a property for $125,000. The owner paid Action Realty 6 percent, which Action Realty shared with the salesperson on a 4:3 ratio. If the salesperson's share was 4 and Action's share was 3, how much money did the salesperson receive?

   (a) $4,285
   (b) $4,343
   (c) $7,142
   (d) $3,214

3. An investor purchase property for 11% below market value. Four months later he sold the property for 5% above market value. What was his percent of profit?

   (a) 16%
   (b) 18%
   (c) 15%
   (d) 17%

4. A building now 18 years old has a total economic life of 40 years. If the original value of the building was $275,000, what is the value today?

   (a) $50,000
   (b) $123,750
   (c) $151,250
   (d) $61,111

5. An apartment building produces a monthly net income of $3,600. If the owner paid $440,000 for the building what is her annual rate of return?

   (a) 8.18%
   (b) 10.18%
   (c) 9.8%
   (d) 11.8%

6. An investor purchased an office building for $750,000. What is the amount of net annual income necessary to provide a 14% return on this investment?

   (a) $105,000
   (b) $64,500
   (c) $186,666
   (d) $122,340

7. What amount of interest will the mortgagor pay on a 20 year mortgage loan of $55,000 at 13½% interest with monthly payments of $664.40 if he pays off the loan over the full term?

   (a) $104,456
   (b) $184,184
   (c) $74,250
   (d) $148,500

8. A broker received a commission of 11% in the sale of the tract illustrated. If the property sold for $2,300 per acre, what was the commission amount?

   (a) $4,517
   (b) $9,409
   (c) $9,034
   (d) $4,704

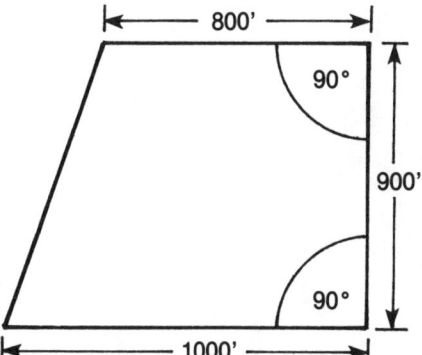

9. A property owner is having a concrete patio poured at the rear of his house. The patio is to be rectangular in shape and will be 24 feet by 12 yards. The patio is to be six inches thick. The labor cost for the project is $3.25 per square yard and the material cost is $1.25 per cubic foot. What will be the total cost of the patio?

   (a) $852
   (b) $312
   (c) $492
   (d) $936

10. A house had an assessed value of $45,000 and the lot had an assessed value of $9,000. The property was taxed at 80% of assessed value at a rate of $3.10 per $100. If the assessed valuation is to be increased by 20%, what will be the amount of taxes to be paid on the property?

    (a) $2008.80
    (b) $1674.00
    (c) $1607.04
    (d) $518.40

11. A house valued at $60,000 was insured for 85% of value. The annual premium was 60 cents per $100 of the face amount of the policy. The home owner paid a 3-year premium on February 28. On April 30 the following year he closed the sale of his home. The buyer is having this policy endorsed to him. What will be the cost to the buyer?

    (a) $357
    (b) $306
    (c) $510
    (d) $561

12. A percentage lease stipulates a minimum rent of $1000 per month and 2% of the annual gross sales of the lessee over $440,000. The total rent paid by the end of the year was $24,000. What was the lessee's gross business income for the year?

    (a) $464,000
    (b) $1,040,000
    (c) $1,640,000
    (d) $600,000

Sample Salesperson's Test   18

The questions on the sample salesperson's test and the sample broker's test are representative of the types of questions appearing on the ETS Uniform Licensing Examinations. These questions, however, have not been obtained from the ETS nor been approved by the ETS in any way. They contain approximately the same percentage of questions by subject matter as indicated in chapter 2 of the text.

Since the state test portion of the ETS examinations varies from jurisdiction to jurisdiction, it has not been included in either of the sample tests.

1. A salesperson associated with Lighthouse Realty effects a sale of property listed by Point Hazard Realty. In this transaction the salesperson is an agent of which of the following?

    (a) Seller
    (b) Lighthouse Realty
    (c) Buyer
    (d) Seller and buyer

2. Which of the following statements is/are correct?
    I. A principal is responsible for acts of his or her agent while engaged in activities concerning the agency.
    II. An agent is in a fiduciary relationship to his or her principal.

    (a) I only
    (b) II only
    (c) both I and II
    (d) neither I nor II

3. If a salesperson listed and sold a property for $90,000 and received 60% of the 7% commission paid to her employing broker, how much did the salesperson receive?

    (a) $2,520
    (b) $2,646
    (c) $5,400
    (d) $3,780

4. Sara Seller was satisfied with all of the terms of an offer to purchase her property from Bill Buyer except the date of possession, which she changed from April 9 to April 10. Which of the following is(are) correct?
    I. Sara's acceptance created a valid contract.
    II. Sara did not accept Bill's offer.

    (a) I only
    (b) II only
    (c) both I and II
    (d) neither I nor II

5. A sandwich lease is created by

    (a) Devise
    (b) Subletting
    (c) Surrender
    (d) Recording

6. At the time of listing a property, the owner specified that he wished to net $65,000 after satisfying a mortgage of $25,000 and paying a 7% brokerage fee. For what price should the property be listed?

    (a) $96,774
    (b) $94,550
    (c) $90,000
    (d) $96,300

7. When an option is exercised it becomes which of the following?

   (a) Lease
   (b) Offer
   (c) Multiple listing
   (d) Contract of sale

8. An agreement that is a financing instrument and a contract of sale is called a(n)

   (a) Option
   (b) Lease
   (c) Contract for deed
   (d) Exclusive agency

9. A real estate broker sold a tract of land for $1,600 per acre and earned a 9% commission. How much did the broker receive? (answers rounded)

   (a) $1,983
   (b) $952
   (c) $992
   (d) $661

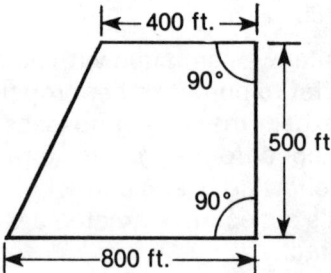

10. An agreement in which one party to a previous agreement agrees to receive something different and the other party agrees to do something different from that agreed to in a previous contract is

    (a) Novation
    (b) Assignment
    (c) Accord and satisfaction
    (d) Carry over contract

11. Which of the following is a test used to determine whether or not a real estate broker is legally entitled to a commission?

    (a) Acceptance
    (b) Accountability
    (c) Assignment
    (d) Assumption

12. A buyer made an offer to purchase seller's land if the buyer decided to buy a tract adjoining seller's land. Which of the following describes this offer?

    (a) Indefinite
    (b) Illusory
    (c) Unilateral
    (d) Fraudulent

13. Failure to comply with the terms of an offer as to the manner of communicating acceptance will result in which of the following?

    (a) Termination
    (b) Extension
    (c) Acceptance
    (d) Duress

14. A real estate agent must provide
    I. Copies of listing contracts to listing sellers.
    II. Copies of offers and contracts of sale to buyers and sellers.

    (a) I only
    (b) II only
    (c) both I and II
    (d) neither I nor II

15. The best type of listing contract from the standpoint of both the agent and the seller is which of the following?

    (a) Open
    (b) Exclusive agency
    (c) Net
    (d) Exclusive right to sell

16. In making an FHA-insured loan of $45,000 a lending institution charged sufficient discount points to increase the yield on the loan from an FHA-permitted maximum of 14% to 14¾%. The cost of the points was

    (a) $5,400
    (b) $1,800
    (c) $1,350
    (d) $2,700

17. If the monthly payment on a $60,000 fully amortizing mortgage loan at 12% APR for a 20-year term is $661.20, how much is the principal reduced by the first monthly payment?

    (a) $600.00
    (b) $612.20
    (c) $61.20
    (d) $72.00

18. If the prospective buyers are a young couple entering the third year of their individual professional careers with conservative expectations of income appreciation of 15% per year for the next few years, what type of mortgage loan would be appropriate when the couple can make only a modest downpayment on a $60,000 home?

    (a) FHA 222
    (b) FHA 245
    (c) Uninsured conventional
    (d) Participation

19. The monthly payment of principal and interest on a thirty-year mortgage at 13% for $40,000 is $442.80. How much interest will the borrower pay over the thirty-year term?

    (a) $144,000
    (b) $40,000
    (c) $159,408
    (d) $119,408

20. Which of the following most accurately describes the major purpose of a deed of trust?

    (a) Secure the payment of a note
    (b) Convey a title to the trustee
    (c) Provide for equity of redemption
    (d) Prevent assumption

21. The acceleration clause provides for which of the following?

    (a) Equity of redemption
    (b) Prepayment penalty
    (c) Right of lender to require immediate payment of principal balance when borrower is in default
    (d) Alienation by borrower

22. Which of the following liens have priority to mortgage foreclosure sale proceeds?

    (a) Mortgage lien
    (b) Income tax lien
    (c) Real property tax lien
    (d) Mechanics lien

23. An alienation clause makes a mortage

    (a) Defeasible
    (b) Unassumable
    (c) Incontestable
    (d) Adjustable

24. Pledging real property to secure payment of a mortgage debt is described as

    (a) Hypothecating
    (b) Amortizing
    (c) Liquidating
    (d) Participating

25. All of the following are prepaid items EXCEPT

    (a) Real property taxes
    (b) Hazard insurance
    (c) Property owner's assessment
    (d) Broker's commission

26. All of the following FHA programs are limited to insuring loans for the purchase or construction of single-family, owner-occupied dwellings EXCEPT

    (a) 245
    (b) 203B-2
    (c) 203B
    (d) 222

27. Which of the following is/are ways that a veteran borrower can have eligibility fully restored?
    I. Dispose of the property and pay off the VA-guaranteed loan.
    II. Sell the property to a qualified veteran who assumes the VA-guaranteed loan.

    (a) I only
    (b) II only
    (c) both I and II
    (d) neither I nor II

28. All of the following are financing instruments EXCEPT

    (a) Deed in trust
    (b) Note
    (c) Junior mortgage
    (d) Contract for deed

29. Nonjudicial foreclosure is also called

    (a) Friendly foreclosure
    (b) Foreclosure by action
    (c) Strict foreclosure
    (d) Foreclosure under power of sale

30. A mortgage providing that the lender will participate in the profit when the pledged property is sold is called

    (a) Shared-appreciation mortgage
    (b) Participation mortgage
    (c) Adjustable mortgage
    (d) Wrap around mortgage

31. A blanket mortgage usually contains which of the following?

    (a) Closed-end clause
    (b) Release clauses
    (c) Good-faith estimate
    (d) Due-on-sale clause

32. What will be the FHA commitment to insure if the FHA appraisal is $45,000 and the FHA estimate of buyer's closing costs is $1,000?

    (a) $43,250
    (b) $44,200
    (c) $44,120
    (d) $43,150

33. Which of the following regulates the advertisement of credit terms available for a house offered for sale?

    (a) RESPA
    (b) Fannie Mae
    (c) Equal Credit Opportunity Act
    (d) Regulation Z

34. Which of the following is limited to purchasing FHA-insured and VA-guaranteed mortgages?

    (a) Fannie Mae
    (b) Freddie Mac
    (c) Maggie Mae
    (d) Ginnie Mae

35. A gift of real property by will is a

    (a) Remise
    (b) Demise
    (c) Devise
    (d) Bequest

36. Which of the following provides the grantee with the greatest assurance of title?

    (a) Special warranty
    (b) Deed of gift
    (c) General warranty
    (d) Grant deed

37. Which of the following is(are) a benefit of recording a deed?
    I. It protects the grantee against future conveyances by the grantor.
    II. It protects the grantee against the grantor's creditors.

    (a) I only
    (b) II only
    (c) both I and II
    (d) neither I nor II

38. Which of the following requires the grantor to execute a deed of confirmation if necessary?

    (a) Covenant of seisin
    (b) Covenant for further assurances
    (c) Covenant against encumbrances
    (d) Covenant of right to convey

39. Which of the following statements about the rollover rule is(are) correct?
    I. It is mandatory if the transaction qualifies.
    II. It may be used only once in a lifetime.

    (a) I only
    (b) II only
    (c) both I and II
    (d) neither I nor II

40. All of the following are rights of a life tenant EXCEPT

    (a) Encumber
    (b) Devise
    (c) Alienation
    (d) Waste

41. Which of the following statements is(are) correct?
    I. An easement provides right of possession.
    II. An estate for years is a freehold estate.

    (a) I only
    (b) II only
    (c) both I and II
    (d) neither I nor II

42. Leasehold estates are created by which of the following?

    (a) Remise
    (b) Deed
    (c) Demise
    (d) Devise

43. The owner(s) of the real property may hold title in all of the following ways EXCEPT

    (a) Tenants in common
    (b) Lessees
    (c) Severalty
    (d) Joint tenants

44. A claim, lien, charge, or liability attached to and binding upon real property is a(n)

    (a) Encumbrance
    (b) Community property
    (c) License
    (d) Syndication

45. A cooperative is managed by which of the following?

    (a) Board of directors
    (b) Association
    (c) Partnership
    (d) Tenants

46. An owner of a condominium office
    I. May pledge his or her property as security for a mortgage loan.
    II. Is assessed by the property owners association.

    (a) I only
    (b) II only
    (c) both I and II
    (d) neither I nor II

47. Time sharing is associated with which of the following?

    (a) Cooperatives
    (b) Profits
    (c) Joint ventures
    (d) Condominiums

48. Which of the following is a deductible expense for homeowners when calculating federal income tax liability on their principal residence?

    (a) Mortgage principal
    (b) Real property taxes
    (c) Energy credits
    (d) Real estate commission

49. The Fair Housing Act of 1968 prohibits discrimination in the rental of all of the following EXCEPT

    (a) Offices
    (b) Apartments
    (c) Houses
    (d) Residential lots

50. The Fair Housing Act of 1968 prohibits all of the following EXCEPT

    (a) Discriminatory advertising
    (b) Use of brokerage services
    (c) Steering
    (d) Redlining

51. Inducing an owner to list property by telling the owner that persons of a particular national origin are moving into the neighborhood is called

    (a) Steering
    (b) Redlining
    (c) Blockbusting
    (d) Profiteering

52. Exemptions to the Fair Housing Act of 1968 are lost if
    I. Discriminatory advertising is used.
    II. Real estate brokerage services are used.

    (a) I only
    (b) II only
    (c) both I and II
    (d) neither I nor II

53. A property manager's fee consists of a base fee plus which of the following?

    (a) A percentage of the rental income received
    (b) A percentage of the gross potential income
    (c) A percentage of the net income
    (d) A percentage of the stabilized budget

54. Which of the following statements about property managers is(are) correct?
    I. Property managers are in a fiduciary relationship to property owners.
    II. Property managers must have a real estate license.

    (a) I only
    (b) II only
    (c) both I and II
    (d) neither I nor II

55. A person living on the managed premises as a salaried employee engaged to and lease apartments is called a(n)

    (a) Property manager
    (b) Rental agent
    (c) Employee manager
    (d) Resident manager

56. The monthly accounting by the property manager is called

    (a) Stabilized budget
    (b) Property management report
    (c) Management budget
    (d) Financial report

57. All of the following are required of property managers EXCEPT

    (a) Showing and leasing property
    (b) Deciding owner's objectives
    (c) Collecting rent
    (d) Providing for the protection of tenants

58. A buyer assumed a seller's existing 11%, $80,000 first deed of trust on the settlement date of June 12. The seller made the monthly payment on June 1 with interest in advance. Which of the following is a correct settlement statement entry for the interest?

    (a) $439.92 seller's cr.
    (b) $293.28 buyer's cr.
    (c) $439.92 seller's db.
    (d) $293.28 seller's db.

59. Which of the following types of listing contracts give the broker commission entitlement if the listed property is sold by anyone during the listing term?

    (a) Net
    (b) Open
    (c) Exclusive agency
    (d) Exclusive right to sell

60. A real estate salesperson advised a prospective buyer that the property the buyer was considering was scheduled for annexation into the city limits. This disclosure constituted which of the following?

    (a) Disloyalty to principal
    (b) Misrepresentation
    (c) Required disclosure to buyer
    (d) Violation of disclosure of information by agent

61. After inspecting a property, the prospective buyer told the salesperson that she liked the property but would not pay the listed price of $75,000. Knowing that the owner was very anxious to sell, the salesperson suggested that the prospective buyer make an offer of $70,000. Which of the following statements about this situation is(are) correct?
    I. The salesperson violated his obligation as an agent.
    II. Since the salesperson knew the owner was anxious to sell, he acted correctly.

    (a) I only
    (b) II only
    (c) both I and II
    (d) neither I nor II

62. A salesperson received two offers for a listed property within a ten-minute period. One offer was 2% less than the listed price and the other was 6% less than the listed price. The salesperson should present to the seller

    (a) neither offer
    (b) both offers
    (c) highest offer
    (d) lowest offer

63. The closing of the purchase of a commercial property was on April 18. The real property taxes in the amount of $5,760 for the tax year that began June 1 of the previous year had been paid by the seller. Which of the following is the correct closing statement entry for taxes?

    (a) $5,088 buyer's cr.
    (b) $672 seller's cr.
    (c) $672 seller's db.
    (d) $5,088 buyer's db.

64. The amount of a purchase money mortgage appears in the
    I. Seller's closing statement
    II. Buyer's closing statement

    (a) I only
    (b) II only
    (c) both I and II
    (d) neither I nor II

65. A seller had paid an annual hazard insurance premium of $540 for a policy effective on February 12. At settlement on April 16 of the same year, the buyer purchased the policy from the seller. This transaction is correctly entered on the settlement statements as

    (a) $96 seller's cr.
    (b) $444 buyer's cr.
    (c) $96 buyer's cr.
    (d) $444 seller's cr.

66. The amount of earnest money appears on closing statements as a

    (a) Credit to buyer
    (b) Debit to seller
    (c) Credit to seller
    (d) Debit to buyer

67. When listing real property for sale, a real estate agent does which of the following?

    (a) Competitive market analysis
    (b) Makes an appraisal to estimate market value
    (c) Estimates residual income
    (d) Correlates reproduction cost

68. An apartment building produces an annual net income of $10,800 after deducting $72 per month for expenses. What price for the property would provide a buyer with a gross return of 12%?

    (a) $90,000
    (b) $116,641
    (c) $129,600
    (d) $97,200

69. An apartment building contains 30 units. Each unit rents for $200 per month. The vacancy rate is 4%. Annual expenses are $3,000 for maintenance, $1,100 insurance, $1,600 taxes, $1,200 utilities, $13,000 interest, and 15% of the gross effective income for management fee. What was the investor's net rate of return for the first year if he paid $260,000 for the property?

    (a) 6.69%
    (b) 14.94%
    (c) 11.64%
    (d) 8.59%

70. If a rental property provides the owner with an 11% return on her investment of $780,000, what is the net annual income from the property?

    (a) $70,909
    (b) $141,025
    (c) $85,800
    (d) $70,512

71. Which of the following methods is used to estimate the value of land on which an apartment building is located?

    (a) Cost approach
    (b) Income approach
    (c) Market data
    (d) Replacement cost

72. Gross rent multipliers are used in connection with which of the following?

    (a) Condominiums
    (b) Schools
    (c) Vacant land
    (d) Income property

73. Adherence to which of the following has the effect of maximizing land value?

    (a) Principle of contribution
    (b) Principle of change
    (c) Principle of anticipation
    (d) Principle of highest and best use

74. Which of the following statements about zoning is(are) correct?
    I. In exclusive-use zoning, property may use only the uses specified for that particular zoned area.
    II. If a nonconforming structure is destroyed, then it may be replaced by another nonconforming structure.

    (a) I only
    (b) II only
    (c) both I and II
    (d) neither I nor II

75. Restrictive covenants are which of the following?

    (a) Conditions
    (b) Encumbrances
    (c) Public land-use controls
    (d) Zoning classifications

76. Which of the following statements is(are) correct?
    I. Spot zoning may be valid or invalid.
    II. Restrictive covenants are enforced by court injunction.

    (a) I only
    (b) II only
    (c) both I and II
    (d) neither I nor II

77. Which of the following statements about real property taxes is(are) correct?
    I. The tax rate is applied to assessed value to calculate the tax bill.
    II. Real property taxes are the largest source of revenue for local governments.

    (a) I only
    (b) II only
    (c) both I and II
    (d) neither I nor II

78. If the market value of a property is $90,000, the tax rate is 90 mills, and the assessment is 70%, what is the amount of the annual tax bill?

    (a) $5,670
    (b) $567
    (c) $8,100
    (d) $7,000

79. The back line of which lot on the accompanying plat lies most nearly in the direction of due north?

    (a) 12
    (b) 7
    (c) 6
    (d) 14

80. A salesperson sold one-quarter of the southeast quarter of section 12 for $1,800 per acre. If the salesperson's commission was 60% of the 10% commission her broker received, how much did the salesperson earn?

    (a) $17,280
    (b) $4,320
    (c) $11,520
    (d) $2,880

Sample Salesperson's Test

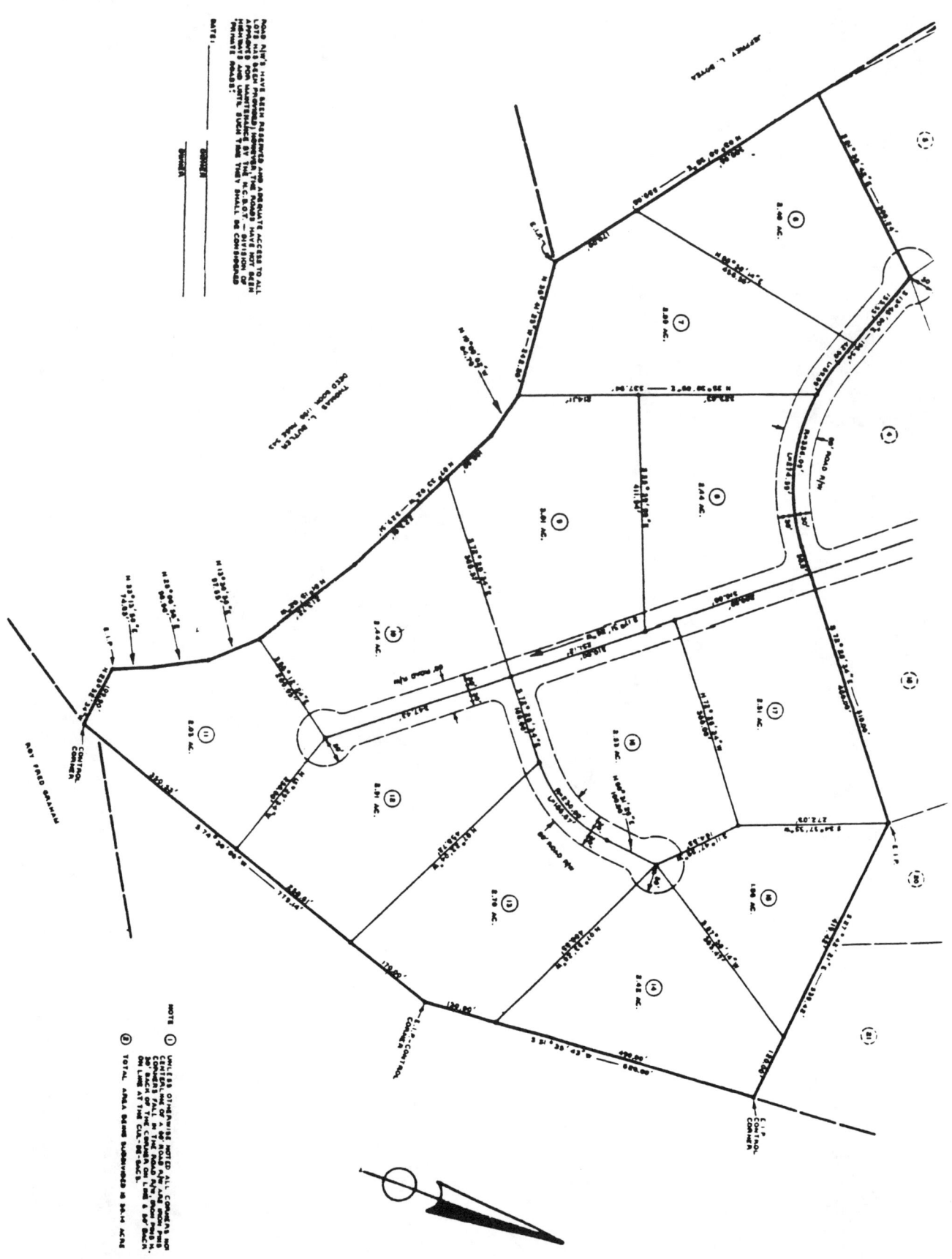

Sample Broker's Test

19

The questions on the sample broker's test and the sample salesperson's test are representative of the types of questions appearing on the ETS Uniform Licensing Examinations. These questions, however, have not been obtained from the ETS nor been approved by the ETS in any way. They contain approximately the same percentage of questions by subject matter as indicated in chapter 2 of the text.

Since the state test portion of the ETS examinations varies from jurisdiction to jurisdiction, it has not been included in either of the sample tests.

1. Mary Beaver, a salesperson associated with Leisure Homes Realty, advised a seller that his property would sell for at least $150,000. Relying on this price quotation, the seller listed the property at a price of $150,000. Comparable sales and listings of competitive properties at the time were in the range of $105,000 to $110,000. The seller refused several offers between $106,000 and $112,000 during the 120-day term of the listing contract. The seller eventually sold his property for $98,000 due to depressed economic conditions existing since the expiration of the listing with Leisure Homes. Which of the following statements about these events is(are) correct?
   I. Mary Beaver committed an act of misrepresentation and may be liable for the resulting financial loss incurred by the seller.
   II. Since Mary is an agent of Leisure Homes Realty, Leisure Homes may be held liable for the seller's damages.

   (a) I only
   (b) II only
   (c) both I and II
   (d) neither I nor II

2. While a broker was inspecting a property for listing, the property owner told the broker that the house contained 2,400 square feet of heated living area. Relying on this information, the broker listed the property and represented it to prospective buyers as containing 2,400 square feet. After purchasing the property, the buyer accurately determined that there were only 1,850 square feet and sued for damages for the difference in value between 2,400 square feet and 1,850 square feet. Which of the following is(are) correct?
   I. The broker is not liable because he relied on the seller's positive statement as to the square footage.
   II. The seller is not liable because the broker, not the seller, represented the property to the buyer as containing 2,400 square feet.

   (a) I only
   (b) II only
   (c) both I and II
   (d) neither I nor II

3. The sales associates of Executive Realty, Ltd. obtained several excellent listings in Exclusive Estates by advising home owners that a number of Chinese families were moving into Exclusive Estates and therefore their property values would be substantially depressed. This activity is most accurately described as which of the following?

   (a) Steering
   (b) Blockbusting
   (c) Soliciting
   (d) Redlining

4. A real estate salesperson earned $48,000 in commissions in one year. If she received 60% of the 6% her broker received, what was her average monthly sales volume?

   (a) $133,333
   (b) $111,111
   (c) $80,000
   (d) $66,666

5. The type of listing contract that is most beneficial to the broker and the seller is which of the following?

   (a) Exclusive right to sell
   (b) Net
   (c) Open
   (d) Exclusive agency

6. A real estate broker is responsible for all of the following EXCEPT?

   (a) Acts of sales associates while engaged in the brokerage activities.
   (b) Maintaining a trust, or escrow, account.
   (c) Adherring to commission schedule recommended by the local board of REALTORS®.
   (d) Respresenting property honestly, fairly, and accurately to prospective buyers.

7. A triangular tract of land is 8,000 feet deep and has highway frontage of 4,000 yards. If Ajax Realty Company listed this property at 9% commission and sold it for $1,600 per acre, what amount of commission did Ajax receive?

   (a) $158,678
   (b) $105,785
   (c) $218,160
   (d) $317,355

8. When listing a home for sale the broker advised the seller that since he owned only one house the listing was exempt from the prohibitions of the Fair Housing Act of 1968. Which of the following statements about the broker's advice is(are) correct?
   I. The broker acted correctly in advising the seller about the exemption.
   II. The broker should always give good legal advice to sellers and buyers.

   (a) I only
   (b) II only
   (c) both I and II
   (d) neither I nor II

9. A broker deposited a buyer's check for earnest money in the amount of $6,000 in her escrow account. Prior to the closing and at the request of the seller, the broker paid $1,200 from the escrow account to pay for the cost of damage repairs caused by termites in the house. This expense was necessary so the seller could provide the required termite certificate to the buyer at the closing. Which of the following statements about this transaction is(are) correct?
   I. Since the $1,200 disbursement from the broker's escrow account was made at the seller's request and benefitted both buyer and seller, the broker acted properly.
   II. The broker's action constituted an act of comingling and as such was improper.

   (a) I only
   (b) II only
   (c) both I and II
   (d) neither I nor II

10. A salesperson associated with Metro Realty, Inc. obtained an offer for a property listed by Preferred Real Estate Company that she gave to Sam Slicker, the listing agent with Preferred, for presentation to the property owner. Realizing that the amount of the offer was such that it would probably not be accepted, Sam increased the amount by $3,000 prior to presentation. Which of the following statements correctly characterizes Sam's action?
    I. Sam should have obtained the approval of Metro Realty before changing the offer to make the change a proper and appropriate act.
    II. Sam's action was in violation of his fiduciary obligations and was completely improper.

    (a) I only
    (b) II only
    (c) both I and II
    (d) neither I nor II

11. In the process of preparing an offer for commercial property, the broker was asked by the two purchasers to recommend the most beneficial way for them to take title to the property. Which of the following should be the broker's recommendation?

    (a) Tenants in common
    (b) In severalty
    (c) Ask an attorney
    (d) Ask the listing broker

12. On the broker's recommendation, a seller accepted an offer that was 8% below the listed price. The broker did not disclose to the listing seller that the buyer was the broker's brother-in-law. Which of the following is(are) correct?
    I. The broker violated his obligations as agent of the seller.
    II. The fact that the buyer is related to the broker is not required to be divulged to the seller.

    (a) I only
    (b) II only
    (c) both I and II
    (d) neither I nor II

13. Which of the following is least likely to be present at the final settlement of a real estate transaction?

    (a) Deed of trust
    (b) Disclosure statement
    (c) Statement of record
    (d) Termite certificate

14. All of the following usually only appear in the seller's closing statement EXCEPT

    (a) Broker's fee
    (b) Deed preparation
    (c) Prepayment penalty
    (d) Earnest money

15. If the closing date is November 10 and the seller had paid the real property taxes of $2,880 for the current tax year of January 1 thru December 31, which of the following will be the correct closing statement entry for taxes?

    (a) Seller's debit $2,480
    (b) Seller's credit $400
    (c) Buyer's credit $400
    (d) Buyer's debit $2,480

16. RESPA requires lending institutions to provide borrowers with which of the following at the time an application is made for a mortgage loan for housing?

    (a) Good faith estimate
    (b) HUD Form No. 1
    (c) Disclosure statement
    (d) Nonrecourse note

17. The buyer assumed a seller's 11%, $74,000 mortgage at closing on July 12. The seller had made the mortgage payment of $773.34, including principal and interest for July, on July 1. Which of the following is the correct closing statement entry for interest?

    (a) Buyer's credit $406.98
    (b) Seller's credit $271.32
    (c) Buyer's debit $406.98
    (d) Seller's debit $271.32

18. A sales contract provided that the buyer was to pay $65,000 for a seller's property by giving a purchase money mortgage for $30,000 and the balance in cash at closing. The buyer made a good faith deposit of $6,500 when he made the offer. The seller's share of the real property taxes credited to the buyer was $850. The buyer's other closing costs totaled $900. What amount must the buyer pay at closing?

    (a) $35,050
    (b) $27,700
    (c) $27,650
    (d) $28,550

19. Which of the following individuals brings the earnest money to the final settlement?

    (a) Broker
    (b) Buyer
    (c) Lender
    (d) Attorney

20. Which of the following is most likely to have been prepared by the broker?

    (a) Deed
    (b) Closing statement
    (c) Certificate of occupancy
    (d) Lien waivers

21. A property manager's responsibilities include all of the following EXCEPT
    (a) Maintenance
    (b) Collecting rents
    (c) Comingling
    (d) Negotiating leases

22. Which of the following is(are) basic responsibilities of a property manager?
    I. Producing the best possible net operating income for the owner.
    II. Maintaining and increasing the value of the property.

    (a) I only
    (b) II only
    (c) both I and II
    (d) neither I nor II

23. What net annual operating income must a property manager produce from a property to provide an 8% return to the owner who paid $763,000 for the property?

    (a) $95,375
    (b) $61,040
    (c) $104,849
    (d) $9,538

24. Which of the following most accurately describes a property manager?

    (a) Fiduciary
    (b) Trustee
    (c) Escrow agent
    (d) Resident manager

25. A management proposal usually contains which of the following?
    I. Schedule of property inspections.
    II. Accounting procedures.

    (a) I only
    (b) II only
    (c) both I and II
    (d) neither I nor II

26. Which of the following is an accounting of the funds received and disbursed by a property manager?

    (a) Property management agreement
    (b) Property management report
    (c) Property analysis
    (d) Property management proposal

27. The owner of an apartment building wished to sell the building and realize the maximum financial gain. A property manager would most probably advise which of the following?
    I. Convert the building to a condominium and sell time shares.
    II. Sell the building to an investor to operate as apartments.

    (a) I only
    (b) II only
    (c) both I and II
    (d) neither I nor II

28. An owner's office building was producing a net annual operating income of $140,000. If the owner had paid $1,166,666 for the property, what rate of return was she receiving on her investment?

    (a) 8.3%
    (b) 14%
    (c) 16.3%
    (d) 12%

29. The mutual promises in a bilateral contract supply which of the following?

    (a) Voidability
    (b) Legality
    (c) Consideration
    (d) Competency

30. All of the following statements about options are correct EXCEPT

    (a) They must be in writing to be enforceable.
    (b) They are binding upon optionor and optionee.
    (c) When exercised they become contracts of sale.
    (d) Optionor and optionee must be competent.

31. Which of the following is both a contract of sale and a financing instrument?

    (a) Installment land contract
    (b) Sale and leaseback
    (c) Lease with option to purchase
    (d) Executed contract

32. A lease providing for rental changes based on changes in the CPI is which of the following?

    (a) Escalated
    (b) Graduated
    (c) Percentage
    (d) Index

33. Deed restrictions that are enforced by a suit for damages or by an injunction are

    (a) Conditions
    (b) Conveyances
    (c) Covenants
    (d) Considerations

34. Public land-use controls in the form of subdivision ordinances are an exercise of

    (a) Power of eminant domain
    (b) General plan for development
    (c) Police power
    (d) Interstate Land Sales Full Disclosure Act

35. A property owner in a recently zoned area was permitted to continue to use his property in a manner that did not comply with the zoning requirements. this use is described as which of the following?

    (a) Exclusive-use zoning
    (b) Deviation
    (c) Nonconforming use
    (d) Private control of land use

36. The covenant for further assurances may require the grantor to execute which of the following?

    (a) Deed of confirmation
    (b) Executor's deed
    (c) Certificate of title opinion
    (d) Deed of devise

37. A life tenant may convey her life estate by executing which of the following?

    (a) Quit claim deed
    (b) Deed of confirmation
    (c) Judicial deed
    (d) Certificate of title registration

38. A deed is made eligible for recording on the public record by which of the following?

    (a) Abstract
    (b) Avoidance
    (c) Alienation
    (d) Acknowledgement

39. A real estate broker may do all of the following EXCEPT

    (a) Have a buyer's deed recorded
    (b) Make a title examination
    (c) Act as agent of the grantee to accept deed delivery
    (d) Execute a certificate of title opinion

40. Which of the following provides the exclusive right of possession and control of real property?

    (a) Easement
    (b) Leasehold
    (c) License
    (d) Encumbrance

41. One co-owner of real property automatically received a deceased co-owner's share of ownership. This is called

    (a) Intestate succession
    (b) Inheritance by devise
    (c) Right of survivorship
    (d) Inheritance by descent

42. Four brothers received title to a large tract of land from their grandfather who gave each brother a one-fourth undivided interest with equal rights to possession of the land. All four received their title on their grandfather's seventieth birthday. The brothers most likely hold title in which of the following ways?

    (a) In severalty
    (b) Joint tenants
    (c) Tenants by the entirety
    (d) As remaindermen

43. John and his wife, Mary, lived in a community property state. Mary inherited a large shopping mall in the city where they lived. Which of the following statements about Mary's ownership of the mall is(are) correct?
    I. Mary holds title as separate property.
    II. Mary may encumber or convey the title without John's participation in a mortgage or deed.

    (a) I only
    (b) II only
    (c) both I and II
    (d) neither I nor II

44. Which of the following statements about the creation of a condominium is(are) correct?
    I. A Declaration, Articles of Association, and Association By-Laws must be recorded on the public record in the county where the property is located.
    II. A parking garage with rental spaces can be converted to condominium ownership.

    (a) I only
    (b) II only
    (c) both I and II
    (d) neither I nor II

45. Which of the following correctly designates the type of ownership existing in a cooperative apartment?

    (a) Personal property
    (b) Real property
    (c) Periodic tenancy
    (d) Separate property

46. Which of the following is(are) correct?
    I. Owners of condominium apartments are assessed by the Property Owners Association for their share of the cost of operating and maintaining the common areas.
    II. Stockholders occupying apartments under a lease pay fees as specified in the lease for the maintenance and operation of the common areas of a cooperative.

    (a) I only
    (b) II only
    (c) both I and II
    (d) neither I nor II

47. A part of an owner's property was taken by the state for the construction of a building. Which of the following statements about this event is(are) correct?
    I. The property owner must be compensated for the difference in market value of the property before and after the partial condemnation.
    II. The building to be constructed may be for the sole use of a private corporation.

    (a) I only
    (b) II only
    (c) both I and II
    (d) neither I nor II

48. An easement that may exist only in adjoining land is

    (a) Easement in gross
    (b) Dedicated easement
    (c) Prescriptive easement
    (d) Appurtenant easement

49. A property with a market value of $80,000 is assessed at 75%. What is the tax rate per $100 if the tax bill is $900?

    (a) $1.125
    (b) $1.50
    (c) $15.00
    (d) $11.25

50. An encroachment is which of the following?

    (a) Lien
    (b) Party wall
    (c) Trespass
    (d) Fixture

51. In estimating the value of an office building containing 22,400 square feet, an appraiser established the annual rental income to be $400,000. The appraiser also learned that monthly expenses averaged $16,700. If the average investor in this type of property was realizing a net return of $13.5%, what would be the appraiser's estimate of the value of the property?

    (a) $2,962,962
    (b) $1,484,444
    (c) $1,478,518
    (d) $2,964,600

52. A competitive market analysis is performed when?

    (a) Assessing property
    (b) Pricing property
    (c) Appraising property
    (d) Condemning property

53. For which of the following types of property would the market data approach be the most relevant appraisal method?

    (a) Farm land
    (b) Library
    (c) Condominium office
    (d) Mobile home park

54. The principle providing that the highest value of a property has a tendency to be established by the cost of purchasing or constructing a building of equal utility and desirability is the principle of

    (a) Highest-and-best use
    (b) Competition
    (c) Supply and demand
    (d) Substitution

55. A property with road frontage adjoining Dick and Jane's land, which had no road frontage, was offered for sale. The value of the available property to Dick and Jane is most accurately described as

    (a) Market value
    (b) Objective value
    (c) Appraised value
    (d) Subjective value

56. Which of the following is(are) included in a competitive or comparative market analysis?
    I. Properties that have sold recently.
    II. Properties currently on the market.

    (a) I only
    (b) II only
    (c) both I and II
    (d) neither I nor II

57. An appraiser who was estimating the value of a four-story government building determined that each floor measured 90 feet by 80 feet with a replacement cost of $60 per square foot. She also observed that the building had depreciated 25% as the result of physical and functional obsolescence. Other site improvements were estimated to have depreciated 20% from a new value of $160,000. The appraiser also estimated the land associated with the building to be worth $362,000. What is the correct value estimate of the property value by the cost approach?

    (a) $814,000
    (b) $1,786,000
    (c) $1,818,000
    (d) $846,000

58. A building now twenty-one-years-old has a total economic life of forty years. If the original value of the building was $1,200,000, what is the value today?

    (a) $570,000
    (b) $228,571
    (c) $630,000
    (d) $252,631

59. Which of the following is the most likely result of the homogeneous development of a residential subdivision?

    (a) Overinflate values
    (b) Maximize values
    (c) Stabilize values
    (d) Depress values

60. Which of the following approaches to value would be the most appropriate method for estimating the value of a condominium apartment?

    (a) Cost approach
    (b) Income approach
    (c) Comparable approach
    (d) Gross rent multiplier

61. An owner's compensation for a condemnation of part of his property is based on which of the following?

    (a) The value of the amount of property condemned as a percentage of the entire property value before condemnation.
    (b) The value per front foot of the area condemned.
    (c) The assessed value of the condemned area as established by the assessor for the governmental agency condemning the property.
    (d) The difference in value of the owner's property before and after the condemnation.

62. If a property producing an annual gross income of $290,000 sold for $2,465,000, what is the GRM?

    (a) 8.5
    (b) 11.8
    (c) 7.2
    (d) 8.0

63. The monthly payment necessary to fully amortize a fifteen-year mortgage loan of $50,000 at 11% APR is $568.50. How much interest will the mortgagor pay over the fifteen-year term?

    (a) $102,330
    (b) $52,330
    (c) $17,083
    (d) $69,413

64. In the preceding question, how much of the borrower's monthly payment was applied to the reduction of principal in the second month?

    (a) $110.37
    (b) $457.32
    (c) $111.18
    (d) $458.33

65. A lender charged a 2% loan origination fee and three discount points to make a 95% conventional insured mortgage loan in the amount of $47,500. What was the cost of these charges to the borrower?

    (a) $1,425
    (b) $1,188
    (c) $2,375
    (d) $922

66. Which of the following statements about promissory notes is(are) correct?
    I. They are only executed by the borrower.
    II. They provide evidence that a valid debt exists.

    (a) I only
    (b) II only
    (c) both I and II
    (d) neither I nor II

67. Which of the following enables the mortgagor to avoid a record of foreclosure after default and prior to a foreclosure sale?

    (a) Statutory redemption
    (b) Deed in lieu of foreclosure
    (c) Deed of trust
    (d) Foreclosure by action

68. All of the following are ways in which a seller may finance the sale of her property for a buyer EXCEPT

    (a) Wrap around mortgage
    (b) Contract for deed
    (c) FHA-insured mortgage
    (d) Purchase money first mortgage

69. Bill and Betty Brown executed and delivered a $50,000 trust deed to Ajax Financial Associates at 10:30 A.M. on April 1. At 11:30 A.M. on the same day they gave a $10,000 mortgage pledging the same property to Fidelity Finance, Inc. Fidelity's mortgage was recorded a 1:10 P.M. that day and the mortgage to Ajax was recorded at 1:42 P.M. on April 1. Which of the following statements about these mortgages is(are) correct?
    I. Since the mortgage to Ajax was executed and delivered first, Ajax holds the first mortgage.
    II. Fidelity has the second mortgage because it was executed and delivered after the mortgage given to Ajax.

    (a) I only
    (b) II only
    (c) both I and II
    (d) neither I nor II

70. Which of the following statements about deeds of trust is(are) correct?
    I. The legal title to property securing the payment of a note is held by a trustee.
    II. The beneficiary is the lender.

    (a) I only
    (b) II only
    (c) both I and II
    (d) neither I nor II

71. Regulation Z specifies that the only specific credit term that may appear in an advertisement of a house for sale without the requirement of a full disclosure is which of the following?

    (a) SAM
    (b) APR
    (c) PLAM
    (d) RESPA

72. In the sale of their home Van and Vera Vendor were required to satisfy their existing first mortgage of $40,000 so that the buyers could obtain a first mortgage to finance their purchase. The Vendor's closing statement contained a debit in the amount of $800 because the Vendors paid off their loan prior to the full term. From this information it can be determined that the Vendor's mortgage contained a(n)

    (a) Acceleration clause
    (b) Alienation clause
    (c) Prepayment clause
    (d) Defeasance clause

73. A developer gave the seller a $385,000 purchase money first mortgage to secure payment of part of the purchase price for a tract of land. The developer was able to convey unencumbered titles to the first six lot purchasers by paying only $8,000 on the purchase money mortgage because the mortgage contained

    (a) Release clauses
    (b) Due on sale clauses
    (c) Prepayment clauses
    (d) Mortgaging clauses

74. In the purchase of an office building, the buyer gave the seller a mortgage for $200,000 more than the seller's first mortgage and took title to the property subject to the first mortgage. The purchase money mortgage required payments of interest only for the first five years at which time the principal had to be paid and a new purchase money mortgage created. Which of the following statements about these financial arrangements is(are) correct?
    I. The purchase money mortgage is a wrap around term mortgage.
    II. For this arrangement to work satisfactorily, the seller's first mortgage must not contain an alienation clause.

    (a) I only
    (b) II only
    (c) both I and II
    (d) neither I nor II

75. None of the following programs are limited to insuring or guaranteeing mortgage loans for the purchase or construction of only single-family dwellings EXCEPT

    (a) VA
    (b) FHA 245
    (c) FHA 203B
    (d) FHA 221 (D) 2

76. Which of the following statements about the secondary mortgage market is(are) correct?
    I. It provides liquidity for mortgages held by lending institutions.
    II. It benefits mortgage loan applicants.

    (a) I only
    (b) II only
    (c) both I and II
    (d) neither I nor II

77. Which of the following statements is(are) correct?
    I. Three homeowners may effect a tax-free exchange of their homes.
    II. If one homeowner receives boot in addition to a home from another exchangor, he or she will be taxed only on the amount of boot received.

    (a) I only
    (b) II only
    (c) both I and II
    (d) neither I nor II

78. A property placed in service on January 1, 1980 is depreciated by the sum-of-the-year's-digits method. If the property had a depreciable value of $20,000 and a useful life of fifteen years, what was the amount of depreciation taken for 1981? (Answers are rounded.)

    (a) $2,500
    (b) $2,333
    (c) $1,714
    (d) $2,166

79. Which of the following statements about ACRS is(are) correct?
    I. A double declining balance depreciation can be used for depreciable property placed in service after 1980.
    II. ACRS provides for depreciation by the straight line method over a specified number of years.

    (a) I only
    (b) II only
    (c) both I and II
    (d) neither I nor II

80. In the sale of a capital asset held for twelve months, the seller realized a gain of $242,000. The amount of taxable gain is

    (a) $242,000
    (b) $96,800
    (c) $145,200
    (d) $193,600

Appendix A
Real Estate Construction Illustrated

The purpose of Appendix A is to provide an elementary understanding of the principles, terminology, and methods of residential construction. The material is confined to wood-frame construction which is the most typical construction method for houses.

Location on Site

The location of the house on the building site is an item that must be given serious consideration by the builder. The proper location can have a significant effect on value. Also such things as the required setback from the street and side and rear property lines are of definite importance. Also, a location that makes the most advantage of available views, privacy, and ease of ingress and egress adds to the value as well as the enjoyment of the home.

Footings

Once the site is definitely established and the batter boards have been erected to lay out the perimeter of the foundation and the height of the foundation walls, the trenches are dug for the footings. The footings are normally made of poured concrete. The concrete must be poured on soil which has not been disturbed and is below the frost line. The width of the footing has to be at least twice the width of the foundation wall which will be erected upon it. The depth of the footing should be at least six inches and it should be as deep as the foundation wall is thick. The purpose of the footings is to support the foundation wall and the load that will be placed upon the foundation wall. The footings should provide an adequate base for the structure so as to avoid excessive settling of the house.

Foundation Walls

Foundation walls are usually constructed of concrete blocks. Sometimes these blocks are faced with brick from the footing to the top of the foundation wall. The best protection against termite infestation is the use of a chemical compound by a licensed exterminator in the area within the foundation walls as well as in the ground immediately adjoining the exterior of the foundation walls. This chemical treatment of the soil within the foundation and without establishes a barrier through which termites are not able to penetrate.

Sometimes the foundation consists of a concrete slab instead of a foundation wall. In the case of the concrete slab it is poured directly on the ground and there is no excavation, that is no crawl space at all. The slab provides the floor of the dwelling and the support for the exterior and interior walls. The concrete slab method is less expensive than the foundation wall construction.

The foundation walls should contain adequate ventilation. The house must be ventilated under the floor to avoid dry rot and decay. This ventilation is provided by vents in the upper part of the foundation wall all around the perimeter of the house.

Flooring and Framing

The top of the foundation wall is finished off with a course of solid concrete block. On top of this course of solid block rests the foundation sill or subsill. This wooden subsill is anchored to the foundation wall by anchor bolts and is used as a bearing and nailing surface.

The box sill rests on the subsill and is usually 2" x 8" lumber whereas the subsill would more likely be 2" x 6" lumber. The box sill runs around the top of the foundation wall attached to the subsill.

Across the span of the foundation are found the floor joists. These joists should be made from 2" x 8" or 2" x 10" lumber and should be 12" or 16" on center depending on the bearing load. Depending on the area to be spanned, the joists are put in double or even triple to support the load. Additionally, there are columns within the foundation area on concrete footings and made from concrete blocks for the floor joists to rest upon where there would otherwise be a span of too great a length to be supported.

On top of the floor joists is the subflooring. This is made of plywood sheets or boards. Around the perimeter of the house 2" x 4" strips are nailed to the subflooring. These are called bottom plates or sole plates. The wall studs which are 2" x 4" usually on 16" centers stand upright on the bottom plate. On top of these studs around the perimeter of the dwelling are the top plates which are two 2" x 4" on top of each other.

The ceiling joists span the structure between the outer walls. The ceiling joists rest upon the top plates and are therefore supported by the exterior walls and the interior wall framing.

The interior wall framing consists of two 2" x 4" on 16" centers placed on bottom plates affixed to the subflooring.

Above the subflooring is the finished floor. This might be a highly finished wood surface or material placed on the subfloor to support wall-to-wall carpeting.

Roof Construction

The roof construction consists of roof rafters, normally 2" x 8" or 2" x 10" which rest upon the top plates of the exterior walls of the house. The rafters are joined at the peak of the roof and are fastened to the ridge board. The roof rafters are covered by boards or exterior plywood sheets. On top of this material building paper or felt is nailed. The shingles are then put on top of the felt or builders paper. To provide satisfactory roof drainage and to avoid the shingles being blown up by the wind, the pitch of the roof, that is the degree of slant of the roof, should not be less than 4" in every 12'

The roof should extend at least 12" beyond the exterior walls of the structure. The larger this extension, or overhang, the more protection there is from sun and rain for the exterior walls as well as the windows. The area under the roof extension is called the soffit. The area of material facing the outer edge of the roof extension is called the facia.

Exterior Finishes

The exterior of the dwelling may be covered with a great variety of materials. Some choices are brick, board and batten, ship lap siding, or stone. These are some examples of the broad range of the possibilities in this area.

Insulation

The house should be properly insulated to control heat, cold, sound and moisture. There should be sufficient insulation in the side walls as well as overhead to make the home comfortable in summer and in winter. If the dwelling has an electric heating system there should also be insulation under the subflooring. Electric heat requires more insulation than other types of heat to minimize the heating cost. A variety of insulation materials are used such as fiberglass, mineral wool, and vermiculite.

Interior Finishes

We should next turn our attention to the interior finish of the dwelling. In most homes constructed today the interior walls are finished by using a dry wall construction. This construction consists of panels of sheetrock board material. These sheetrock panels, when properly finished, look as good or better than plaster and the age old problem of plaster cracks is eliminated. Wood paneling, either in sheets or individual boards, makes a very attractive interior finish. Often a home will contain a combination of sheetrock and wood paneling.

The most durable and satisfactory finish in bathrooms has been ceramic tile. This tile is used on the floors as well as a wainscot up to waist high or so around the bathroom wall and head high around the tub and shower area. The use of fiberglass tubs, showers, or tub and shower combinations has gained in popularity in recent years. The installation of these fiberglass units eliminates the necessity for ceramic tile around the tub or shower area.

A good deal of attention should be given to the finished carpentry on the interior of the house. The quality of the materials as well as the quality of the workmanship in the construction of window frames, baseboards, door casings, quality of doors, and hardware are all items that are strong indications of the quality of construction of the dwelling.

Floor Plans

The layout and design of the floor plan that provides functional utility is of prime importance. Good floor planning greatly increases the amenities of family living. This includes adequate closets and storage space, an entrance hall to protect the living room from the immediate front door area, the proper placing of windows as well as the size of the windows to provide sufficient light and ventilation for all the rooms. Additionally, the grouping of the bedroom and bathroom areas to provide privacy is important. These rooms should be grouped in one area or wing of the house. The kitchen should be designed to provide an efficient as well as attractive work area. The kitchen should be located near a rear entrance for access to the outside. Rooms should be of a reasonably good size and should be sized proportionately to each other. Hallways should be at least three feet wide.

Electrical Systems

Care should be taken to ascertain whether or not the electrical system is adequate. In modern homes the great number of electrically operated appliances makes adequate wiring of extreme importance. Modern construction requires a 110/220 volt wiring system that has a capacity of 150-200 amps. The system is fitted with circuit breakers. There should be sufficient electrical wall receptacles for the use of the household. They should be spaced at regular intervals in every room.

Plumbing

The adequacy and quality of the plumbing system is another important facet to be investigated in establishing the quality of construction. Copper piping is quite superior to galvanized piping. Each bathroom should be vented to the exterior by the use of a metal pipe through the roof's surface. The venting of the trap in the kitchen sink is also necessary. All water fixtures should have separate cutoffs so that a repair could be effected without shutting down the entire system.

Heating and Air Conditioning

The heating and air conditioning should be a central system with a warm or cool air circulating through ducts to each room in the house. Additionally, each room should have a duct for air return to the furnace. Modern construction frequently utilizes a heating system of electric cable panels in the ceiling. This type of heating has proven to be quite adequate. It has the advantage of providing even heat as well as being clean. As previously stated, for this type of heat particular attention should be given to providing adequate insulation.

Summary

In summary every real estate broker and real estate salesperson should learn to distinguish those features in a dwelling that show quality construction as well as those things which indicate construction of inferior quality. As a suggestion, those not familiar with construction techniques might well spend some time looking at homes in various stages of construction in their areas. In doing so, a knowledge of the construction process and the various qualities of workmanship and materials can be gained.

The drawing appearing in the text illustrates a typical wall section of a single family dwelling. Notice that on this drawing the various components of the wall section are identified and the dimensions of the materials are shown.

Terminology

Bridging—Short wooden pieces placed between timbers to help hold them in place.

Column—A vertical shaft used to support the frame not supported by a foundation wall.

Concrete Slab—A foundation of poured concrete.

Fascia—The wood covering attached to the end of the roof rafters at the outer end.

Floating Slab—A slab and footings poured in separate forms.

Footing—A concrete base used to support a foundation wall.

Foundation Wall—Bearing wall, set on footings, that supports the structure of a house.

Gable Roof—One consisting of two inclined planes joined over the center line of a house and resting on the two opposite roof plates on top of the studs. The triangular end walls are called gables.

Gambrel Roof—Similar to a gable roof except each of two sides consists of two inclined planes. The upper planes are relatively flat and the lower planes are quite steep.

Header—Timber used to support the free ends of joists, studs, or rafters over openings in the frame.

Hip Roof—One consisting of four inclined planes joined to form a rectangle.

Joists—Horizontal timbers to support a floor or ceiling.

Mansard Roof—One like a gambrel roof except there are two planes on each of four sides.

Monolithic Slab—A concrete slab poured in one piece to form an entire foundation.

Pilasters—Rectangular concrete or concrete block columns attached to a foundation wall to provide additional support to the frame.

Plates—Timbers placed horizontally on top of studs in a wall framework.

Sill—Wood member of the frame attached to the foundation wall.

Soffit—The covering, usually plywood, on the under side of a roof over-hang.

Stud—A verticle 2" x 4" or 2" x 6" timber used in the framework of a wall.

Sub-Flooring—Material on which the finished flooring is laid.

Truss—A triangular framework to provide support over a long span as in roof construction.

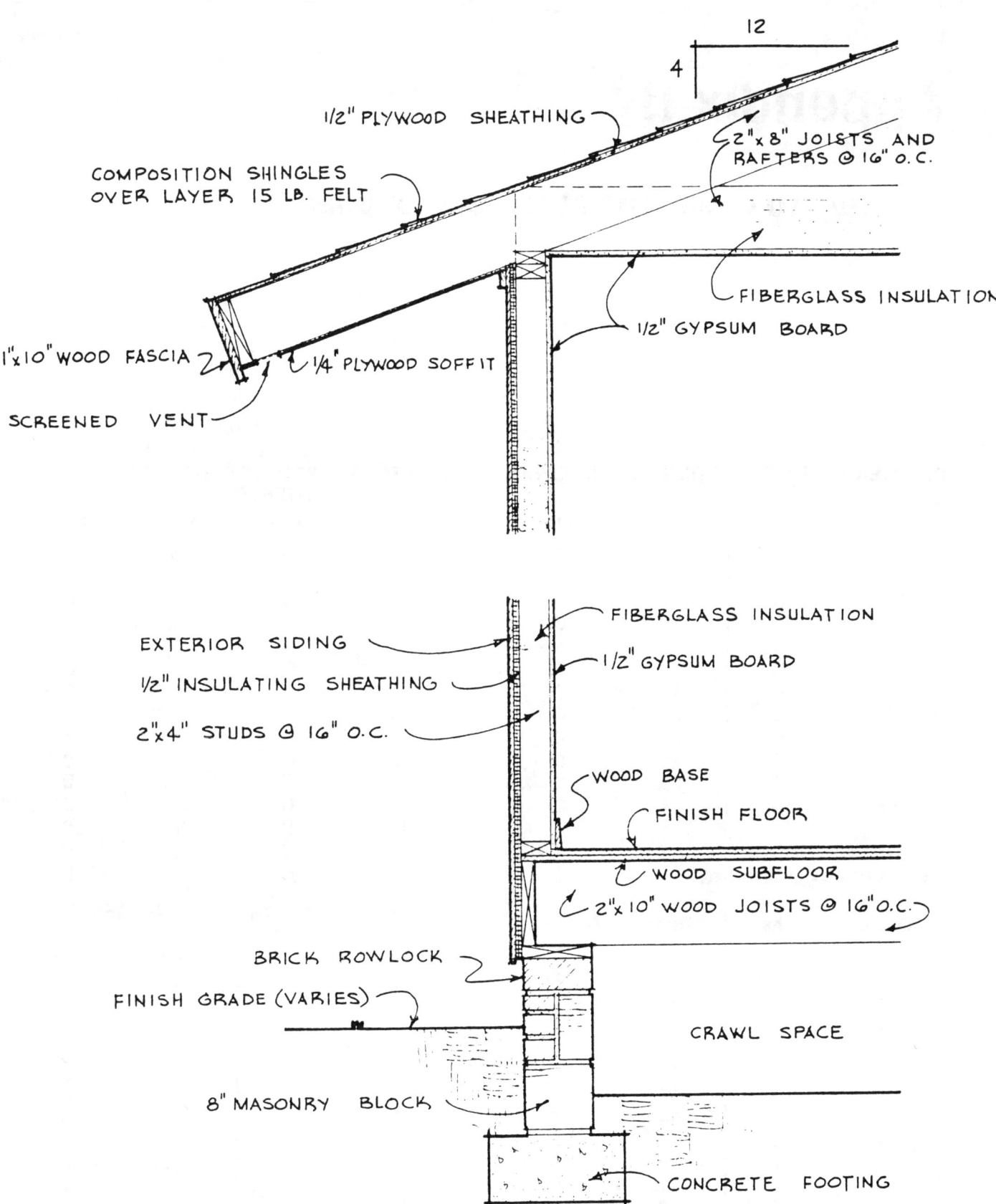

WALL SECTION

Appendix B

Answers to questions at the end of chapters.

CHAPTER 3 — INTRODUCTION TO REAL ESTATE

Ques.	Ans.	Ques.	Ans.
1.	C	13.	D
2.	B	14.	C
3.	C	15.	C
4.	C	16.	C
5.	D	17.	A
6.	C	18.	B
7.	D	19.	B
8.	B	20.	C
9.	D	21.	B
10.	C	22.	D
11.	C	23.	C
12.	B	24.	C

CHAPTER 4 — LICENSING

Ques.	Ans.	Ques.	Ans.
1.	C	17.	C
2.	C	18.	B
3.	C	19.	D
4.	C	20.	C
5.	C	21.	D
6.	C	22.	A
7.	C	23.	C
8.	D	24.	B
9.	C	25.	C
10.	C	26.	C
11.	A	27.	D
12.	D	28.	B
13.	D	29.	C
14.	C	30.	C
15.	C	31.	C
16.	B	32.	D

CHAPTER 5 — PROPERTY OWNERSHIP AND INTERESTS

Ques.	Ans.	Ques.	Ans.
1.	C	16.	C
2.	B	17.	B
3.	C	18.	B
4.	D	19.	C
5.	D	20.	C
6.	C	21.	C
7.	A	22.	B
8.	B	23.	B
9.	C	24.	A
10.	C	25.	C
11.	D	26.	D
12.	C	27.	D
13.	B	28.	B
14.	C	29.	C
15.	C	30.	D

CHAPTER 6 — CONTRACTS AND AGENCY

Ques.	Ans.	Ques.	Ans.
1.	C	16.	C
2.	C	17.	C
3.	D	18.	D
4.	C	19.	D
5.	A	20.	A
6.	D	21.	C
7.	B	22.	C
8.	B	23.	C
9.	C	24.	A
10.	D	25.	A
11.	C	26.	B
12.	A	27.	B
13.	C	28.	D
14.	B	29.	D
15.	C	30.	A

Appendix

CHAPTER 7 — TRANSFER OF TITLE

Ques.	Ans.	Ques.	Ans.
1.	B	14.	B
2.	C	15.	C
3.	A	16.	C
4.	C	17.	D
5.	D	18.	B
6.	D	19.	A
7.	B	20.	C
8.	A	21.	C
9.	D	22.	C
10.	D	23.	D
11.	C	24.	C
12.	A	25.	B
13.	A		

CHAPTER 8 — REAL ESTATE FINANCE

Ques.	Ans.	Ques.	Ans.
1.	D	19.	B
2.	C	20.	A
3.	D	21.	D
4.	B	22.	D
5.	A	23.	D
6.	B	24.	D
7.	A	25.	D
8.	D	26.	D
9.	A	27.	C
10.	C	28.	B
11.	C	29.	C
12.	B	30.	A
13.	B	31.	D
14.	C	32.	B
15.	D	33.	D
16.	A	34.	B
17.	A	35.	C
18.	C		

CHAPTER 9 — CLOSING REAL ESTATE TRANSACTIONS

Ques.	Ans.	Ques.	Ans.
1.	C	7.	A
2.	A	8.	B
3.	B	9.	C
4.	D	10.	B
5.	D	11.	D
6.	A		

CHAPTER 10 — VALUATION OF REAL ESTATE

Ques.	Ans.	Ques.	Ans.
1.	D	12.	B
2.	B	13.	B
3.	A	14.	D
4.	C	15.	C
5.	B	16.	D
6.	C	17.	B
7.	A	18.	D
8.	A	19.	B
9.	C	20.	D
10.	A	21.	D
11.	B	22.	C

CHAPTER 11 — LAND USE CONTROLS

Ques.	Ans.	Ques.	Ans.
1.	C	9.	A
2.	D	10.	C
3.	B	11.	A
4.	D	12.	B
5.	B	13.	C
6.	B	14.	C
7.	D	15.	D
8.	B		

CHAPTER 12 — FAIR HOUSING

Ques.	Ans.	Ques.	Ans.
1.	B	6.	D
2.	C	7.	C
3.	C	8.	B
4.	D	9.	C
5.	B	10.	B

CHAPTER 13 — PROPERTY MANAGEMENT AND INSURANCE

Ques.	Ans.	Ques.	Ans.
1.	C	6.	C
2.	C	7.	A
3.	A	8.	B
4.	C	9.	D
5.	C	10.	B

CHAPTER 14 — TAX IMPLICATIONS OF REAL ESTATE OWNERSHIP AND TRANSACTIONS

Ques.	Ans.	Ques.	Ans.
1.	C	12.	C
2.	C	13.	A
3.	A	14.	D
4.	B	15.	B
5.	D	16.	C
6.	C	17.	A
7.	A	18.	C
8.	B	19.	C
9.	C	20.	B
10.	D	21.	D
11.	C	22.	B

ANSWERS TO REVIEW PROBLEMS IN CHAPTER 15 — MATH APPEAR IN THE SOLUTIONS AT THE END OF THE CHAPTER.

NO ANSWERS TO CHAPTER 16 WHICH IS A GLOSSARY OF TERMINOLOGY.

CHAPTER 17 — DIAGNOSTIC TEST

Chapter 3 — Introduction		Chapter 4 — Licensing		Chapter 5 — Ownership and Interests		Chapter 6 — Contracts & Agency	
Ques.	Ans.	Ques.	Ans.	Ques.	Ans.	Ques.	Ans.
1.	A	1.	C	1.	B	1.	A
2.	C	2.	B	2.	B	2.	B
3.	B	3.	D	3.	D	3.	B
4.	D	4.	C	4.	A	4.	A
5.	C	5.	C	5.	B	5.	D
6.	C	6.	C	6.	C	6.	B
7.	B	7.	D	7.	A	7.	C
8.	D	8.	A	8.	C	8.	C
9.	A	9.	C	9.	B	9.	D
10.	C	10.	C	10.	A	10.	B
				11.	D	11.	A
				12.	D	12.	C
				13.	B	13.	B
				14.	C	14.	C
				15.	D	15.	B

Appendix

Chapter 7 — Transfer of Title

Ques.	Ans.
1.	D
2.	A
3.	C
4.	B
5.	C
6.	A
7.	D
8.	C
9.	D
10.	D

Chapter 8 — Finance

Ques.	Ans.
1.	A
2.	B
3.	A
4.	A
5.	D
6.	A
7.	B
8.	B
9.	D
10.	C
11.	C
12.	D
13.	C
14.	A
15.	A

Chapter 9 — Closing Real Estate Transactions

Ques.	Ans.
1.	B
2.	A
3.	C
4.	B
5.	D

Chapter 10 — Valuation

Ques.	Ans.
1.	D
2.	A
3.	A
4.	C
5.	C
6.	A
7.	A
8.	A
9.	A
10.	C

Chapter 11 — Land-Use Controls

Ques.	Ans.
1.	B
2.	B
3.	A
4.	B
5.	B
6.	C
7.	A
8.	C

Chapter 12 — Fair Housing

Ques.	Ans.
1.	C
2.	D
3.	A
4.	C
5.	B
6.	

Chapter 13 — Property Management and Insurance

Ques.	Ans.
1.	A
2.	D
3.	C
4.	D
5.	B

Chapter 14 — Tax Implications

Ques.	Ans.
1.	C
2.	C
3.	A
4.	C
5.	D
6.	D
7.	B
8.	C
9.	B
10.	D

Chapter 15 — Real Estate Math

Ques.	Ans.
1.	D
2.	A
3.	B
4.	C
5.	C
6.	A
7.	A
8.	D
9.	A
10.	C
11.	D
12.	B

CHAPTER 18 — SAMPLE SALESPERSON'S TEST

Ques.	Ans.	Ques.	Ans.	Ques.	Ans.	Ques.	Ans.
1.	B	21.	C	41.	D	61.	A
2.	C	22.	C.	42.	C	62.	B
3.	D	23.	B	43.	B	63.	B
4.	B	24.	A	44.	A	64.	C
5.	B	25.	D	45.	A	65.	D
6.	A	26.	C	46.	C	66.	A
7.	D	27.	C	47.	D	67.	A
8.	C	28.	A	48.	B	68.	D
9.	C	29.	D	49.	A	69.	B
10.	C	30.	A	50.	B	70.	C
11.	A	31.	B	51.	C	71.	C
12.	B	32.	B	52.	C	72.	D
13.	A	33.	D	53.	A	73.	D
14.	C	34.	D	54.	C	74.	A
15.	D	35.	C	55.	D	75.	B
16.	D	36.	C	56.	B	76.	C
17.	C	37.	C	57.	B	77.	C
18.	B	38.	B	58.	A	78.	A.
19.	D	39.	A	59.	D	79.	D
20.	A	40.	D	60.	C	80.	B

CHAPTER 19 — SAMPLE BROKER'S TEST

Ques.	Ans.	Ques.	Ans.	Ques.	Ans.	Ques.	Ans.
1.	C	21.	C	41.	C	61.	D
2.	D	22.	C	42.	B	62.	A
3.	B	23.	B	43.	C	63.	B
4.	B	24.	A	44.	C	64.	C
5.	A	25.	C	45.	A	65.	C
6.	C	26.	B	46.	C	66.	C
7.	A	27.	A	47.	A	67.	B
8.	D	28.	D	48.	D	68.	C
9.	D	29.	C	49.	B	69.	D
10.	B	30.	B	50.	C	70.	C
11.	C	31.	A	51.	C	71.	B
12.	A	32.	D	52.	B	72.	C
13.	C	33.	C	53.	A	73.	A
14.	D	34.	C	54.	D	74.	C
15.	B	35.	C	55.	D	75.	B
16.	A	36.	A	56.	C	76.	C
17.	C	37.	A	57.	B	77.	D
18.	D	38.	D	58.	A	78.	B
19.	A	39.	D	59.	B	79.	B
20.	B	40.	B	60.	C	80.	A

Index

Abandonment, 49
Abstract Continuation, 101
Abstract of Title, 101
Accelerated Depreciation, 218
Acceleration Clause, 113
Access, 48
Accord and Satisfaction, 61
Acknowledgement, 78, 94
Acquisition, 124
Acquisition Cost, 124
Acre, 248
Action to Quiet Title, 92
Actual Age, 169
Actual Eviction, 84
Actual Notice, 95
Adjoining Lands, 47
Adjustable Rate Mortgage (ARM), 118
Adjusted Sales Price, 212
Adjustments, 170
Administrator, 92
Administratrix, 92
Administrators Deed, 92
Ad Valorem, 35
Adverse Possession, 91
Affirmative Easement, 48
Age 55-and-Over Exclusion, 212
Agency, 63
Agent, 63
Agreement, 57
Air Rights, 33
Alienation, 91
Alienation Clause, 113
Allodial System, 34
Amortization Schedule, 117
Amortizing Mortgage, 116
Annual Percentage Rate (APR), 130
Anticipation, 167
Appraisal, 169
Appraisal Process, 169
Appraisal Report, 175
Appreciation, 245
Approaches to Value, 169
Appurtenance, 47
Appurtenant Easement, 47

Appears, 150, 240
Artificial Person, 43
Asking Price, 69
Assessed Value, 165
Assessment, 165
Assessor, 35
Assignee, 60
Assignment, 60
Assignment of a Lease, 82
Assignor, 60
Assumable Mortgage, 115
Attestation, 94
Attorney-at-Law, 20
Attorney-in-Fact, 20
Auction, 114
Availability, 8

Bail Bond, 50
Balloon Mortgage, 116
Bargain and Sale Deed, 69
Base Lines, 106
Base Rent, 83, 246
Basis, 211, 221
Beneficial Title, 112
Beneficiary, 92, 113
Bequest, 92
Bilateral Contract, 58
Blanket Mortgage, 120
Blockbusting, 192
Bona Fide, 195
Book Value, 165
Boot, 221
Breach of Contract, 61
Broker, 4, 62
Bundle of Rights, 36
Building Codes, 185

Capital Asset, 209
Capital Gain, 209
Capital Gains Tax, 209
Capital Improvement, 210
Capital Loss, 209

Capitalization, 173
Capitalization Rate, 173
Carry-Over Clause, 69
Cash Flow, 173
Certificate of Eligibility, 127
Certificate of Occupancy, 185
Certificate of Reasonable Value, 126
Certificate of Title Opinion, 101
Chain, 248
Chain of Title, 101
Change, 168
Civil Action, 194
Civil Rights Act of 1866, 194
Closed-End Mortgage, 116
Closed Mortgage, 116
Closing, 141
Closing Costs, 142
Closing (or Settlement) Statement, 141
Cloud on a Title, 99
Cluster Zoning, 183
Code of Ethics, 11
Coinsurance Clause, 201
Collateral, 111
Color of Title, 91
Commercial Property, 119, 214
Comingling, 21
Commission, 65
Commissioner's Deed, 101
Commitment, 74
Common Areas, 41
Community-Based Planning, 185
Community Planning, 183
Community Property, 40
Comparable, 169
Comparison Approach, 169
Competent Parties, 58
Competition, 167
Component Depreciation, 218
Composite Depreciation, 218
Condemnation, 35
Condemnation Value, 165
Condominium, 41
Condominium Declaration, 42
Conformity, 167
Consideration, 60
Construction Loan, 121
Construction Mortgage, 121
Constructive Eviction, 84
Constructive Notice, 95
Consumer Price Index (CPI), 83
Contract, 57
Contract for Deed, 76
Contract Rent, 166
Contribution, 167
Cooperative, 42
Cooperating Broker, 65
Coownership, 39
Corporation, 43
Corporeal, 36
Cost Approach, 174
Counteroffer, 60
Covenant, 96
Covenant against Encumbrances, 96
Covenant for Further Assurances, 96
Covenant of Quiet Enjoyment, 96

Covenant of Right to Convey, 96
Covenant of Seisin, 96
Covenant of Warranty, 96
Coventional Life Estates, 37
Conventional Loan, 123
Conveyance, 36
Credit, 142
Creditor, 50
Cul-de-Sac, 104
Cumulative-Use Zoning, 184
Curable Depreciation, 168
Curtesy, 37

Damages, 62
Debit, 142
Debt Service, 173
Declaration of Restrictions, 182
Declining Balance Depreciation, 216
Decree, 75
Dedication, 48
Deed, 92
Deed in Lieu of Foreclosure, 114
Deed in Trust, 44
Deed of Bargain and Sale, 99
Deed of Confirmation, 99
Deed of Gift, 101
Deed of Release, 99
Deed of Surrender, 99
Deed of Trust, 111
Deed Restrictions, 181
Default, 74
Defeasance Clause, 112
Defeasible, 36
Defeasible Fee, 36
Deficiency Judgment, 115
Demise, 45
Density, 181
Department of Housing and
  Urban Development, 194
Depreciation, 168
Depreciation, 214
Depreciable Asset, 215
Depreciation Methods, 215
Depreciated Value, 215
Descent, 92
Devise, 92
Devisee, 92
Disclosure Statement, 130
Discount Points, 129
Discriminatory Advertising, 192
Disintermediation, 132
Dominant Tenement, 47
Dower, 37
Due-on-Sale Clause, 113
Duress, 59

Earnest Money, 71
Easement, 46
Easement in Gross, 47
Economic Life, 169
Economic Obsolescence, 168
Economic Rent, 166
Effective Age, 169

Index

Effective Demand, 164
Effective Interest Rate, 130
Emblements, 33
Eminent Domain, 35
Enabling Acts, 183
Encroachment, 46
Encumbrance, 46
Enforceable, 57
Environmental Impact Statement, 186
Equal Credit Opportunity Act (ECOA), 132
Equity of Redemption, 114
Escalation Clause, 83
Escalated Lease, 83
Escheat, 35
Escrow Account, 127
Escrow Account, 64
Estate in Real Property, 35
Estate at Sufferance, 45
Estate at Will, 45
Estate for Years, 45
Estate from Year-to-Year, 45
Estate in Fee, 36
Estovers, 39
Eviction, 84
Exclusive Agency Listing, 67
Exclusive-Right-to-Sell Listing, 67
Exclusive-Use Zoning, 184
Executed Contract, 58
Execution, 70
Executor, 92
Executory Contract, 58
Executrix, 92
Exercise of Option, 81
Express Contract, 57

Fair Market Value, 163
Fair Housing Act of 1968, 198
Fannie Mae, 133
Federal Home Loan Bank System, 122
Federal Home Loan Mortgage Corporation (Freddie Mac), 134
Federal Housing Administration (FHA), 123
Federal National Mortgage Association (Fannie Mae), 133
Federal Reserve System, 130
Fee Simple Absolute, 36
Fee Simple Determinable, 36
Fee Simple Subject to a Condition Subsequent, 36
Feudal System, 34
FHA, 123
FHA Loan, 123
FHA Mutual Mortgage Insurance, 123
Fiduciary, 63
First Mortgage, 121
Final Settlement, 141
Finance Charge, 130
Fixed Lease, 83
Fixed-Rate Mortgage, 116
Fixing Up Expenses, 211
Fixture, 34
Flat Lease, 83
Flexible Loan Insurance Program (FLIP Mortgage), 118

Foreclosure, 114
Forfeiture Clause, 76
Fraud, 59
Freehold Estate, 36
Friendly Foreclosure, 114
Fully Amortizing Mortgage, 116
Functional Obsolescence, 168

Gain Realized, 212
General Lien, 50
General Warranty Deed, 96, 98
Good Faith Estimate, 131
Government National Mortgage Association (Ginnie Mae), 133
Government Survey System, 106
Graduated Lease, 83
Graduated Payment Adjustable Mortgage (GPAM), 118
Graduated Payment Mortgage (GPM), 116
Grant Deed, 99
Grantee, 93
Granting Clause, 94
Grantor, 93
Gross Effective Income, 172
Gross Income, 172
Gross Lease, 83
Gross Potential Income, 172
Gross Rent Multiplier, 174
Ground Lease, 83

Habendum Clause, 94
Heirs, 92
Highest and Best Use, 166
Holding Period, 209
Homeowner's Association, 42
Homeowner's Policy, 201
Homeowner's Warranty (HOW), 203
Home Buyer's Guide, 131
Homogeneous, 181
Horizontal Property Act, 41
Housing and Urban Development (HUD), 194
HUD Form No. 1, 131
Hypothecate, 111

Illusory Offer, 59
Implied Contract, 58
Immobility, 8
Inchoate, 46
Income Approach, 170
Income Property, 170
Incompetent, 58
Incorporeal, 36
Incurable Depreciation, 168
Index Lease, 83
Indestructibility, 8
Ingress and Egress, 46
Injunction, 183
Installment Land Contract, 76
Installment Sale, 213
Instrument, 111
Insurable Interest, 201
Insurance Value, 165

Insured Conventional Loan, 123
Interest, 35, 116
Interim Financing, 121
Intermediate Theory, 111
Interstate Land Sales Full
  Disclosure Act, 186
Intestate, 92
Intestate Succession, 92

Joint Tenancy, 39
Joint Venture, 44
Judgment, 50
Judgment Lien, 50
Judicial Deed, 101
Judicial Foreclosure, 114
Junior Mortgage, 121

Land, 33
Land Capacity, 166
Land Contract, 76
Land-Use Regulations, 181
Landlocked, 48
Land Trust, 44
Lease, 45, 81
Leased Fee, 45, 81
Leasehold Estates, 45
Leasehold Mortgage, 121
Leasehold Title Insurance, 102
Legal Capacity, 58
Legal Description, 93
Legal Life Estates, 37
Lessee, 82
Lessor, 82
Levy, 50
License, 49
Lien, 49
Lien Theory, 111
Life Estate, 37
Life Estate in Remainder, 37
Life Estate in Reversion, 37
Life Estate Per Autre Vie, 37
Life Tenant, 37
Like Kind Property, 221
Limited Partnership, 43
Liquidity, 132
Lis Pendens, 50
Listing Contract, 62, 67, 68
Loan Commitment, 74
Loan-to-Value Ratio, 123
Location (SITUS), 9
Long-Term Capital Gain Tax, 209
Long-Ter Capital Gain Tax, 209
L.S., 94

Management Agreement, 200
Management Plan, 199
Management Proposal, 200
Marketable Title, 99
Market Data Approach, 169
Market Value, 163
Material Fact, 59
Mechanics Lien, 50

Metes and Bounds, 102
Mill, 245
Mineral Lease, 33
Mineral Rights, 33
Minor, 58
Misrepresentation, 59
Modification by Improvement, 9
Mortgage, 111
Mortgage Assumption, 115
Mortgage Banker, 122
Mortgage Broker, 122
Mortgage Guarantee Insurance
  Corporation (Maggie Mae), 134
Mortgage Loan Value, 165
Mortgagee, 111
Mortgagee's Title Insurance Policy, 102
Mortgage Clause, 112
Mortgagor, 111
Multiple Exchange, 222
Multiple Listing, 67
Mutual Assent, 58
Mutual Rescission, 61
Mutual Savings Banks, 122

Narrative Appraisal Report, 176
NARELLO, 19
National Association of REALTORS®, 19
Negative Easement, 48, 181
Net Income, 172
Net Lease, 83
Net Listing, 66
Net Salvage Value, 215
Nonconforming Use, 184
Nonjudicial Foreclosure, 114
Nonrecourse, 115
Notary Public, 94
Nonhomogeneity, 8
Notice of Lis Pendens, 50
Novation, 61
Null and Void, 57

Obsolescense, 168
Offer, 59
Offeree, 59
Offeror, 59
Offer and Acceptance, 59
Open-End Mortgage, 116
Open-Ended Listing Contract, 63
Open Listing, 67
Open Mortgage, 116
Operator Budget, 200
Operating Expenses, 172, 219
Operating Statement, 172
Operation of Law, 61
Opinion of Title, 101
Option to Purchase, 79
Optionee, 79
Optionor, 79
Ordinance, 183
Origination, 128
Ownership, 36
Ownership in Severalty, 39
Owner's Title Insurance Policy, 102

Index

Package Mortgage, 120
Participation Mortgage, 119
Partially Amortizing Mortgage, 116
Partition, 39
Party Wall, 46
Percentage Lease, 83
Periodic Tenancy, 45
Personal Property, 7
Physical Deterioration, 168
Planned Unit Development (PUD), 183
Planning, 183
Plat, 103
Plat Books, 103
Pledge, 111
Police Power, 35
Population Density, 181
Power of Attorney, 20
Prepaid Items, 128
Prepayment Penalty, 113
Prescription, 48
Prescriptive Easement, 48
Price Level Adjusted Mortgage (PLAM), 119
Primary Mortgage Market, 132
Principal, 62
Private Land-Use Control, 181
Private Mortgage Insurance (PMI), 123
Probate, 92
Profit à Prendre, 49
Promissory Note, 111
Property Management Report, 201
Property Manager, 199
Proration, 144, 239
Proprietary Lease, 42
Public Land-Use Control, 183
Public Record, 45, 95
Purchase Money Mortgage, 121

Quantity Survey, 174
Quarter Section, 106
Quiet Enjoyment, 96
Quiet Title Action, 92
Quit Claim Deed, 99

Range, 106
Rate of Return, 173, 242
Ratify, 58
Ready, Willing, and Able, 70
Real Estate, 33
Real Estate Broker, 19
Real Estate Commission, 20
Real Estate Investment Trust (REIT), 44, 122
Real Estate Market, 11
Real Estate Salesperson, 19
Real Estate Settlement Procedures Act (RESPA), 131
Real Property, 33
Realty, 7
Realized Gain, 212
Reappraisal Lease, 83
REALTOR®, 11
Recapture, 218
Reciprocity, 25
Recording, 95

Redlining, 192
Reentry, 36
Referral Fee, 66
Regulation Z, 130
Release Clause, 120
Remainder, 37
Remainderman, 37
Renegotiable Rate Mortgage, 118
Replacement Cost, 174
Reproduction Cost, 174
Residual Income, 166
Restrictive Covenants, 181
Reversion, 37
Revocation, 60
Right of First Refusal Clause, 82
Right of Survivorship, 39
Right to Emblements, 33
Rollover Rule, 209
Run-with-the-Land, 47
Sale and Leaseback, 84
Sales Contract, 71
Salvage Value, 215
Savings and Loan Associations, 122
Scarcity, 164
Second Mortgage, 121
Secondary Mortgage Market, 132
Section, 106
Seisin, 96
Separate Ownership, 39
Servient Tenement, 47
Setback, 182
Settlement, 141
Settlement Costs, 142
Severalty Ownership, 39
Shared Appreciation Mortgage (SAM), 119
Short Term Capital Gain, 209
Short Term Capital Gain TAx, 209
Situs, 9
Special Assessment, 50
Special Warranty Deed, 99
Specific Lien, 49
Specific Performance, 75
Spot Zoning, 185
Stabilized Budget, 200
Statute of Frauds, 62
Statute of Limitations, 61
Statutory Foreclosure, 114
Steering, 192
Strict Foreclosure, 114
Straight Line Depreciation, 216
Subdivision Regulation (Ordinance), 185
Sublet, 82
Subordinate, 121
Substitution, 166
Supply and Demand, 167
Survivorship, 38

Taking Title Subject to a Mortgage, 115
Tax Credit, 208
Tax Deductible Expense, 207
Tax Free Exchange, 221
Tax Shelter, 218
Taxable Gain, 215
Taxation, 35

Tenancy by the Entirety, 40
Tenancy in Common, 39
Term Mortgage, 116
Testate, 92
Testator, 92
Testatrix, 92
Title, 36
Title Examination, 101
Title Insurance, 102
Title Theory, 111
Title Transfer Tax, 101
Torrens System, 95
Trade Fixtures, 34
Transferability, 164
Trespass, 46
Trust Deed, 111
Trustee, 112
Trustor, 112
Trapezoid, 237
Truth in Lending Law, 130

Undisclosed Principal, 65
Undivided Interest, 39
Undue Influence, 59
Unencumbered Property, 46
Uniform Commercial Code (U.C.C.), 34

Unilateral Contract, 58
Uninsured Conventional Loan, 123
Unintentional Misrepresentation, 59
Unities of Title, 40
Useful Life, 215
Utility, 163

VA Loan, 126
Vacancy Rate, 172
Valid Contract, 57
Value in Exchange, 163
Value in Use, 163
Valuable Consideration, 60
Variable Rate Mortgage (VRM), 118
Variance, 184
Void Contract, 57
Voidable Contract, 57
Voluntary Alienation, 92

Waste, 39
Words of Conveyance, 94
Wrap Around Mortgage, 122

Zoning, 183